COLLECTED WOR

BERNARD LONERGAN

VOLUME 7

THE ONTOLOGICAL AND PSYCHOLOGICAL

CONSTITUTION OF CHRIST

COLLECTED WORKS
OF BERNARD
LONERGAN

*THE ONTOLOGICAL AND
PSYCHOLOGICAL CONSTITUTION
OF CHRIST*

translated from the fourth edition of
De constitutione Christi ontologica
et psychologica
by Michael G. Shields

Published for Lonergan Research Institute
of Regis College, Toronto
by University of Toronto Press
Toronto Buffalo London

ISBN 0-8020-3637-6 (cloth)
ISBN 0-8020-8474-5 (paper)

Printed on acid-free paper

National Library of Canada Cataloguing in Publication Data

Lonergan, Bernard J.F.
  The ontological and psychological constitution of Christ

(Collected works of Bernard Lonergan ; v. 7)
Includes bibliographical references and index.
ISBN 0-8020-3637-6 (bound). ISBN 0-8020-8474-5 (pbk.)

I. Jesus Christ–Psychology. 2. Hypostatic union. I. Shields, Michaels G.
II. Crowe, Frederick E. III. Doran, Robert M., 1939– IV. Lonergan
Research Institute. v. Title. VI. Series: Lonergan, Bernard J.F.
Collected works of Bernard Lonergan ; v. 7.

BT213.L6513 2001   232'.8   C2001-903603-5

The Lonergan Research Institute gratefully acknowledges the financial assistance of the JESUIT COMMUNITY OF REGIS COLLEGE, TORONTO, toward the publication of this volume of the Collected Works of Bernard Lonergan.

University of Toronto Press acknowledges the financial assistance to its publishing program of the Canada Council for the Arts and the Ontario Arts Council.

University of Toronto Press acknowledges the financial support for its publishing activities of the Government of Canada through the Book Publishing Industry Development Program (BPIDP).

Contents

General Editors' Preface

The full history of Lonergan's work in Christology (courses, writings, occasional lectures) will be more appropriately given in the preface to volume 8 of the Collected Works. For this volume 7, it will be enough simply to sketch that history and then focus on the history and content of the volume, and regarding content especially on the two areas he named ontological and psychological.

First, then, the sketch. Lonergan taught courses on Christology at Regis College (then College of Christ the King) in Toronto in the academic years 1948–49 and 1952–53; at the Gregorian University in Rome 1953–54, 1955–56, 1957–58, 1959–60, 1961–62, 1963–64, and 1964–65. When ill health forced his retirement from the Gregorian he did not give up his interest in Christology, but taught a course on this topic the year he was Stillman Professor, Divinity School, Harvard, in 1971–72; back at Regis College in 1972–73 he began a course in Christology but was not able to finish it. There were also several extracurricular articles or lectures.

His Christological writings, published or unpublished, began with notes in Latin for his students: 'De conscientia Christi,' 8 pages at Regis in 1952; 'De ratione convenientiae eiusque radice ...,' twelve legal-size pages at the Gregorian 1953–54; *De constitutione Christi ontologica et psychologica*, also at the Gregorian in 1956, with reprints in 1958, 1961, and 1964; *De Verbo incarnato*, again at the Gregorian in 1960, with new editions in 1961 and 1964. When he left the Gregorian in 1965 he took with him a considerable sheaf of a work that was to have been a supplement to *De Verbo incarnato*; it remains unfinished in the archives. His course at Harvard was tape-recorded, as was the beginning of his course at Regis in 1973; the tapes have not yet been transcribed. The

extracurricular articles or lectures were published in various journals or collective works.

The following comments can be made about the printing history of the volume. In a letter from Rome dated 11 April 1956, Lonergan speaks of having completed the work the previous Monday (9 April); at that time he was hoping to have it ready for his students before examination time, and in a letter of 12 June he states that the book had indeed appeared; this, however, was too late to meet his original purpose, so the book was not included in the material for examinations.

According to the information on the back of the title page of the 1964 so-called 'fourth edition,' the work was first published in 1956, then reprinted by photographic process (*anastatice*) in 1957, 1958, 1961, and 1964. Extant in the archives are copies of all except that of 1957, and they enable us to reconstruct the printing history. As for the 1957 printing, the fact is confirmed by a letter from Rome dated 19 December 1958: 'DCCOP was reproduced photomechanically last year'; but this was not regarded as an 'edition,' since the 1958 printing is called 'second edition.'

The 'fourth' edition (1964) was the first to carry the formal permission of church authorities: 'Imprimi potest,' 16 July 1964, and 'Imprimatur,' 23 July 1964. It is also the first to be copyrighted in Lonergan's name, previous printings having only 'Proprietà letteraria.' Those first three printings were regarded simply as notes for students, and were so identified: 'Ad usum auditorum'; but the fourth was regarded as a published work. The 1964 printing is also the first to carry the note, p. 7, referring the reader to Lonergan's *De Verbo incarnato* 1960, 1961, 1964, and to his article 'Christ as Subject,' 1959 (see below, p. 7).

It is odd that the extant copies have no marginal notes by Lonergan (one copy corrects a typographical error on p. 12, but it had been in the Regis College Library, and the correction is obviously the work of a library reader): odd because he must have had a copy to mark errata. Further, a list of corrigenda was sent him within a year (acknowledged in a letter of 19 March 1958), and though they could not be conveniently entered for the photocopying, Lonergan would hardly have thrown them away. It is possible that those charged with packing his belongings when unexpectedly in 1965 he was unable to return to Rome threw away a dog-eared copy that maybe seemed of little value; but it is more likely that Lonergan himself threw it away when Latin theology grew out of style and there seemed no question of reprinting the book.

Turning now to the content of the present volume, we note that this work is not a Christology or a textbook for his course (in evidence of that, scripture does not enter this supplement, though it occupies a large part of his courses – see the series *De Verbo incarnato*). It is, as the title page states, a 'supplement.'

A supplement to what? A textbook was essential in the schools of the time, and it was Lonergan's practice, when he was not ready to publish his own textbook, to use one that was at hand, and supplement it on selected questions with his own notes. It is clear that from 1953 up to 1959 he used for his Christology a textbook by Charles Boyer, fellow professor at the Gregorian, and the director of Lonergan's doctoral dissertation some years earlier; a letter dated 22 December 1959 says, 'Next term's De Verbo Inc is a problem as Boyer's text is out of print and something has to be given to the mob.' (Another letter, 27 December 1955, separating his handling of scripture from that of Boyer, confirms this historical point.) Lonergan solved his problem by producing at last his own textbook, *De Verbo incarnato*, 1960.

Meanwhile, the present volume served to present his ideas on the ontological constitution of Christ (parts 1 to 4) and on the psychological constitution of Christ (parts 5 and 6). The *Prooemium* gives a very useful survey of the sub-questions to be treated: old and new notions of the person (part 1), the metaphysics of the constitution of the person (part 2), the relation of theology as a science to metaphysics as a science (part 3 – ideas on method make their expected appearance here), the application of this to the constitution of Christ (part 4), the view of consciousness as experience of the subject (part 5), and the application of this to Christ (part 6).

The relative importance of the questions treated may be gauged from the fact that the last three of six parts take up two-thirds of the volume. Part 4 is not very different from what Lonergan had taught on the ontological constitution of Christ while he was at Regis in Toronto. Parts 5 and 6, however, break ground that is relatively new in his history, and the question treated there will continue to interest him from now on. Today there is a little flood of books on consciousness; they manage, quite understandably, to ignore Lonergan's Latin volumes on that topic (not so understandably they ignore also his *Insight*); with this translation, one may hope for some modification of that attitude.

Matching Lonergan's new interest, the editors of the Collected Works also embark on a new venture: publication of one of Lonergan's Latin works. This involves a quite different approach, and it was of some importance to choose the right test case; here *De constitutione Christi ontologica et psychologica* was clearly indicated. Besides the intrinsic interest of his views on consciousness, there is the practical appeal that it is a slim volume and for that reason better serves as an experiment than the huge volumes in Latin on the Trinity or Christology.

The Latin text used here is the latest, that of 1964. The changes are very few from the 1956 edition to the fourth printing in 1964. In fact, only one change occurs in the text itself, and it is sufficient to indicate it here. It corresponds to what can be found here in English on p. 197, lines 20–21, and in Latin on p. 196,

lines 14–15. On p. 103, lines 16–18, of the 1956 edition Lonergan wrote, 'tum apud *Theological Studies*, 1946–49, tum in foliis multiplicatis, De processionibus divinis, 1955, omnino ...,' and that becomes in 1964, 'tum apud *Theological Studies*, 1946–49, tum opere, *De Deo trino, Pars systematica*, 1964, pp. 186 ss., omnino ...' (The pages 'De processionibus divinis' to which he refers obviously were an earlier version of some material that appears in *De Deo trino*.) Several footnotes in the present text indicate changes in Lonergan's footnotes from 1956 to 1964.

Two points special to this volume should be mentioned here. The Gregorian University text has paragraphs in larger print and other paragraphs in smaller print. That distribution has been maintained here only in the Latin text. There is evidence, though, that it may have been of some importance to Lonergan, and was not simply the result of an editor's decision: in one of Lonergan's own copies of another Latin text, *Divinarum personarum conceptionem analogicam evolvit B. Lonergan*, 2nd ed., 1959, pp. 76–77, there is a marginal note in Lonergan's hand in which he indicates that small print should be used in the next edition; that edition, *De Deo trino: Pars systematica*, 1964, casts precisely that same material into smaller print.

The other point has to do with the question of inclusive language. One new possibility, denied us in publishing his English works, opened up with translation from the Latin: the opportunity to use inclusive language. This was not possible in every use of gender language. For one thing, the scriptural use of 'Son' prevented it quite often. Also, after trying other possibilities we eventually settled on expressions such as 'Christ, God and man,' 'Christ as man,' and 'Christ the man.' And sometimes the structure of English would not admit it (as the translators of the New Revised Standard Version of the Bible, who were sensitive to the issue, also found).

Otherwise our edition follows the now familiar pattern of the Collected Works, taking the *Oxford American Dictionary* and the *Chicago Manual of Style* as our authorities, using DB (DS) in references to Denzinger's *Enchiridion*, and so on. Lonergan's notes (not frequent in this volume) were checked as usual. There are fewer editorial notes, and there is no need for a list of loci in Aquinas, who will of course appear in the index. Marietti numbers were supplied for references to the *Summa contra Gentiles*, replacing numbers that Lonergan had arrived at by simply counting paragraphs.

The editors owe a heavy debt of gratitude to Michael Shields for his painstaking work of translation as well as for his willing acceptance of their modification of his English style; his scholarly background in the classics was a bonus in our task. It is appropriate also to record our thanks to the late John Hochban who, after two retirements, took on a third career in the Lonergan Research Institute. Finally,

Professor Charles C. Hefling of Boston College, who read the manuscript for University of Toronto Press, offered a number of extremely helpful comments and suggestions.

FREDERICK E. CROWE
(for the General Editors)

Translator's Foreword

Work on this translation of *De constitutione Christi ontologica et psychologica* was begun early in 1987 as a collaborative effort on the part of the Reverend John I. Hochban, s.j., and myself. Hochban had for many years taught theology at Regis College and was thus a colleague of Lonergan's for much of that time. He also had an excellent background in classics and was well versed in both classical and medieval Latin.

The original publication runs to 150 pages and falls into two almost equal parts, the ontological and the psychological. We decided, therefore, that Hochban would work on the former part while I would undertake the latter. He had done a preliminary draft of a translation of most of the ontological part when in May 1987 he suffered a fatal heart attack. It fell to me, therefore, to complete the translation and produce it in typescript form in order to make it available to students. In 1990 at Boston College this typescript was attractively re-formatted in a two-column desktop edition.

Nine years later, the editors of the Collected Works of Bernard Lonergan decided that the time had come to publish this work, the projected Volume 7 of the collection. The two editors and I subjected the translation to a careful and thorough revision. Since it was decided to publish the Latin text along with the English translation, this final revision is intended to be a fairly literal translation, so that by comparing the translation with the original, a person with some knowledge of Latin might have access to what Lonergan actually wrote. Similarly, we decided to keep the paragraphing of the original in order to facilitate this comparison.

In the Latin book there are numerous misprints that remained uncorrected through all four editions; I hope we have succeeded in eliminating these from

the Latin text in this book. Also, Lonergan was overly fond of the subjunctive mood, and in a few places where the subjunctives cannot be justified we have changed them to the indicative. We have also taken the liberty of changing words like *eumdem* and *quemdam* to the more correct *eundem* and *quendam*.

Still, Lonergan was an exceptionally fine Latinist, and could write Latin prose in the styles of the best classical authors – see, for example, his book review in the style of Cicero in *Gregorianum* 16 (1935). Fortunately the Latin of this book owes more to Aquinas than to Cicero. It is simple and unadorned, yet not without a certain elegance. At the same time, words like *confrontatio* and *metabolismus* give it a definitely contemporary ring.

Certain recurrent terms presented some difficulty in knowing how best to translate them. Taking our cue from Lonergan himself, we have translated the important phrases 'ex parte obiecti' and 'ex parte subiecti' as 'on the side of the object' and 'on the side of the subject.'[1]

The word *ratio* is notoriously difficult to translate, since it can mean so many different things; for 'sub ratione ...' we used 'under the formality of ...'[2]

On the other hand, after much deliberation we decided to leave *notionalis*, referring to the acts proper to each of the divine persons, as 'notional,' even though that English word normally has a different meaning. *Notionalis* is a technical term in trinitarian theology with a long history going back through Aquinas to Augustine. It refers to the cause of our knowing the distinction of persons within the one God. Contemporary English works on the Trinity continue to use the term 'notional' in this sense.

The crucial distinction between *cognitio* and *notitia* (page 218 in the Latin text) we have rendered as the distinction between knowledge and awareness. 'Knowledge' is an obvious translation of *cognitio*, and for *notitia* we found 'awareness' in several passages referring to consciousness.[3]

I well remember reading *De constitutione Christi ontologica et psychologica* with keen interest as a theological student in the seminary not long after it was published.

1 Bernard Lonergan, *Insight: A Study of Human Understanding* (CWL 3), ed. Frederick E. Crowe and Robert M. Doran (Toronto: University of Toronto Press, 1992) 349.

2 See Bernard Lonergan, 'Christ as Subject: A Reply,' in *Collection* (CWL 4), ed. Frederick E. Crowe and Robert M. Doran (Toronto: University of Toronto Press, 1988) 168.

3 See Lonergan, *Insight* 344; *Method in Theology* (latest printing, Toronto: University of Toronto Press, 1999) 8–10; *Verbum: Word and Idea in Aquinas* (CWL 2), ed. Frederick E. Crowe and Robert M. Doran (Toronto: University of Toronto Press, 1997) 86, 88, 198 n. 28; *A Third Collection*, ed. Frederick E. Crowe (Mahwah, NJ: Paulist Press, 1985) 55.

It is very gratifying, therefore, to have been engaged in the task of making this valuable treatise available to a wider public.

MICHAEL G. SHIELDS

THE ONTOLOGICAL AND PSYCHOLOGICAL

CONSTITUTION OF CHRIST

Prooemium

Supplementi Finis

In quaestionibus christologicis etiam speculativis investigandis ita iam pridem fervet opus ut non solum tota quaedam quaestio et nova et minime detrectanda de humana Christi conscientia vehementer disputetur, sed etiam de constitutione Christi ontologica theoriae perantiquae nova quadam ratione et explorentur et probentur.

Qua de causa, ne auditores in tanta sententiarum varietate quasi inermes relinquamus, ita notiones, principia, methodos scripto exponere volumus ut ab omnibus qui debitam adhibuerint diligentiam perspici possit et unde sententiae tam diversae sint ortae et quemadmodum inter eas eligendum videatur.

Quare quae hisce paginis traduntur, nisi per modum supplementi non sunt legenda. Per consueta enim manualia tum ea quae ipsam fidem respiciant tum celebriores auctorum sententiae speculativae iam notae supponuntur. E recentioribus autem opinionibus non omnes exponendas selegimus (quamvis ipsi ex omnibus aliquid saltem didicisse fateamur), sed eas praecipue quae directe vel indirecte ad methodum principiaque illustranda conferre viderentur.

Denique tandem, sicut ad haec componenda nos adduxit non scribendi otium sed munus docendi, ita non perfectio opusculi sed instantia examina nobis suadent ut quae celerius conscripsimus ad usum auditorum privatum in lucem edamus.[1]

Preface

The Aim of This Supplement

For some time now there has been considerable ferment among those investigating speculative questions in Christology. The result is that a lively dispute has arisen over a new and unavoidable question, namely, the human consciousness of Christ. As well, time-honored theories about the ontological constitution of Christ are being examined and demonstrated from a new perspective.

Accordingly, lest students find themselves all at sea in such a welter of opinions, I should like in this book to expound notions, principles, and methods in such a way that all who apply themselves diligently will be able to learn both the origin of opinions so diverse and how to choose from among them.

Hence, this book is to be read merely as a supplement. I am presuming as already known what is contained in the usual theological textbooks both about matters of faith and about the speculations of the better-known authors. I have chosen to expound, not all the more recent opinions (though I acknowledge having learned at least something from each of them), but those especially which directly or indirectly appear to contribute to the clarification of methods and principles.

Finally, it was because of teaching obligations that I was led to write the book and not because I had nothing else to do. Likewise, it was the imminence of examinations and not the desire to finish this rather hastily written volume that has urged me to publish it for the use of my students.[1]

---

1 [A letter of 11 April 1956 from Lonergan to Frederick Crowe indicates that Lonergan finished the manuscript on 9 April. The book was already published by

Argumenti Natura

Cum de Christo Deo et homine agatur, quaestio simul theologica atque anthropologica est. Cum quaestio iam disputetur, etiam methodologica est. Cum
nonnullis visum sit solutionem per investigationes patristicas atque conciliares
exquirere, etiam historica fieri potest. Quaestionem theologicam, metaphysicam,
psychologicam, atque methodologicam evitari non posse iudicavimus, et iis usi
sumus principiis quae sub aspectu historico quibusdam in articulis[2] exposuimus et
anno proximo sub aspectu speculativo elaborata publici iuris faciemus.[3] Quaestionem autem historicam, nempe, patristicam atque conciliarem, fructuosius investigari credimus postquam theoreticus est exploratus notionum nexuumque
campus.

Divisionis Ratio

Cum 'conscium' seu 'psychologicum' non addat super ens (secus enim nihil prorsus esset), primo de constitutione Christi ontologica agendum est (*partes I–IV*) et
deinde de constitutione eiusdem psychologica (*partes V–VI*).

Circa constitutionem Christi ontologicam, duo maxime quaeruntur, nempe,
cur natura humana assumpta non sit persona humana (*partes I–II*), et cur Christus
Deus et homo sit unus idemque (DB 148), nisi mente non divisus (DB 219), unum
suppositum, unum ens, una res (*partes III–IV*).
Circa constitutionem personae finitae, et traditionalis personae notio ita vindicatur ut quemadmodum se habeat ad notiones recentiores perspici possit (*pars I*),

The Nature of the Argument

When we deal with Christ, God and man, we are addressing a question that is at once theological and anthropological; and since the question is still under discussion, it has a methodological aspect as well. In fact, it could also be a historical question, since some believe that a solution is to be sought by investigating the teaching of the Fathers and the councils. In my judgment the theological, metaphysical, psychological, and methodological question must be faced, and I have made use of principles that I have previously expounded from a historical viewpoint in a series of articles[2] and that I shall elaborate from a speculative viewpoint in a book to be published next year.[3] The historical question, that dealing with the Fathers and the councils, can, in my opinion, be more profitably investigated after one has explored the theoretical area of notions and their interconnections.

Rationale of the Division

Although 'the conscious' or 'the psychological' is not something over and above being (for otherwise it would be absolutely nothing), I shall treat first the ontological constitution of Christ (parts 1–4) and then his psychological constitution (parts 5–6) .

As to the ontological constitution of Christ, two questions stand out, namely, why the assumed nature is not a human person (parts 1–2) and why Christ as God and as man is one and the same (DB 148, DS 300), divided only in reflective thought (DB 219, DS 428), one supposit, one being, one reality (parts 3–4).

As to the constitution of a finite person, the traditional notion of person is explained in such a way that one can see how it is related to more recent ideas

---

the time he wrote again on 12 June, but appeared too late for the original purpose of helping students prepare for their examinations; so the book was not made part of the examination material.]

2 'The Concept of *Verbum* in the Writings of St. Thomas Aquinas,' *Theological Studies* 7 (1946) 349–92; 8 (1947) 35–79, 404–44; 10 (1949) 3–40, 359–93 [in book form, first as *Verbum: Word and Idea in Aquinas*, ed. David B. Burrell (Notre Dame: University of Notre Dame Press, 1967), and now, with the same title, ed. Frederick E. Crowe and Robert M. Doran (CWL 2, Toronto: University of Toronto Press, 1997)].

3 *Insight: A Study of Human Understanding* (London: Longmans, Green & Co. 1957) [second rev. ed., 1958; fifth ed. ed. Frederick E. Crowe and Robert M. Doran (CWL 3, Toronto: University of Toronto Press, 1992); Lonergan left in the later editions of *De constitutione Christi* the words 'anno proximo' (next year) from the 1956 edition].

et omisso constitutivi formalis nomine maxime ambiguo, ex ipsa ratione metaphysicae ut scientiae deducuntur non solum ontologica personae finitae constitutio sed etiam qua ratione tot alii ad sententias tam diversas pervenerint
(*pars II*).

Circa constitutionem ontologicam unitatis Christi, cum explicatum fuerit quemadmodum theologia ut scientia ad metaphysicam ut scientiam se habeat (*pars
III*), tria determinantur, nempe, in quaenam elementa constitutiva resolvatur Verbum incarnatum, quibusnam principiis haec multa in unum hypostaticum coalescere possint, quaenam denique mysterii intelligentia ex hac resolutione atque
compositione haberi possit (*pars IV*).

Circa constitutionem Christi psychologicam, primo explicatur quod hactenus
praetermissum videtur, nempe, conscientiam non esse obiecti perceptionem sed
experientiam subiecti (*pars V*), et deinde ita concluditur Christum esse subiectum
unum tum ontologicum duarum naturarum tum psychologicum duarum conscientiarum, ut etiam satis clare appareat quanam necessitate dialectica inter se
coniungantur multae et diversae sententiae hac in re propositae (*pars VI*).

N.B. Eandem ac hanc doctrinam alia tamen ratione alioque ordine notis cy-
clostylice impressis exposuimus (*De Verbo incarnato*, Rome, 1960, 1961, 1964).
Accedit articulus anglice conscriptus: 'Christ as Subject,' *Gregorianum* 40 (1959)
242-70.[4]

(part 1). Then, leaving aside that highly ambiguous term 'formal constitutive,' from the very nature of metaphysics as a science we deduce not only the ontological constitution of a finite person but also the reason why so many others reach such different conclusions (part 2).

As to the ontological constitution of the unity of Christ, after we have explained how theology as a science is related to metaphysics as a science (part 3), three points will be determined: namely, the constitutive elements into which the incarnate Word is resolved; the principles whereby these elements can be united into one hypostatic unit; and the understanding that can be attained of the mystery as a result of this resolution and composition (part 4).

As to the psychological constitution of Christ, we must first of all explain something that up to now has been ignored, namely, that consciousness is not the perception of an object but the experience of a subject (part 5). We shall then conclude that Christ is one subject, ontologically of two natures and psychologically of two consciousnesses. In this way it will become sufficiently clear what type of dialectical necessity unites the many different opinions that have been proposed in this matter.

Note: I have set forth this same material, though for a different reason and in a different order, in a set of mimeographed notes, *De Verbo incarnato* (Rome, 1960, 1961, 1964). There is also an article, 'Christ as Subject: A Reply,' *Gregorianum* 40 (1959) 242–70.[4]

---

4 [This note was added in the fourth edition, 1964. A translation of *De Verbo incarnato* will appear as volume 8 in CWL. The 1961 edition of *De Verbo incarnato* was unchanged except for pagination, but considerable revision appears in some parts of the 1964 edition. 'Christ as Subject' can now be found in CWL 4, *Collection*, ed. Frederick E. Crowe and Robert M. Doran (Toronto: University of Toronto Press, 1988) 153–84.]

PARS I

De Notione Personae

Cum persona sit subsistens distinctum in natura intellectuali, primo dicendum erit de ipsa intellectuali natura tum ex parte obiecti in quod tendit haec natura (*sectio 1*, de ente) tum ex parte subiecti quod a tendentia adeo elevata facile deficit (*sectio 2*, de ex-sistentia).

Deinde, cum subsistens sit ens simpliciter unum, de uno (*sectio 3*) agendum erit et de subsistente (*sectio 4*) ut deinceps de subsistente distincto seu de supposito (*sectio 5*) et de ipsa personae ratione (*sectio 6*) agatur.

Sectio Prima: De Ente

Circa ens sunt tria dicenda, nempe, de eius quidditate, de eius intentione, et de eius extensione seu denotatione.

1 *Quidditas* entis est qua intellecta totum ens intelligitur. Quae quidem quidditas est ipsa divina essentia.

Nam intellecta divina essentia, (1) intelligitur aliquod ens, cum haec essentia cum esse identificetur, et (2) intelligitur totum ens, tum quia Deus, comprehensa sua essentia, omne prorsus ens perfectissime cognoscit, tum quia beati, visa Dei essentia, et ipsum Deum et alia in Deo pro perfectione visionis intuentur.[1]

PART 1

The Notion of Person

Since a person is a distinct being subsisting in an intellectual nature, we must first speak of an intellectual nature both from the side of the object toward which this nature tends (§ 1, Being) and from the side of the subject who easily falls short of so lofty an aim (§ 2, *Existenz*).

Next, since a subsistent being is one in the strictest sense of the word, we shall deal with the notion of 'one' (§ 3) and with the notion of 'subsistent' (§ 4), so that we may then go on to deal with the notion of 'distinct subsistent' or 'supposit' (§ 5) and with the formality of 'person' (§ 6).

1 Being

With regard to being, three points are to be treated: the quiddity of being [1–2], the intention of being [3–4], and the extension or denotation of being [5].

1 The *quiddity* of being is that by which, when understood, being in its totality is understood. That quiddity is the divine essence itself.

For, once the divine essence is understood, (1) some being is understood, since this essence is identified with 'to be,' and (2) being is understood in its totality, both because God by comprehending the divine essence understands perfectly every being whatsoever, and because the blessed in heaven seeing God's essence behold both God and other beings in God in proportion to the perfection of the vision they possess.[1]

---

1 Thomas Aquinas, *Summa theologiae*, 1, q. 14, aa. 5, 6; q. 12, aa. 8–10.

At intellecta finita qualibet essentia, non intelligitur ens. Nam finita essentia esse non includit. Qua de causa, finita essentia intellecta, non intelligitur esse; et esse non intellecto, non intelligitur ens. Iterum, cum finita essentia intelligatur, in ea non perspiciuntur nisi proprietates hypotheticae seu ab esse abstractae.[2]

2 Unde secundum quidditatem dividitur ens dupliciter.

Primo modo, in ens per essentiam et ens per participationem.

Ens per essentiam est cuius essentia est suum esse, vel (gnoseologice) cuius essentia intellecta totum ens intelligitur.

Ens per participationem est cuius essentia non est suum esse, vel (gnoseologice) cuius essentia intellecta non intelligitur ens sed proprietates hypotheticae ex essentia profluentes perspiciuntur.

Alio modo, in ens quidditative et ens analogice.

Ens quidditative est ens prout innotescit mediante divina essentia intellecta.

Ens analogice est ens prout innotescit tum intelligendo essentias finitas tum eas comparando cum esse in iis recepto.[3]

3 *Intentio* entis aut est intendens aut intenta.

Intentio quae ens intendit nihil est aliud quam ipsa intellectus acies secundum finalitatem suam naturalem seu secundum orientationem suam radicalem atque

But when you understand any finite essence, you do not understand being. For a finite essence does not include 'to be.' Accordingly, if you understand a finite essence, you do not understand 'to be'; and if you do not understand 'to be,' you do not understand being. Again, when you understand a finite essence, you apprehend merely properties that are hypothetical or that are abstracted from 'to be.'[2]

2 Thus, with respect to quiddity being is divided in two ways.

First, it is divided into being by essence and being by participation.

Being by essence is being whose essence is its own 'to be'; or, to put it in cognitional terms, it is being through the understanding of whose essence being is understood in its totality.

Being by participation is being whose essence is not its own 'to be'; in cognitional terms, it is being through the understanding of whose essence you do not understand being but apprehend only the hypothetical properties derived from its essence.

Another division is into being known quidditatively and being known analogously.

Being known quidditatively is being as known through the mediation of an understanding of the divine essence.

Being known analogously is being as known through understanding finite essences and comparing them with the 'to be' received in them.[3]

3 The *intention* of being is either intending or intended.

The intention intending being is simply the cutting edge of the intellect in accordance with its natural finality, that is, in accordance with its radical dynamic

---

2 See also Thomas Aquinas, *Summa contra Gentiles*, 2, c. 98, § 1835; *Summa theologiae*, 1, q. 54, aa. 1–3; q. 79, a. 2.

3 See Lonergan, *Insight*, chapters 12 and 19. [This is the reference given in this note in the 1961 and 1964 editions. The 1956, 1957, and 1958 printings refer rather to Lonergan's 'opusculum,' *De divinis processionibus*, which was the first *quaestio* of an intended supplement *De sanctissima Trinitate*. This opusculum was issued in 1955. The references in the note that appears in these early printings of *De constitutione Christi* are to sections 12–14 and 21–24 of *De divinis processionibus*. Sections 12–14 are part of the second article of this *quaestio*, 'De imagine Dei in homine,' part of which became the second appendix ('De actu intelligendi') in *Divinarum personarum conceptionem analogicam evolvit B. Lonergan, S.I.* (Rome: Gregorian University Press, 1957, 1959) and then in *De Deo trino: Pars systematica* (Rome: Gregorian University, 1964). In the latter work the material referred to here is found at pp. 275–85. Sections 21–24 of *De divinis processionibus* appear at the beginning of article 3, 'Ex imagine in exemplar aeternum,' which is not repeated as such anywhere in *Divinarum personarum* or *De Deo trino*.]

dynamicam. Intellectus enim est 'quo est omnia facere et fieri.' Quare, cum 'omnia' respiciat, ens respicit. Cum 'omnia' respiciat secundum facere et fieri, ens respicit secundum finalitatem vel secundum orientationem dynamicam. Cum denique ipse intellectus definiatur tamquam 'quo est omnia facere et fieri,' haec finalitas est naturalis et haec dynamica orientatio est radicalis.

Praeterea, naturalis haec finalitas atque dynamica orientatio (1) non est inconscia sicut habitudo gravis ad locum deorsum, (2) non est sensibiliter tantum conscia sicut habitudo esurientis ad cibum, sed (3) est intellectualiter atque rationaliter conscia, cum ipsa sit illa admiratio quam Aristoteles initium iudicavit omnis scientiae et omnis philosophiae. Ex hac enim admiratione oriuntur quaestiones omnes sive circa rerum essentias (Quid sit, Propter quid ita sit) sive circa earum esse (An sit, Utrum ita sit).

Iam vero si finalitas quaedam atque dynamica orientatio est intellectualiter et rationaliter conscia, est veri nominis intentio. Quae tamen intentio, cum cognitionem non constituat sed in cognitionem per quaestiones ducat, intentio est non intenta sed intendens.

Secundum quam intentionem intendentem, ens nobis per se atque naturaliter innotescit[4] et nobis ignotum esse non potest.[5] Praeterea, cum ipsa haec intentio intendens et naturalis sit et ignota esse non possit, specifice una atque eadem est in omnibus prorsus hominibus; quod enim naturale est, et ante habetur quam evolvatur cultura hellenica neque ideo amovetur quod scholastici contemnantur.

4 Intentio autem entis intenta, seu entis conceptio explicita, alia in aliis est. Aliter enim apud Parmenidem, aliter apud Platonem, aliter apud Aristotelem, aliter apud Avicennam, aliter apud Aquinatem, aliter apud Scotum, aliter apud Hegel concipitur ens.[6]

Cuius diversitatis ratio atque causa est quod ens est conceptus maxime fundamentalis ex quo plurima derivantur. Iam vero satis facilis est scientia quae conclusiones ex praemissis deducat. Neque difficilis est intelligentia qua innotescant principia; cognitis enim terminis statim principia perspiciuntur. Sed difficillima est sapientia cuius est omnia ordinare et de omnibus iudicare; et ideo difficillimum est ita primos terminos seligere ut vera principia

orientation. For the intellect is 'that by which it is possible to make and become everything.' Hence, since the intellect regards 'everything,' it regards being; and since it regards 'everything' with respect to making and becoming, it regards being in accordance with its finality or dynamic orientation. Finally, since the intellect is defined as 'that by which it is possible to make and become everything,' this finality is natural and this dynamic orientation is radical.

Furthermore, this natural finality and dynamic orientation (1) is not unconscious, like that of a heavy object with regard to the law of gravity, nor (2) is it only sensitively conscious, such as the desire of a hungry being for food, but (3) it is intellectually and rationally conscious, since it is that sense of wonder that Aristotle considered to be the beginning of all knowledge and all philosophy. For from this wondering all questions arise, whether about the essences of things (What is it? Why is it so?) or about their existence (Is it? Is it so?).

Now, if a finality and dynamic orientation is intellectually and rationally conscious, it is rightly called 'intention.' However, since this intention does not constitute knowledge but leads to it through questioning, it is an intending intention, not an intended one.

Through this intending intention, being becomes known to us of itself and naturally[4] and cannot be unknown to us.[5] Moreover, since this intending intention itself is natural and cannot go unknown, it is specifically one and the same in every single human being; for what is natural both existed before the rise of Greek culture and does not cease to exist just because the Scholastics are scorned.

4 On the other hand, the intended intention of being, the explicit concept of being, differs with different thinkers. Parmenides, Plato, Aristotle, Avicenna, Aquinas, Scotus, Hegel[6] – they all conceive being differently.

This diversity stems from the fact that being is the most fundamental concept of all, one from which many consequences flow. A science that deduces conclusions from premises is easy enough. Nor is that understanding difficult by which principles become known, for as soon as the terms are known, the principles are grasped. But that sapiential knowledge whose function it is to order all things and make judgments about all things is extremely difficult; and therefore it is very difficult to choose primitive terms in such a way that true principles are

---

4 Thomas Aquinas, *Summa contra Gentiles*, 2, c. 83, § 1678.
5 Thomas Aquinas, *De veritate*, q. 11, a. 1, ad 3m.
6 [At least by the time of a 1962 institute on 'The Method of Theology,' lecture 5, Lonergan had added Heidegger to this list of philosophers with different conceptions of being.]

perspiciantur et non solum verae sed etiam omnes verae conclusiones deducantur. Et cum haec difficultas in conceptu maxime fundamentali maxima sit, mirum esse non potest multos clarissimosque viros circa intentionem entis intentam seu entis conceptionem erravisse.[7]

Attamen ex iis quae de quidditate entis deque eiusdem intentione intendente diximus, tuto ad explicitam eius conceptionem proceditur.

Cum enim ipsa intellectus acies 'omnia' respiciat, sequitur conceptionem entis esse conceptionem totius realitatis totius universi; si enim minima quaelibet pars vel aspectus omitteretur, iam non ad 'omnia' attenditur.

Cum duplici quaestione (Quid sit, An sit) ad singula cognoscenda procedatur, sequitur conceptionem entis esse conceptionem cuiusdam compositi quod essentia (quid sit) et esse (an sit) constet.

Cum intentio intendens cognitionem non constituat sed tantummodo in cognitionem per quaestiones ducat, sequitur conceptionem entis vacuam quidem videri sed esse plenissimam. Vacua quidem videtur, nam per solam intentionem intendentem nihil adhuc cognoscitur. Est autem plenissima, nam conceptio entis non id quod iam cognoscitur sed id in quod intenditur dicit atque significat; et cum omnia intendat, cum ad totam realitatem totius universi cognoscendam pergat, plenissima sane est.

Ulterius sequitur differentias entis non addere super ens; si enim adderent, aliquid praeter ens significarent; sed praeter ens non est nisi nihil; et ideo differentiae entis super ens addere non possunt.

Ulterius sequitur ens non esse genus; nam id est genus quod in se suas differentias non iam includat;[8] etc., etc.

5 Consideratis ergo et quidditate entis et eius intentione tum intendente tum intenta, remanet ut de eius extensione seu denotatione dicatur.

Secundum extensionem ergo sumitur ens vel collective vel distributive. Collective enim ens dicit 'omnia.' Distributive autem ens dicit 'totam uniuscuiusque realitatem.'

grasped, and that not only true but also all true conclusions are deduced from them. Since this most fundamental concept presents the most formidable difficulty, it is no wonder that many brilliant thinkers have gone astray in this matter of the intended intention, or concept, of being.[7]

Now, however, from what we said about the quiddity and the intending intention of being, we may safely go on to consider the explicit concept of being.

Since the cutting edge of the intellect regards 'everything,' it follows that the concept of being embraces the total reality of the entire universe; for if even the least part or aspect is left out, it no longer regards 'everything.'

Since the process whereby we gain knowledge of each single thing involves two questions (What is it? and Is it?), it follows that the concept of being is the concept of a composite consisting of essence (what it is) and existence (that it is).

Since the intending intention does not constitute knowledge but only leads to knowledge through questioning, the concept of being may seem to be empty, yet in fact it is the fullest of all. It seems empty because through the intending intention alone nothing is yet known. On the other hand, it is the fullest of all, because the concept of being denotes and signifies not what is already known but that towards which the intending intention tends; and since it intends everything, since it drives on to know the full reality of the entire universe, it is indeed the fullest of all concepts.

Further, it follows that the differences of being are not something over and above being. If they were, they would indicate something other than being; but apart from being there is nothing at all, and so the differences of being cannot be over and above being.

Again, it follows that being is not a genus; for a genus does not include its differences within itself. Etc., etc.[8]

5 Now that we have dealt with the quiddity of being and its intending and intended intention, we must say a word about its extension or denotation.

With regard to its extension, being is understood either collectively or distributively. Collectively being denotes 'everything'; distributively it denotes 'the total reality of each single thing.'

---

7 See Thomas Aquinas, *Summa theologiae*, 1-2, q. 66, a. 5, ad 4m.

8 [See Lonergan, *Insight* 386: 'Inasmuch as the notion of being is prior to all other cognitional contents, it is like a genus awaiting division by the addition of differences. But inasmuch as the notion of being anticipates, penetrates, and includes all other contents, it differs from the genus, which is a determinate content quite distinct from the content of its differences.' Lonergan's 'Etc., etc.' here probably refers to other points about being that are discussed in this same section (6) of chapter 12 of *Insight*.]

Praeterea, secundum quod ens sumitur distributive, vel strictius vel latius dicitur.

Strictius, ens est id quod est. Ita Deus, angeli, homines, animalia, plantae, mineralia, quia ipsa sunt, entia strictius dicuntur.

Latius, ens est quod quodammodo ordinatur ad id quod est. Ita latius entia dicuntur (1) principia intrinseca entis finiti, (2) accidentia, (3) possibilia, (4) entia rationis tantum. Quorum nullum est illud ipsum quod est; et tamen horum omnia quodammodo ordinantur ad id quod est. Nam (1) principia entis ipsa non sunt sed iis aliquid est; (2) accidentium non est esse sed inesse; (3) possibilia non sunt sed esse possunt; et (4) entia rationis non esse naturale sed intentionale tantum habent.

6 Quibus perspectis, sequentia facile concludes.

Primo, adeo ens non est abstractum ut illud ipsum sit quo concretum intendere et significare possimus. Qui enim concretum dicit, rem secundum totam eius realitatem dicit. Sed nemo inter homines ullam rem secundum totam eius realitatem cognoscit. Qua de causa, non cognoscendo sed tendendo per intentionem entis intendentem concretum dicimus et significamus.

Deinde, ens est maximum non solum extensione sed etiam intentione. Quod autem Scotistas et Hegelianos decipit ut ens intentione minimum dictitent, in eo est quod per solam entis intentionem intendentem, quamvis potentia omnia cognoscamus, actu tamen nihil cognoscimus.

Tertio, cum ens omnia respiciat, non ita est philosophis relinquendum ut ab omni alia scientia exuletur. Sicut enim sola philosophia non est omnium scientia, ita etiam sola philosophia non est entis scientia.

Quarto, eatenus theologia de ente tractat quatenus de Deo et de omnibus quae ad Deum referuntur tractat. Deus enim est ens per essentiam, quo omisso, omittitur entis intelligibilitas intrinseca. Et visio Dei beata atque absolute supernaturalis est sola notitia creaturae possibilis qua ei innotescere potest ens quidditative. Denique qui de omnibus tractat prout ad Deum referuntur, de omnibus quodammodo tractat et ideo de ente.

Quinto, intentio entis intendens est ipsum lumen nostri intellectus. Per hanc enim intentionem atque lumen et (1) sensibilia intellectualiter admiramur et (2) a sensibilibus qua sensibilibus avertimur et (3) in quaestiones circa totum verum intelligibile convertimur.

Moreover, if being is taken distributively, it can be understood in a stricter or a broader sense.

In a stricter sense, being is that which is. Thus God, angels, humans, animals, plants, and minerals are beings in the stricter sense because they themselves are.

More broadly speaking, a being is that which is in some way or other related to what is. Thus the following are called beings in a wider sense: (1) the intrinsic principles of a finite being, (2) accidents, (3) things that are possible, (4) 'beings of reason,' beings that exist only in the mind. None of these is that which itself is, and yet all of these are in some way or other related to what is. For (1) the principles of being do not themselves exist, but something exists through them; (2) accidents do not exist, they inhere, exist-in; (3) possible beings do not exist but can exist; and (4) beings of reason have not a natural but only an intentional act of existence.

6 Granted the foregoing, these conclusions readily follow.

First, far from being abstract, being is precisely that by which we can intend and signify the concrete. When you speak of something concrete, you are speaking of a thing in its total reality. But no human being knows anything in its total reality. Accordingly, we denote and signify the concrete not by knowing it but by intending it through the intending intention of being.

Second, being is the greatest not only in extension but also in intention. The followers of Scotus and Hegel maintain that being is minimal in intention. But what leads them astray is the fact that by the intending intention of being alone, although potentially we know everything, we actually know nothing.

Third, since being includes everything it must not be considered the sole preserve of philosophers to the exclusion of all other branches of knowledge. For just as philosophy alone is not the science of all reality, so too philosophy alone is not the science of being.

Fourth, theology deals with being insofar as it deals with God and everything that is related to God. For God is being by essence, and if you eliminate God, you eliminate the intrinsic intelligibility of being. And the absolutely supernatural beatific vision of God is the only knowledge possible to a creature whereby being can be known quidditatively. Finally, to deal with everything as it is related to God means in some way to deal with everything and therefore with being.

Fifth, the intending intention of being is the very light of our intellect. For by this intention and light (1) we wonder intellectually about sensible things; (2) we are turned away from sensible things as sensible; and (3) we are turned to questions about the entire range of intelligible truth.

Sexto, lumen nostri intellectus est participata quaedam similitudo lucis increatae.[9]

Septimo, Verbum divinum est ens per essentiam intellectualiter genitum, et Verbum incarnatum est ens per essentiam intellectualiter genitum atque incarnatum. Unde dicitur: 'Erat lux vera quae illuminat omnem hominem venientem in hunc mundum' Ioan., 1, 9;[10] et 'Ego in hoc natus sum et ad hoc veni in mundum, ut testimonium perhibeam veritati: omnis qui est ex veritate, audit vocem meam' Ioan., 18, 37;[11] et caetera apud Ioannem de luce et tenebris.

Octavo, quia intentio entis intenta in aliis alia est, ideo historicus inter diversas scholas philosophicas et theologicas distinguere debet.

Quia autem intentio entis intendens est una eademque specifice in omnibus, nihil ineptius fingi potest quam quae saepius dicantur, nempe, revelationem divinam omni entis intentione caruisse, quam intentionem ex Hellenismo, Gnosticismo, Platonismo, Aristotelismo fuisse in Christianismum invectam.

Iterum, quia intentio entis intendens est homini naturalis et omnibus communis, ad eam maxime attendere debet theologus quippe quod haec intentio in fontibus secundum ipsorum fontium sensum deesse non potest. Et pari ratione idem est dicendum de notionibus potentiae, formae, et actus prout postea definientur.

Sectio Secunda: De Ex-sistentia[12]

7 Quaerebat S. Kierkegaard utrum ipse vere et realiter existeret Christianus. Quaerunt et philosophi recentissimi quid sit proprie, genuine, authentice hominem esse.

Sixth, the light of our intellect is a participated likeness of uncreated light.[9]

Seventh, the divine Word is being by essence intellectually begotten, and the incarnate Word is being by essence intellectually begotten and incarnate. Hence we read, 'He was the true light that enlightens everyone coming into the world' (John 1.9),[10] and 'For this was I born and for this have I come into the world, to bear witness to the truth. Everyone who is of the truth hears my voice' (John 18.37).[11] See also other Johannine passages that speak of light and darkness.

Eighth, since the intended intention of being has been understood by various people in various ways, a historian must distinguish between the different philosophical and theological schools.

On the other hand, because the intending intention of being is specifically one and the same in all, one can imagine nothing more absurd than what is heard all too often, namely, that divine revelation lacked any intention of being, that the intention of being was imported into Christian thought from Hellenism, Gnosticism, Platonism, Aristotelianism.

Again, because the intending intention of being is part of human nature and common to all, the theologian must pay particular attention to it for the reason that, in keeping with the meaning of the sources of revelation themselves, this intention cannot be absent from those sources. And for the same reason this holds also for the notions of potency, form, and act as they will be defined later.

2 Existenz[12]

7 Kierkegaard used to ask whether he was really and truly a Christian. Contemporary philosophers ask what it means to be a human being in the proper, genuine, authentic sense.

---

9 Thomas Aquinas, *Summa theologiae*, 1, q. 84, a. 5.

10 [NRSV: 'The true light, which enlightens everyone, was coming into the world.']

11 [NRSV: 'For this I was born, and for this I came into the world, to testify to the truth. Everyone who belongs to the truth listens to my voice.']

12 [The choice of *Existenz* to translate 'De ex-sistentia' is based on Lonergan's usage in the 1964 lecture '*Existenz* and *Aggiornamento*,' where *Existenz* is coupled with 'on being oneself.' See *Collection* (Toronto: University of Toronto Press, 1988 [CWL 4]) 222. 'On being oneself' was a key theme in Lonergan's 1957 lectures on existentialism, published in CWL 18; there, however, he tended to limit the use of the word *Existenz* to discussions of the philosophy of Karl Jaspers, in which it is a key technical term. Elsewhere in this section his *ex-sistere* is rendered *to 'exist'* (that is, using inverted commas) and similarly for cognate terms, while *Existenz* is used to translate *ex-sistentia*. Usually Lonergan's Latin word 'exsistentia' does not have this dramatic significance, and then it has been changed to 'existentia.' The same holds for the verb 'exsistere,' which becomes 'existere.' But when Lonergan added a hyphen, as here, his spelling of the Latin word is retained.]

Quibus in quaestionibus non de quolibet esse rei quaeritur sed de eius existentia prout ipsa res normative concipitur. Non enim Kierkegaard sufficiens duxit se esse in Dania natum et ideo vi iuris publici ad ecclesiam officialem Daniensem quippe Christianam pertinere. Neque auctores contemporanei illum proprie hominem ducunt qui documenta nativitatis clarissima, imo indubitabilia, afferre possit. Sed hominem utrum existat quaerunt prout, ut voce Augustini utar, sempiternis rationibus esse debeat.

Quae quidem quaestio minime superfluit. Cum enim homo definiatur animal rationale, nihilominus per prius animal quoddam sat evolutum efficitur quam actu rationale esse incipiat. Non enim parvulos nisi septennes ad aetatem rationis pervenisse iudicamus; neque adolescentes pleni iuris habemus ante annum vigesimum primum; qui autem spectacula publica conducunt iis maxime placere student qui aetatem mentalem duodecim annorum habeant quia ista mentalis aetas maxime communis inter adultos homines mulieresque aestimetur.

Quod si quis non populares opiniones sed ipsam rei rationem audire mavult, ordinem rerum hierarchicum inspicere atque intelligere debet. In elementis enim chimicis ita dominantur leges chimiae propriae ut tamen omnes leges physicae observentur. In plantis ita dominantur leges biologiae propriae ut tamen omnes leges et physicae et chimicae observentur. In animalibus ita dominantur leges quae in psychologia sensitiva stabiliantur ut tamen nulla lex vel physica vel chimica vel biologica violetur. Unde forte concludes eiusmodi esse hieriarchicum rerum ordinem ut unumquodque genus superius quasi per quandam Aufhebung et leges inferiores retineat et easdem etiam tollat. Perfecte enim retinentur leges inferiores cum perfecte observentur; et perfecte etiam tolluntur cum dominio altioris cuiusdam syntheseos perfecte subordinentur.

Quae tamen conclusio, etsi de aliis verissima sit, in homine tamen exceptionem statim patitur. Quamvis enim in homine vigeant leges physicae, chimicae, biologicae, et psychicae, ipsa tamen altior in eo synthesis non actualis sed potentialis est. Eiusmodi enim est homo, non ut ratio parti suae inferiori necessitate quadam naturali dominetur, sed ut ratio dominari debeat. Quod dominium cum ipse homo per propriam rationem et propriam libertatem efficere debeat ut vere et proprie et authentice et genuine homo sit, ad hominem pertinet ut ipse se ex potentialitate sui ex-sistere faciat.

Cuius ex-sistentiae paradoxon statim elucet. Non enim per intellectum sapientia, intelligentia et scientia actuatum neque per voluntatem virtutibus iam ornatam homo ex-sistere conatur, sed per notam illam tabulam rasam et per voluntatem virtutibus orbatam hominem incipere oportet ut tandem denique addiscat quid esse debeat et talem se efficere velit qualis esse debeat.

These questions deal not with just any existence of a thing but with its existence as that thing is conceived normatively. Kierkegaard did not think it sufficient to be born in Denmark and thus by the law of the land to belong to the official Danish Christian Church. Nor do contemporary writers regard one to be a human being in the proper sense just because one can produce a clear and authentic birth certificate. Rather they ask whether human beings exist as they ought to 'according to the eternal reasons,' to borrow a phrase from Augustine.

This question is by no means pointless. While a human being is defined as a rational animal, still we must be sufficiently well developed as animals before we begin to act rationally. We do not regard children as having reached the age of reason until they are seven years old, nor do we judge young people to have reached majority until the age of twenty-one. And producers of public entertainment aim at adapting their shows to the mentality of twelve-year-olds, since that is reckoned to be the average mental age of the adult population.

But if you prefer to disregard popular opinion and get at the heart of the matter, you must investigate and understand the hierarchic order of things. In chemical elements the laws proper to chemistry prevail, while leaving intact the laws of physics. In plants the laws of biology prevail, but without violating any of the laws of chemistry and physics. In animals the laws of animal psychology prevail, but in such a way that no law of chemistry, physics, or biology is violated. From this you will perhaps conclude that the hierarchic order of things is such that each higher genus, as if by a kind of *Aufhebung*, retains lower laws while at the same time doing away with them. For the lower laws are completely retained, since they are perfectly observed; but they are also completely dispensed with since they are wholly subordinated to the overriding control of a higher synthesis.

Now while this conclusion holds true for all other beings, we immediately note an exception in the case of human beings. Although physical, chemical, biological, and psychic laws are operative in us, the higher synthesis itself is not actual but potential. For we are not made in such a way that by some natural necessity our reason *must* rule over our lower nature, but that it *ought* to do so. Such dominion must be achieved through the exercise of one's reason and personal freedom in order for one to become a true, proper, authentic and genuine human being. It is up to each one, therefore, out of the potentiality each one has, to achieve his or her own *Existenz*.

The paradox inherent in this *Existenz* comes to light immediately. For human beings do not strive to 'exist' through intellects already actuated by wisdom, understanding, and knowledge, nor through wills already endowed with virtues. Rather, one has to begin from that famous *tabula rasa* and from a will devoid of virtues so that one may at last learn what one ought to be and will to make oneself what one ought to be.

Quibus perspectis, illud sane mirum esse non potest rarissimos ex-sistere homines, rarissimos esse qui didicerint illud re vera esse 'reale' seu 'realiter reale' quod mediantibus conceptibus atque iudiciis sub nomine entis innotescat, rarissimos pariter esse qui per quandam sensitivae animae noctem ita sint purgati ut bono intelligibili atque vero et totaliter et efficaciter et perseveranter sese dederint.

8 Quae cum ita sint, si quis aliis subvenire voluerit, et (1) ipse ex-sistat necesse est ne caecus caecum ducat et (2) in aliis magis convertendis quam convincendis incumbat. Cum enim qualis quisque sit, talis ei videatur finis,[13] sequitur sane non solum qualis quis in appetendo sit talem ei videri appetitionis finem sed etiam qualis quis in apprehendendo sit talem ei videri apprehensionis finem.

Inquantum ergo homo sensibilibus immergitur seu, uti recentius dicitur, inquantum in sphaera aesthetica subiectivitatis existentialis versatur, eatenus unumquodque ei reale videtur quatenus sensibile est, et eatenus unumquodque ei nihil videtur quatenus sensus fugit.

Inquantum autem homo a sensibilibus emersus ad intelligibilia convertitur, eatenus unumquodque ei reale videtur quatenus est (i.e., quatenus intus-legendo et affirmando innotescere potest), et eatenus unumquodque ei nihil videtur quatenus non est.

Ex quo factum est ut qui non ex-sistant ens esse nihil aestiment, et qui ex-sistant non-ens esse nihil iudicent. Quae tamen positiones clarae, distinctae, et inter se contradictoriae ne concipiantur quidem nisi ab iis qui aliquatenus ex-sistere inceperint cum hoc ipsum quod problema exacte innotescit ad eius solutionem plus dimidium reputari soleat.

9 Quantum autem ad adiutoria attinet quibus homo converti possit ut ex-sistere incipiat, tum inter media et finem distinguendum est, tum inter directa media et indirecta, tum inter naturalia et supernaturalia.

Et media quidem naturalia et indirecta satis obvia sunt. Qui enim loquitur, intellectu rationeque utatur necesse est; qui intellectu rationeque utitur, non solum ad sensibilia attendit sed etiam circa intelligibilia et vera occupatur; qua de causa, et antiqui Graeci loquaces et mediaevales disputationibus dediti, quasi ipsa natura humana manuducente, ad ens pervenerunt. E contra, recentiores qui solitarii systemata excogitaverint, de

Once this is grasped, it can surely come as no surprise that very few 'exist,' that very few have learned that 'the real' or the 'really real' is what becomes known under the name of being through the mediation of concepts and judgments, that very few have come through a kind of dark night of the senses so purified as to surrender themselves wholeheartedly, effectively, and perseveringly to the intelligible and true good.

8 This being the case, if you wish to be of service to others, it is necessary (1) that you 'exist' yourself, so that it is not a matter of the blind leading the blind, and (2) that you try to effect a conversion in others rather than to prove them wrong. For since the type of person you are determines how you see your aim in life,[13] it surely follows not only that the type of person you are in desiring determines how you will see the aim of your desiring but also that the type of person you are in apprehending determines how you will see the aim of your apprehending.

To whoever, therefore, is immersed in the world of the senses – or, as they say nowadays, to one living in the aesthetic sphere of existential subjectivity – things will be seen as real only insofar as they are perceptible to the senses; and they will be seen as nothing insofar as they cannot be so perceived.

But to the extent that one emerging from the world of the senses is converted to the intelligible world, things will be seen to be real insofar as they *are* (that is, insofar as they can be known by being understood and affirmed), and things will be seen to be nothing insofar as they are not.

And so it happens that those who do not 'exist' regard being as nothing, while those who do 'exist' judge non-being to be nothing. Such clear, distinct, and mutually contradictory positions, however, would not even be conceived except by those who have already begun to 'exist' to some extent, since a problem clearly grasped is a problem half solved.

9 As to what can help one to be converted and so begin to 'exist,' we must distinguish between end and means, between direct and indirect means, and between natural and supernatural means.

Means that are natural and indirect are clear enough. When you speak, you have to use your mind and reason; and when you use your mind and reason, you have not only to attend to the data of sense but you are also concerned with the intelligible and the true. For this reason both the ancient Greeks with their love of talk and the medievals with their passion for disputation arrived at being,

13 [See Aristotle, *Nicomachean Ethics*, III, 5, 1114a 30; Thomas Aquinas, *Summa theologiae*, 1, q. 83, a. 1, obj. 5.]

meditationibus suis profundissimis saepius ea deprompserunt quae eos sensismo haud liberatos manifestarent.

Iterum, qui persona humana cum personis humanis agit, et ipse intellectu et ratione utatur necesse est et de iis cogitet qui pariter intellectu et ratione utantur. Ex quo fit ut ipso hoc exercitio illa exsurgat atque confirmetur orientatio quae orientationi animalibus propriae opponatur. Homo enim quatenus non ex-sistit centrum quoddam apprehensionum atque appetitionum est ad quod alia omnia tamquam utilia vel inutilia referantur; neque intellectus et ratio adeo in eo dominantur ut potius cum caeteris animalis organis enumerentur; quod enim cervis est velocitas et leonibus fortitudo et serpentibus dens veneno plenus, hoc hominibus intellectus reputatur. Quatenus e contra homo ex-sistere inceperit, et universum esse ordinem quendam intelligit, et se huius ordinis partem subordinatam iudicat, et bonum privatum communi bono postponendum esse addiscit. Quibus perspectis, sicut et loquacitas Graecorum et mediaevalis disputationum amor, ita etiam modernus personae cultus inter adiutoria est recensendus quae apta nata sint ut homo convertatur atque ex-sistat.

Attamen media huiusmodi naturalia, quia indirecta sunt, etiam illa carent efficacia ut omnem excludant deceptionem. Non enim eo modo agunt ut ipsum morbum detegant atque expellant; sed potius illos et fines proponunt et illa adiuncta inducunt et illas actiones laudant unde saepe felicem fore eventum sperari possit. Quamvis enim Graeci antiqui ad ens pervenerint, post et Academia in scepticismum et Lycaeum in empiricismum declinaverunt. Quamvis mediaevales profundissima de ente invenerint, saeculorum decimi quarti et quinti decadentiam, conceptualismum, nominalismum, scepticismum impedire non valuerunt. Et sicut Stoici olim doctrinam moralem vere elevatam ita profitebantur ut tamen a materialismo non recesserint, similiter nostri temporis personalistae veras virtutes ita laudant ut tamen a disciplinis proprie scientificis despiciendis et contemnendis non abstineant.

10 Qua de causa, mediis indirectis etiam ea quae directe ipsum finem respiciant coniungi oportet. Finis autem est ut ex-sistat homo, ut de potentialitate dominii in exercitium dominii completi atque perfecti transeat rationalitas humana. In quem finem medium directum est conversio quaedam et intima et radicalis, conscia atque deliberata. In quam conversionem primus generatim est gressus ut quisque apud se et suspicetur et inveniat et saltem sibi profiteatur se nondum esse conversum. Si enim acutissimum Augustini ingenium per multos annos nihil reale nisi corpus aestimabat, qui minoris sint ingenii ideo

led along as it were by human nature itself. Modern thinkers, on the other hand, who have worked out their systems in isolation, more often than not have drawn from their profound musings ideas indicating that they have hardly been liberated from a kind of sensism.

Again, when human persons interact with one another, they must use their intellect and reason and also be aware that the others are likewise using theirs. Through this exercise there arises and develops an orientation that is the opposite of that which characterizes animals. For to the extent to which one does not 'exist,' one is a kind of focal point of thoughts and desires in relation to which everything else is judged useful or useless. Intellect and reason are of so little importance as to be deemed comparable to animal faculties; for the intellect is considered to be to a human being what swiftness is to a deer, bravery to a lion, or venemous fangs to a snake. But when one has begun to 'exist,' one understands that there is a certain order to the universe and concludes that one is a subordinate part of that order, and so learns to put the common good before one's own private good. On this basis, therefore, the present-day esteem for the person must be reckoned among the aids that contribute to personal conversion and *Existenz*, just as in an earlier time the Greek fondness for talk and the medieval passion for disputation had done.

However, since natural means of this kind are indirect, they are also not so effective as to exclude all possibility of self-deception. For they do not act in such a way as to diagnose the disease and cure it; rather they propose the goals, provide the circumstances, and favor those actions from which more often than not a happy outcome may be hoped for. Although the ancient Greeks did arrive at being, later on the Academy fell into skepticism and the Lyceum into empiricism. And although the medievals plumbed the depths of being, in the fourteenth and fifteenth centuries they were unable to stem the tide of decadence, conceptualism, nominalism, and skepticism. Just as in former times the Stoics had propounded a truly lofty doctrine of morality and yet remained materialists, so too the personalists of our day, while they praise true virtue, nonetheless do not refrain from looking down on and holding in contempt disciplines that are truly scientific.

10 For this reason, means that directly regard the goal must be added to indirect means. The goal is that a human being 'exist,' that human rationality go from a potency to dominate to actually exercising complete and perfect control. To this end the direct means is a certain deep and radical conversion that is conscious and deliberate. Normally the first step towards this conversion is that one suspect, discover, and admit, at least to oneself, that one is not yet converted. For if the keen mind of Augustine thought for years that only material bodies were real,

communiter ab Augustino differunt, non quod ipsi re vera ens esse reale et non-ens esse nihil perspectum habeant, sed quia inconstantes atque confusi neque umquam ipsum problema clare et distincte conceperunt et multo minus decisive resolverunt.

Quibus mediis naturalibus et indirectis et directis, longe efficaciora sunt supernaturalia. Quamvis enim naturaliter nobis indita sit intentio illa entis intendens quae et participata quaedam similitudo sit lucis increatae et naturale illud desiderium quod non quiescat donec ens-per-essentiam per essentiam suam cognoscatur,[14] tamen in hunc finem per media naturalia non proceditur[15] sed et ipsa hominis iustificatio, qua pars sensitiva rationi et ratio Deo subdatur,[16] est supernaturalis effectus gratuiti amoris divini[17] secundum quod Deus in nobis operatur ut cum Deo cooperari possimus.[18]

Et supernaturalis haec conversio, quae naturalem in se includit, quamvis principaliter in finem vitae aeternae dirigatur, nihilominus ea secum fert quae hominem etiam hac in vita ex-sistere faciant. Nam qui fidem catholicam profitetur, iam parvulus spiritualia esse realia addiscit; qui dogmatibus catholicis adhaeret, per vera ad realia pertingit; qui concilio Vaticano obtemperat, illam mysteriorum intelligentiam quam concilium laudat spernere non potest; qui duce ecclesia theologiam quaerit quae secundum principia, methodum, et doctrinam S. Thomae Aquinatis tradatur,[19] cum tota haec theologia in quaestionibus ponendis et solvendis consistat, saltem suspicari debet per quaestiones ad cognitionem hominem procedere.

Quae cum ita sint, negari non potest tum ipsam nostram fidem tum suo etiam loco theologiam catholicam ita totam hominis mentem penetrare atque dirigere ut tam efficaciter quam profunde eum invitet, alliciat, imo fere cogat ad ex-sistendum. Et tamen 'qui iustus est, iustificetur adhuc' (DB 803). Qui gratiam recepit quae hominem sanum, rectum, iustum faciat, per gratiam laboret ut gratia augeatur.[20] Quo enim magis ratio Deo subditur et pars sensitiva rationi, eo minus pars sensitiva rationalem hominis partem obscurat atque obnubilat. Quo minus a vita sensitiva perturbatur ratio,

those less gifted than Augustine generally differ from him not in that they perceive that being is the really real and that non-being is nothing, but rather in the fact that through their confusion and indecision they have never clearly and distinctly conceived the problem, much less definitively settled it.

Supernatural means are far more efficacious than these natural means, direct or indirect. Although we are naturally endowed with that intending intention of being that is a participated likeness of uncreated light, and with that natural desire that is not at rest until being-by-essence is known through its essence,[14] still we do not proceed toward this end by natural means.[15] Our justification, by which the sensitive element of our being is subject to our reason and our reason to God,[16] is the supernatural effect of the free gift of divine love[17] inasmuch as God operates in us so that we may be able to cooperate with God.[18]

This supernatural conversion which, although primarily directed towards the goal of eternal life, includes natural conversion, also carries along with it that by which one can 'exist' even in this life. One who was brought up in the Catholic faith learned even as a child that spiritual things are real; one who holds to Catholic dogmas arrives at what is real by what is true; one who agrees with the [First] Vatican Council cannot make light of that understanding of the mysteries commended by the Council; and one who, following the lead of the church, pursues theology according to the principles, method, and doctrine of St Thomas Aquinas,[19] must at least suspect that we advance in knowledge by questioning, since the whole of Thomas's theology consists in asking questions and answering them.

Since this is so, it cannot be denied that our faith and, in its proper place, Catholic theology penetrate and direct the whole human mind in such a way as effectively and profoundly to invite, entice, and almost force one toward *Existenz*. And yet, 'let one who is just be further justified' (DB 803, DS 1335). One who has received the grace that makes a human being whole, righteous, and just should strive, with the help of grace, that grace be further increased.[20] The more completely reason is subject to God and the sense appetite to reason, the less does the sensitive element obscure and darken the rational. The less reason is perturbed

14 Thomas Aquinas, *Summa theologiae*, 1-2, q. 3, a. 8.
15 Ibid. q. 5, a. 5.
16 Ibid. q. 113, a. 1.
17 Ibid. q. 110, a. 1.
18 Ibid. q. 111, a. 2.
19 [The 1917 Code of Canon Law (1366, §2) imposed on Catholic philosophy and theology an injunction to follow 'Angelici Doctoris rationem, doctrinam, et principia.' Lonergan repeated his own wording of the injunction in the very last sentence of this book: 'principia, doctrina, methodus S. Thomae Aquinatis ...']
20 Ibid. q. 114, a. 8.

eo efficacius fides rationem illuminare potest. Quo efficacius fides rationem illuminat, eo fructuosius ratio per fidem illustrata aliquam Deo dante mysteriorum intelligentiam attingit.

11 Quibus perspectis, etiam quae sequuntur adnotanda sunt.

Primo, quae brevissime de ratione ex-sistentiae scripsimus, nisi per summa capita rem non tangunt. Nam inter extrema quae tum in coherenti quodam sensismo tum in intel-lectualismo pariter coherenti consistant, multi et diversi sunt gradus intermedii. Neque opinandum est singulos homines in determinato quodam gradu constanter vivere sed potius inter diversos gradus plus minus oscillari. Sicut enim superficies oceani nunc mi-noribus nunc fluctibus agitatur maioribus, sicut ipsa aquarum altitudo fluxu augetur et refluxu minuitur, ita etiam de perfectionis gradibus quibus homines ex-sistant ratiocinan-dum est.

Deinde, hac rei complexitate et quaestionis obscuritate perspectis, arbitretur nemo se hisce notulis esse paratum ad eos intelligendos auctores qui nomen existentialistarum audi-ant. Quid enim singuli per ens dicere velint, nisi singulis diligentissime investigatis accurate determinari non potest.

Tertio, potius theologicam quam philosophicam esse hanc de ex-sistentia quaestionem multis probatur argumentis. Nam qui hominem prout de facto est intelligere studet, hominem peccato originali infectum et gratia Dei adiutum et huic gratiae vel cooperan-tem vel resistentem investigat. At peccati originalis et divinae gratiae intelligentia non a philosophis sed a theologis est quaerenda. Praeterea, in actuali rerum ordine per unum revelationis remedium duplicem Deus intendit finem, nempe, et ut veritates supernatu-rales innotescant, et ut naturales veritates ab omnibus expedite, firma certitudine et nullo admixto errore cognosci possint (DB 1786). Quare qui a revelatione divina praescindant, qui empirice et concrete procedant, qui hominum massam magis respiciant quam id quod per se humana natura facere posset, specie quidem hominem considerare videntur prout est, sed re vera illud omittunt quod ad conditionem hominis sublevandam et divina sapi-entia conceperit et bonitas divina sit largita.

Quarto, alio etiam sensu ad theologum pertinet ut de ex-sistentia quaerat. Quod enim ex philosophis inter se dissentientibus et multa diversaque opinantibus oritur problema criticum, non simpliciter abest a theologis qui de omni fere quaestione speculativa in di-versas abeant partes ut sine fructu qui perspiciatur et sine fine qui exspectetur disputent. Praeterea, si ideo philosophi dissentiunt quod alius alio perfectionis gradu ex-sistit, non solum theologi suspicari possunt se eodem morbo non perfecte esse liberatos, sed etiam et

by the life of the senses, the more effectively will faith be able to enlighten reason. And the more effectively faith enlightens reason, the more fruitfully will reason, thus enlightened, attain with God's help some understanding of the mysteries of faith.

11 With all this well understood, the following points should also be noted.

First, what we have very briefly written about the meaning of *Existenz* merely touches the surface. There are many different intermediate stages between the extremes of a coherent sensism and an equally coherent intellectualism. And one must not think that each individual lives consistently at one fixed stage but rather that we more or less go back and forth between stages. Just as the surface of the ocean is disturbed now by smaller and now by larger waves, and just as the water level falls and rises with the ebb and flow of the tides, so ought we to think of the various levels of perfection at which persons may 'exist.'

Second, once the complexity of the matter and the obscurity of the problem are grasped, do not imagine that with these notes you are ready to understand those authors who go by the name of existentialists. For what each one of them means by 'being' can be determined only by a painstaking investigation of that particular thinker.

Third, there are many arguments to prove that this question of *Existenz* is theological rather than philosophical. For whoever strives to understand human beings as they actually are is investigating creatures infected by original sin and helped by God's grace, and as either cooperating with or resisting that grace. But it is theologians and not philosophers whose task it is to seek an understanding of original sin and of divine grace. Furthermore, in the actual order of things, by the one remedy of revelation God had a twofold end in view, namely, that supernatural truths might become known and that natural truths could be known with relative ease, with certitude, and with no trace of error (DB 1786, DS 3005). Hence, those who disregard divine revelation and proceed empirically and concretely, who regard only the mass of humanity rather than what human nature can do by itself, may appear to be considering human beings as they are, but in fact are ignoring what divine wisdom has devised and divine goodness has bestowed to alleviate the human condition.

Fourth, there is also another sense in which the question of *Existenz* belongs to the theologian. For the critical problem which has arisen from the many disagreements and opposing views of philosophers is not simply absent in theologians: the latter, in their investigation of almost every speculative question, take up different positions with the result that they argue fruitlessly and inconclusively. Furthermore, if philosophers disagree because they 'exist' at different levels, theologians

eniti debent, cum de actuali hominis conditione altiores causas rationesque investigent, ut tum sibi tum philosophis subveniant.

Quinto, illud denique omnino praetermitti non oportet multas obiectiones quae contra theologiam thomisticam urgeri soleant et non ex-sistentibus existere gravissimas et ex-sistentibus evanescere. Quamvis enim vetera novis augere atque perficere conveniat,[21] in primis enitendum est ut vetera re vera intelligantur. Quem in finem nihil efficacius conducere scio quam intima illa atque radicalis conversio qua quis, umbris quasi depulsis, sibi fateatur reale esse intelligibile, verum, ens, bonum.

Quod sane non ita est intelligendum quasi sensus, imaginatio, affectus essent derelinquendi. Nihil enim hac in vita intelligit homo nisi intellectum suum ad phantasmata convertit. Et quamvis ipse Deus per negationem omnis materialitatis et sensibilitatis concipiatur, non tamen ad Dominum nostrum Iesum Christum, hominem materialiter individuatum, acceditur nisi hic locus hocque tempus sensibus innotescunt et per imaginationem continuuntur donec ad Palestinam, Bethlehem, Nazareth, Ierusalem ante duo millia annorum perveniatur. Sed postquam per partem sensitivam ad corpus Domini pervenimus, etiam intellectu perspicere oportet eum esse hominem anima intellectiva animatum, et fide credere oportet eum non solum hominem sed etiam Deum esse, et theologia aliquatenus intelligere oportet quid denique tandem significet unam esse personam in duabus subsistentem naturis et sibi per duas conscientias innotescentem.

Sectio Tertia: De Uno

12 Distinguuntur unum transcendentale, unum naturale (seu formale, seu unum per se), et unum praedicamentale.

Unum praedicamentale est principium numeri et primo innotescit experiendo; e.g., oculis cernendo digitos distinguo primum, alterum, tertium, etc.

Unum naturale seu formale seu per se est quod primo innotescit in prima intellectus operatione; e.g., acervus lapidum dicitur unum per accidens quia in eo nullum unitatis principium intelligibile deprehenditur sed tantum iuxtapositio spatialis; sed homo vel animal dicitur unum per se quia non solum oculis

not only can suspect that they have not been entirely free of the same malady, but also should strive to help both themselves and the philosophers, since they are investigating the deeper causes and reasons for the human condition as it actually is.

Fifth, we must not overlook the fact that the numerous objections which are usually brought up against Thomist theology are most serious for those who do not 'exist,' but completely disappear for those who do. While it is true that the old should be expanded and perfected by the new,[21] it is crucial that we strive really to understand the old. I know of nothing that can lead to this more effectively than that interior and radical conversion whereby one emerges from the shadows and admits to oneself that the real is the intelligible, the true, being, the good.

That does not mean, of course, that the senses, imagination, and affectivity are of no account. For we understand nothing in this life unless we turn our intellects to phantasms. And although we conceive God by denying all materiality and all that is perceptible by the senses, we cannot approach our Lord Jesus Christ, a man individuated by matter, save by beginning from this particular time and place familiar to us through our senses and then proceeding by our imagination until we arrive at the Palestine, the Bethlehem, the Nazareth, and the Jerusalem of two thousand years ago. But after arriving at the corporeal reality of the Lord by means of our senses, we ought to grasp by our mind that he is a man animated by a rational soul and believe by faith that he is not just man but also God. And finally, by theology we ought to understand to some extent what it means to be one person subsisting in two natures and being aware of himself through two consciousnesses.

3 The Meanings of 'One'

12 We distinguish three meanings of 'one': 'transcendental one,' 'natural one' (that is, the formal 'one,' or one per se), and 'predicamental one.'

'Predicamental one' is the principle of number, and it first becomes known through experience. For example, seeing my fingers I distinguish the first, the second, the third, and so on.

'Natural or formal one,' one per se, is what first becomes known in the first operation of the intellect. Thus a pile of stones is said to be one-by-accident, since no intelligible principle of unity is apprehended in it but only spatial juxtaposition. A human being, on the other hand, or an animal is said to be one per se, not only

---

21 [The reference is to the phrase 'vetera novis augere et perficere,' in Pope Leo XIII's encyclical *Aeterni Patris*; see *Acta sanctae sedis* 12 (1879) 91–115, at 111.]

cernitur iuxtapositio spatialis partium sed etiam intellectu intus legitur unum proprie intelligibile.

Unum transcendentale est indivisum in se et divisum a quolibet alio; et hoc unum primo innotescit in secunda intellectus operatione, secundum quod obiectum iudicii necessario subest principiis identitatis et contradictionis; quodcumque enim rationabiliter affirmatur vel negatur, sibi idem et cum nullo alio confusum necessario est.

Sectio Quarta: De Subsistente

13 Quod strictius est ens, etiam strictius est unum (transcendentale). Cuius ratio est quod unum super ens non addit nisi negationes, unde tota perfectio unitatis in perfectione entitatis suum fundamentum habeat necesse est.

Quod unum super ens non addit nisi negationes ex definitione unius constat. Unum enim est indivisum in se et divisum a quolibet alio. Sed 'indivisum in se' non dicit nisi negationem divisionis internae; et 'divisum a quolibet alio' non dicit nisi negationem identificationis vel confusionis cum quolibet alio.

Quod plenius verificatur definitio 'unius' in ente strictius quam in ente latius dicto, ex brevi quadam comparatione constat.

Entia enim strictius dicta non solum concipiuntur et affirmantur secundum principia identitatis et non-contradictionis sed etiam in sua realitate ontologica sunt in se indivisa et a quolibet alio divisa. Mineralia enim et plantae et animalia et homines et angeli seorsum ab invicem sunt et propria existentia gaudent.

Entia vero latius dicta ita concipiuntur atque affirmantur secundum principia identitatis et contradictionis ut in sua realitate ontologica non plene ab omni alio dividantur; neque hoc iis accidit tantum sed ex ipsa eorum natura sequitur.

Accidentia enim ex ipsa sua natura substantiae insunt, et ideo non a quolibet alio simpliciter dividuntur. Principia entis intrinseca ex ipsa sua natura inter se coalescunt ad unum ens (strictius) efformandum; et ideo simpliciter dividuntur neque ab invicem neque a toto quod constituunt. Possibilia nihil sunt praeter potentiam agentis vel materiae, et ideo a tali potentia non dividuntur realiter. Entia denique rationis nihil sunt extra mentem, et ideo realiter a mente dividi non possunt.

because I perceive a spatial juxtaposition of parts but also because with my mind I grasp a unit that has its own proper intelligibility.

'Transcendental one' is undivided in itself and divided from everything else; and this 'one' first becomes known in the second operation of the intellect, inasmuch as the object of judgment is necessarily subject to the principles of identity and contradiction. For whatever is reasonably affirmed or denied is necessarily identical with itself and not confused with anything else.

4 The Subsistent

13 That which is being in the stricter sense is also one in the stricter, that is the transcendental, sense. The reason for this is that 'one' adds nothing but negations to being, and therefore the whole perfection of unity necessarily has its foundation in the perfection of being.

That 'one' adds nothing to being except negations is clear from the definition of 'one.' For what is one is undivided in itself and divided from everything else; but 'undivided in itself' merely denies internal division, and 'divided from everything else' merely denies identification with or admixture of anything else.

That the definition of 'one' is more fully verified in being in the stricter sense than in being in a broader sense is clear from a simple comparison.

Beings in the stricter sense are not only conceived and affirmed according to the principles of identity and non-contradiction, but in their ontological reality they are also undivided in themselves and divided from everything else. For minerals, plants, animals, human beings, and angels exist apart from one another and all have their own proper existence.

On the other hand, beings taken in a broader sense are so conceived and affirmed according to the principles of identity and contradiction that in their ontological reality they are not completely divided from one another; and this is not something that just happens to them, but follows from their very nature.

For accidents of their very nature inhere in a substance, and for that reason are not simply divided from everything else. The intrinsic principles of being by their very nature come together to form one being in the strict sense, and so are simply divided neither from each other nor from the whole they constitute. Things that are possible are nothing apart from the potency of the agent or that of matter, and hence they are not really distinct from that potency. Finally, 'beings of reason' are nothing outside the mind, and so they cannot be really separated from the mind.

14 Quibus perspectis, ad systematicam subsistentis notionem pervenitur. Communiter enim subsistens describitur id quod per se et in se est, ens completum, totum in se, a quolibet alio simpliciter divisum, seorsum et separatim existens. Unde ad refellendam sententiam Platonicam quaeri solet utrum universalia subsistant, scilicet, utrum sint entia extra mentem existentia, separata (*khôrista*), substantiae (*ousiai*). Iam vero omnia quae de subsistente dicuntur ad hoc reducuntur quod subsistens est ens strictius dictum. Si enim est ens, quodammodo existit et quodammodo est indivisum in se et divisum a quolibet alio. Si vero est ens strictius dictum, est id quod est, substantiale seu ens per se (secus esset accidentale vel aliquid minus), in se indivisum et quidem ex ipsa sua natura, a quolibet alio simpliciter divisum et ideo seorsum et separatim existens.

Unde elucet (1) quod entia strictius dicta (ea quae sunt) subsistunt, et ideo mineralia, plantae, animalia, homines, angeli subsistere dicuntur; (2) quod entia latius dicta (ea quibus quodammodo tantum competit esse) non subsistunt, et ideo accidentia, principia entis intrinseca, possibilia, et entia-rationis-tantum non subsistere dicuntur; (3) quod anima humana separata aliquatenus a ratione subsistentis deficit cum homo in animam et corpus divisus non sit 'indivisum in se';[22] (4) quod accidentia eucharistica sine subiecto a divina virtute sustentata aliquatenus ad rationem subsistentis appropinquant cum plenius ab omni alio dividantur quam accidentibus competit; (5) quod Christus, Deus et homo, cum sit unum ens strictius dictum (nempe, unum quod est et Deus et homo), etiam est unum subsistens.

Sectio Quinta: De Subsistente Distincto seu De Supposito Reali

15 Distincta sunt quorum unum non est aliud.

In rebus creatis eo ipso quod habetur subsistens, etiam habetur subsistens distinctum.

In divinis autem ratione distinguitur inter Deum et Patrem, Deum et Filium, Deum et Spiritum. Pater, Filius, et Spiritus sunt subsistentia distincta. Deus autem, prout ratione distinguitur a personis, est subsistens quodammodo indistinctum.

Suppositum dupliciter dicitur: primo modo, est suppositum reale, puta, hunc hominem existentem; altero modo, est suppositum hypotheticum tantum quod a vero et falso, et ideo ab esse et non esse praescindit.

14 With these observations in mind, we come now to the systematic notion of the subsistent. Ordinarily the subsistent is described as that which exists per se and in itself, a complete being, a whole in itself, simply divided from and existing separately and apart from everything else. Hence, in refutation of the Platonic view, the usual question asked is whether universals subsist, that is to say, whether they are beings that exist outside the mind, separate entities (*khôrista*), substances (*ousiai*). Now everything that is predicated of a subsistent comes down to the fact that a subsistent is a being in the strict sense. For if it is a being, somehow or other it exists and somehow or other it is undivided in itself and divided from everything else. And if it is a being in the strict sense, it is that which is, substantial, being per se (otherwise it would be something accidental or something less), undivided in itself and this by its very nature, and simply divided from all else and so existing separately and apart.

From all this it is evident (1) that beings in the strict sense (things which are) subsist, and therefore minerals, plants, animals, human beings, and angels are said to subsist; (2) that beings in the broader sense (things to which existence belongs only in a certain way) do not subsist, and therefore accidents, the intrinsic principles of being, possible beings, and beings of reason are not said to subsist; (3) that the separated human soul falls somewhat short of being a subsistent in the true sense, since a human being who has been separated into body and soul is not 'undivided in itself';[22] (4) that the Eucharistic accidents, which by divine power are sustained without a subject, come somewhat closer to being truly subsistent, since they are more completely divided from everything else than is the case with accidents; and (5) that Christ, God and man, one being in the strict sense (a one, that is, which is divine and human), is also one subsistent.

5 The Distinct Subsistent or Real Supposit

15 Things are distinct when one is not the other.

Among created things, a subsistent is by that very fact a distinct subsistent.

In God, however, there is a notional distinction between God and the Father, between God and the Son, and between God and the Spirit. The Father, the Son, and the Spirit are distinct subsistents; but God, as notionally distinct from the persons, is in some way an indistinct subsistent.

A supposit is understood in two ways: first, as a real supposit, this existing human being, for example; and secondly, as a merely hypothetical supposit which prescinds from truth and falsity, and therefore from existence and non-existence.

22 See Thomas Aquinas, *Summa theologiae*, 1, q. 75, a. 2, ad 1m.

Suppositum reale est subsistens distinctum.

Suppositum hypotheticum est id quod intercedit inter conceptus universales concretos et conceptus universales abstractos, puta, inter hominem et humanitatem, inter centaurum et centauritatem.[23]

16 Quae distinctio cum multis difficultatem faciat breviter est enucleanda.

Primo obicitur quod cum 'esse' iudicio innotescat cumque aliud sit iudicare et aliud concipere, nullus datur conceptus tou esse et ideo, cum suppositum reale includat esse, nullus datur conceptus suppositi realis.

Respondetur: esse non cognoscitur nisi per iudicium, concedo; esse non cogitatur nisi per iudicium, nego. Aliud sane est supponere (hypothesim facere) quod centauri existunt; aliud autem est falso affirmare eos existere. Caeterum, quandocumque quaeritur, An sit, ante concipitur existentia quam per iudicium cognoscitur.

Deinde obicitur: definitio dicit essentiam rei; sed esse non pertinet ad essentiam cuiuslibet creaturae; ergo esse non est ponendum in definitione cuiuslibet creaturae.

Respondetur: definitio stricte dicta essentiam rei declarat, concedo; definitio late dicta solam rei essentiam declarat, nego. Et pariter distinguitur conclusio.

Notate definitionem late dictam fieri per additionem et quidem dupliciter: primo modo per additionem definitorum: altero modo per additionem definiti et non definibilis. Primo modo definitur 'homo albus' definiendo et hominem et album et has definitiones addendo. Altero modo definitur 'hic homo' definiendo 'homo' et addendo 'hic' quod definitionem non admittit.

Tertio obicitur: sed id quod quaeritur est definitio stricte dicta suppositi; ergo nulla solutio.

Respondetur: id quod quaeritur est definitio vera. Quare si suppositum reale est tantummodo essentia quaedam, definiendum est per modum essentiae, nempe, per definitionem stricte dictam; si autem suppositum reale non est tantummodo quaedam essentia, definiendum est per modum eius quod non est essentia tantum, nempe, per definitionem latius dictam.

Iam vero patet suppositum reale non esse tantummodo essentiam. Si enim dico Petrum esse album, loquor de supposito; sin autem dico essentiam Petri esse albam, loquor de

A real supposit is a distinct subsistent.

A hypothetical supposit is one that comes in between concrete universal concepts and abstract universal concepts, such as, for example, between 'man' and 'humanity,' or between 'centaur' and 'centaurity.'[23]

16 Since it is frequently a source of difficulty, this distinction calls for a brief clarification.

Objection 1: Since *esse*, the act of existence, is known by judgment and since to judge is not the same as to conceive, there is therefore no concept of *esse*; and so, since a real supposit includes *esse*, there is no such thing as a concept of a real supposit.

Reply: That the act of existence is not known except through a judgment, we agree; that the act of existence is not an object of thought except through a judgment, we deny. It is surely one thing to suppose, to make a hypothesis, that centaurs exist, but quite another to state falsely that they do exist. Besides, whenever the question, Is it? is asked, existence is conceived before it becomes known through a judgment.

Objection 2: A definition denotes the essence of a thing; but the act of existence does not belong to the essence of any creature whatsoever; therefore, the act of existence should not be included in the definition of any creature.

Reply: That a definition strictly so called denotes the essence of a thing, we agree; that a definition in the broader sense denotes only the essence of a thing, we deny; and we distinguish the conclusion accordingly.

Note that a definition in the broad sense is formed by addition, and this in two ways: first, by adding defined terms, and secondly, by adding a defined term and a non-definable term. In the first way, a 'white man' is defined by defining 'man' and 'white' and then combining the two. In the second way, 'this man' is defined by defining 'man' and adding to it the term 'this,' which is incapable of definition.

Objection 3: But what we are seeking is a strict definition of supposit; therefore, the previous objection still stands.

Reply: What is being sought is a true definition. Hence if a real supposit is merely a kind of essence, it should be defined the way an essence is, namely, by a strict definition; but if a real supposit is not merely a kind of essence, it has to be defined in the same way as that which is not merely an essence, namely, by a definition in the broader sense.

Now it is obvious that a real supposit is not merely an essence. If I say that Peter is white, I am speaking of a supposit; but if I say that Peter's essence is

23 [For more on 'hypothetical supposit,' see below, p. 69.]

essentia; et cum primum sit verum et alterum falsum, sequitur suppositum non esse essentiam; et idem concludi potest ubicumque praedicatum non essentiale sed accidentale est.

Quarto obicitur: omnis scientia fundatur in essentiis et ideo saltem omnis definitio scientifica essentiam vel essentiale dicit per definitionem stricte dictam.

Respondetur: omnis scientia quae non etiam sapientia sit, transeat; illa scientia quae etiam est sapientia, metaphysica nempe, in essentiis fundatur, distinguo: quoad se, concedo, quoad nos, nego. Et explico.

Circa scientiam quae sapientia non est distinguitur cum Aristotele[24] inter scientiam in potentia quae est de universalibus et abstractis et scientiam in actu quae est de individuis et concretis; porro, concedi potest quod scientia in potentia in essentiis et essentialibus tantum fundatur; sed concedi non potest quod scientia in actu in essentiis et essentialibus tantum fundatur.

Circa scientiam autem quae etiam est sapientia distinguitur inter scientiam Dei et beatorum et scientiam nostram. Scientia Dei et beatorum utique in essentia Dei fundatur: comprehensa enim essentia Dei, omnia etiam alia secundum omnes prorsus eorum determinationes perfecte cognoscuntur; immediate autem visa Dei essentia, pro perfectione visionis caetera entia etiam videntur. Praeterea, scientia nostra metaphysica etiam fundatur quoad se in essentia Dei, nam solus Deus est ens per essentiam et in solo ente per essentiam fundatur quoad se scientia de toto ente. Nihilominus, quoad nos, nostra scientia hac in vita non proxime fundatur in Dei essentia, nam hac in vita quid sit Deus nescimus; neque fundatur in essentiis entium per participationem, cum ex istis essentiis non habeantur nisi scientiae particulares, puta, physicam, chimiam, biologiam, psychologiam; sed fundatur in entibus per participationem quae considerantur inquantum sunt, inter se ordinantur, et in ultimas eorum causas reducuntur.[25]

white, I am speaking of an essence; and since the first is true and the second false, it follows that a supposit is not an essence; and the same conclusion may be drawn wherever the predicate is not essential but accidental.

Objection 4: All science is founded on essences, and therefore at least every scientific definition expresses an essence or that which is essential, by a definition in the strict sense.

Reply: That all science that is not also wisdom is so founded, we let pass; that that science which is also wisdom, namely metaphysics, is founded upon essences, we distinguish as follows: with respect to itself, we agree; with respect to us, we deny. Let us explain.

As to science that is not wisdom, we distinguish with Aristotle[24] between science in potency, which deals with the universal and the abstract, and science in act, which deals with the singular and the concrete; furthermore we can concede that science in potency is founded upon essences and essentials only, but we cannot concede that science in act is founded upon essences and essentials only.

With regard to the science that is also wisdom, we distinguish God's knowledge and the knowledge possessed by the blessed from our knowledge. God's knowledge and that of the blessed are, of course, founded upon the divine essence; for once that essence is known comprehensively, all other things are known in all their details. In the immediate vision of God's essence, however, all other things are seen in proportion to the perfection of one's vision. Furthermore, considered in itself our metaphysical science is also founded on God's essence, for God alone is being by essence, and it is only on a being that exists by its very essence that the science of all being, considered in itself, is founded. Nevertheless, with respect to us, our knowledge in this life is not proximately founded on God's essence, for in this life we do not know what God is; nor is it founded on the essences of beings-by-participation, because only particular sciences, such as physics, chemistry, biology, and psychology are derived from those essences. But our knowledge is founded on beings-by-participation considered as existing, as interrelated, and as resolved into[25] to their ultimate causes.

24 Aristotle, *Metaphysics*, XIII, 10, 1087a 15–25.

25 [Latin variants of 'reducere ad' and 'reducere in' will sometimes be translated by corresponding forms of 'to resolve into.' This will be so whenever (as in the present instance) the meaning refers to the *via resolutionis*, the way of analysis that begins with what is 'first for us' and seeks its causes or reasons or explanation, and so when 'reducere in' or 'reducere ad' could equally well have been 'resolvere in' (which Lonergan also uses). There are a few occasions where 'reducere' should be translated 'reduce' (see, for example, below, p. 51), but at other times, as in the present case, the meaning is better captured by 'resolve.']

17 Quibus perspectis quam sit nefasta opinio essentialistarum concludes. Si enim omnis conceptus, omnis definitio, omnis scientia solas respicit essentias, aut impossibilis est metaphysica aut vacua. Si enim obiectum metaphysicae ponitur in Dei essentia, cum essentia Dei sit nobis ignota, metaphysica evadit nobis impossibilis. Sin autem obiectum metaphysicae ponitur in aliis essentiis, metaphysica nihil dicit nisi aggregationem aliarum scientiarum quarum nulla metaphysica est.

E contra, si obiectum metaphysicae dicitur, non ens in quantum essentiam habet, sed ens inquantum ens, seu id quod est inquantum est, necessario sequitur quod dantur conceptus et definitiones et saltem una scientia quae non solum essentias et essentialia respiciunt. Qua sane in scientia ille conceptus atque illa definitio maxime necessaria erit quae id quod est, seu suppositum reale, quid sit manifestat atque declarat.

Sectio Sexta: De Persona

18 Inde a S. Thoma persona definitur subsistens distinctum in natura intellectuali.

Natura (sensu Aristotelico) est principium motus et quietis in eo in quo est (motus vel quies) primo et per se et non secundum accidens.[26]

Natura (alio quodam sensu mediaevali) est essentia substantialis prout ad operationes refertur.

Intellectualis est natura quae intelligendo et volendo circa totum ens operari potest. Nec quidquam refert utrum 'natura' sumatur sensu Aristotelico an sensu posteriori.

Persona, ergo, est id quod subsistit ut distinctum in natura intellectuali.

Quia ergo persona subsistit, quae non subsistunt personae non sunt; et ideo a ratione personae excluduntur principia entis intrinseca, accidentia, possibilia, et entia rationis.

Quia persona est subsistens distinctum, quod subsistit quin sit usquequaque distinctum, persona non est; et ideo Deus, qui est ipsum esse subsistens, non est quarta quaedam persona praeter Patrem, Filium, et Spiritum sanctum.

Quia persona est subsistens distinctum in natura intellectuali, creaturae non-intellectuales non sunt personae; et ideo a ratione personae excluduntur animalia bruta, plantae, et mineralia.

17 From this you can gather how pernicious is the opinion of the essentialists. For if every concept, every definition, every science regards only essences, then metaphysics is either impossible or empty. If the object of metaphysics is placed in God's essence, metaphysics becomes impossible for us, since we do not know God's essence; and if the object of metaphysics is placed in other essences, metaphysics means nothing but a congeries of other sciences none of which is metaphysics.

On the other hand, if the object of metaphysics is said to be, not being as having an essence, but being as being, that which is precisely insofar as it is, then it necessarily follows that there are concepts and definitions and at least one science that are concerned with more than just essences and essentials. And indeed in this science the most necessary concept and definition will be that which clearly manifests and clarifies what a 'that-which-is,' a real supposit, is.

6 Person

18 Beginning with St Thomas, 'person' has been defined as 'a distinct subsistent in an intellectual nature.'

'Nature', in the Aristotelian sense, is the principle of motion and rest in that in which it (motion or rest) exists of itself and not by accident.[26]

'Nature' in another sense, a medieval sense, is a substantial essence considered in relation to operation.

A nature is intellectual when by understanding and willing it can operate within the entire realm of being. It makes no difference, either, if 'nature' is taken in the Aristotelian or in the later sense.

A person, therefore, is that which subsists as distinct in an intellectual nature.

Accordingly, since a person subsists, beings that do not subsist are not persons; therefore the intrinsic principles of being, accidents, possible beings, and 'beings of reason' are all excluded from the formality of person.

Because a person is a distinct subsistent, whatever subsists without being distinct in every respect is not a person. Thus God, who is subsistent existence itself, is not some fourth person in addition to the Father, the Son, and the Holy Spirit.

Because a person is a distinct subsistent in an intellectual nature, creatures that are non-intellectual are not persons; animals, plants, and minerals are thus excluded from the formality of person.

26 Aristotle, *Physics*, II, 1, 192b 21–22.

Relinquitur ergo ut definitio data omni solique conveniat, cum personae omnes et soli sint Pater, Filius, Spiritus sanctus, angeli, et homines.

19 Attamen obicitur datam definitionem id praeterire quod personas essentialiter constituit, nempe, relationes interpersonales.

Respondetur: omnem personam intra systema quoddam relationum interpersonalium ita versari ut personae infinitae per tales relationes constituantur et personae finitae tales relationes per modum proprietatis consequentis habeant, conceditur; personam finitam per tales relationes constitui, negatur.

Ideo relationes interpersonales trinitariae personas constituere possunt quia ipsae relationes sunt subsistentes. Relationes autem interpersonales et finitae ideo subsistere non possunt quia operationes (quae necessario sunt accidentales)[27] consequuntur. Neque quisquam arbitratur personas non subsistere.

Denique tandem, quamvis multa magni momenti de relationibus interpersonalibus ex psychologia, sociologia, ascetica, historiae theoria etc., colligi possint, ad praesentem quaestionem iam satis amplam sufficiant quae vere essentialia sint.

Our definition, therefore, applies to all persons and only to them, since the Father, the Son, the Holy Spirit, angels, and human beings are all persons and the only persons.

19 Yet it may be objected that our definition disregards the essential constituents of persons, namely, interpersonal relations.

To this objection we reply that while we agree that every person lives within a certain network of interpersonal relations in such a way that infinite persons are constituted by these relations and finite persons have these relations as a consequent property, nevertheless we deny that a finite person is constituted by such relations.

In the Trinity, then, interpersonal relations are able to constitute persons because the relations themselves subsist. But finite interpersonal relations cannot subsist because they result from operations, which are necessarily accidental.[27] And no one denies that persons subsist.

Finally, although much of importance can be gathered about interpersonal relations from psychology, sociology, ascetical studies, the theory of history, and so forth, for the present question, already lengthy enough, let us be satisfied with those points that are truly essential.

27 Thomas Aquinas, *Summa theologiae*, 1, q. 54, aa. 1–3.

De Constitutione Personae Finitae

---

20 Ideo quaeritur quaenam sit constitutio personae finitae ut determinari possit cur natura humana a Verbo assumpta non sit persona. Ipsa ergo quaestio philosophica est sed propter finem ulteriorem atque theologicum ponitur.

Cur auctores hac in re tot tamque diversas emiserint sententias, triplicem maxime invenio causam. Primo, quia alii aliter personae definitionem intelligunt. Deinde, quia ipso nomine 'constitutivi formalis' decipiuntur. Tertio, quia circa ipsum intentum decepti, methodice procedere non possunt.

Circa primum vero iam actum est.

Circa alterum animadvertendum est, cum aliter metaphysica et aliter theologia scientiae rationem habeat, aliter etiam et aliter his in scientiis constitutivum formale intelligi oportet. Qui enim in metaphysica constitutivum formale quaerit, rei existentis causam realem, intrinsecam, ab ipsa re realiter et inadaequate distinctam quaerit; quae quidem causa non solum forma esse potest sed etiam potentia ad formam vel actus formam consequens vel ipsa horum principiorum aptitudo atque naturalis necessitas ut in unum coalescant. Qui autem in ipsis divinis constitutivum formale quaerit, non causam sed rationem quaerit cum ipsius Dei non sint causae. Qui denique inter haec tam diversa non distinguit, iam ad parvum illum in initio errorem pervenerit qui in fine magnus erit.

Circa tertium denique non per aliam proceditur methodum ad constitutiva formalia personae finitae determinanda quam universaliter in metaphysica ad principia entis finiti invenienda.

PART 2

The Constitution of a Finite Person

---

20 The reason for our inquiry into the constitution of a finite person is to enable us to determine why the human nature assumed by the divine Word is not a person. The question is therefore philosophical, but it is posed with a further theological end in view.

There are, I find, three reasons why authors have expressed so many diverse opinions in this matter. First, they do not understand the definition of person in the same way; second, they are led astray by the term 'formal constitutive'; and third, being mistaken about the purpose of the inquiry, they are unable to proceed methodically.

The first point has already been dealt with.

As to the second, it must be noted that since metaphysics and theology are not sciences in the same sense, the term 'formal constitutive' must be understood in them in different ways. When you seek a formal constitutive in metaphysics, you are looking for a cause of an existing reality, a cause that is real, intrinsic, and really and inadequately distinct from that reality itself; and this cause can be not only a form but also a potency to a form or an act consequent upon form, or the aptitude and natural necessity of these principles to come together to form one being. But when you seek a formal constitutive in matters pertaining to God, you are looking not for a cause but for a reason, since God has no causes. Finally, if you do not distinguish between these very different formal constitutives, you will have already fallen into the sort of slight initial error that in the end becomes very serious.

As to the third reason, the procedure for determining the formal constitutives of a finite person is no different from that universally followed in metaphysics for discovering the principles of finite being.

Quibus perspectis, dicendum videtur (1) quid sit causa, (2) an sint causae, (3) quemadmodum causae in unum coalescant, (4) propter quid persona finita sit persona, et (5) quibusnam inter se differant diversae quae proponuntur sententiae.

Sectio Prima: De Causis

21 Causa (id quod influit esse in aliud) aut extrinseca aut intrinseca est.

Causa extrinseca aut est finis (id cuius gratia aliquid fit vel est), aut exemplar (id secundum quod aliquid fit vel est), aut efficiens (id a quo aliquid fit vel est).

Causa intrinseca aut est natura aut constitutiva. Est natura inquantum una pars ad aliam refertur, puta forma ad operationem. Est constitutiva inquantum omnes partes ad totum referuntur; ita Socrates est *homo* per formam humanam, est *hic* per materiam individualem, *existit* per esse suum, *potest intelligere* per intellectum possibilem, *peritus* est philosophiae per habitum sapientiae, *actu intelligit* per suum intelligere.

Causae intrinsecae et constitutivae sunt potentia, forma, actus; quae ulterius in substantiales et accidentales dividuntur.

Potentia se habet ad formam, sicut oculus ad visum, vel sicut auris ad auditum, vel sicut materia ad animam, vel sicut intellectus possibilis ad speciem impressam, vel sicut voluntas ad habitum in voluntate receptum.

Forma se habet ad actum, sicut visus ad visionem, vel sicut auditus ad auditionem, vel sicut anima ad esse et vivere, vel sicut species impressa ad intelligere, vel sicut habitus in voluntate receptus ad velle.

Essentia est quae ex potentia et forma componitur (vel, in immaterialibus, quae forma sola consistit).

Essentia-simpliciter est cuius definitio nihil ponit praeter ipsum definitum; ita homo qui et animal est et rationalis definitur animal rationale.

Essentia-secundum-quid est cuius definitio aliquid ponit praeter ipsum definitum; ita simitas, quae est curvitas quaedam sed nasus non est, definitur curvitas in naso.

Substantia est essentia-simpliciter. Abeat ergo notio vulgaris secundum quam substantia est ignotum quid sub accidentibus latens. Sicut enim substantia per se est, ita per se intelligitur et per se definitur.

With this in mind, we must go on to treat the following points: (1) what a cause is, (2) whether there are causes, (3) how causes come together to form one being, (4) what makes a finite person a person, and (5) in what respects various opinions that are proposed differ from one another.

1 Causes

21 A cause (that which exerts an influence on the existence of something else) is either extrinsic or intrinsic.

An extrinsic cause is either an end (that on account of which a thing is done or is) or an exemplar (the model according to which a thing is done or is) or an agent (that by which a thing is done or is).

An intrinsic cause is either a nature or a constitutive. It is a nature in that one part is related to another, as when form is related to operation. It is a constitutive in that all parts are related to the whole. Thus Socrates is *a human being* because of a human substantial form, he is *this* because of individuating matter, he *exists* because of his own act of existence, he *can understand* because of his possible intellect, he is an *expert* in philosophy because of his habit of wisdom, and he *actually understands* because of his act of understanding.

Intrinsic constitutive causes are potency, form, and act; and these are further divided into substantial and accidental.

Potency is related to form as the eye is to eyesight (the ability to see), as the ear is to hearing (the ability to hear), as matter is to the soul, as the possible intellect is to the impressed species, or as the will is to a habit received in the will.

Form is related to act as one's eyesight is to seeing, as one's hearing is to actually hearing sounds, as soul is to existing and living, as an impressed species is to an act of understanding, or as a habit received in the will is to an act of willing.

Essence is composed of potency and form, or, in the case of immaterial creatures, consists of form only.

Essence simply understood is that whose definition expresses nothing beyond that which is defined; thus a human being, who is animal and rational, is defined as a rational animal.

Essence in a qualified sense is that whose definition expresses something beyond that which is defined; thus snubness, which is a kind of curvature but not a nose, is defined as a curvature of the nose.

A substance is an essence simply understood. Let us, then, forget the commonly held idea that substance is some unknown reality lying hidden under accidents. Just as substance exists per se, so too is it understood and defined per se.

Accidens est essentia-secundum-quid. Abeat ergo notio vulgaris secundum quam accidentia solis sensibus innotescunt. Sunt enim essentiae quaedam, et sicut in alio sunt, ita sine hac inhaesione neque intelliguntur neque definiuntur.

Substantiales dicuntur non solum essentia-simpliciter sed etiam potentia et forma quibus essentia componitur et actus qui eam consequitur.

Accidentales pariter dicuntur non solum essentia-secundum-quid sed etiam potentia et forma quibus essentia componitur et actus qui eam consequitur.

22 Quae omnia ut recte intelligantur, sequentia sunt accurate notanda.

Primo, scientia est certa per causas cognitio, et ideo ut consideratio sit metaphysica non sufficit ut de ente agatur sed etiam requiritur ut ens in causas suas ultimas resolvatur.

Differt ergo metaphysica a grammatica quae non ens inquantum ens sed orationem considerat eamque non in causas ultimas resolvit sed in functiones grammaticales, nempe, nomina, verba, pronomina, adiectiva, adverbia, praepositiones, coniunctiones, etc.

Differt etiam metaphysica a logica quae non ens inquantum ens sed argumenta et propositiones considerat eaque resolvit non in causas ultimas sed in praemissas et conclusiones, in subiecta universalia et particularia, in copulam affirmativam et negativam, et in praedicata quae dicunt genus, differentiam, essentiam, proprium, et accidens.

Differt ulterius metaphysica ab analysi attributorum in transcendentalia (ens, unum, verum, bonum) et praedicamentalia (quid, quantum, quale, ad quid, ubi, quando, actio, passio, situs, habitus). Quamvis enim haec attributa ens respiciant, causas entis minime dicunt.

Unde concludes:

Minime confundendus est actus (causa intrinseca et constitutiva) cum factione (exercitium causalitatis extrinsecae et efficientis), quamvis utrumque grammatice per verbum in voce activa exprimatur, v.g., esse, videre, intelligere, creare, producere, movere.

Neque confundi oportet essentiam sensu metaphysico et essentiam sensu logico. Metaphysice enim essentia est causa quaedam intrinseca, constitutiva, realis, concreta, individua, quae ex hac potentia et hac forma constituitur; sed logice essentia est universalis et abstracta et genere cum differentia specifica componitur.

An accident is an essence in a qualified sense. Let us, then, forget the commonly held idea that accidents are known only through the senses. They are essences of a sort, and just as they inhere in another, so too they can neither be understood nor be defined apart from this inherence.

It is not only an essence simply understood that is referred to as substantial, but also the potency and form of which it is composed and the act that is consequent upon it.

Similarly it is not only an essence in a qualified sense that is called accidental, but also the potency and form of which the essence is composed and the act that is consequent upon it.

22 For a correct understanding of all this, the following points should be carefully noted.

First, science is certain knowledge through causes, and hence for a study to be metaphysical it is not sufficient that it deal with being; there is the further requirement that being be resolved into its ultimate causes.

Metaphysics, therefore, differs from grammar, which considers, not being as being, but speech, and does not resolve speech into its ultimate causes, but rather into its grammatical functions, namely, nouns, verbs, pronouns, adjectives, adverbs, prepositions, conjunctions, and so on.

Metaphysics differs also from logic. Logic does not deal with being as being but with arguments and propositions, resolving them not into their ultimate causes but into premises and conclusions, into universal subjects and particular subjects, into affirmative and negative copulas, and into predicates that express genus, difference, essence, property, and accident.

Again, metaphysics differs from the analysis of attributes into transcendentals (being, one, true, good) and predicaments or categories (substance, quantity, quality, relation, place, time, action, passion, posture, habit). Although these attributes refer to being, they do not in any way express the causes of being.

From this we may draw the following conclusions.

Act (an intrinsic constitutive cause) must by no means be confused with making (the exercise of extrinsic efficient causality), although grammatically both are expressed by a verb in the active voice – for example, to be, to see, to understand, to create, to produce, to move.

Essence in the metaphysical sense must not be confused with essence in the logical sense. In the metaphysical sense essence is an intrinsic, constitutive, real, concrete, individual cause composed of this potency and this form; but in logic essence is universal and abstract and is composed of genus and specific difference.

Neque confundi oportet accidens sensu metaphysico et accidens sensu logico. Metaphysice enim accidens est essentia quaedam atque causa neque semper a subiecto separari potest; v.g., intellectus in homine est accidens quod tamen ab homine separari non potest. Logice autem accidens contra essentiam dividitur et illud est quod adesse vel abesse potest salva essentia.

Neque confundi oportet analysin in causas entis ultimas cum analysi in transcendentalia et praedicamenta. Quare qui nihil aliud intendit quam reductionem[1] entis in praedicamentum substantiae vel qualitatis vel actionis vel relationis, ad quaestiones metaphysicas non attendit.

Neque confundi oportet substantiam sensu metaphysico cum substantia sensu praedicamentali. Metaphysice enim substantia est essentia simpliciter quae est causa quaedam entis intrinseca. Sed praedicamentum substantiae respicit suppositum sive reale sive hypotheticum.

Deinde, et illud notandum est quod potentia, forma, actus multipliciter dicuntur. Supra,[2] sensus quidam fundamentalis per analogias est declaratus, cui tamen accedunt tum alii sensus tum sequens qui ad praesens negotium multum refert. Potentia enim ad actum comparatur sicut perfectibile ad perfectionem; et secundum hoc, cum unum idemque sit et perfectibile et perfectum, ponitur theorema fundamentale compositionis metaphysicae, nempe, unum idemque est in potentia prima per potentiam et in actu primo per formam, et unum idemque est in potentia secunda per formam et in actu secundo per actum, et unum idemque est in potentia per substantiam et in actu per accidentia sua.

Tertio, quae analogiis proportionis declarantur, dupliciter considerari possunt: primo modo, inquantum tali proportioni subsunt, et sic consideratio est abstracta; alio modo, ut quae tali proportioni subsunt, et sic consideratio est concreta. Porro, cum universalia non subsistant, omne ens concretum sit necesse est; et cum causae effectibus proportionari debeant, etiam omnis causa entis sive intrinseca sive extrinseca pariter concreta sit necesse est. Quare omnis consideratio metaphysica ita analogiis sive entis sive potentiae, formae, et actus uti debet ut non primo modo abstracto sed altero modo concreto ens eiusque causae intendantur.

Accident in the metaphysical sense must not be confused with accident in the logical sense. In metaphysics an accident is a certain essence and cause, and it cannot always be separated from its subject; in a human being, for example, intellect is an accident but one which cannot be separated from him or her. In logic an accident is opposed to essence, and is that which can be present or absent without affecting the essence of a thing.

The analysis of being into its ultimate causes must not be confused with analysis into transcendentals and predicaments. Thus if you have no purpose in mind other than to reduce[1] being to the predicament of substance or quality or action or relation, you are not dealing with questions that are metaphysical.

Substance in the metaphysical sense must not be confused with substance in the predicamental sense. Metaphysically substance is an essence simply understood, which is an intrinsic cause of a being, whereas the predicament 'substance' refers to a supposit either real or hypothetical.

Second, this too must be borne in mind, that potency, form, and act can be taken in many difference senses. We have explained above[2] a certain basic sense by way of analogies. However, other meanings can be added to the above, including the following one, which is very important in our present investigation. Potency is related to act as the perfectible to the perfection; and thus since one and the same thing is both perfectible and perfected, we have the fundamental theorem of metaphysical composition, namely, that one and the same thing is in first potency through potency and in first act through form, and that one and the same thing is in second potency through form and in second act through act, and that one and the same thing is in potency through substance and in act through its accidents.

Third, things explained by analogies of proportion can be considered in two ways: first, as to the fact that they fall under such proportion, and then the consideration is abstract; second, as those things that fall under such proportion, and then the consideration is concrete. Furthermore, since universals do not subsist, every existing being must be concrete; and since causes must be proportioned to their effects, every cause of being, intrinsic or extrinsic, must likewise be concrete. Every metaphysical consideration, therefore, has to make use of analogies, either of being or of potency, form, and act, if it is to consider a being and its causes not according to the abstract first way, but according to the second way, which is concrete.

1 [See above, p. 39, note 25.]
2 [See above, p. 47.]

Sectio Secunda: An Sint Causae Intrinsecae

23 Quae quaestio non in tota sua amplitudine est a nobis consideranda sed ad duo tantum restringenda, nempe, utrum essentia finita ab esse contingente realiter distinguatur, et utrum modi vel aliae et similes entitatulae praeter causas intrinsecas supra enumeratas sint reales et realiter distinctae.

24 *Circa primum sic arguitur*: Quorum diversa est intelligibilitas, eorum diversa est realitas. Atque diversa est intelligibilitas essentiae finitae et esse contingentis. Ergo diversa est eorum realitas.

Improprie dicitur intelligibile id quod concipi potest; et sic nihil, peccatum, irrationale, inintelligibile, quia concipiuntur, etiam intelligibilia improprie dicuntur.

Proprie dicitur intelligibile id quod intelligendo (intus legendo) innotescit; intelligere vero seu intus legere est ille actus qui rarius in tardioribus et frequentius in acutioribus evenit.

Intelligibile-proprie dupliciter dicitur: intelligibile in se seu intrinsece est id ipsum quod intelligendo innotescit; intelligibile in alio seu extrinsece est id quod intelligitur non in se sed inquantum ad aliud refertur. Primo modo intelligibilia sunt forma, proportio potentiae ad formam, proportio formae ad actum, habitudo effectus ad causam extrinsecam. Alio modo intelligibilia sunt potentia quae in forma intelligitur, contingens quod ad causam extrinsecam reducitur.

Unde ad praemissam minorem: Diversa est intelligibilitas essentiae finitae et esse contingentis. Essentia enim finita est intrinsece intelligibilis; est id quod intelligendo innotescit; quod valet non solum de essentia quae cum sola forma identificatur sed etiam de essentia quae ex potentia et forma componitur, cum potentia in forma intelligatur. E contra, esse contingens non est intrinsece intelligibile; non enim intelligendo sed iudicando innotescit esse contingens; neque hoc esse intelligitur donec ad causam extrinsecam non contingentem reducatur.

Unde ad praemissam maiorem: Quorum diversa est intelligibilitas, eorum diversa est realitas. Reale enim est id ipsum quod innotescit mediantibus verbis interioribus. Quod si quis dixerit intelligibilitatem extrinsecam non in ipsa re sed tantum in mente inveniri, tollit argumentum ex contingentia rerum ad primam causam. Pariter, si quis dixerit intelligibilitatem intrinsecam non in ipsa re sed in sola mente inveniri, tollit obiectivitatem omnium scientiarum quae in intrinseca rerum intelligibilitate fundantur.

2 The Reality of Intrinsic Causes

23 We cannot treat this question in its totality but must restrict our consideration to two points, namely, whether a finite essence is really distinct from a contingent act of existence, and whether there are real and really distinct modes or other such 'thinglets' in addition to the intrinsic causes already mentioned.

24 *On the first point*, our argument is as follows: things that differ in intelligibility differ in reality; but a finite essence and a contingent act of existence differ in intelligibility; therefore, they differ also in reality.

Improperly speaking, the intelligible is whatever can be conceived; thus, nothing, sin, the irrational, the unintelligible, because they are conceivable, are said to be intelligible, but only in an improper sense.

Properly speaking, the intelligible is what becomes known by understanding (*intelligendo, intus legendo,* 'grasping inwardly'); to understand, or 'grasp inwardly,' is an act which occurs rarely in the slower-witted but more frequently in the more intelligent.

What is properly intelligible can be either (1) what is intelligible in itself, intrinsically, the thing itself that becomes known by understanding, or (2) what is intelligible in something else, extrinsically, that which becomes known not in itself but as related to something else. Form, the proportion of potency to form, the proportion of form to act, and the relationship of an effect to its extrinsic cause are intelligible in the first way. Potency, which is understood in form, and the contingent, which is resolved into its extrinsic cause, are intelligible in the second way.

The *minor premise* of the above syllogism, that a finite essence and a contingent act of existence differ in intelligibility, we substantiate as follows. A finite essence is intrinsically intelligible: it is that which becomes known through understanding. And this holds not only for an essence that is identical with form alone, but also for an essence composed of potency and form, since potency is understood in form. On the other hand, a contingent act of existence is not intrinsically intelligible: it becomes known not by understanding but by judging, nor is this act of existence understood until it is resolved into a non-contingent extrinsic cause.

The *major premise*, that things which differ in intelligibility differ in reality, we substantiate as follows. The real is that which becomes known through the mediation of inner words. If you say that extrinsic intelligibility resides not in the thing itself but only in the mind, you destroy the argument for the existence of a first cause from contingent beings. Similarly, if you say that intrinsic intelligibility resides not in the thing itself but only in the mind, you destroy the objectivity of all sciences, which are founded on the intrinsic intelligibility of things.

Denique tandem contradictorie opponuntur in se seu intrinsece intelligibile, et non in se seu non intrinsece intelligibile; neque contradictoria de eodem praedicari possunt; et ideo non idem realiter est esse contingens quod essentia finita.

Dices: contradictoria de eodem praedicantur secundum diversos aspectus; ita homo est mortalis secundum corpus et immortalis secundum animam. *Respondetur*: ubi diversi aspectus compositionem realem supponunt, puta compositionem formae et materiae, *concedo*; ubi compositionem realem non supponunt, *nego*.

25 Deinde quaeritur utrum praeter causas entis intrinsecas supra enumeratas sint modi vel aliae et similes entitatulae; et sic arguitur.

Radix proportionis inter potentiam et formam est proportio inter (1) sensibile et (2) intelligibile quod in sensibili perspicitur; et radix proportionis inter formam et actum est proportio inter (1) intelligibile in sensibilibus intellectum et (2) affirmationem (est, ita) iudicii. Iam vero omnis nostra directa cognitio in experientiam, intelligentiam, et iudicium reducitur; experientiae correspondet potentia, intelligentiae correspondet forma, iudicio correspondet actus; et ideo quod ponitur praeter potentiam, formam, et actum aut in haec reducitur aut penitus non cognoscitur. Quod si modus ad potentiam vel formam vel actum reducitur, non est causa ultima et ad metaphysicam non pertinet. E contra si modus penitus non cognoscitur, melius de eo tacetur.

Sectio Tertia: Quemadmodum Unum per Multas Causas Constituatur

26 Consideratio metaphysica duplici procedit via. Primo, enim, analysis ens concretum in causas suas resolvit (via resolutionis); deinde, synthesis causas in ens concretum constituendum componit (via compositionis).

Neque analysis magnam facit difficultatem uti brevi exemplo illustratur. Sit Petrus hic homo existens scientia praeditus et actu intelligens: tunc resolvitur Petrus ut 'hic' in materiam (potentiam substantialem), ut 'homo' in animam humanam (formam substantialem), ut 'existens' in esse (actum substantialem), ut 'scientia praeditus' ad habitum (formam accidentalem) in intellectu possibili (potentia accidentali) receptum, ut 'actu intelligens' in intelligere (actum accidentalem). Et similiter in aliis procedi potest: quodcumque enim

Finally, the intelligible-in-itself or intrinsically intelligible, and the intelligible-not-in-itself or non-intrinsically intelligible, are contradictories, and contradictories cannot be predicated of the same subject; therefore, in the real order, contingent act of existence and finite essence are not the same thing.

It may be *objected* that contradictories can be predicated of the same subject under different aspects; thus, for example, a human being is mortal with respect to the body but immortal with respect to the soul. To this *we reply* that this is true where the different aspects imply a real composition, such as that of matter and form; but it is not the case where no real composition is supposed.

25 On the second point, whether there are such things as 'modes' or other 'thinglets' in addition to the above-mentioned intrinsic causes of being, we state our position in the following way.

The root of the proportion between potency and form is the proportion between (1) the sensible data and (2) the intelligible that is grasped in the sensible data; and the root of the proportion between form and act is the proportion between the intelligible understood in the sensible data and the affirmation ('It is,' 'Yes') by the judgment. Now, all our direct knowledge is reduced to experience, understanding, and judgment. Potency corresponds to experience, form to understanding, and act to judgment; and so anything affirmed apart from potency, form, and act is either reduced to one of these or is entirely unknown. But if a 'mode' is reduced to potency or form or act, it is not an ultimate cause and so does not belong to metaphysics; if, on the other hand, it is entirely unknown, it is better to say nothing about it.

3 One as Constituted by Many Causes

26 Metaphysical considerations can proceed in two ways: first, by analysis, the way of resolution, which resolves concrete being into its causes; second, by synthesis, the way of composition, which combines the causes to constitute a concrete being.

Analysis creates no great difficulty, as the following example illustrates. Suppose that Peter is this existing human being endowed with knowledge and actually understanding: then, as 'this,' Peter is resolved into matter (substantial potency), as 'human being' into a human soul (substantial form), as 'existing' into an act of existence (substantial act), as 'endowed with knowledge' into a mental habit (accidental form) received in the possible intellect (accidental potency), and as 'actually understanding' into an act of understanding (accidental act). The same

scientifice stabilietur, erit hypothesis in multis verificata; et prout est hypothesis in formam resolvitur; prout verificatur in actum resolvitur; et prout in multis invenitur, in potentiam resolvitur.

Synthesis autem hanc obviam facit difficultatem quod ex multis ad unum non proceditur nisi multa apta nata sunt coalescere ad unum efformandum. Et ideo quaeri solet utrum causae entis intrinsecae atque constitutivae per se aut per aliud (puta gluten quoddam intermedium) in unum coalescant. Cui quaestioni respondemus eas se ipsis uniri modo inter se proportionentur sicut potentia ad actum.

Quod primo declaratur secundum theorema fundamentale compositionis metaphysicae, nempe, unum idemque esse quod per potentiam est perfectibile et per actum est perfectum. Nisi enim conceditur haec identitas, nihil umquam procedi potest ex perfectibili ad perfectum; et si ipsis factis ad hanc identitatem concedendam cogimur, statim sequitur criterion quo determinari potest quaenam potentia ad quemnam actum proportionetur, nempe, potentiam ad actum proportionari ubi idem sit quod per potentiam est perfectibile et quod per actum est perfectum.

Praeterea, inutiliter adduceretur quodlibet intermedium ad uniendum sive potentiam ad formam sive formam ad actum sive substantiam ad accidentia. Si enim tale intermedium ad hanc unionem perficiendam requiritur, pariter aliud intermedium requiritur ad uniendum potentiam ad intermedium et aliud ad uniendum intermedium ad formam; et sic in infinitum regreditur. Sin autem ulterius intermedium non requiri dicitur, pari ratione dici potest neque primum requiri intermedium.

27 Denique tandem solvi possunt argumenta quae in contrarium adducuntur. Arguitur enim quod saltem modaliter differt potentia non actuata a potentia actuata; et similiter quod saltem modaliter differt accidens actu inhaerens ab accidente eucharistico quod non actu inhaeret.

Respondetur: realiter aliud est quod sola potentia constat, et realiter aliud est quod et potentia et actu constat; quae realis differentia est inter actum et non-actum. Nec quidquam aliud est potentia actuata nisi potentia eius quod non solam potentiam sed etiam actum habet. Fallacia autem in eo consistit quod non distinguitur inter causas ultimas (potentiam et actum) et id quod in causas reducitur (actuationem).[3]

procedure can be applied to other cases; for whatever is scientifically established will be a hypothesis verified in several instances. As hypothesis it is resolved into form; as verified it is resolved into act; and as found in several instances it is resolved into potency.

With regard to synthesis, however, there is the obvious difficulty that there is no proceeding from the many to one unless the many are naturally suited to come together to form one. And so the question that regularly comes up is whether the intrinsic constitutive causes of being come together to form one thing by themselves or through something else, such as some sort of intermediary glue. Our answer to this question is that they are united by themselves, provided they are proportioned to each other as potency and act.

This can be explained, first of all, according to the fundamental theorem of metaphysical composition, namely, that it is the very same thing that is perfectible by potency and perfected by act. Unless this identity is conceded, nothing can ever proceed from being perfectible to being perfected; and once we are compelled by the facts themselves to concede this identity, we immediately have the criterion whereby we can determine which potency is proportioned to which act, namely, the principle that a potency is proportioned to an act when it is the same thing that is perfectible by a potency and perfected by an act.

Furthermore, there would be no point in bringing in some kind of intermediary to unite either potency and form or form and act or substance and accidents. For if such an intermediary is needed to bring about this union, another intermediary is needed to unite the potency to the intermediary, and still another to unite the intermediary to the form, and so on ad infinitum. But if no additional intermediary is required, then for the same reason neither is the first.

27 We are now at last in a position to counter the opposing arguments. It is argued that unactuated potency is at least modally distinct from actuated potency; and likewise that an accident that actually inheres in a subject is at least modally distinct from a Eucharistic accident, which does not actually inhere.

To this we reply that there is a real difference between what is composed of potency alone and what is composed of potency and act, and that this real difference is the difference between non-act and act. An actuated potency is nothing else than the potency of something that possesses not only potency but also act. The fallacy lies in thinking that there is a distinction between ultimate causes (potency and act) and that which is resolved into its causes (actuation).[3]

3 [The Latin of the last sentence ('Fallacia autem in eo consistit ...') is cryptic. The fallacy referred to consists, not in failing to distinguish between the ultimate

Similiter, respondendum est quod realiter aliud est id quod solo accidente constat, et realiter aliud est id quod et accidente et substantia constat; quae realis differentia est inter substantiam et non-substantiam. Nec quidquam aliud est accidens actu inhaerens nisi accidens eius quod etiam substantialia habet. Fallacia denique est eadem: actualis enim inhaesio non est tertia quaedam causa ultima praeter substantiam et accidens, sed consectarium quoddam quod in substantiam et accidens tamquam in causas suas reducitur.

Sectio Quarta: De Constitutione Personae Finitae

28 *Ad terminos*:

Persona: subsistens distinctum in natura intellectuali.

Subsistens: id quod est; ens strictius dictum; unum strictius dictum seu quod simpliciter in se est indivisum et simpliciter a quolibet alio divisum.

Distinctum: distincta sunt quorum unum non est aliud.

Natura: principium intrinsecum prout ad operationem refertur.

Intellectualis: natura quae circa totum ens operari potest.

Finita persona[4]: ens per participationem seu ens cuius esse non est sua essentia.

Constituitur persona inquantum (1) assignantur causae intrinsecae quibus componitur et (2) applicantur leges secundum quas ex his multis fit unum.

29 *Primus gressus*: causae intrinsecae assignantur.

Ad personam finitam constituendam requiruntur:

(1) substantialis essentia naturae intellectualis, secus nulla est persona;

Similarly, we answer that there is a real distinction between what consists of an accident alone and what consists of accident and substance, and that this real difference is between non-substance and substance. An actually inhering accident is nothing other than an accident of that which also has substantial components. It all comes down to the same fallacy: the actual inhering is not some third kind of ultimate cause over and above substance and accident, but is, as it were, a consequence resolvable into substance and accident as into its causes.

4 The Constitution of a Finite Person

28 *Explanation of the Terms*

Person: a distinct subsistent in an intellectual nature.

Subsistent: that which is; a being in the strict sense; one in the strict sense; that which is simply both undivided in itself and divided from everything else.

Distinct: things are distinct when one is not the other.

Nature: the intrinsic principle as related to operation.

Intellectual: a nature that can operate throughout the entire range of being.

Finite[4]: a being by participation; a being whose act of existence is not its essence.

Determining the constitution of a finite person means (1) assigning the intrinsic causes by which it is composed and (2) applying the laws that govern the composition of a unit out of these several causes.

29 *Step 1*: Assigning the intrinsic causes.

To constitute a finite person the following are required.

(1) A substantial essence of an intellectual nature; otherwise there would be no person;

---

causes (potency and act) and a resultant actuation, as a literalistic translation might have it, but in making a distinction where there is none. Lonergan's meaning is, 'The fallacy consists in this, that they distinguish between potency-and-act and actuation, whereas potency-and-act and actuation are not distinguished.' In the next paragraph, dealing with the parallel case of substance and accident, the same fallacy is quite clearly stated as supposing the resultant actual inherence of an accident to be some third ultimate cause over and above substance and accident, when in fact it is resolvable into those causes and hence not distinct from them. For a fuller treatment of this fallacy see Lonergan, *De Verbo incarnato* (Rome: Gregorian University Press, 1960) 343–44, (1964) 250–51, where Lonergan makes reference to Maurice de la Taille, 'Actuation créée par acte incréée,' *Recherches de science religieuse* 18 (1928) 260–68, where this theorem is applied to the *lumen gloriae*, sanctifying grace, and the hypostatic union.]

4 [Lonergan's Latin has 'Finita persona' (Finite person), but the definition is that of a finite being.]

(2) esse, secus deest subsistens, id quod est, ens strictius;

(3) esse in essentia receptum, secus persona non est finita;

(4) esse proprium, secus est esse alterius et impeditur tum 'indivisum in se' tum 'divisum a quolibet alio';

(5) accidentia saltem inseparabilia, secus tollitur et ipsa essentia.

30 *Alter gressus*: applicantur leges compositionis.

Lex compositionis est ut causae intrinsecae ita inter se proportionentur ut unum idemque sit per diversas causas perfectibile et perfectum.

Sed una eademque persona finita est perfectibilis per essentiam substantialem naturae intellectualis et perfecta per esse suum proprium; et iterum una eademque persona est perfectibilis per haec substantialia et perfecta per sua accidentia.

E contra, si esse non esset proprium huic essentiae, esset alterius; et tunc per essentiam esset hic in potentia, et per esse ille alter esset in actu; et ita tolleretur unum strictius dictum (simpliciter indivisum in se et simpliciter divisum a quolibet alio).

31 *Nota*: quid per esse proprium intelligitur.

Esse est actus substantialis seu actus essentiae substantialis; vicissim, essentia substantialis est potentia ad actum qui dicitur 'esse.'

Porro, duplex est potentia, alia naturalis, et alia obedientialis. Naturalis est potentia inquantum est ad actum qui qualis sit per naturam rei determinatur. Obedientialis est potentia inquantum est ad actum qui qualis sit ultra naturam rei secundum divinum beneplacitum determinatur.

Esse ergo est proprium essentiae si ad essentiam comparatur tamquam ad potentiam naturalem; et esse non est proprium essentiae si ad essentiam comparatur tamquam ad potentiam obedientialem.

Sectio Quinta: Sententiarum Differentiae

32 Concordat Scotus inquantum videt personam esse ens strictius dictum, ens strictius dictum esse simpliciter divisum a quolibet alio, et ideo humanitatem Christi non esse personam humanam quia non simpliciter dividitur a Verbo

(2) an act of existence; otherwise there would be no subsistent, no that-which-is, no being in the strict sense;

(3) an act of existence received in an essence; otherwise the person would not be finite;

(4) a proper act of existence; otherwise it would have another's act of existence and could be neither 'undivided in itself' nor 'divided from everything else';

(5) at least inseparable accidents; otherwise the essence itself would not exist.

30 *Step 2*: Applying the laws of composition.

The law of composition is that intrinsic causes be proportionate to one another in such a way that by different causes one and the same thing is perfectible and perfected.

But one and the same finite person is perfectible by the substantial essence of an intellectual nature and perfected by the act of existence proper to it; and again, one and the same person is perfectible by these substantial principles and perfected by its accidents.

On the other hand, if the act of existence were not proper to this essence, it would belong to another; and then through essence it would be 'this' in potency, and through the act of existence it would be 'that other' in act; and thus there would be no 'one' in the strict sense, as something simply undivided in itself and divided from everything else.

31 *Note*: The meaning of 'proper act of existence.'

The act of existence is substantial act, the act of substantial essence. Conversely, substantial essence is potency to the act that is called 'the act of existence.'

Moreover, there are two kinds of potencies, natural and obediential. A natural potency is one that is directed to an act whose character is determined by the very nature of the thing in question. An obediential potency is one that is directed to an act whose character, in a manner determined by the divine good-pleasure, exceeds the nature of the thing.

An act of existence, therefore, is proper to an essence if it is related to that essence as to its natural potency; but if it is related to it as to an obediential potency, that act of existence is not proper to that essence.

5 How Other Opinions Differ from Ours

32 Scotus agrees with our opinion in that he holds that a person is a being in the strict sense, that a being in the strict sense is simply divided from everything else, and accordingly that the humanity of Christ is not a human person because

assumente; pariter videt Scotus ens strictius dictum esse simpliciter indivisum in se, hominem in animam et in corpus divisum non esse indivisum in se, et ideo animam separatam non esse personam. Qua de causa minime negamus Scotum recte sensisse personam negare tum actualem ab alio assumptionem tum aptitudinalem cum alio coniunctionem.

Differt autem sententia Scoti a nostra inquantum Scotus, duplici negatione contentus, resolutionem in causas metaphysicam omisit. Quare haec sola quaestio cum Scotistis est disputanda, nempe, utrum scientia sit certa rerum *per causas* cognitio.

33 Concordat etiam Tiphanus inquantum videt personam esse ens strictius dictum, ens strictius dictum esse simpliciter indivisum in se, et ideo personam esse realitatem substantialem completam, totam in se, alteri non communicabilem. Quibus omnibus consentimus.

Differt autem sententia Tiphani a nostra inquantum Tiphanus, eiusmodi declaratione contentus, metaphysicam in causas resolutionem omisit. Quare cum Tiphano sicut et cum Scoto haec sola quaestio est disputanda, nempe, utrum scientia sit certa rerum *per causas* cognitio.

34 Concordat nobiscum Suarezius inquantum non solum quaerit quid per nomen personae significetur sed etiam determinat principium intrinsecum unde persona constituatur.

Differt autem sententia Suarezii a nostra inquantum Suarezius notas atque demonstratas entis finiti causas constitutivas praetermittit ut modum quendam existentialem inveniat. Quod nobis ideo non placet quia demonstratum credimus tum ens finitum in potentiam, formam et actum reduci, tum modos similesque entitatulas omnes non esse nisi fictiones fallaciis fundatas. Quare cum Suarezio haec sola est quaestio disputanda, nempe, utrum aliunde directe cognoscamus quam per experientiam, intelligentiam atque iudicium; si enim adest quartus gressus in nostra cognitione, etiam adest quartum principium constitutivum in obiecto nostrae cognitioni proportionato, i.e., in omni ente materiali; sin autem quartus gressus in cognitione non invenitur, dicendus est modus Suarezii aliud esse non posse nisi fictio fallaciis fundata. Neque aliter sentiendum est sive de modo Caietani essentiali, sive de modo D. Maritain,[5] sive de actuatione quam forte distinguit P. de la Taille et ab actu et a potentia.[6]

it is not simply divided from the Word who assumes it. Likewise Scotus holds that being in the strict sense is that which is simply undivided in itself, that a human being divided into body and soul is not undivided in itself, and therefore that a separated soul is not a person. For this reason we do not at all deny that Scotus was right in maintaining that 'person' precludes both actual assumption by another and the aptitude to be joined with another.

However, Scotus's view differs from ours in that, content with these two negations, he neglected the metaphysical resolution into causes. Hence our only dispute with the Scotists is whether or not science is the certain knowledge of things *through their causes*.

33 Tiphanus also concurs with our opinion in that he holds that a person is a being in the strict sense, that a being in the strict sense is simply undivided in itself, and therefore that a person is a complete substantial reality, whole in itself, and not communicable to another. With all this we agree.

But the opinion of Tiphanus differs from ours in that, content with the above statement, he neglected the metaphysical resolution into causes. Hence, as with Scotus, our only argument with Tiphanus is whether science is the certain knowledge of things *through their causes*.

34 Suarez also agrees with us in that he not only seeks the meaning of the word 'person,' but also specifies the intrinsic principle whereby a person is constituted.

But his opinion differs from ours in that he disregards the known and proven constitutive causes of a finite being to come up with some sort of existential mode. We find this unacceptable, because we believe we have shown that a finite being is resolved into potency, form, and act, and that modes and all similar 'thinglets' are but figments founded on fallacies. Hence our only quarrel with Suarez is whether there is another source of our direct knowledge apart from experience, understanding, and judgment; for if there is a fourth step in the cognitional process, there is also a fourth constitutive principle in the object proportionate to our knowledge, that is, in every material being. But if there is no fourth step in our knowing, this Suarezian mode cannot be said to be anything other than a figment founded on fallacies. And the same must be said of Cajetan's essential mode, of Maritain's mode,[5] and of the actuation that de la Taille would seem to consider distinct from act and potency.[6]

5 Jacques Maritain, 'Sur la notion de subsistence,' *Revue thomiste* 54 (1954) 242–56.
6 [On de la Taille, see above, p. 59, note 3.]

35 Concordat nobiscum Caietanus (1) inquantum realem ponit distinctionem inter essentiam substantialem et esse contingens, (2) inquantum realem ponit distinctionem inter essentiam substantialem (seu naturam) et personam, et (3) inquantum optime scit modum non esse causam sive intrinsecam sive extrinsecam.

Differt autem sententia Caietani a nostra tum quaestione tum methodo: quaestione quidem quia de praedicamento substantiae primae (hic homo, hic bos) quaerit inquantum a natura seu essentia substantiali (hac humanitate, hac bovinitate) distinguitur; methodo autem inquantum praedicamentum in essentiam et modum essentialem reducit. Nostra enim methodus est generalis methodus metaphysica quae entia concreta in causas suas ultimas resolvit ut ex iisdem causis eadem entia componat; et ideo non de praedicamentis quaerimus sed de entibus, neque praedicamenta in modos reducimus sed entia in causas resolvimus.

Quod si quis dixerit idem esse de praedicamento quaerere ac de ente cum praedicamentum significet ens, respondetur:

Idem est si praedicamentum consideratur praecise inquantum ens respicit, conceditur; idem est si praedicamentum consideratur praecise inquantum ab esse et non-esse praescindit, negatur.

Si enim hoc secundo modo sumitur praedicamentum substantiae primae, necessaria quodammodo est conclusio Caietani quod persona addit modum essentialem super essentiam; sin autem primo modo sumitur praedicamentum substantiae primae, cum ens sit id quod est, satis est obvium ideo 'ens' et 'subsistens' et 'personam' ab essentia finita realiter distingui quia 'ens' super essentiam addit esse.

36 Instaret tamen quispiam: nisi ratio personae iam in essentialibus continetur, frustra ab esse mendicatur; esse enim non addit super determinationes essentiae finitae sed tantummodo ipsas essentiae determinationes actuat.[7]

Ad additam rationem respondetur: esse non addit determinationes in ratione naturae, *conceditur*; esse non addit determinationes in ratione entis, *subdistinguitur*; non addit determinationes potentiales, *conceditur*; non actuat determinationes potentiales, *negatur*.

Quod sic illustrari potest: conceditur esse non addere determinationes in ratione naturae quia non per suum esse sed per suam essentiam Socrates est in natura intellectuali; conceditur esse non addere determinationes potentiales in ratione entis quia non per suum esse sed per suam essentiam substantialem Socrates est cui competit esse

35 Cajetan's opinion is the same as ours in that (1) he maintains a real distinction between substantial essence and contingent act of existence, (2) he affirms a real distinction between substantial essence (or nature) and person, and (3) he knows very well that a mode is neither an intrinsic nor an extrinsic cause.

But his opinion differs from ours both in the question it poses and in its method: in the question, because he asks how the predicament of first substance ('this man,' 'this ox') differs from nature or substantial essence ('this humanity,' 'this bovinity'); and in its method, in that he reduces this predicament into essence and essential mode. Our method is the general method of metaphysics, which resolves concrete beings into their ultimate causes so that it may reconstitute these same beings from these same causes. And so our concern is not with predicaments but with beings. We do not reduce predicaments into modes; we resolve beings into their causes.

To anyone who would say that inquiring about predicaments is the same as inquiring about being, since predicament signifies being, we would reply as follows.

If a predicament is considered precisely as referring to being, we agree, but if a predicament is considered precisely as prescinding from existence and non-existence, we disagree.

For if the predicament of first substance is taken in the second sense, Cajetan's conclusion that person adds an essential mode to essence somehow follows necessarily. But if the predicament of first substance is taken in the first sense, since being is that-which-is, it is clear enough that 'being' and 'subsistent' and 'person' are really distinct from a finite essence for the simple reason that 'being' adds to essence the act of existence.

36 Someone might further argue that unless the formality of person is already contained in the essential elements, there is no point in looking for it in the act of existence, since 'to be' adds nothing to the determinations of a finite essence, but merely actuates those determinations.[7]

With respect to the reason adduced, we agree that the act of existence adds no determinations in what pertains to nature. But in what pertains to being, although the act of existence does not add potential determinations to it, it does actuate those potential determinations.

This can be illustrated as follows. We agree that the act of existence adds no determinations in what pertains to nature, because Socrates, for example, has an intellectual nature not through his act of existence but through his essence. We also agree that the act of existence adds no potential determinations in what

7 See Herman Diepen, 'La critique du Basilisme selon saint Thomas d'Aquin,' *Revue thomiste* 50 (1950) 313.

per se; negatur esse non actuare determinationes potentiales in ratione entis quia esse proprium facit ut actu sit per se illud cui per essentiam substantialem competit esse per se.

Unde *ad ipsam obiectionem* respondetur: frustra ab esse mendicatur ratio personae nisi haec ratio iam in essentialibus continetur, *distinguitur*: si ratio personae ad rationem naturae reducitur, *conceditur*; si ratio personae ad rationem entis reducitur, *subdistinguitur*; si ratio personae est tantummodo potentialis determinatio in ratione entis, *conceditur*; si ratio personae est actuata determinatio in ratione entis, *negatur*.

Iam vero ratio personae est actuata determinatio in ratione entis; persona enim est subsistens seu ens strictius dictum seu id quod est.

37 *Instatur*: ratio nullius creaturae includit esse.

Respondetur: 'Ratio quam significat nomen est rei definitio'[8] et ideo sicut de definitione ita etiam de ratione distinguendum est: ratio stricte dicta nullius creaturae includit esse, *conceditur*, nam ratio stricte dicta dicit solam essentiam, et nulla essentia finita includit esse; ratio late dicta nullius creaturae includit esse, *subdistinguitur*: si creatura non existit, *conceditur*; si creatura existit, *negatur*, nam ratio late dicta super essentiam addit vel accidens vel individuum vel etiam existens.

Caeterum quantum ad ulteriora argumenta quae ex essentialismo repetuntur, satis iam est dictum; quantum autem ad auctoritatem S. Thomae quam Caietanus invocat, quaeritur vel unus locus S. Thomae ubi personalitas ad modum quendam essentialem reducitur.

Dixerit tamen quispiam sententiam Caietani necessario ex diversis locis S. Thomae concludi.

pertains to being, because it is not through his act of existence but through his substantial essence that 'to exist per se' belongs to Socrates. But we deny that the act of existence does not actuate the potential determinations in what pertains to being, because a proper act of existence brings it about that that to which, through its substantial essence, existence belongs per se actually exists per se.

Accordingly, our *answer to the objection itself* is as follows. We have to distinguish the statement that there is no point in looking for the formality of person in the act of existence unless this formality is already contained in the essential elements. The statement is true if the formality of person is reducible to the formality of nature. But if the formality of person is reducible to the formality of being, a further distinction is required. The objection would hold if 'person' is understood only as a potential determination in what pertains to being, but not if by 'person' is meant an actuated determination in what pertains to being.

Now, in fact, the formality of 'person' is an actuated determination in what pertains to being; for a person is a subsistent, a being in the strict sense, that-which-is.

37 But the objection is urged that the act of existence is not included in the formal determination of any creature.

To this further objection we reply that 'the formality that a noun signifies is the definition of the thing,'[8] and therefore that as a definition is distinguished, so also must a formality be distinguished. We agree that the formal determination, in the strict sense, of any creature does not include its act of existence, since formal determination in the strict sense indicates only essence, and no finite essence includes the act of existence. We also agree that in the case of a non-existent creature, formal determination taken in the broad sense does not include existence, but we deny that this is so if the creature actually exists, since formal determination in the broad sense adds to essence either an accident or an individual or even an existing being.

Regarding further arguments derived from essentialism, enough has been said. As to the authority of St Thomas that Cajetan appeals to, one looks in vain for a single passage in which Aquinas reduces personhood to some kind of essential mode.

It might be objected, however, that Cajetan's opinion is a necessary conclusion from various passages in St Thomas.

8 [Lonergan: 'ratio quam significat nomen est definitio'; Thomas: 'ratio vero significata per nomen est definitio' (*Summa contra Gentiles*, 1, c. 12, referring to Aristotle; see *Metaphysics*, IV, 7, 1012a 23–24).]

Respondetur: Non necessario concluditur ex hoc effato, 'esse pertinet ad ipsam constitutionem personae.'[9]

Quibus perspectis, haec duo cum Caietano sunt disputanda, primo, utrum resolutio metaphysica sit in causas ultimas reales, deinde, utrum id quod in causas reales resolvatur sit ens reale et ideo concretum.

38 Concordat nobiscum Capreolus tum inquantum entia realia et concreta in causas suas reales resolvit tum inquantum inter subsistens et non-subsistens per esse proprium discernit.

Differt autem sententia Capreoli a nostra tum inquantum quaestionem de supposito finito reducimus ad quaestionem generalem de compositione entis finiti tum inquantum illud explicite agnoscimus non esse ens strictius et unum strictius quod essentia finita et esse non proprio componatur.

Quantum autem ad eos qui Capreolum idem quod Caietanus sensisse iudicant, notate essentialismum influere posse non solum in iudicia de entibus sed etiam in iudicium de scriptis.[10]

39 Aliae denique recenter sunt propositae sententiae duae quae, quamvis immediate ipsam unionem hypostaticam respiciant, tamen propter naturam argumentorum quae afferuntur hoc in loco melius considerantur.

Quarum prima est a H. Diepen elaborata,[11] qui post dubitationem quandam initialem ad sententiam Caietani de notione personae conversus est.[12] Circa personae constitutionem maxime distinguere videtur inter *suppositum hypotheticum* et *esse*.

Ipsum hoc nomen, suppositum hypotheticum, non adhibet sed ex ipsa hac notione facile deducuntur omnia fere quae affirmat. Si enim quis de 'hoc homine' ita cogitat ut a vero et falso, esse et non esse, praescindat, tunc illud cogitat (i) quod ad ordinem mere possibilem

We simply answer that such a conclusion does not necessarily follow from Thomas's statement that 'to be belongs to the very constitution of a person.'[9]

From all this, then, we have these two points of difference with Cajetan: first, whether metaphysics resolves being into ultimate real causes, and second, whether what is resolved into real causes is real, and therefore concrete, being.

38 Capreolus is in agreement with our position both in resolving real concrete beings into their real causes and in making a proper act of existence what distinguishes 'subsistent' from 'non-subsistent.'

But his opinion differs from ours both inasmuch as we reduce the question of a finite supposit to the general question of the composition of finite being, and inasmuch as we explicitly recognize that what is composed of a finite essence and an act of existence that is not proper to it is neither a being nor one in the strict sense of those terms.

As for those who maintain that Capreolus held the same view as Cajetan, we simply note that essentialism can influence not only judgments about beings but also judgments about books.[10]

39 Finally, two other views have been proposed recently, and while they have immediate reference to the hypostatic union, nevertheless because of the nature of the arguments advanced, it will be better to deal with them here.

The first of these is that worked out by Herman Diepen.[11] After some initial reservations he eventually came over to Cajetan's notion of person.[12] Regarding the constitution of a person he appears to draw an especially sharp distinction between a *hypothetical supposit* and *the act of existence*.

He does not actually use the term 'hypothetical supposit,' but practically everything he says can be readily deduced from this notion. For if one thinks about 'this human being' in such a way as to prescind from truth and falsehood, from existence and non-existence, then one is thinking about (1) what pertains to the merely

---

9 Thomas Aquinas, *Summa theologiae*, 3, q. 19, a. 1, ad 4m. See Cajetan's arguments, *In IIIm*, q. 4, a. 2, §§ 4–27, Leonine ed., vol. 11 (Rome: Ex Typographia Polyglotta, 1903) 75–81. Louis de Raeymaeker has collected the passages in St Thomas and explained them briefly in his *Metaphysica generalis*, vol. 2 (Louvain: E. Warny, 1932) 360–74.

10 See D. Foucher, *Personne et existence chez le Père Billot*. Dissertatio 2367 (Rome: Gregorian University Press, 1955).

11 Diepen, 'La critique du Basilisme selon saint Thomas d'Aquin,' *Revue thomiste* 50 (1950) 290–329; 'L'unique Seigneur Jésus-Christ,' ibid. 53 (1953) 28–80; 'Les implications métaphysiques du mystère de l'Incarnation,' ibid. 54 (1954) 257–66.

12 Diepen, 'L'unique Seigneur ...' 34–38.

seu idealem pertinet, nam ab esse et non esse praescinditur; (ii) quod significat non hominis partem sed totum hunc hominem; (iii) quod significat non essentiam individuam
tantum (hanc humanitatem) sed essentiam individuam et personificatam (hunc hominem);
(iv) quod est potentia quaedam ad realitatem; quod enim concipimus, hoc etiam re vera
esse potest; (v) quod ad ordinem realem transit inquantum extra causas in realitate et sub
realitate ponitur, scilicet, inquantum hic homo est; (vi) quod per talem transitum totam
suam realitatem accipit; (vii) quod per talem transitum nullam prorsus determinationem
sui mutat, nam quod concipitur, si vere concipitur, exacte correspondet ei quod in realitate
invenitur; (viii) quod ideo est totum id quod in realitate invenitur.[13]

Iam vero id quod ponit rem extra causas, productive quidem est causa efficiens, sed formaliter est esse seu existentia seu actus entis seu actus essendi. Ergo componuntur essentia
personificata (quam etiam nominat 'ens,' 'id quod est,' 'id cui competit esse,' 'hypostasis')
et esse. Quae compositio est realis inter potentiam realem et actum realem, ita tamen
ut totum quod componitur sit unum de componentibus (nempe, essentia personificata) et
compositi tota realitas sit aliud de componentibus (nempe, esse).[14]

Quod si conceditur, admitti non potest unicum esse idque divinum in Christo Deo et
homine, cum humana Christi natura nullam prorsus actualitatem realem haberet.[15]

40 Ab hac ergo sententia differt nostra tum circa notionem personae tum circa
personae constitutionem tum circa unionem hypostaticam.
    Differentia circa notionem personae eadem est ac supra ponitur ubi de notione
Caietani agitur.
    Differentia circa personae constitutionem tum methodum tum conclusiones
respicit. Quoad methodum desideramus clariores distinctiones (i) inter quaestiones historicas et quaestiones speculativas, (ii) in ipsis speculativis inter quaestiones stricte metaphysicas et alias, et (iii) in stricte metaphysicis inter causas reales
quae constituunt et rem realem quae constituitur. Quoad argumenta et conclusiones, (i) distinguimus inter suppositum hypotheticum et suppositum reale, (ii)
notamus non iam sermonem fieri de supposito hypothetico cum ex ordine conceptionum ad ordinem realem transeatur, ideoque (iii) arbitramur argumenta

possible or ideal order, for one is prescinding from existence and non-existence, (2) what denotes not a part of a human being but this whole human being, (3) what denotes not only an individual essence (this humanity) but an individual and 'personified' essence (this human being), (4) what is a certain potency to reality, since what we conceive can in fact exist, (5) what passes into the real order inasmuch as in reality and as real it stands outside its causes, that is, inasmuch as this human being exists, (6) what receives its whole reality as a result of such transition, (7) what in no way changes any determination of itself as a result of such transition, for what is conceived, if it is rightly conceived, corresponds exactly to what is found in reality, (8) what, therefore, is the whole of what is found in reality.[13]

Now, what makes a thing stand outside its causes is, as producer, the efficient cause, but formally it is existence, the act of existence, the act of a being, or the act of existing. Therefore 'personified' essence (which he would also call 'being,' 'that-which-is,' 'that to which existence belongs,' 'hypostasis') and act of existence are combined. This is a real composition of real potency and real act, composed in such a way, however, that the whole that is combined is one of the components, namely, a personified essence, and the whole reality of the composite is another of the components, namely, an act of existence.[14]

But if this is granted, it is impossible for there to be in Christ, God and man, only one act of existence and that divine, since the human nature of Christ would have no real actuality whatsoever.[15]

40 Our opinion, therefore, differs from Diepen's on the notion of person, on the constitution of a person, and on the hypostatic union.

Concerning the notion of person, our difference is the same as that explained above in dealing with the view of Cajetan.

Concerning the constitution of a person, our difference of opinion has to do with both method and conclusions. As to method, we need clearer distinctions (1) between historical and speculative questions, (2) in speculative questions themselves, between strictly metaphysical questions and others, and (3) in strictly metaphysical questions, between the real constitutive causes of a reality and the reality they constitute. As to Diepen's arguments and conclusions, (1) we distinguish between a supposit that is hypothetical and a supposit that is real, (2) we note that no further mention is made of a hypothetical supposit once the transition is made from the conceptual order to the real order, and hence (3) we believe the author's

13 Diepen, 'La critique ...' 297, 313, 317; 'L'unique Seigneur ...' 35, 37, 57–61.
14 See the Diepen references cited above.
15 Diepen, 'La critique ...' 296–313; 'L'unique Seigneur ...' 41–62.

auctoris aequivocatione laborari. Nam suppositum hypotheticum a vero et falso, ab esse et non esse praescindit et ideo in rebus est nihil prorsus; suppositum autem reale esse includit inquantum esse est causa quaedam intrinseca et constitutiva; reale denique dupliciter dicitur sicut et ens, nam strictius reale est ens quod est, et latius reale est principium entis intrinsecum quod ipsum quidem non est sed eo aliquid (ens-quod) est; quo sensu latiori sed vero non solum esse sed etiam essentia sunt realia.

Quantum autem ad unionem hypostaticam attinet, ita defendemus unicum esse in Christo ut esse divinum sit unica causa constitutiva ipsius unionis, ut humanitas Christi proprio et proportionato esse careat, ut tamen eadem humanitas esse quodam creato non proprio actuetur non quidem ut existat sed ut sit actu assumpta.

41 Ultima denique consideranda est sententia quam medio aevo excogitavit Ioannes Baconthorp et nuperrime resuscitavit B. Xiberta.[16]

In eo est quod distinguit causam et duplicem effectum formalem. Causa est plena actuatio naturae substantialis. Effectus formalis primarius est ut omnia praeter subsistentiam habeantur. Effectus formalis secundarius est ut etiam habeatur subsistentia. Asseritur quod divina omnipotentia effectum formalem secundarium impedire potest ut natura humana Christi non sit persona creata; quo effectu impedito, persona Verbi naturam hanc assumit tamquam suam, inquantum eminenter supplet vices personae non per modi cuiusdam additionem sed per perductionem totius naturae assumptae ad plenam realitatem.

Distinctio quae inter effectum primarium et secundarium intercedit in eo esse videtur quod primarius est 'nuda constitutio rei in ratione naturae' et secundarius est functio quaedam ordinis transcendentalis unde natura realis suis notis determinata efficitur 'plenum ens inter caetera entia.'

Quod autem ab auctore assumitur tamquam ab omnibus agnitum atque affirmatum, non simpliciter verum credimus, nempe, 'distinctio effectus formalis primarii et secundarii, amborum realis identitas cum forma, ordo naturae existens inter eos ratione cuius verificari queat effectus primarius impedito secundario: haec omnia saepe repetuntur in philosophia

arguments to be equivocal. For a hypothetical supposit prescinds from truth and falsity, from existence and non-existence, and so in terms of reality it is nothing at all. But a real supposit includes the act of existence in that the act of existence is an intrinsic constitutive cause; and so, finally, just as being is understood in two senses, so also is the real; for in the strict sense the real is a being that exists, and in a broader sense the real is an intrinsic principle of being that of itself does not exist but is that by which some thing (that-which) does exist; and in this broader but true sense not only the act of existence but also essence are real.

As for the hypostatic union, we shall defend a single act of existence (*esse*) in Christ, in such a way as to maintain that the divine act of existence is the sole constitutive cause of the union itself, that the humanity of Christ lacks its own proper and proportionate act of existence, and yet that the same humanity is actuated by a created act of existence not proper to it – not, indeed, in order that it exist, but rather that it be actually assumed.

41 The last opinion under consideration is that proposed by the medieval theologian John Baconthorp and recently revived by B. Xiberta.[16]

This opinion makes a distinction between a cause and a double formal effect. The cause is the complete actuation of a substantial nature. The primary formal effect is that everything apart from subsistence be effected. The secondary formal effect is that subsistence also be effected. It is asserted that divine omnipotence can prevent the secondary formal effect, so that the human nature of Christ not be a created person; and with the prevention of this effect, the person of the Word assumes this nature as his own. The Word does this by supplying in a higher fashion the role of person, not by the addition of some kind of mode, but by drawing the entire assumed nature to its full reality.

This distinction between primary and secondary effects seems to be that the primary formal effect is 'the bare constitution of a thing in what pertains to nature' while the secondary formal effect is some sort of function of a transcendental order whereby a real nature, determined by its characteristic features, becomes 'a full-fledged being among other beings.'

However, we simply do not accept as true what Xiberta assumes as acknowledged and affirmed by everyone, namely, that 'the distinction between the primary and the secondary formal effect, the real identity of both with the form, the natural order between them whereby the primary effect can be verified while the secondary effect is prevented – all these are frequently found in philosophy and

16 Bartolomé M. Xiberta, *Tractatus de Verbo incarnato*, vol. 1 (Madrid: Consejo Superior de Investigaciones Cientificas, Instituto 'Francisco Suarez,' 1954) 257–58, 264–67.

et in theologia."[7] Posita enim forma, etiam ponitur omne quod realiter identificatur cum ipsa forma; qua de causa contradictorium esse credo asserere ita poni posse formam ut effectus secundarius cum forma realiter identificatus non ponatur. Quantum autem ad exempla ab auctore allata, intentum suum probare non videntur; dicit substantiam definiri non 'ens per se' sed 'id cui competit esse per se,' accidens definiri non 'ens in alio' sed 'id cui competit esse in alio,' quia effectus formales secundarii, nempe, subsistere, actu inhaerere, divina virtute impediri possunt; sed remanet ab eo probandum quod (i) subsistere est effectus formalis secundarius qui realiter identificatur cum forma quae est substantia, (ii) actu inhaerere est effectus formalis secundarius qui realiter identificatur cum forma quae est accidens, (iii) et utraque haec identificatio realis communiter et in philosophia et in theologia recipitur et docetur.

Differt ergo nostra sententia inquantum dicimus (i) subsistere non realiter identificari cum essentia substantiali individua sed advenire inquantum realiter distinctum esse proprium ei coniungitur, (ii) inhaerere non realiter identificari cum accidente sed advenire inquantum existit substantia realiter ab accidente distincta cui accidens inhaeret, (iii) realem distinctionem inter substantiam et accidens communiter recipi et doceri tum in philosophia tum in theologia catholica, (iv) aliquam distinctionem a parte rei inter substantiam et subsistentiam communiter a Thomistis et Suarezianis doceri.

theology."[17] For once you have the form, everything that is really identical with that form is also present; hence it seems to us a contradiction to say that you can have a form without the secondary effect that is really identical with it being also present. Nor do the examples given by the author seem to prove his point. He says that substance is not defined as 'being per se' but as 'that to which it belongs to be per se,' and that an accident is defined not as 'being in another' but as 'that to which it belongs to be in another,' because the secondary formal effects, namely, subsistence and actual inherence in another, can be prevented by divine power. But it still remains to be proved (1) that subsistence is a secondary formal effect really identical with the form which is substance, (2) that actual inherence in another is a secondary formal effect really identical with the form which is an accident, and (3) that both of these real identities are commonly accepted and taught in philosophy and theology.

Therefore our position differs from the above in that we maintain (1) that subsistence is not really identical with an individual substantial essence but comes to it inasmuch as a really distinct and proper act of existence is conjoined to it, (2) that actual inherence in another is not really identical with an accident, but comes to it inasmuch as there exists a substance that is really distinct from the accident and in which that accident inheres, (3) that a real distinction between substance and accident is commonly accepted and taught both in philosophy and in Catholic theology, and (4) that some distinction in reality between substance and subsistence is the common teaching of Thomists and Suarezians.

17 Ibid. 265.

De Intelligentia Theologica

---

42 Intellectus humani duplex maxime distinguitur obiectum: nam et aliud est ens in quod cognoscendum tamquam in finem procedit intellectus; et aliud est quidditas in materia corporali existens per quam intellectus movetur ut intelligat.

Qua de causa, illud omnibus scientiis commune est quod in ens cognoscendum procedunt, et illud singulis est proprium quod eatenus ad ens perveniunt quatenus ab hac illave quidditate moventur.

Porro, ut illas omittamus scientias quae a quidditatibus finitis moveantur ut entia per participationem cognoscantur, summa quaedam est quidditas seu essentia quae, cum entis per essentiam sit, ad omnem omnium scientiam proportionatur.

Per hanc ergo quidditatem et ipse Deus se comprehendit et omnia in se intelligit. Per immediatam huius quidditatis visionem beati et ipsum Deum vident et caetera in Deo pro perfectione visionis intuentur. At nos hac in vita inquirentes nisi mediate Deum non cognoscimus, et ideo mediate tantum a divina essentia movemur ad ens cognoscendum.

Quod tamen dupliciter contingit. Uno modo, per revelationem illam naturalem secundum quam singulae creaturae et maxime ipse totius universi ordo similitudinem quandam Dei exprimunt; unde oriuntur et metaphysica et theologia naturalis. Alio modo, per revelationem formalem atque supernaturalem qua Deus ipse nobis loquitur et qualis sit ipse dicit; unde oritur theologia dogmatica quae ideo scientia subalternata dicitur et in imperfecta quadam etsi fructuosissima fidei intelligentia consistit.

PART 3

Theological Understanding

---

42 There is a most important distinction between the two objects of the human intellect: being, toward the knowledge of which the intellect proceeds as to its goal, and quiddity existing in corporeal matter, by which the intellect is moved to understand.

Hence, what is common to all sciences is that they move toward the knowledge of being, and what is proper to and distinctive of each of them is that they arrive at being differently depending on whether they are moved by this or that quiddity.

Furthermore – to say nothing of sciences that are moved by finite quiddities toward a knowledge of beings by participation – there is a supreme quiddity or essence which is that of being by essence and is thereby proportionate to all knowledge of all things.

Through this quiddity, therefore, God knows himself comprehensively and understands all things in himself. Through the immediate vision of this quiddity the blessed both see God and behold everything else in God in proportion to the degree of perfection of the vision they possess. But in our quest for knowledge in this life we know God only mediately, and therefore it is only mediately that we are moved by God's essence towards the knowledge of being.

This process occurs in two ways. One way is through natural revelation, whereby individual creatures and especially the order of the whole universe express some likeness to God; here we find the origin of both metaphysics and natural theology. The other way is through formal supernatural revelation whereby God speaks to us and tells us what God is like; here we find the origin of dogmatic theology, which is thus called a subalternate science and which consists in an imperfect yet most fruitful understanding of the faith.

Quae quidem dogmatica theologia in positivam et speculativam dividi solet.[1] Inquantum enim idem verum revelatum sub ecclesiae magisterio secundum diversitatem culturarum, temporum, locorum, quasi in diversis linguis aliter et aliter est expressum, inquantum praeterea idem verum revelatum secundum oeconomiam divinae gratiae maiori semper intelligentia, scientia, sapientia apprehendi potest (DB 1800), theologiae positivae oritur munus ut sub diversis quasi indumentis culturalibus et in ipsa eiusdem veri evolvente intelligentia semper inveniatur idem dogma, idem sensus, eademque sententia.[2]

Quod tamen haud fieri posset, nisi accederet theologia speculativa. In illo enim 'quoad nos,' quod differentiis historicis multiplicatur, idem verum non discerneret theologia positiva, nisi id ipsum, quod 'quoad se' semper idem manet, perspexisset atque quam accuratissime expressisset theologia speculativa. Finis ergo theologiae speculativae proprius est ut verbum Dei revelatum ita intelligatur et 'quoad se' enuntietur ut in diversitatibus culturalibus et historicis praeteritis idem semper verum eluceat et in futuris facilius retineatur.

Qua de causa, theologia speculativa et philosophia ita sunt similes ut tardioribus etiam identicae videantur. Nam et utraque disciplina in ens cognoscendum tamquam in finem procedit, et utraque mediate a quidditate ipsius entis per essentiam movetur, et utraque ad id cognitionis genus pervenit quod a sensibus est remotum cum per causas et rationes ad 'quoad se' pertingat, et utraque propter concretam universalitatem obiecti regimen quoddam atque influxum in caeteras disciplinas exercet. Ex quo factum est ut quibusdam etiam theologis visum sit S. Thomam in *Contra Gentiles* et *Summa theologiae* et *Quaestionibus disputatis* multo magis philosophum quam theologum fuisse.

Quos sane fugit quantum intercedat inter motionem intellectus philosophicam et theologicam, cum aliud sit mediantibus ipsis creaturis et aliud longe sit mediante revelatione divina moveri. Quam ob causam, etsi utraque disciplina mediate

This dogmatic theology is customarily divided into positive and speculative theology.[1] Because the same revealed truth, under the guidance of the teaching church, finds different forms of expression as if in different languages, according to the diversity of cultures, times, and places, and moreover because that same revealed truth, through the economy of divine grace, can be apprehended by ever-increasing understanding, knowledge, and wisdom (DB 1800; DS 3020), there arises the task of positive theology to find the same dogma, the same meaning, the same pronouncement[2] under diverse cultural dress, as it were, and in the developing understanding of the same truth.

However, positive theology could hardly perform this task without the assistance of speculative theology. For it would not discern the same truth in the manifold historical variations of things in relation to us unless speculative theology had grasped and with all possible accuracy expressed that very thing which in respect to itself remains ever the same. The proper aim, therefore, of speculative theology is so to understand the revealed word of God and so to formulate the 'in respect to itself' that the same truth is clearly discernible amid cultural variations and in different periods in the past, and is more easily preserved for the future.

For this reason, the similarities between speculative theology and philosophy might lead the less perceptive to imagine them even to be identical. Both disciplines have the knowledge of being as their goal, both are moved mediately by the quiddity of being-by-essence, both arrive at a type of knowledge far removed from the senses since by way of causes and reasons they reach the 'in respect to itself,' and, because of the concrete universality of their object, both exercise a certain control and influence over other disciplines. This has led even some theologians to think that in his *Summa contra Gentiles*, *Summa theologiae*, and *Quaestiones disputatae* St Thomas was much more a philosopher than a theologian.

Of course, what escapes the notice of these theologians is the vast difference between the intellectual processes involved in philosophy and those involved in theology. To be moved by the mediation of creatures is one thing; to be moved by the mediation of divine revelation is something quite different. Therefore,

---

1 [Lonergan here gives the expressions 'dogmatic theology,' 'positive theology,' and 'speculative theology' a somewhat different meaning from the usual sense that they have in his work. In *De Deo trino: Pars systematica* (1964), chapter 1, for example, dogmatic theology and systematic theology are distinguished from one another, rather than systematic (or speculative) theology being considered a division of dogmatic theology; and in the same text positive theology is distinct from both dogmatic and systematic theology. The usage of *De Deo trino* is the more common one in his writings during this period.]

2 [DS 3020: '... *in eodem scilicet dogmate, eodem sensu eademque sententia.*' For the wording of the translation, see Lonergan, *Method in Theology* 323.]

a quidditate entis per essentiam moveatur, et utraque in ens cognoscendum tamquam in finem procedat, tamen cum theologia plenius moveatur, etiam plenius finem attingit; unde multae quaestiones materialiter similes in philosophia incipiuntur et tamen non ante intelliguntur quam plenior atque profundior theologica investigatio perficiatur. Praeterea, etsi utraque disciplina, quia scientifica est, causas rationesque quaerat, longe tamen aliter in theologia proceditur cum verum revelatum omnem intellectum creatum excedat. Denique, etsi utraque disciplina regimen quoddam in alias inquisitiones omnes exerceat, latius sane patet influxus theologicus, cum solum verum revelatum conducere possit ad Deum prout in se est, ad actualem universi ordinem, ad actualem hominis statum, aliquatenus intelligenda.

His ergo praemissis, ad ipsam praesentem quaestionem methodologicam accedendum est. Cum enim superius methodum pure philosophicam adhibuerimus ad notionem constitutionemque personae finitae determinandam, nunc aliam methodum aliquatenus similem at minime identicam introducere oportet. Ubi enim philosophia ab ente concreto incipit ut causas reales quaerat et inventas ita componat ut ad idem ens concretum iterum redeat, ibi theologia a vero divinitus revelato incipit ut rationem fides illustret unde ratio per fidem illuminata quandam imperfectam veri revelati intelligentiam percipere possit. Incipiunt ergo ab ente concreto philosophus, sed a vero revelato theologus; procedunt per resolutionem in causas philosophus, sed per illuminationem rationis theologus; terminantur ad intelligentiam entis compositi philosophus, sed ad intelligentiam imperfectam veri revelati theologus. Quae ut enucleatius declarentur, quaeruntur (1) quaenam sit analogia inter scientiam metaphysicam et scientiam theologicam, (2) quotuplex sit verum divinum et in quasnam rationes reducatur, (3) qualis denique sit adeptio imperfectae illius intelligentiae theologicae.

Sectio Prima: De Methodorum Analogia

43 *Quod circa divina neque fit resolutio in causas neque ex causis compositio.*

Deus enim non est ens compositum et contingens. Quia ergo simplex est, circa eum non fit resolutio in causas intrinsecas. Et quia est omnino necessarius, circa eum non fit resolutio in causas extrinsecas. Denique tandem, ubi deest omnis resolutio in causas sive intrinsecas sive extrinsecas, etiam deest omnis ex causis compositio.

although each discipline is moved mediately by the quiddity of being-by-essence and proceeds towards a knowledge of being as its goal, still because theology is more completely moved, it attains the goal more completely. The result is that many questions [in the two disciplines] that are materially alike originate in philosophy but are understood only after a fuller and more profound investigation by theology. Again, although each discipline, being scientific, seeks causes and reasons, theological procedure is far different, since revealed truth surpasses every created intellect. Finally, although each discipline exercises a certain control over all other investigations, the influence of theology is much wider, since only revealed truth can lead to some understanding of God as God is, of the actual order of the universe, and of the actual state of humankind.

With these preliminary remarks, then, let us go on to consider the question at hand, that of methodology. We had recourse above to a purely philosophical method to determine the notion and constitution of a finite person, but now we must bring in a somewhat similar but by no means identical method. For where philosophy begins with concrete being to seek its real causes and having found them puts them together again in order to arrive back at the same concrete being, theology begins with a divinely revealed truth so that faith may enlighten reason and then that reason, thus enlightened, may be able to attain some understanding, albeit imperfect, of revealed truth. Thus the philosopher begins with concrete being, the theologian with revealed truth; the philosopher proceeds by resolution into causes, the theologian by the illumination of reason; the philosopher arrives at an understanding of composite being, the theologian at an imperfect understanding of revealed truth. In order to explain all this more clearly, we ask the following questions: (1) What is the analogy between metaphysical science and theological science? (2) How many kinds of divine truth are there, and into what principles are they resolved? (3) What is the nature of the acquisition of this imperfect theological understanding?

1 The Analogy of Methods

43 *Divine realities admit neither of resolution into causes nor of composition from causes.*

God is not a composite and contingent being. Because God is simple, there is no resolution of God into intrinsic causes. Because God is absolutely necessary, there is no resolution of God into extrinsic causes. Finally, where there is no resolution into either intrinsic or extrinsic causes, there is also no composition from causes.

Unde concludes: non univoce dicitur scientia circa Deum et circa creaturas. Scientia enim est certa rerum per causas cognitio. Sed non sunt causae Dei. Et ideo Deus non scitur per causas Dei.

44 *Quod multa quae de Deo cognoscimus vera ita inter se ordinantur ut aliud alterius ratio esse perspiciatur.*

Nos multa de Deo cognoscere vera constat tum ex multis thesibus theologiae naturalis tum ex multis quae de Deo in symbolis fidei et conciliorum decretis declarantur.

Quae multa ita inter se ordinari ut aliud verum alterius ratio esse perspiciatur constat tum ex nexu thesium in theologia naturali tum ex nexu mysteriorum de quo concilium Vaticanum loquitur (DB 1796).

Ideo autem nos multa vera de Deo simplici cognoscimus, quia imperfectus est noster cognoscendi modus. Sicut enim Deus etiam composita per cognitionem simplicem cognoscit, ita nos etiam simplicia per cognitionem compositam cognoscimus.

Ideo vero nos multa ita inter se ordinamus ut aliud alterius ratio esse perspiciatur, quia multa illa non tantum ut multa cognoscimus sed etiam aliquatenus intelligimus. Intelligentis enim est multa per unum apprehendere, et ideo quo magis intelligimus multa quae de Deo cognoscimus, eo magis illa multa ad unum reducimus et per unum apprehendimus.

45 *Quod rationes quibus inter se ordinantur vera de Deo cognita, hac in vita perfecte intelligere non possumus.*

Hac enim in vita quid sit Deus intelligere non possumus; omnis enim intellectio est per speciem quae rei intellectae proportionatur; sed nulla finita species essentiae seu quidditati divinae proportionatur; neque hac in vita nostris intellectibus illabitur ipsa divina essentia per modum speciei intelligibilis.[3]

Proinde, essentia divina non intellecta, neque attributa divina intelliguntur. Omnis enim intellectio attributi vel proprietatis in eo consistit quod necessaria consequentia attributi ex essentia perspicitur; et ideo ubi non intelligitur ipsa essentia, neque intelliguntur attributa. Praeterea, cum omne attributum divinum

From this we conclude that the word 'science' about God and about creatures is not predicated univocally. Science is the certain knowledge of things through their causes. But God has no causes. And so God is not known through causes of God.

44 *The many truths we know about God are interrelated in such a way that one truth is understood as being the reason for another.*

That we know many truths about God is clear from the many theses of natural theology as well as from the numerous statements about God found in the creeds and conciliar decrees.

That these many truths are related to one another in such a way that one truth is understood as being the reason for another is clear from the interconnection of the theses in natural theology as well as from the connection among the mysteries that is referred to by the [First] Vatican Council (DB 1796; DS 3016).

It is because of the imperfection of our way of knowing that we know many truths about God who is simple. Just as God by simple divine knowledge knows also beings that are composite, so we through a knowledge that is composite know also simple realities.

But it is because we not only know these many truths as many but also to some extent understand them that we arrange them among themselves so that one is understood as being the reason for another. It is the mark of intelligence to apprehend unity in multiplicity; therefore the more we understand the many truths we know about God, the more we reduce those many truths to a unity and apprehend them through this unity.

45 *We cannot in this life perfectly understand the reasons whereby known truths about God are interrelated.*

In this life we cannot understand what God is. All understanding takes place through a species that is proportionate to that which is understood; but no finite species is proportionate to the divine essence or quiddity, and in this life the divine essence does not enter into our intellects as an intelligible species.[3]

Furthermore, if the divine essence is not understood, then neither are the divine attributes. For every understanding of an attribute or property consists in grasping that attribute as necessarily flowing from the essence; so, when the essence is not understood, neither are the attributes. Moreover, since every divine attribute is

3 Thomas Aquinas, *Summa theologiae*, I, q. 12.

cum ipsa divina essentia realiter identificetur, fieri non potest ut, essentia non intellecta, attributum intelligatur.

Reliquum est ergo ut nostra de Deo cognitio hac in vita sit analogica, scilicet, ut intellectis rebus creatis per vias affirmationis, negationis, et eminentiae ad similitudinariam quandam Dei cognitionem perveniamus. At omnis cognitio analogica est imperfecta; et maxime imperfecta est analogica de Deo cognitio 'quia inter creatorem et creaturam non potest tanta similitudo notari, quin inter eos maior sit dissimilitudo notanda' (DB 432).

Qua de causa, cum singula quae de Deo concipiamus nisi analogice non cognoscamus, etiam rationes quibus haec inter se ordinantur analogiarum imperfectionem effugere non possunt. Quas enim rationes perspicimus, non in intellecta divina essentia sed in analogice conceptis perspicimus; imo quod in Deo est necessaria identitas, in nostra cognitione non identitas sed nexus est, neque ipse hic nexus semper est necessarius quoad nos.

Unde concludes: imperfecta nostra mysteriorum intelligentia (quam Vaticanum fructuosissimam affirmat, DB 1796) in eo consistit quod divina analogice concipimus et analogice concepta ita inter se ordinamus ut aliud alterius ratio sit. Ita in tractatu de Deo trino analogice concipimus processiones, relationes, et personas ut ex processionibus ad relationes et ex relationibus ad personas concludamus; quae omnia cum simul per modum unius apprehenduntur imperfectam quandam Dei trini intelligentiam constituunt.

Ulterius concludes: cum rationes a theologis inventae nisi imperfecte intelligi non possint, insipientis est obicere ipsam huius intelligentiae imperfectionem.

46 *Quod omnis verorum ordinatio est duplex.*

Dupliciter enim ordinantur quae de rebus creatis scimus, cum scientia sit certa rerum per causas cognitio et primo ipsas res in causas resolvamus ut deinde ex causis res componamus. Praeterea, huic resolutionis viae correspondet via inventionis, utputa scientiam chimicam ex sensibilibus incipi et ad tabulam periodicam progredi; viae autem compositionis correspondet via doctrinae et disciplinae, utputa manuale scientiae chimicae ex tabula periodica incipi ut plus ter centena millia compositorum explicet.

really identical with the divine essence, no attribute can be understood unless the essence is also understood.

We can only conclude, therefore, that our knowledge of God in this life is analogical, that is to say, that through an understanding of created realities we attain a knowledge of God, as it were by similitude, according to the steps of affirmation, negation, and eminence. But all analogical knowledge is imperfect; and our analogical knowledge of God is especially so, 'because between Creator and creature no similarity can be found so great but that their dissimilarity is even greater' (DB 432, DS 806).

Hence it follows that, since we know only analogically every single item that we conceive about God, the reasons whereby these items are related to one another cannot be free from the imperfection inherent in analogies. For we grasp these reasons, not in an understanding of the divine essence but in what has been analogically conceived. Indeed, what in God is a necessary identity, in our knowledge is not an identity but a nexus, and even this nexus itself is not always necessary with respect to us.

From all this we conclude that our imperfect understanding of the mysteries, which Vatican I declared to be very fruitful (DB 1796, DS 3016), consists in the fact that we conceive divine realities analogously and once they are so conceived we relate them among themselves in such a way that one grounds another. So, for example, in the treatise on the Trinity we analogously conceive the processions, relations, and persons in such a way that from the processions we conclude to the relations and from the relations we conclude to the persons. And when all these are apprehended together as a unity, they constitute an imperfect understanding of the triune God.

We may draw the further conclusion that since the reasons discovered by theologians can be understood only imperfectly, it is foolish to find fault with the imperfection of this understanding.

46 Every ordering of truths is twofold.

There are two ways of ordering what we know about created things. Science is certain knowledge of things through their causes. First we resolve things into their causes, and then we compose them from their causes. Furthermore, the way of discovery corresponds to the way of resolution, and so chemistry, for example, begins from sensible things and moves toward the periodic table; but the way of teaching and learning corresponds to the way of composition, and so a chemistry textbook begins from the periodic table to go on to explain more than 300,000 chemical compounds.

Dupliciter pariter ordinantur quae naturaliter de Deo cognoscimus. Primo enim ex rebus creatis ad Deum ascendimus; deinde autem, posito primo quodam vero circa Deum, attributa divina concludimus et res creatas sub luce quadam divina explicamus.

Dupliciter denique ordinantur quae supernaturaliter de Deo cognoscimus. Primo enim fides rationem illuminat; deinde ratio per fidem illustrata aliquam mysteriorum intelligentiam attingit. Iam vero cum fides rationem illuminat, ab iis incipitur quae sunt notiora quoad nos, nempe, ab iis quae a Deo revelata in verbo Dei scripto et tradito sunt contenta. Cum autem ratio per fidem illustrata aliquam mysteriorum intelligentiam attingit, incipitur a rationibus theologicis quae sunt notiora quoad se et concluditur ad ipsa revelata per rationes intellecta. In quibus omnibus per circulum ferimur: fides enim rationem illuminat inquantum ex revelatis concluduntur rationes theologicae; et ratio mysteria aliquatenus intelligit inquantum ex iisdem rationibus ad eadem revelata mysteria concluditur.

Quibus perspectis, illuminationem rationis per fidem dices viam inventionis theologicae, intelligentiam vero fidei per rationem esse viam doctrinae seu disciplinae theologicae.

Ulterius concludes, cum simile sit rem in causas et verum in rationes reducere, etiam similem esse viam resolutionis scientificae et viam inventionis theologicae; et cum simile sit rem ex causis componere et verum ex rationibus deducere, etiam similem esse viam compositionis scientificae et viam doctrinae seu disciplinae theologicae.

Quod si harum viarum exempla quaesiveris, nota S. Thomam in *Summa theologiae* in via disciplinae procedere;[4] in *Summa contra Gentiles*, lib. I–III, similiter in via disciplinae arguere (unde citatur sacra scriptura non ad praemissas stabiliendas sed ad conclusiones confirmandas); denique in *Summa contra Gentiles*, lib. IV, partim in via inventionis,[5] partim in via doctrinae.[6]

Nota ulterius quam Scotus Scotique sequaces intelligentiam mere negativam nominant ne existere quidem posse si mentem S. Thomae sequeris. Omnis enim conceptus seu verbum interius ex actu quodam intelligendi procedit; unde definitio rei ex intellecta rei essentia oritur, et conceptus analogicus eatenus haberi potest quatenus intelligitur essentia

There are likewise two ways of ordering what we know naturally about God. First we ascend to God from a knowledge of created things; then, having established some primary truth about God, we conclude to divine attributes and go on to explain created reality in the light of the divine.

Finally, there are also two ways of ordering what we know about God supernaturally. First faith enlightens reason; then reason enlightened by faith attains some understanding of the mysteries. Now when faith is enlightening reason, we start from what is more evident with respect to us, namely, from what has been revealed by God and is contained in the word of God in scripture and tradition. But when reason enlightened by faith is attaining some understanding of the mysteries, we begin from theological principles that are more evident with respect to themselves, to arrive at those same revealed truths now understood through these principles. In all this we move in a circle: faith enlightens reason when we conclude to theological principles from revealed truths; and reason arrives at some degree of understanding of the mysteries when we conclude to these same revealed mysteries from these same principles.

In view of this, the illumination of reason by faith is referred to as the way of theological discovery, while the understanding of faith by reason is referred to as the way of theological teaching or learning.

Since there is a similarity between resolving a being into its causes and resolving a truth into its principles, we may further conclude that there is also a similarity between the way of scientific resolution and that of theological discovery; and since there is a similarity between composing a thing from its causes and deducing a truth from its principles, there is also a similarity between the way of scientific composition and the way of theological teaching or learning.

For examples of these ways, notice that in his *Summa theologiae* St Thomas proceeds by the way of teaching;[4] in the *Summa contra Gentiles*, books 1–3, he develops his argument in the same way (hence he quotes scripture not to establish premises but to confirm his conclusions); and finally, in book 4 of the *Summa contra Gentiles* his argument proceeds partly by the way of discovery[5] and partly by the way of teaching.[6]

Note also that that understanding which Scotus and his followers call purely negative cannot even exist according to the thought of St Thomas. For every concept or inner word proceeds from some act of understanding; thus, the definition of a thing proceeds from understanding its essence, and an analogous concept

4 Ibid., Prologue.
5 Chapters 2–9 and 27–39, where he argues from scripture.
6 Chapters 10–14 and 40–49, where he proceeds to an understanding of the mysteries.

rei partim similis et partim dissimilis. Qua de causa, antequam S. Thomas rationes adver-
sariorum solvere nitatur, analogicam quandam generationis divinae intelligentiam atque
conceptionem quaerit;[7] quae quidem analogica intelligentia positiva est quamvis ex ea non
concludatur nisi contradictionis absentia. Scotus autem et Scoti sequaces cum conceptum
non ex actu intelligendi sed ex mechanismo quodam inconscio ortum credant, primo conceptus habent et deinde vel nexus positivos perspiciunt vel contradictionem adesse non
perspiciunt; qua de causa per non-intelligentiam absentia contradictionis iis innotescere
potest.

47 *Quod theologia est scientia analogice dicta.*

Notissima est distinctio Aristotelica inter causam essendi et causam cognoscendi.
Causa enim essendi est ens quoddam quod esse in aliud ens influit, sive extrinsece per modum finis vel per modum efficientis, sive intrinsece per modum principii quo causatum constituitur. Causa autem cognoscendi non ens est sed verum
quoddam quod alterius veri ratio est; quae quidem ratio facit ut nos sciamus, sed
non necessario correspondet enti quod aliud ens causat. Ita si dicitur luna esse
sphaerica quia tales pertransit phases, illud 'quia' denotat causam cognoscendi
sed non causam essendi, cum phases lunae eiusdem sphaericitatem non causent;
si autem dicitur luna tales phases pertransire quia sphaerica est, illud 'quia' denotat causam cognoscendi et etiam causam essendi; sphaericitas enim lunae non
solum nobis explicat phasium successionem sed etiam hanc successionem aliquatenus causat, siquidem discus circularis et planus aut totus illuminaretur aut
nullatenus.

Iam vero in scientiis rerum creatarum ponuntur et causae cognoscendi et causae essendi: quamvis enim in via resolutionis a causis cognoscendi incipiatur,
tamen ad causas essendi concluditur; quae causae essendi in via compositionis
tamquam causae cognoscendi adhibentur.

In theologia vero inquantum ipse Deus consideratur, non ponuntur nisi causae
cognoscendi. Deus enim cum simplex omnino atque necessarius sit, causas essendi
sive extrinsecas sive intrinsecas non admittit. Cum tamen nostra de Deo cognitio
per multa vera rationibus inter se ordinata constituatur, verum quod est ratio
alterius etiam causa aliud cognoscendi est. Et cum duplex sit omnium verorum

can be had insofar as the essence of the thing is understood to be partly similar and partly dissimilar. This is why St Thomas, before attempting a refutation of his adversaries' arguments, seeks some analogical understanding and conception of divine generation;[7] and this analogical understanding is positive even though what is concluded from it is only the absence of contradiction. For Scotus and his followers, however, concepts are thought to emerge not from an act of understanding but from some kind of unconscious mechanical process in which first you have concepts and then you either apprehend a positive nexus or else you do not apprehend the presence of any contradiction. For them, therefore, the absence of contradiction can be known through non-understanding.

47 *Theology is a science in an analogous sense.*

The Aristotelian distinction between the cause of being and the cause of knowing is quite well known. A cause of being is some being that is a source of existence for another being, either extrinsically as final cause or efficient cause, or intrinsically as a constitutive principle of that which is caused. The cause of knowing, on the other hand, is not a being but a truth that is the reason grounding another truth. This reason causes us to know, but it does not necessarily correspond to a being which causes another being. Thus if you say that the moon is a sphere because it goes through certain phases, that 'because' denotes the cause of knowing but not the cause of being, since the phases of the moon do not cause its sphericity. But if you say that the moon goes through phases because it is spherical, 'because' denotes both the cause of knowing and the cause of being; for the sphericity of the moon not only explains to us the succession of its phases but also to some extent causes this succession, since a flat circular disc would be illuminated either totally or not at all.

Now in sciences dealing with created realities, both causes of knowing and causes of being are posited. For although in the way of resolution one begins from the causes of knowing, nevertheless one arrives at the causes of being; and in the way of composition those causes of being are in turn used as causes of knowing.

But in theology, whenever God is the object of inquiry, we have only the causes of knowing, since for God, who is utterly simple and necessary, there are no causes of being whether intrinsic or extrinsic. However, since our knowledge of God consists of numerous truths related to one another by various reasons, a truth that is the reason for another truth is also the cause of our knowing that other

7 *Summa contra Gentiles*, 4, cc. 10–14.

ordinatio, nempe, ex notioribus quoad nos ad notiora quoad se, et ex notioribus quoad se ad notiora quoad nos, aliae in theologia sunt causae cognoscendi notiores quoad nos (ex quibus incipitur inquantum fides rationem illuminat in via inventionis theologicae), et aliae sunt causae cognoscendi notiores quoad se (ex quibus incipitur inquantum ratio per fidem illustrata fidei mysteria aliquatenus intelligit in via doctrinae theologicae).

Proinde quamvis inter se differant quantum ad rem, tamen quantum ad nostram cognitionem similes sunt et causae essendi scientificae et eae causae cognoscendi theologicae quae quoad se sunt notiores. Sicut enim scientificus ex intellecta rei essentia ad intellecta rei attributa concludit, ita etiam theologus ex essentia Dei analogice concepta ad attributa Dei analogice concepta procedit.

Quae quidem differentia circa rem et similitudo circa cognitionem nostram est analogia inter scientias alias atque theologiam. Sicut enim scientia est certa rerum per causas essendi cognitio, ita etiam theologia est certa Dei per causas-cognoscendi-notiores-quoad-se cognitio. Praeterea, ex hoc ipso quod theologia est scientia analogice dicta, sequitur theologiam non conferre nisi intelligentiam Dei imperfectam. Perfecta enim simplicis atque necessarii intelligentia, pariter simplex atque necessaria intuitio intellectualis est. Et ideo si theologia de Deo multa rationibus ordinata cognoscit, etiam necesse est theologiam analogice Deum concipere et per nexus inter concepta simplex sibique identicum imperfecte contemplari.

Quibus perspectis concludes quo sensu dicitur Deus per suam scientiam scire, per suam voluntatem velle, per actum purum constitui, etc. Quae enim nomina verbaque in creaturis ad causas essendi significandas adhibentur, in divinis causas significant cognoscendi quae quoad se sunt notiores.

Sectio Secunda: Quemadmodum Consideretur Verum Divinum

48 *Quod quadrupliciter dividuntur quae de Deo cognoscimus vera.*

Vera enim de Deo cognita dividuntur ratione subiecti in communia et propria.

truth. And since there is a twofold ordering among all truths, namely, from what is more evident with respect to us to what is more evident with respect to itself, and from what is more evident with respect to itself to what is more evident with respect to us, there are in theology some causes of knowing that are more evident with respect to us, namely, those from which we begin when faith is enlightening reason by the way of theological discovery, and there are other causes of knowing that are more evident with respect to themselves, namely, those from which we begin when reason enlightened by faith acquires some understanding of the mysteries of faith by the way of theological teaching.

Accordingly, although the causes of being in science and those causes of knowing in theology that are more evident with respect to themselves are different with regard to the status of their referents, they are nevertheless similar as far as our knowledge is concerned. For just as the scientist arrives at understanding the properties of something once he or she has understood its essence, so too the theologian proceeds to the attributes of God conceived analogously once he or she has analogously conceived God's essence.

Now this difference with respect to their referents but similarity with respect to our knowledge is the analogy between theology and other sciences. As science is certain knowledge of things through the causes of their being, so too theology is certain knowledge of God through the more-evident-in-themselves causes of knowing. Besides, from the fact that theology is a science in an analogous sense it follows that theology provides only an imperfect understanding of God. For a perfect understanding of that which is simple and necessary is an equally simple and necessary intellectual intuition. And so, if theology knows many things about God that are rationally connected, it is also necessary that theology conceive God analogically and that the simple and self-identical reality be imperfectly contemplated through the connections among the conceived elements.

From all this we may draw a conclusion as to the sense in which God may be said to know by divine knowledge, to will by divine will, to be constituted by pure act, and so forth. For the nouns and verbs that are used to denote the causes of being in created things, in matters of divinity denote the causes of knowing that are more evident with respect to themselves.

2 Ways of Considering Truths about God

48 *There is a fourfold division of the truths that we know about God.*

Truths about God are divided into common and proper, in accord with their respective subjects.

Communia sunt quae vere de tribus pariter personis divinis dicuntur, v.g., et Patrem et Filium et Spiritum esse, intelligere, amare, esse Deum, Dominum, Creatorem, etc.

Propria sunt quae vere de una alterave persona sed non communiter de tribus dicuntur, e.g., Patrem generare, Filium gigni, Patrem Filiumque spirare, Spiritum sanctum spirari seu procedere.

Iterum vera de Deo cognita dividuntur ratione nexus in necessaria et contingentia.

Necessaria sunt quae aliter esse non possunt, v.g., Deum esse aeternum, spiritualem, immutabilem, trinum, etc.

Contingentia sunt quae aliter esse possent, v.g, Deum hunc mundum creasse et conservare, cum liberrimo consilio creasset Deus; Deum scire hunc mundum existere, si enim non creasset, existentem non cognovisset; Deum velle hunc mundum existere, si enim non libere eum esse elegisset, neque eum esse voluisset, etc.

49 *Quod necessaria et communia in divinam essentiam resolvuntur.*

Sensus asserti: sicut Socrates est homo per formam humanam, sicut existit per esse proprium, ita omnia vera divina necessaria et communia in divinam essentiam resolvuntur ut Deus per suam essentiam sit aeternus et per suam essentiam sit immutabilis, etc.

Probatio asserti: ubi adest perfectio infinita, superfluit alia ratio; atqui divina essentia est perfectio infinita; ergo superfluit alia ratio cuiuscumque praedicati divini necessarii et communis.

Probatio altera: necessaria et communia distinguuntur a divina essentia neque realiter neque ratione cum fundamento in re; et ideo ea in divinam essentiam resolvere valet per principium identitatis.

Obicitur: hac in vita nescimus quid sit Deus; et ideo vera in divinam essentiam resolvere est ea in ignotum resolvere.

Respondetur: sicut scimus de Deo non quid sit sed quid non sit, ita non requiritur ut dicamus quaenam sit causa sed dicere sufficit quaenam causa non sit; et ideo cum necessaria et communia in divinam essentiam resolvuntur, sensus est Deum esse talem et talem per nihil aliud quam per suam essentiam.

Obicitur: cum non sint causae Dei, inanis est divinorum in causas resolutio.

Respondetur: non sunt causae Dei, *distinguo*: causae essendi, *concedo*, causae cognoscendi, *nego*.

Common truths are those that are predicated equally of the three divine persons; for example, we say that the Father, the Son, and the Spirit exist, understand, love, are God, Lord, Creator, and so forth.

Proper truths are those that are truly predicated of one or other divine person but not of all three in common; for example, the Father generates, the Son is generated, the Father and Son spirate, the Holy Spirit is spirated or proceeds.

Truths about God are divided into necessary and contingent, in accord with the character of the nexus that they affirm.

Necessary truths are those that cannot be otherwise; for example, God is eternal, spiritual, immutable, triune, and so on.

Contingent truths are those that could be otherwise; for example, that God created and conserves this world, since God created it with the utmost freedom; that God knows that this world exists, for had it not been created, God would not have known it as existing; that God wills this world to exist, for had it not been freely chosen, God would not have willed its existence, and so on.

49 *Truths that are necessary and common are resolved into the divine essence.*

This assertion means that just as Socrates is a human being by reason of his human form, and just as he exists by his own act of existence, so too all necessary common truths about God are resolved into the divine essence, so that it is by the divine essence that God is eternal, immutable, and so forth.

Proof of this assertion: where there is an infinite perfection, no other reason is needed; but the divine essence is an infinite perfection; no other reason, therefore, is needed to ground any necessary common truth predicated of God.

A second proof: necessary common truths are not distinct from the divine essence either in reality or conceptually with a basis in reality; therefore by the principle of identity they are resolved into the divine essence.

Objection: in this life we do not know what God is; to resolve truths into the divine essence, therefore, is to resolve them into something unknown.

To this we reply that just as we do not know what God is but do know what God is not, so it is not necessary for us to say what the cause is, but it suffices to say what it is not; and therefore since necessary common truths are resolved into the divine essence, the meaning is that God is such and such by the divine essence and by nothing else.

A second objection: since God has no causes, it is pointless to resolve divine truths into causes.

To this we reply that although there are no causes of God's being, there are causes of our knowledge of God.

Inanis est divinorum in causas resolutio, in causas essendi, *concedo*, in causas cognoscendi, *nego*, nam notitia Dei rite ordinata non est inanis.

50 *Quod necessaria et propria in relationes subsistentes resolvuntur.*

Ex tractatu de Deo trino constat (1) quattuor esse relationes reales in divinis, nempe, paternitatem, filiationem, spirationem activam, et spirationem passivam; (2) quarum tres realiter inter se distinguuntur, nempe, paternitas, filiatio, et spiratio passiva, et (3) has relationes reales esse subsistentes, nempe, sicut deitas est Deus ita paternitas est Pater, filiatio est Filius, spiratio passiva est Spiritus sanctus.

Probatio asserti fit per partes.

Necessaria et propria non resolvuntur in divinam essentiam prout est tribus personis communis; ita enim propria non essent propria sed communia. Si enim Pater generaret quia Deus est, cum Filius etiam Deus sit, pariter Filius generaret; sed si Filius generaret, esset Pater, et ita tolleretur distinctio personarum.

Necessaria et propria non resolvuntur in aliud quod non est Deus; nam persona divina non necessario est aliquid per rem creatam.

Necessaria et propria resolvuntur in relationes subsistentes, nam hae relationes realiter identificantur cum divina essentia et realiter inter se distinguuntur; quia realiter cum essentia identificantur, necessariae sunt sicut et essentia necessaria est; quia realiter inter se distinguuntur, secernunt ea quae sunt propria uni personae ab iis quae aliis sunt propria.

51 *Quae communia et contingentia de Deo vere dicuntur, in ipso Deo super divinam essentiam non addunt nisi relationem rationis, sed extra Deum terminum creatum atque convenientem important.*

Relatio est 'ad aliquid'; relatio realis dicit ordinationem realem; relatio rationis dicit ordinationem conceptam; v.g., pater ad filium realiter ordinatur, sed Creator ad creaturam tantummodo concipitur ut ordinatus.

Terminus est aut operationis aut relationis. Ita scitum est terminus sciendi, volitum est terminus volendi, productum est terminus productionis, et correlativum est terminus relationis.

Quod contingentia non addunt in ipso Deo ullam realitatem super divinam essentiam, constat ex eo quod Deus est ens simplicissimum et prorsus necessarium. Quia enim Deus est simplex, nulla in eo invenitur compositio; quia autem Deus est necessarius, nulla in eo invenitur entitas contingens.

Therefore, while it would be pointless to resolve divine truths into causes of being, it is by no means pointless to resolve them into causes of knowing, for a properly ordered knowledge of God is not pointless.

50   *Truths that are necessary and proper are resolved into the subsistent relations.*

From the treatise on the Trinity it is clear (1) that there are four real relations in God, namely, paternity, filiation, active spiration, and passive spiration, (2) that three of these are really distinct, namely, paternity, filiation, and passive spiration, and (3) that these real relations are subsistent, that is, that just as divinity is God, so paternity is the Father, filiation the Son, and passive spiration the Holy Spirit.

The assertion will be proved step by step.

Necessary proper truths are not resolved into the divine essence since the divine essence is common to all three persons, and in that case proper truths would be common, not proper. If the Father generated by reason of being God, then so would the Son, since the Son too is God; but if the Son were to generate, the Son would be the Father, and so there would be no distinction of persons.

Necessary proper truths are not resolved into something else that is not God, since what a divine person is by necessity is not due to any created thing.

Necessary proper truths are resolved into the subsistent relations, for these relations are really identical with the divine essence and really distinct from one another. Because they are really identical with the divine essence, they are necessary as the essence is necessary; because they are really distinct from one another, they separate what are proper to one person from what are proper to others.

51   *Common contingent truths predicated of God add nothing to the divine essence except a relation of reason, but imply an appropriate created term outside God.*

A relation is a 'being toward something.' A real relation indicates a real ordination; a relation of reason indicates an ordination that is conceived in the mind. A father, for example, is really related to his son, while the Creator is only conceived as being ordered to a creature.

A term belongs either to an operation or to a relation. Thus, what is known is the term of knowing, what is willed is the term of willing, what is produced is the term of production, and a correlative is the term of a relation.

That what is contingent adds no reality in God to the divine essence is clear from the fact that God is an utterly simple and altogether necessary being. Because God is simple, there is in God no composition; because God is necessary, there is in God nothing contingent.

Quod contingentia important terminum creatum et convenientem, constat ex eo quod verum contingens qua contingens adaequationem veritatis habere non potest nisi per ens contingens.

Quod in Deo ponenda est relatio rationis ad talem terminum contingentem, constat ex eo quod veritas contingens de ipso Deo praedicatur; nisi enim conceptu saltem Deus ad ens contingens refertur, veritas contingens de ipso Deo praedicari non potest.

Sequitur nota solutio difficultatum circa immutabilitatem atque libertatem Dei. Eo enim quod Deus libere eligit creare, non datur mutatio entitativa in Deo sed terminativa extra Deum.

52 *Propria et contingentia quae de divina persona vere praedicantur, in ipsa persona divina super relationem subsistentem non addunt nisi relationem rationis, sed extra Deum important terminum creatum et convenientem qui ad divinam relationem subsistentem realiter refertur.*

Exemplo sit Filium incarnari. Quod proprium est, cum neque Pater neque Spiritus sanctus incarnatus est. Quod etiam contingens est, cum fieri potuisset Verbum non incarnari.

Quod nisi relatio rationis nihil intra Deum additur relationi subsistenti, constat ex eo quod relatio divina subsistens realiter identificatur cum immutabili divina essentia.

Quod importatur terminus ad extra creatus et conveniens, constat ex eo quod veritas contingens qua contingens adaequationem veritatis habere non potest nisi per ens quoddam contingens.

Quod hic terminus realiter refertur ad divinam relationem subsistentem, constat ex eo quod secus deesset adaequatio veritatis inter intellectum et rem; v.g., intellectu diceretur quod *solus* Filius est incarnatus, sed re nihil haberetur quod huic vero corresponderet.

53 *Terminus ad extra conveniens (qui in veris de Deo contingentibus importatur) simultaneus est tum cum relatione rationis in Deo agnita tum cum vero contingenti quod de Deo affirmatur; sed simpliciter posterior est in ordine reali sive comparatur ad divinam essentiam sive ad divinam relationem subsistentem.*

Simultaneus est cum relatione rationis quae in Deo agnoscitur, quia correlativa sunt simultanea. V.g., non prius concipitur Deus ut Creator quam concipiatur Dei creatura.

That contingent truths imply the existence of an appropriate created term is clear from the fact that a contingent truth, as contingent, would necessarily lack the correspondence of truth if no appropriate contingent being existed.

That a relation of reason to such a contingent term must be attributed to God is clear from the fact that a contingent truth is predicated of God; for a contingent truth cannot be predicated of God unless God is related at least conceptually to a contingent being.

From this there follows the well-known solution to the difficulties about God's immutability and freedom. The fact that God freely chooses to create does not involve an entitative change in God but a terminative change outside God.

52 *Proper contingent truths predicated of a divine person add to the subsistent relation only a relation of reason in the divine person, but imply an appropriate created term outside God that is really related to the divine subsistent relation.*

Take for example the incarnation of the Son. Incarnation is proper to him, for neither the Father nor the Holy Spirit is incarnate. But the Son's incarnation is also a contingent fact since it was possible for the Word not to become incarnate.

That within God nothing apart from a relation of reason is added to the subsistent relation is clear from the fact that a divine subsistent relation is really identical with the immutable divine essence.

That an appropriate external created term is implied is clear from the fact that a contingent truth, as contingent, can have the correspondence of truth only through some contingent being.

That this term is really related to the divine subsistent relation is clear from the fact that otherwise the correspondence of truth between the intellect and reality would be lacking. For example, in the intellect one would be saying that *only* the Son was made flesh while there would be nothing in reality to correspond to this true statement.

53 *The appropriate external term implied in contingent truths about God is simultaneous with the relation of reason acknowledged in God and with the contingent truth affirmed of God; but it is simply posterior in the real order whether in relation to the divine essence or in relation to a divine subsistent relation.*

It is simultaneous with the relation of reason acknowledged in God, because correlatives are simultaneous; for example, you cannot conceive God as Creator without conceiving God's creation.

Simultaneus est vero contingenti quod de Deo affirmatur, quia veritas est adaequatio inter intellectum et rem, et non prius habetur verum contingens quam habeatur ens contingens.

Posterior est in ordine reali si comparatur ad divinam essentiam, nam Deus est absolute independens neque ulla creatura indiget sive per modum conditionis praeviae sive per modum concausae simultaneae. V.g., mundus non praerequiritur ut Deus mundum concipiat, eligat, faciat; neque ullo modo adiuvat mundus ut Deus eum concipiat, eligat, faciat; sed simpliciter posterior est divina scientia, divina voluntate, divina potentia, quae omnia cum divina essentia realiter identificantur.

Posterior est in ordine reali si comparatur ad divinam relationem subsistentem, nam talis relatio realiter identificatur cum divina essentia et ideo pariter ab omni creatura est absolute independens. Praeterea, eiusmodi relatio subsistens est relatio originis in divinis quae non ad creaturas sed ad oppositam relationem in divinis necessario refertur.

Sectio Tertia: Intelligentia Theologica Concrete Illustratur[8]

54 *Quod infinitum, quamvis negative concipiatur, positive tamen etsi extrinsece et imperfecte intelligi potest.*

Infinitum negative concipitur cum idem dicat quod non-finitum.

Infinitum positive intelligi potest. Ex conceptu enim negativo deducuntur multae conclusiones negativae quae tamen, inquantum per modum unius apprehenduntur, positive intelliguntur. Intelligere enim est multa per unum apprehendere, et positive intelligere est multorum per unum apprehensio quae re vera existit.

Quae positiva infiniti intelligentia est extrinseca et imperfecta. Perfecta enim et intrinseca unius infiniti intelligentia est unius per unum apprehensio infinita.

Quibus perspectis, ad positivam illam etsi imperfectissimam intelligentiam procedendum est. Quod quidem eatenus fiet quatenus conclusiones multae superius determinatae quodammodo per modum unius apprehendentur.

It is also simultaneous with the contingent truth affirmed of God, because truth is the correspondence between intellect and reality, and so there cannot be a contingent truth prior to a contingent being.

It is posterior in the real order in relation to the divine essence, since God is absolutely independent and does not need any creature either by way of a previous condition or by way of a simultaneous co-cause. For example, the world is not a prerequisite in order for God to conceive, choose, and create the world; nor does the world in any way help God to conceive, choose, and create. It is purely and simply posterior to divine knowledge, divine will, divine power, all of which are really identical with the divine essence.

It is posterior in the real order in relation to a divine subsistent relation, since such a relation is really identical with the divine essence and so likewise absolutely independent of any created thing. Furthermore, such a subsistent relation is a relation of origin in God that is necessarily related not to creatures but to the opposite divine relation.

3 Concrete Examples of Theological Understanding[8]

54 *The infinite, though conceived negatively, can be understood positively, albeit extrinsically and imperfectly.*

The infinite is conceived negatively since it means the same as the non-finite.

The infinite can be understood positively. For from a negative concept many negative conclusions are deduced which nevertheless are understood positively inasmuch as they are apprehended as a unity. To understand is to apprehend many things as one, and a positive understanding is a really existing apprehension of many things as one.

This positive understanding of the infinite is extrinsic and imperfect; for a perfect and intrinsic understanding of the one infinite is the infinite apprehension of that one as one.

With this in mind, we must now proceed to this positive albeit very imperfect understanding. This will occur insofar as the many conclusions arrived at above are somehow apprehended as a unity.

---

8 [Lonergan's Table of Contents had simply 'De intelligentia theologica' ('Theological Understanding'), but the section title in the text is 'Intelligentia theologica concrete illustratur.' The corresponding change was made in the Table of Contents here.]

Iam vero quae de entibus finitis cognoscimus vera resolvimus et in causas extrinsecas finales atque efficientes, et in causas intrinsecas, substantiales nempe accidentalesque potentias, formas, actusque. Quae autem de ente infinito cognoscimus vera etiam in alia extrinseca et alia intrinseca reducimus; sed extrinseca non sunt causae vel finales vel efficientes sed tantummodo termini qui in ordine reali simpliciter posteriores sunt; intrinseca autem non sunt substantia et accidens sed ipsa divina essentia et relationes divinae subsistentes.

His ergo stabilitis differentiis, statim oriuntur difficultates multaeque obiectiones quae primis quidem initiis nihil sunt nisi vaga quaedam et fere inconscia dissatisfactio intellectualis. At si plene consciae redduntur, si accurate exprimuntur, si systematice solvuntur, tandem denique nos eo conducunt ut per modum unius intelligibilis apprehendamus et omnes illas differentias et omnium difficultatum solutiones systematicas; quae sane apprehensio nihil est aliud quam extrinseca et imperfecta quaedam infiniti intelligentia.

55 Primo ergo quaeratur utrum Deus sit entitative idem sive creat sive non creat; et simul quaeratur utrum vere et realiter Deus omnia creet, conservet, gubernet, etsi sit idem prorsus entitative ac esset si neque crearet neque conservaret neque gubernaret.

Ex antecessis affirmative respondendum est ad utramque quaestionem. Ne tamen affirmativa hac responsione sis contentus sed etiam imperfectam quandam huius rei intelligentiam quaere.

Recole ergo quod agens qua agens non mutatur, quod actio est in passo, quod transitus de otio in actum metaphorice tantum est mutatio. Per accidens quidem in corporibus moventibus haec non verificantur cum corpora non moveant nisi tangunt et non tangant nisi simul tanguntur. Quod tamen accidit non moventi qua moventi sed qua corpori moventi. Intellectus enim agens noster et quandoque agit et quandoque non agit; neque hoc ullam in ipso intellectu agente mutationem importat. Si enim lege qualibet metaphysica movens qua movens vel agens qua agens mutaretur, omne movens moveretur; si omne movens moveretur, nullus esset motor immobilis; si nullus esset motor immobilis, nullus esset motus, quod est contra factum. Agens ergo qua agens non mutatur; et tamen vere et realiter agit; quod si verum est de omni agente et movente qua tali, verum etiam est de primo agente et de primo movente.

Now the truths we know about finite beings we resolve into their extrinsic causes, final and efficient, and into their intrinsic causes, namely, their substantial and accidental potencies, forms, and acts. On the other hand, truths we know about an infinite being we also resolve into elements, some extrinsic and some intrinsic; but the extrinsic elements are not final or efficient causes but only terms that in the real order are simply posterior, and the intrinsic elements are not substance and accident but the divine essence itself and the subsistent divine relations.

Having established these differences, there immediately arises a host of objections and difficulties that at first may seem to be but the expression of a rather vague and almost unconscious intellectual dissatisfaction. But if fully adverted to, clearly expressed, and systematically solved, they ultimately lead us to the point where we apprehend as an intelligible unity all those differences and the systematic solutions to all those difficulties. This apprehension, of course, is simply an extrinsic and imperfect understanding of the infinite.

55 Our first question, then, is whether God is entitatively the same whether he creates or does not create; and at the same time we ask whether God really and truly creates, conserves, and governs all things, even while remaining entitatively exactly the same as would be the case if he neither created nor conserved nor governed.

On the basis of what we have been saying, we must answer both questions in the affirmative. However, do not rest content with this affirmative answer; rather, try to obtain some imperfect understanding of this matter.

Recall, therefore, that an agent qua agent does not undergo change, that action is in the recipient, and that the transition from rest to action is a change only in a metaphorical sense. It just so happens that these principles are not verified in the case of material bodies moving other bodies, since bodies do not move others unless they touch them and they do not touch them unless they themselves are touched at the same time. But this is accidental to a mover as such; it applies to a mover, not as mover but as bodily mover. Our agent intellect sometimes acts and sometimes does not; but this does not imply any change in the agent intellect itself. If by some metaphysical law or other a mover qua mover or an agent qua agent were to undergo a change, then every mover would be itself moved; but if every mover were itself moved, there would be no such thing as an unmoved mover, and if there were no unmoved mover there would be no motion at all, which goes against the facts. An agent, therefore, qua agent, does not change, and yet it really and truly acts; and if this is true of every agent and mover as such, it is also true of the first agent and mover.

56 Deinde quaeratur utrum Deus sit entitative idem, sive scit et vult hunc mundum esse, sive scit et vult hunc mundum non esse; et simul quaeratur utrum vere et realiter ille sciat et velit qui per eundem entitative actum contradictoria divisim sciat et velit.

Ex antecessis sane ad utramque quaestionem affirmative est respondendum; et iterum ultra hanc responsionem affirmativam ad aliquam captandam intelligentiam procedere oportet.

Considerandum ergo est quod aliud facit actus finitus qua actus et aliud facit qua finitus. Actus enim sciendi vel volendi, quatenus actus est, quoddam scire vel velle constituit. Sed actus sciendi vel volendi, quatenus finitus est, quoddam nescire et quoddam non-velle constituit. Eo enim quod quis finite scit, non omnia sed hoc tantum vel illud scit; et eo quod quis finite vult, non omnia sed hoc tantum vel illud vult.

Ex quo fit ut Petrus Paulusve, quia per actus finitos sciunt et volunt, alia et alia obiecta per alios et alios actus sciunt et volunt. Sed eadem ratione fit ut Deus, quia per actum infinitum scit et vult, per eundem actum omnia sciat et omnia velit. Neque sequitur contradictio ex eo quod idem entitative esset actus divinus sive hunc mundum esse scit et vult sive hunc mundum non esse scit et vult; quae enim contingentia de Deo dicuntur vera, terminum ad extra contingentem important; neque idem habetur terminus ad extra sive Deus hunc mundum esse scit et vult sive eum non esse scit et vult. Neque tollitur veritas et realitas divinae scientiae et volitionis: si enim vere et realiter per actus finitos scit et vult Petrus Paulusve, quanto magis vere et quanto magis realiter per infinitum scire et infinitum velle scit et vult Deus.

57 Tertio quaeritur utrum vere et realiter Filius Dei sit homo et quidem sit subiectum conscientiae humanae, si idem entitative in divinis maneat sive incarnetur sive non incarnetur.

Iterum sane affirmative respondendum est, nam vere et realiter Filius Dei incarnatus est, et tamen Verbum Dei qua Verbum necessario in divinis immutatum manet.

Neque alia est difficultas circa hoc quam anthropomorphica quaedam translatio ex entibus finitis ad Deum infinitum. Petrus enim quia est ens, est; sed quia est ens finitum, non est nisi hic homo. Deus autem non est ens quoddam finitum quod omnino a se excludat ut etiam aliud sit praeter Deum; sed Deus est ens infinitum quod eminenter in se includit omnem perfectionem tum omnium actualium tum omnium possibilium. Praeterea, sicut Deus per eundem infinitum

56 Next we might ask whether God is entitatively the same whether he knows and wills this world to exist or knows and wills this world not to exist; and at the same time we might ask whether there is really and truly knowing and willing in one who in an act that is entitatively the same knows and wills separately two contradictory things.

Of course, from all that we have been saying, our answer to both questions is once more in the affirmative; and again we must go beyond this affirmative answer to get some measure of understanding.

Note, therefore, that a finite act does one thing as act and something else as finite. An act of knowing or of willing, as an act, constitutes a certain knowing or willing. But an act of knowing or of willing, as finite, constitutes a certain ignorance or a certain non-willing; for by the fact that one's knowledge is finite, one knows not everything but only this or that, and by the fact that one's willing is finite, one wills not everything but only this or that.

For this reason Peter or Paul, because their acts of knowing and willing are finite, know and will different objects by different acts. But for the same reason God, whose act of knowing and willing is infinite, knows everything and wills everything by the same act. Nor is there any contradiction in saying that the divine act would be entitatively the same whether God knows and wills this world to exist or knows and wills it not to exist. For contingent truths predicated of God imply the existence of a contingent term outside God, and that term is not the same whether God knows and wills this world to exist or knows and wills it not to exist. Nor does this do away with the truth and reality of God's knowing and willing; for if Peter or Paul really and truly knows and wills by finite acts, it is all the more true to say that God really and truly knows and wills by an infinite act of knowing and of willing.

57 Our third question is whether the Son of God is really and truly man and indeed the subject of a human consciousness if, whether he becomes incarnate or not, he remains entitatively the same in what regards divinity.

Again, of course, our answer must be affirmative, for the Son of God was really and truly made flesh, and yet the Word of God as Word necessarily remains unchanged in what regards divinity.

The only difficulty in this matter is a certain anthropomorphic transfer from finite beings to the infinite God. Because Peter is a being, he exists; but because he is a finite being, he exists only as this human being. But God is not a finite being such as would prevent God from being something else besides God; rather, God is an infinite being that by way of eminence includes in itself all the perfection of all beings, both actual and possible. Furthermore, just as God by the same infinite

actum non solum necessaria sed etiam contingentia scit, sicut Deus per eundem infinitum actum non solum necessaria vult sed ea etiam quae contingenter vult, ita etiam Deus per eundem infinitum actum essendi non solum necessario est Deus sed etiam est id quod contingenter factus est.

Quae si quomodocumque intellexeris, etiam intelliges cur S. Thomas unicum esse Verbo incarnato vindicaverit. Nisi enim per suum esse Verbum esset homo, non ipse sed alius esset homo.

act knows not only necessary but also contingent realities, and just as God by the same infinite act wills not only necessary realities but also contingent ones, so also God by the same infinite act of existence not only is necessarily God but also is what God has contingently become.

With some understanding of this, you will also understand why St Thomas held for a single act of existence in the incarnate Word. For if it were not by the Word's own act of existence that the Word is man, then not the Word but someone else would be that man.

De Constitutione Christi Ontologica

58 Praemissis ergo exercitiis brevioribus quae divisim finitum et infinitum respiciunt, iam ad mysterium acceditur in quo infinitum atque finitum realiter in unum eundemque Christum coniunguntur.

Et primo recolitur verum revelatum a quo incipit et in quod terminatur theologica intelligentia principalis.

Deinde in rationes divinas causasque creatas hoc verum reducitur, nempe, ex parte subiecti assumentis in potentiam actumque assumendi et ex parte obiecti assumpti in potentiam qua assumi potest et in actum quo assumitur.

Tertio, ad ipsum problema acceditur, nempe, quanam ratione vel causa haec multa in unum subsistens realiter coalescere possint. Et diversis consideratis theoriis, nempe, et iis quae ponunt duo entia completa, et iis quae actuationem eminentem invocant, et iis quae a R. P. Diepen et a R. P. Xiberta nuperrime sunt propositae, ad veterem concluditur sententiam secundum quam *principium quod* unionis hypostaticae est persona Verbi et *principium quo* eiusdem est esse Verbi divinum.

Quarto denique, quo facilius multa per unum apprehendantur et imperfecta intelligentia attingatur, ab hoc unionis principio incipitur et caetera ordinate deducuntur.

Sectio Prima: Dogma Recolitur

59 Ad primum brevissime proceditur ea recolendo quae in dogmate catholico praedicantur et inter theologos communiter accipiuntur.

PART 4

The Ontological Constitution of Christ

58 Having gone through the rather brief exercises in which we dealt separately with the finite and the infinite, we come now to the mystery in which the infinite and the finite are in actual fact united in one and the same Christ.

To begin, we recall the revealed truth from which our principal theological understanding begins and in which it terminates.

Next, we resolve this truth into its divine reasons and its created causes: that is, on the side of the assuming subject to the potency and the act of assuming, and on the side of the object assumed to the potency enabling it to be assumed and the act by which it is assumed.

Third, we come to the problem itself, namely, by what reason or by what cause all these can really come together into one subsistent being. And after weighing various theories, namely, those which hold for two complete beings, those which appeal to an eminent actuation, and those which have been quite recently proposed by Fr Diepen and Fr Xiberta, we shall conclude to the older view that the 'principle which' of the hypostatic union is the person of the Word, and the 'principle by which' of this union is the divine act of existence of the Word.

Fourth and finally, in order to facilitate our grasp of many realities in one intelligible whole and thereby arrive at some understanding of the mystery, however imperfect, this principle of the union will serve as our starting point for the systematic deduction of all the other relevant truths.

1 The Dogma of the Incarnation

59 As to the first step, then, let us briefly recall the dogma as it is taught in the Catholic Church and commonly accepted by theologians.

Dogmatis quidem summa haec est: unum eundemque esse et verum Deum et verum hominem; unam nempe divini Verbi personam in duabus subsistere naturis, divina atque humana; et quia persona dividenda non est ut alia sit persona divina et alia persona humana, unio dicitur esse in persona contra Nestorianos; quia vero naturae non sunt confundendae ut ex duabus quodammodo una fiat natura, unio dicitur esse secundum personam contra Monophysitas.[1]

Inter theologos autem illud iam pridem constat Christum nempe esse unum suppositum, unum ens, unam rem (DB 219).

Suppositum enim reale est subsistens distinctum. Sed persona est subsistens distinctum in natura intellectuali. Et ideo quia una tantum est persona, unum tantum sit suppositum necesse est.

Ens vero stricte dictum est id quod est. Sed in Christo Deo et homine unum idemque quod est Deus etiam est homo. Et ideo cum sit unum tantum quod est Deus et homo, Christus sit unum id-quod-est seu unum ens necesse est.

Res denique est id quod habet naturam. Sed in Christo Deo et homine non aliud habet naturam divinam et aliud habet naturam humanam, sed unum habet utramque naturam. Et ideo res una est.

Sectio Secunda: Resolutio in Causas

60 Deinde, ut fides rationem illuminet, incipere oportet ab ente concreto quod fidei proponitur et in rationes eius divinas creatasque causas procedere.

Quod ut ordinatius fiat, dicamus:

(a) unionem hypostaticam esse unionem in persona et secundum personam;

(b) hanc unionem considerari tum in facto esse tum in fieri;

(c) hanc unionem in fieri consideratam nominari assumptionem;[2]

The gist of the dogma is this: one and the same is both truly God and truly man; that is, the one person of the divine Word subsists in two natures, divine and human; and since the person must not be divided so as to have one person who is divine and another who is human, the union is said to be in the person, in contradiction to the opinion of the Nestorians; on the other hand, since the two natures are not to be merged so that a single nature somehow results from the two, the union is said to be on the basis of the person, in contradiction to the opinion of the Monophysites.[1]

The long-standing position among theologians is that Christ is one supposit, one being, one reality (DB 219; DS 428).

A real supposit is a distinct subsistent. But a person is a distinct subsistent in an intellectual nature, and so, since there is only one person, there is necessarily only one supposit.

A being in the strict sense is that which is. But in Christ, God and man, the very same one that is God is also man; and therefore since there is only one reality that is both God and man, Christ is necessarily one that-which-is, that is, one being.

Finally, a thing is that which has a nature. But in Christ, God and man, there is not one thing that has a divine nature and another thing that has a human nature, but the one same thing has both natures. Christ is therefore one thing.

2 Resolution into Causes

60 Next, for faith to enlighten reason, we must begin from the concrete reality proposed for our belief and proceed from there to its divine reasons and created causes.

To do this in an orderly fashion, let us state the following:

(a) that the hypostatic union is a union in the person and on the basis of the person;

(b) that this union is being considered both as an accomplished fact and in its coming-to-be;

(c) that this union considered in its coming-to-be is called 'assumption';[2]

---

1 [On union in the hypostasis and on the basis of the hypostasis (*en hypostasi* and *kath' hypostasin*) see Aloys Grillmeier, *Christ in Christian Tradition*, vol. 1: *From the Apostolic Age to Chalcedon (451)*, trans. John Bowden (Atlanta: John Knox Press, 1975) 434, 482–83, 487. Lonergan's 'in persona' and 'secundum personam' translate these terms into Latin. 'On the basis of the person' seemed the best translation into English of the meaning of 'kath' hypostasin' or 'secundum personam.' At one point (487) the English text of Grillmeier has 'by hypostasis.']

2 Thomas Aquinas, *Summa theologiae*, 3, q. 2, a. 8.

(d) unionem in facto esse et assumptionem differre quidem secundum modum signifi-candi, sed nullatenus differre quoad rem cum unio hypostatica in instanti perficiatur.

Assumptio et proprie et improprie dicitur.

Improprie dicitur assumptio tum de eo quod assumptionem producit tum de eo in quo assumptio producitur. Et quia Deus trinus assumptionem producit, assumptio improprie et active super divinam essentiam addit relationem rationis Dei trini ad naturam assumptam, assumptio autem improprie et passive dicit realem relationem naturae assumptae ad Deum trinum. Haec ergo de assumptione improprie dicta sufficiant cum simillima sint ad ea quae de creatione activa et passiva communiter traduntur.

Proprie autem dicitur assumptio non secundum causas extrinsecas sed secundum causas intrinsecas. Unde distinguuntur et subiectum assumens, quod est solus Filius, et obiectum assumptum, quod est illa natura humana quae ex Maria fuit. Et utrumque, subiectum nempe et obiectum, tum secundum potentiam tum secundum actum sunt consideranda; quod enim assumit etiam assumere potuit, et quod assumitur etiam assumi potuit.

61 Potentia ergo assumendi ex parte subiecti communis est Patri, Filio, et Spiritui sancto. Quamvis enim solus Filius incarnatus sit, tamen omnes et singulae personae incarnari possunt.[3] Quare haec potentia tribus communis in divina essentia fundetur necesse est, et quidem in infinita perfectione huius essentiae. Quod enim infinitum est, restrictiones et limitationes excludit omnes; quod autem omnes restrictiones et limitationes excludit, potest esse quodlibet concipit et vult secundum infinitam suam sapientiam atque bonitatem.

Actus autem assumendi ex parte subiecti in solo Filio invenitur cum solus Filius aliam naturam assumpserit. Qui sane actus non necessarius sed contingens est, cum non incarnari potuerit Filius. Iam vero uti superius demonstratum est, quae contingenter et proprie de persona divina praedicantur vera, super divinam relationem subsistentem non addunt in divinis nisi relationem rationis tantum. Attamen, quamvis nihil addatur nisi relatio rationis, hoc minime est intelligendum quasi actus assumendi ex parte subiecti nihil reale nihilve verum diceret. Considerari enim oportet non solum id quod additur sed etiam id cui additur; et cum Filius infinitam iam perfectionem habeat, cum haec infinitas et realissima sit et verissima, ideo actus assumendi ex parte subiecti et realissimus et verissimus est.

(d) that the accomplished union and the assumption differ in the way we give them meaning but do not differ at all in reality, since hypostatic union takes place in an instant.

Assumption can be understood in a proper and an improper sense.

Improperly speaking, assumption is predicated both of that which effects the assumption and of that in which the assumption is effected. Since the triune God effects the assumption, assumption in the active improper sense adds to the divine essence a 'relation of reason' of the triune God to the assumed nature, while assumption in the passive improper sense denotes a real relation of the assumed nature to the triune God. These remarks about assumption in an improper sense should be sufficient, since this case is quite similar to what is commonly held concerning active and passive creation.

Properly speaking, however, we speak of assumption not with respect to its extrinsic causes but with respect to its intrinsic causes. Hence we distinguish between the subject that assumes, which is the Son alone, and the object assumed, namely, the human nature derived from Mary. Both subject and object must be considered with regard to both potency and act; for that which does assume was able to assume, and that which is assumed was able to be assumed.

61 Thus the potency to assume on the side of the subject is common to the Father, the Son, and the Holy Spirit. For although only the Son became incarnate, it is possible for all and each of the persons to become incarnate.[3] This potency, therefore, which is common to all three persons, must have its foundation in the divine essence, and indeed in the infinite perfection of that essence. For what is infinite excludes all restrictions and limitations; but what excludes all restrictions and limitations can be whatever it conceives and wills in accordance with its infinite wisdom and goodness.

The act of assuming, however, on the side of the subject belongs only to the Son, since only the Son has assumed another nature. This act, of course, is not a necessary but a contingent act, since it was possible for the Son not to become incarnate. Now as we established above, truths contingently and properly predicated of a divine person add nothing to that divine subsistent relation except a relation of reason. Nevertheless, although nothing but a relation of reason is added, this is in no sense to be understood as though the act of assuming expressed nothing real and nothing true on the side of the subject. We have to bear in mind not only what is added but also that to which it is added; and since the Son is already infinitely perfect, and since this infinity is most real and most true, it follows that on the side of the subject the act of assuming is most real and most true.

3 Ibid. q. 3.

Potentia autem ex parte obiecti assumendi in ea invenitur natura quae de facto assumpta est. Nisi enim assumi potuit, non assumeretur.

Actus pariter ex parte obiecti assumendi in ea invenitur natura quae de facto est assumpta. Si enim nuda poneretur potentia et actus negaretur, etiam ipsa assumptio excluderetur.

62 Qualis autem sit illa potentia et qualis ille actus, nunc considerandum est.

Primo ergo constat potentiam illam esse obedientialem et actum illum esse supernaturalem. Nulla enim natura finita naturaliter proportionatur ad unionem hypostaticam, et ideo si natura quaedam finita hypostatice unitur Filio Dei, potentia ad hoc ei inest inquantum omnis natura Deo ad nutum obedit ut de ea fiat quidquid Deo placuerit. Praeterea, huius potentiae actus prorsus supernaturalis est, cum unio hypostatica simpliciter excedit proportionem cuiuslibet essentiae substantialis finitae.

Deinde constat potentiam illam obedientialem esse essentiam humanam individualem quae ex Maria fuit. Quod enim actu est assumptum, illud assumi potuit. Sed essentia illa humana actu est assumpta. Ergo essentia illa assumi potuit. Quod quidem posse assumi nihil aliud est quam potentia obedientialis ad assumptionem.

Tertio distinguendum est inter essentiam illam humanam ut potentiam naturalem ad esse proprium et eandem essentiam ut potentiam obedientialem ad unionem hypostaticam. Quamdiu enim actuatur potentia naturalis, tamdiu excluditur actuatio potentiae obedientialis. Si enim essentia humana recipit esse proprium, constituitur ens stricte dictum et unum stricte dictum; si constituitur unum stricte dictum, habetur simpliciter indivisum in se et simpliciter divisum a quolibet alio; unde habetur subsistens distinctum seu suppositum reale et, cum essentia humana intellectualis naturae sit, etiam habetur persona. Iam vero si habetur persona humana, excluditur unio hypostatica quae est non duarum personarum sed in persona divina et secundum personam divinam. Qua de causa, potentia obedientialis expedita ad unionem hypostaticam consistit in essentia individuali sine proprio esse.

Quarto, actus supernaturalis ad quem essentia-humana-assumenda est in potentia obedientiali aut est actus increatus solus aut est actus creatus cum habitudine ad actum increatum; praeterea, si est actus creatus, aut accidentalis est aut substantialis. Sed non est actus increatus solus; et non est actus creatus accidentalis cum habitudine ad actum increatum; ergo est actus creatus et substantialis.

Non est actus increatus solus. Quae enim de persona divina contingenter dicuntur, adaequationem veritatis non habent sine convenienti termino ad extra.

The potency on the side of the object to be assumed is in that nature that has in fact been assumed. For unless it was able to be assumed, it would not actually be assumed.

Similarly, the act on the side of the object to be assumed is in that nature that has in fact been assumed. For if only the mere potency were present in it and no act, even the assumption itself would be excluded.

62 Let us consider now the nature of this potency and the nature of this act.

First of all, it is clear that this potency is obediential and this act supernatural. No finite nature is naturally proportionate to the hypostatic union; hence if any finite nature is hypostatically united to the Son of God, then the potency for this is in that nature inasmuch as every nature is obedient to God's bidding so that that nature will become whatever God might will. Moreover, the act of this potency is entirely supernatural, since the hypostatic union is absolutely beyond the proportion of any finite substantial essence.

Second, it is clear that this obediential potency is the individual human essence derived from Mary. For what was actually assumed was capable of being assumed; but that human essence was actually assumed; therefore, it was capable of being assumed. And this capability of being assumed is nothing other than the obediential potency to assumption.

Third, we must distinguish between that human essence as a natural potency to its own proper act of existence and that same essence as an obediential potency to the hypostatic union. For the actuation of a natural potency precludes the actuation of obediential potency. If a human essence receives its own proper act of existence, it is constituted both as being in the strict sense and as one in the strict sense. If it is constituted as one in the strict sense, then you have something that is absolutely undivided in itself and absolutely divided from everything else; thus you have a distinct subsistent or real supposit, and since a human essence is intellectual in nature, you also have a person. Now if there is a human person, then hypostatic union, which is a union not of two persons but a union in and on the basis of a divine person, is precluded. For this reason the obediential potency available for hypostatic union consists in an individual essence that lacks its own proper act of existence.

Fourth, the supernatural act to which the human essence to be assumed is in obediential potency is either uncreated act alone or a created act with a relationship to uncreated act; also, if this act is created, it is either accidental or substantial. Now it is not uncreated act alone; nor is it an accidental created act with a relationship to uncreated act; therefore it is a substantial created act.

It is not uncreated act alone, for whatever is predicated contingently of a divine person lacks the correspondence needed for truth unless there is an appropriate

Qua de causa, si ponitur solus actus increatus, eo ipso negatur terminus ad extra conveniens et tollitur veritas incarnationis.

Dices: sufficit essentia humana sine esse proprio tamquam terminus ad extra conveniens.

Respondetur: sufficit ad veritatem huius quod haec natura humana assumi potest a qualibet persona divina, *conceditur*; sufficit ad veritatem huius quod haec natura humana actu est assumpta a solo Filio, *negatur*.

Praeterea, non est actus creatus accidentalis cum habitudine ad actum increatum. Nam actus creatus accidentalis cum habitudine ad actum increatum, si in essentia recipitur, est gratia sanctificans et, si in intellectu recipitur, est lumen gloriae. Sed unio gratiae sanctificantis cum dono increato et unio gloriae cum Deo viso non constituunt unionem hypostaticam. Ergo actus creatus potentiae obedientialis ad unionem hypostaticam non est accidentalis.

Praeterea, actus accidentalis de se non potest facere nisi unionem accidentalem ut Filius Dei huic naturae humanae coniungatur. Sed eiusmodi coniunctio seu *synapheia* Nestoriana est.

Praeterea, si potentia est substantialis, etiam actus est substantialis. Sed potentia est substantialis; est enim essentia seu natura humana quae assumitur. Ergo etiam actus est substantialis ut per eum Filius Dei sit hic homo.

Denique hic actus creatus et substantialis refertur ad personam Filii Dei. Idem enim actus et perficit potentiam obedientialem essentiae humanae ut a Filio Dei actu assumatur et constituit terminum ad extra quo verum est hoc contingens, nempe, Filium Dei actu assumere hanc naturam humanam.

Quibus perspectis, resolutio in causas unionis hypostaticae absolvitur. Unionem enim consideravimus tum improprie secundum causam efficientem et effectum productum, tum proprie secundum subiectum assumens et obiectum assumptum; quod subiectum quodque obiectum tum secundum potentiam tum etiam secundum actum unionis in rationes causasque intrinsecas reduximus.

Sectio Tertia: Compositionis ex Causis Principium

63   Sicut scientificus ideo entia concreta in causas resolvit ut eadem entia ex causis composita intelligat, ita etiam theologus veritates fidei in rationes ideo reducit ut easdem veritates ex rationibus deductas quodammodo intelligat.

Quare cum unionem hypostaticam in quattuor reduxerimus, nempe, ex parte subiecti (1) in potentiam qua assumere potest et (2) in actum quo assumit, et ex

external term. If there is only uncreated act, then by that very fact there is no appropriate external term, and so the truth of the incarnation is precluded.

One may object here that a human essence that lacks its own proper act of existence suffices as an appropriate external term.

To this objection we would answer that, while it suffices for the fact that this human nature can be assumed by any divine person, it does not suffice for the fact that this human nature actually has been assumed by the Son alone.

Again, it is not an accidental created act with a relationship to uncreated act. For an accidental created act with a relationship to uncreated act, if received in the essence, is sanctifying grace; if received in the intellect, it is the light of glory. But the union in sanctifying grace with uncreated Gift and the union in the light of glory with God in the beatific vision do not constitute a hypostatic union. Hence the created act of the obediential potency for the hypostatic union is not accidental.

Again, of itself an accidental act can bring about only an accidental union whereby the Son of God would be joined to this human nature. But that sort of conjunction or *synapheia* is Nestorian.

Again, if the potency is substantial, the act also is substantial. But the potency is substantial: it is the assumed human essence or nature. Therefore the act also is substantial, so that through it the Son of God is this man.

Finally, this created substantial act is related to the person of the Son of God. For the same act both perfects the obediential potency of the human essence so that it is actually assumed by the Son of God and constitutes the external term whereby this contingent fact is true, namely, that the Son of God has actually assumed this human nature.

With these observations we have completed the resolution of the hypostatic union into its causes. We have considered this union both in its improper sense, with regard to its efficient cause and the effect produced, and in its proper sense, with regard to the assuming subject and the object assumed; and we have resolved that subject and that object into the intrinsic reasons and causes of both the potency and the act of the union.

3 The Principle of Composition from Causes

63 As the scientist resolves concrete beings into their causes in order to understand those same beings as composed of their causes, so too the theologian resolves the truths of faith into their reasons in order to gain some understanding of these same truths as deduced from these reasons.

Accordingly, we have resolved the hypostatic union into four elements: on the side of the subject, into (1) the potency whereby it can assume and (2) the act

parte obiecti (3) in potentiam qua assumi potest et (4) in actum quo assumitur, iam ex his multis ad unum componendum procedere oportet. Qua in compositione totum invenitur problema: nam unio hypostatica nullo fere negotio in multa resolvitur; quod autem unum ex multis vere et realiter constituitur, hoc sane mysterium est neque hac in vita a nobis intelligi potest nisi imperfecte.

Ad quam intelligentiam assequendam viis diversis processerunt qui hac de re conscripserunt auctores. Quorum sententias recitare iuvabit. Quamvis enim fieri non possit ut omnes inter se pugnantes vera dixerint, ipsa tamen opinionum successio dialectica critice examinata multum docere solet.

64 Prima ergo sententiarum classis eorum est qui per relationes unionem hypostaticam constitutam voluerint. Ita Scotus, Tiphanus, Suarez et (1) duo agnoverunt, nempe, Verbum divinum et naturam humanam individualem existentem, et (2) haec duo ideo unum suppositum, unum ens, unam rem aestimaverunt quia Verbo quidem accedit relatio rationis, naturae autem humanae accedit realis relatio assumptionis vel etiam modus.

Quae sententiae dupliciter errare videntur. Primo, enim, cum Scotus et Tiphanus causam personae finitae non quaesiverint et Suarez quaesitam non invenerit, fieri non potuit ut hanc causam a natura Christi humana amoverint; et ideo non naturam humanam sed personam humanam assumptam re vera posuerunt. Deinde, sicut causam personae ita etiam causam relationis realis haud sufficienter consideraverunt. Nisi enim fundamentum relationis reale praecesserit, realis relatio haberi non potest. Nemo sane dubitat assumptionem esse realem relationem in natura assumpta, sicut nemo dubitat creationem passivam esse realem relationem in substantia creata. At realis haec relatio creationis passivae non inesset substantiae nisi per prius ex nihilo fuerit producta; et pariter omnino realis relatio assumptionis ex parte obiecti non inesset naturae Christi humanae nisi per prius vere et realiter illa natura fuerit assumpta. Quod tamen assumi quid sit, et totum problema est et his in sententiis vel omittitur vel insufficienter per modum, qui re vera nihil est, explicatur.

65 Altera deinde sententiarum classis eorum est qui analogiam rerum creatarum invocent. Omne enim ens finitum essentia et esse componitur; quae quidem duo ideo unum constituunt quia unum idemque per essentiam est in potentia et per

whereby it does assume; and on the side of the object, into (3) the potency whereby it can be assumed and (4) the act whereby it is assumed. We must proceed now to bring these several elements into one. The whole problem lies in this composition. To resolve the hypostatic union into its several elements is easy enough; but that from this multiplicity a unity really and truly results, here indeed is the mystery, and one that in this life we can only imperfectly understand.

In attempting to gain this understanding, theologians who have written about this matter have proceeded in various ways. It will be helpful to review their opinions. For while those who take different sides in a disputed question cannot all be right, still a critical scrutiny of the dialectical succession of opinions can be quite instructive.

64 The first set of opinions is that of those who maintain that the hypostatic union is constituted by relations. Thus Scotus, Tiphanus, and Suarez (1) acknowledge two factors, namely, the divine Word and an existing individual human nature, and (2) consider these two to be one supposit, one being, one thing because the Word acquires a relation of reason and the human nature a real relation of assumption, or even a 'mode.'

These opinions appear to be mistaken in two ways. In the first place, since Scotus and Tiphanus did not look for the cause of a finite person and Suarez did look for it but never found it, it was impossible for them to remove this factor from the human nature of Christ; consequently they in fact hold for the assumption not of a human nature but of a human person. Second, as they failed to attend to the cause of a person, so also they failed to pay sufficient attention to the cause of a real relation. Without a prior real foundation there can be no real relation. No one, of course, doubts that the assumption is a real relation in the assumed nature, just as no one doubts that passive creation is a real relation in a created substance. But this real relation of passive creation would not exist in a substance if the substance had not first been produced from nothing; and in exactly the same way the real relation of the assumption on the side of the object would not exist in the human nature of Christ unless that nature had first been really and truly assumed. But what this 'being assumed' is – that is the crux of the whole problem, and these opinions either omit it entirely or inadequately explain it by a mode, which is nothing at all in reality.

65 A second set of opinions is held by those who appeal to the analogy of created things. Every finite being is composed of essence and an act of existence; and these two elements constitute a unit because it is one and the same thing that is in potency through its essence and in act through its act of existence:

esse est in actu; idem enim est Petrus qui per essentiam suam in potentia est et per esse suum in actu est. Quod unionis theorema analogice ad unionem hypostaticam applicant. Sicut enim Petrus essentia et esse componitur, ita etiam Verbum incarnatum esse divino et essentia humana componitur; et sicut Petrus est unum suppositum, unum ens, una res, ita pariter Verbum incarnatum est unum suppositum, unum ens, una res. Cum tamen omnis analogia non solum similitudine sed etiam dissimilitudine constat, ultro concedunt essentiam Christi humanam non esse potentiam proportionatam ad esse divinum neque illud esse recipere neque illud esse limitare; esse enim divinum, inquiunt, est actus quidam eminens qui actuat quin recipiatur vel limitetur.

Quae sententia quibusdam difficultatibus laborat.

Primo, enim, cum esse divinum est tribus personis divinis commune, ex hac theoria sequitur non solum Filium sed etiam Patrem atque Spiritum sanctum incarnari. Quod est haereticum.

Deinde, cum esse divinum sit natura divina, unio in esse est unio in natura et unio secundum esse est unio secundum naturam. At unio quae quaeritur est hypostatica, nempe, et in persona et secundum personam.

Tertio, ut radix difficultatum tangatur, speciosior quam solidior videtur analogia in qua fundatur tota haec sententia.

Eatenus enim in Petro aliove ente finito per essentiam et esse constituitur unum ens, quatenus idem prorsus et in potentia est per essentiam et in actu est per esse. At in Verbo incarnato, in quo infinitum et finitum uniuntur, et per esse divinum Deus infinitus est actu, et per essentiam humanam aliquid finitum in potentia sit necesse est; nam fieri non potest ut infinitum-simpliciter in potentia sit. Quare cum aliud sit finitum et aliud prorsus infinitum, non idem per essentiam humanam est in potentia quod per divinum esse est in actu; et ideo, quamvis analogiae quaedam species non sit neganda, in eo tamen deficit quod solum desideratur, nempe, ut ratio quaedam vel causa unionis verae et realis assignetur.

Quarto, ut eadem difficultas aliter urgeatur, eatenus haec theoria aliquam mysterii intelligentiam parit quatenus dicitur quid sit actus eminens et quid sit eminenter actuare. Quibus quaestionibus non solum non satisfit sed neque satisfieri posse videtur. Cum enim ens finitum componatur, et habetur potentia ad actum proportionata, et actus in potentia recipitur atque limitatur. Cum autem actus eminens eminenter tantum actuet, neque habetur potentia ad actum proportionata, neque actus in potentia recipitur, neque actus per potentiam limitatur.

it is the same Peter who is in potency through his essence and in act through his act of existence. Then they apply this theorem of union analogously to the hypostatic union. Just as Peter is composed of essence and existence, so the incarnate Word is composed of the divine act of existence and a human essence; and just as Peter is one supposit, one being, one thing, so too the Word incarnate is one supposit, one being, one thing. However, since every analogy comprises not only similarity but also dissimilarity, they readily concede that the human essence of Christ is not a potency proportionate to the divine act of existence and neither receives that act of existence nor limits it; for the divine act of existence, according to them, is a kind of eminent act that actuates without being received or limited.

This opinion labors under certain difficulties.

First of all, since the divine act of existence is common to the three divine persons, it follows from this theory that not only the Son but also the Father and the Holy Spirit are incarnate; and that is heresy.

Second, since the divine act of existence is identical with the divine nature, a union in the act of existence is a union in the nature, and a union on the basis of the act of existence is a union on the basis of the nature. But the union we are looking for is hypostatic, that is, in the person and on the basis of the person.

Third, at the root of these difficulties is the fact that the analogy on which this entire view is based is more superficial than sound.

For in Peter or any other finite being, one being is constituted of essence and existence only if the same being is in potency through its essence and in act through its act of existence. But in the incarnate Word, in which the infinite and the finite are united, it is the infinite God that is in act through the divine act of existence, and it is necessarily something finite that is in potency through the human essence, since what is purely and simply infinite cannot be in potency. Thus, since it is one thing to be finite and quite another to be altogether infinite, what is in potency through a human essence and what is in act through the divine act of existence are not the same. Therefore, though we may admit some semblance of analogy here, it lacks the one thing we are looking for, namely, the assigning of some reason or cause of a true and real union.

Fourth, to press the difficulty in another way, this theory provides some understanding of the mystery only insofar as it tells us what an eminent act is and what eminent actuation means. But not only does it not answer these questions satisfactorily, it also seems incapable of doing so. For in the composition of a finite being, there is a potency proportionate to an act and an act received in and limited by the potency. But since an eminent act actuates only in an eminent way, neither is there a potency proportionate to the act nor is the act

Quae inter se adeo sunt diversa ut praeter nomina nihil simile detegatur. Quod si similitudo deest, etiam analogia deest; et si analogia deest, fieri non potest ut quis vel acutissimus dicat quid sit actus eminens vel quid sit eminenter actuare.

Quinto, inter fautores huius sententiae nominatur S. Thomas. Quod in confusione quadam fundari videtur.

Aliud enim est affirmare unicum esse in Christo, quod S. Thomas semper fecit quamvis esse quoddam secundarium et substantiale in *Quaestione disputata de unione Verbi incarnati* agnoverit; aliud autem est analogiam statuere inter compositionem entis finiti et unionem hypostaticam. Quam analogiam apud S. Thomam nondum legi. In *C. Gent.* IV, 41, expresse quidem affirmat nullam unionem incarnationi esse similiorem quam unionem animae et corporis; quam tamen similitudinem expresse negat in eo consistere quod anima se habet ad corpus sicut forma ad materiam, et id solum esse simile dicit quod, sicut corpus est animae instrumentum proprium atque coniunctum, ita humanitas assumpta est Verbi instrumentum proprium atque coniunctum.

66 Tertia ergo est sententia quam nuper proposuit H. Diepen quasi dictis S. Thomae magis conformem.[4]

Primo ponit quod in ordine possibilitatis, essentiae, actus primi[5] Christus Deus et homo non solum est unus masculine sed etiam unum neutraliter seu unum ens seu una res subsistens.

Deinde ponit quod actus secundus nihil aliud est quam actualitas pura ordinis possibilis supra indicati.

Tertio addit analogias ut hoc totum intelligi possit, et optimam etsi imperfectam iudicat quae ex toto organico repetitur, nempe, sicut Socrates est animatus per animam suam et capitatus per caput suum, ita Christus est Deus per divinitatem suam et homo per humanitatem suam; iterum, sicut vi unionis a capite tollitur subsistentia propria eique largitur ut sit 'esse capitatum in Socrate subsistente,' ita etiam vi unionis ab humanitate assumpta tollitur subsistentia propria eique largitur ut sit 'esse hunc hominem in Christo subsistente.'[6]

received in potency nor is the act limited by potency. The two cases are so utterly different that the only similarity between them is in terminology. But where there is no similarity, there is no analogy, and without an analogy not even a genius could tell us what an eminent act is and what eminent actuation means.

Fifth, St Thomas is numbered among the proponents of this opinion; that, however, would seem to result from some misunderstanding.

It is one thing to affirm a single act of existence in Christ, as St Thomas always did even though in his *Quaestio disputata de unione Verbi incarnati* he acknowledged a certain secondary substantial act of existence; but it is quite another to set up an analogy between the composition of a finite being and the hypostatic union. I have never found such an analogy in St Thomas. In *Summa contra Gentiles*, 4, c. 41, he expressly states that there is no union more similar to the incarnation than the union of body and soul; however, he expressly denies that this similarity consists in the soul's relation to the body as form to matter, and he points out that the only similarity is in this, that as the body is the proper and conjoined instrument of the soul, so the assumed humanity is the proper and conjoined instrument of the Word.

66 A third opinion has been proposed recently by Herman Diepen as being more in conformity with the statements of St Thomas.[4]

First, he proposes that in the order of possibility, essence, first act,[5] Christ, God and man, is not only one in the sense of one male being, but also in the neutral sense of one being, one subsistent thing.

Next, he states that second act is nothing other than the pure actuation of the above possible order.

Third, to help us understand all this he has recourse to analogies. He considers the best, albeit imperfect, analogy to be that derived from an organic whole; that is, just as Socrates is animated through his soul and is cephalic through having a head, so Christ is God through his divinity and man through his humanity. Then, just as because of its union [with the whole Socrates] the head is denied its proper subsistence while being granted 'the existence of a head in the subsistent Socrates,' so because of the hypostatic union the assumed human nature is denied its proper subsistence while being granted 'the existence of this man in the subsistent Christ.'[6]

4 Diepen, 'La critique du Basilisme ...' 313–24; 'L'unique Seigneur ...' 49–62. [See above, p. 69, note 11.]
5 'La critique ...' 313, 317.
6 Ibid. 317.

Quae quidem sententia in aliquibus videtur imperfecta.

Nam, primo, quam supra indicavimus confusionem inter suppositum hypotheticum et suppositum reale, etiam suo modo hic redit. Deest enim distinctio inter id quod concipitur et id quod vere affirmatur: quando S. Thomas vere affirmat Christum esse unum ens, non iam agitur de ordine possibilitatis, essentiae, actus primi. Pariter deest distinctio inter potentiam obiectivam et potentiam subiectivam: ordo possibilitatis est ordo potentiae obiectivae; ordo essentiae et actus primi est ordo potentiae subiectivae.

Deinde non satis distinguit inter unum naturale et unum simpliciter.

Unum quod in toto organico invenitur est unum naturale, unum per se, unum quod primo innotescit per primam intellectus operationem inquantum in multis sensibilibus unam plantam, unum animal, unum hominem intelligimus.

Porro, unum transcendentale est indivisum in se et divisum a quolibet alio. Quod unum in omnibus prorsus invenitur quatenus concipi et affirmari possunt; quodcumque enim affirmamus secundum principia identitatis (indivisum in se) et non-contradictionis (divisum a quolibet alio) affirmamus.

Iam vero quatenus unum transcendentale uni naturali applicatur, Christus non est unus sed duo cum duas habeat naturas. Et ideo quatenus unio hypostatica secundum unum naturale exponitur, eatenus in haeresin monophysitarum, monenergistarum, monothelitarum aberratur secundum quod sermo sit de duabus Christi naturis, de duabus eius operationibus, de duabus eius voluntatibus, vel etiam de duabus eius conscientiis.

Qua de causa, aliud requiritur cui applicetur unum transcendentale ut habeatur unum simpliciter. Quod aliud diximus ens strictius dictum, id quod est; quemadmodum vero sit simpliciter indivisum in se et simpliciter a quolibet alio divisum, et ideo subsistens, iam explicavimus. Quod unum simpliciter sane Socrati inest, et eatenus tantum valet analogia ab hoc auctore uti etiam a S. Thoma allata.

Tertio, ad scientiam non pervenitur donec causae assignentur, cum scientia sit certa rerum per causas cognitio. At auctor causas praetermittit. Non enim assignat causam cur Socrates subsistat, et ideo non amovit causam cur humanitas assumpta sit persona; non minus ergo quam Scotus vel Tiphanus ponit in toto, quod Christum dicit, hominem subsistentem atque personam. Neque causam assignat ipsius unionis hypostaticae: verum sane catholicum sicut Scotus et Tiphanus enuntiat cum tale asserat totum ut eadem persona et

This opinion, however, would seem to be somewhat flawed.

First of all, the confusion we called attention to above between a hypothetical supposit and a real supposit turns up again here in its own way. The distinction between what is conceived and what is truly affirmed is missing here: when St Thomas truly affirms that Christ is one being, he is no longer dealing with the order of possibility, of essence, of first act. Likewise there is no distinction made here between objective and subjective potency: the order of possibility is the order of objective potency, and the order of essence and first act is the order of subjective potency.

Second, Diepen does not make enough of a distinction between 'natural one' and 'one simply.'

The 'one' that is found in an organic whole is 'natural one,' one per se, one that first becomes known through the first operation of the intellect inasmuch as we grasp one plant, one animal, one human being in a multiplicity of sensible data.

'Transcendental one,' on the other hand, is undivided in itself and divided from everything else. This 'one' is found in all things whatever insofar as they can be conceived and affirmed; for whatever we affirm we affirm on the basis of the principles of identity (undivided in itself) and non-contradiction (divided from everything else.)

If you try to make out that natural unity is transcendental unity, Christ is two, not one, since he has two natures. So too, if you explain the [oneness of the] hypostatic union in terms of natural unity, you join the Monophysites, Monenergists, and Monothelites in heresy, since the right way of speaking is to speak of Christ's two natures, his two operations, his two wills, even his two consciousnesses.

For this reason, if we are going to have 'one simply,' something else is needed to which 'transcendental one' will be applied. This 'something else' we have called being in the strict sense, that which is; and we have already explained how it is simply undivided in itself and simply divided from everything else, and hence subsistent. This 'simply one' is, of course, in Socrates, and only to that extent is this author's analogy valid, as also is that put forth by St Thomas.

Third, since science is the certain knowledge of things through their causes, scientific knowledge is not attained until causes are assigned. But the author makes no mention of causes. He does not assign the cause for Socrates being subsistent, and so he does not remove the cause that would make the assumed humanity a person. Just like Scotus and Tiphanus, he places a subsistent man and a person in the total entity that he calls Christ. Nor does he assign a cause of the hypostatic union itself. Of course, along with Scotus and Tiphanus he states the Catholic doctrine in affirming that this totality is such that the same person is both God

Deus et homo sit; sed causam vel rationem non nominat sed simplici veritatis adaequatione contentus manet. Nihil enim aliud est quam veritatis adaequatio quod una res subsistens prout vere affirmatur etiam a parte rei invenitur.

Quarto, ita causas praetermittit ut causas assignare fiat impossibile. Eatenus enim Christus Deus et homo est unum simpliciter quatenus ultra ordinem essentialem realem aliud invenitur principium reale; secus enim vel cum Nestorianis duas essentias esse duas res vel cum Monophysitis ex duabus essentiis unam fieri essentiam asseritur.

Neque veritati et realitati unionis hypostaticae ab eo consulitur qui hoc aliud principium modum quendam esse ducat; modus enim nisi fallaciis fundari posse non videtur. Relinquitur ergo ut hoc aliud principium rei constitutivum sit esse, existentia, actus essendi; quod tamen hic auctor audire non vult propter rationes quas supra sub nomine essentialismi iam reiecimus.

67 Quarta proinde est sententia quam Ioannes Baconthorp excogitavit et B. Xiberta nuperrime resuscitavit.[7]

Distinguit ergo hic auctor inter unam causam formalem (naturam humanam plene actuatam) et duplicem effectum formalem realiter cum causa formali identificatum, nempe, constitutionem in ratione naturae et constitutionem in ratione entis.

Docet (i) ita poni causam formalem ut (ii) primus effectus formalis habeatur, (iii) secundus effectus formalis divina virtute impediatur, (iv) secundus effectus formalis per Verbum divinum suppleatur.

Ad litteram sumi oportet realem identificationem utriusque effectus formalis cum una causa formali. Non solum enim hoc explicite affirmat[8] sed adeo nullam realem admittit distinctionem inter naturam et ens ut P. Billot reprehendatur quasi in Christo intelligibilitatem humanitatis non autem realitatem posuerit.[9]

Realem tamen distinctionem ponere videtur inter duos effectus formales: non solum conceptu diversas sed etiam re separabiles iudicat functiones ordinis transcendentalis (ens) et ordinis praedicamentalis (natura).[10]

and man; but he states no cause or reason for this, being quite content with the simple correspondence of truth. For it is nothing else than the correspondence of truth that one subsistent thing is found to exist in the real order exactly as it is truly affirmed.

Fourth, he passes over causes in a way that makes it impossible to assign any. For Christ, God and man, is one simply, only because there is present another real principle beyond the real essential order; otherwise you hold either with the Nestorians that the two essences are two things, or with the Monophysites that the two essences become one essence.

Nor do you safeguard the truth and reality of the hypostatic union if you suppose this other principle to be some sort of mode. It does not seem that a mode can be founded on anything except fallacies. It remains, therefore, that this other constitutive principle of a thing is *esse*, existence, the act of being – something that this author will not hear of for reasons that we rejected above when we spoke of essentialism.

67 There is also a fourth opinion, originated by John Baconthorp and recently revived by B. Xiberta.[7]

Xiberta draws a distinction between one formal cause, the fully actuated human nature, and a twofold formal effect that is really identical with the formal cause, namely, constitution in the formality of nature and constitution in the formality of being.

He states (1) that the formal cause is present in such a way that (2) the first formal effect is also present, while (3) the second formal effect is prevented by divine power but (4) is supplied by the divine Word.

The real identity of both formal effects with the one formal cause should be taken literally. He not only explicitly affirms this identity[8] but is so adamant in denying any real distinction between nature and being that he takes L. Billot to task as having affirmed the intelligibility of the humanity of Christ but not its reality.[9]

And yet he seems to admit a real distinction between the two formal effects: he holds that the functions of the transcendental order (being) and those of the predicamental order (nature) are not only conceptually distinct but are in reality even separable.[10]

7 Bartolomé M. Xiberta, *Tractatus de Verbo incarnato*, vol. 1 (Madrid: Consejo Superior de Investigaciones Científicas, Instituto 'Francisco Suarez,' 1954) 257–58, 264–67.

8 Ibid. 265.

9 Ibid. 268.

10 Ibid. 225–32.

Quamvis laudandam suam sententiam iudicet quia rationem specificam actionis Verbi obvolutam relinquit in ineffabili altitudine divinae maiestatis,[11] saltem dici posse videtur Verbum non supplere merum modum Suarezianum, capere humanitatem ex ipsa radice entitatis, totam humanitatis realitatem complecti inquantum ad plenitudinem usque perductam,[12] permeare totam humanitatem ex radice entitatis et quidem tam intime et totaliter ut magis non possit,[13] nihil pure humanum in Christo relinquere,[14] divinorum et humanorum compenetrationem quandam efficere.[15]

Circa hanc sententiam quae sequuntur dicenda videntur.

Primo, magis valeret haec sententia si in ea fieri posset realis distinctio inter transcendentalia prout entibus strictius dictis et entibus latius dictis applicantur. Auctor autem nolle videtur realem distinctionem inter naturam finitam et ens-quod finitum.

Deinde, realis identificatio utriusque effectus formalis cum una causa formali in consequentias absurdas ducere videtur. Nam

(i) poni non potest natura plene actuata quin simul ponantur quae cum ea realiter identificantur; ergo simul etiam ponitur cum natura humana etiam persona humana;

(ii) tolli vel impediri non potest effectus formalis secundarius quin simul tollatur vel impediatur causa formalis quae cum eo realiter identificatur; et ideo impedita persona humana, etiam impeditur natura humana;

(iii) Verbum supplere non potest pro effectu secundario quin simul suppleat pro iis quae realiter cum hoc effectu identificantur; et ideo Verbum supplet non solum pro impedita persona humana sed etiam pro impedita natura humana;

(iv) ita sane ad summam quandam unitatem concluditur, nempe, ipsius Verbi divini, sed quaeritur de unitate Verbi incarnati in quo aliquid realiter finitum, anima et corpore compositum, invenitur.

Tertio, non minus mirae sunt consequentiae si quis ad distinctionem attendit secundum quam attributa praedicamentalia naturae et transcendentalia personae assignat.

Although he believes that his opinion has the merit of leaving the specific nature of the action of the Word shrouded in the ineffable sublimity of the divine majesty,[11] at least it seems possible to say that the Word does not supply a mere Suarezian mode, that it takes the humanity from the very root of its being, that it embraces the whole reality of the humanity as brought to the fullness of its perfection,[12] that it permeates the whole humanity from the root of its being in as complete and intimate a manner as possible,[13] that it leaves nothing merely human in Christ,[14] and that it brings about a kind of interpenetration of the divine and human attributes.[15]

Concerning this opinion we have the following comments.

First of all, this view would have more in its favor if it allowed for a real distinction between transcendentals as they apply to beings in the strict sense and to beings in a broader sense. Its author, however, apparently makes no allowance for a real distinction between a finite nature and a finite 'being which is.'

Second, a real identification of both formal effects with one formal cause appears to lead to absurd consequences. For

(1) you cannot have a fully actuated nature without at the same time having what are really identical with it; therefore with a human nature you would also have a human person;

(2) a secondary formal effect cannot be removed or prevented without at the same time removing or preventing the formal cause that is really identified with it; and therefore by preventing the human person, the human nature would be likewise prevented;

(3) the Word cannot supply the secondary effect without at the same time supplying everything that is really identical with that effect; the Word, therefore, would supply not only the prevented human person but also the prevented human nature;

(4) in this way one does, of course, arrive at some highest degree of unity, that of the divine Word; but the question here is about the unity of the incarnate Word, in whom there is present a really finite element composed of body and soul.

Third, the consequences are no less startling if one turns to the distinction whereby Xiberta assigns predicamental attributes to the nature and transcendental attributes to the person.

11 Ibid. 266–67.
12 Ibid. 266.
13 Ibid. 231.
14 Ibid. 266.
15 Ibid. 290–95.

Nam transcendentalia omnibus prorsus conveniunt: et Verbi divini qua divini existit entitas, unitas, veritas, bonitas; et naturae humanae assumptae qua naturae humanae existit sua entitas, unitas, veritas, bonitas; et Verbi incarnati, quod est unum ens, etiam existit entitas, unitas, veritas, bonitas.

Iam vero si Verbum supplet pro transcendentalibus ipsius humanae naturae, Verbum supplet pro ipsa realitate humanae naturae. Si Verbum supplet pro ipsa realitate humanae naturae, tunc humana natura nullam suam realitatem habet. Sequitur sane mira illa compenetratio quam hic auctor enuntiat atque laudat; at compenetrantur non realitas divina et realitas humana sed realitas divina et attributa praedicamentalia naturae humanae.

Quarto, uti iam pridem contra auctorem obicitur,[16] quo modo ipse docet Scotum in Nestorianismo involvi, eodem modo ipse in monophysismo involvitur. Quod tamen rite intelligendum est.

Sicut enim intentio Scoti nullatenus Nestoriana fuit, ita etiam huius auctoris intentio nullatenus est monophysitica.
Sicut additis principiis in se veris sed a Scoto reiectis ex positione Scoti ad Nestorianismum concludi potest, ita etiam additis principiis in se veris sed ab hoc auctore non agnitis ex eius positione ad monophysismum concludi potest.

Attamen dum positio Scoti summa quadam sollertia ita elaborata est ut periculum conclusionis erroneae praecaveatur, alia longe videtur huius auctoris methodus atque dicendi modus.
Quinto, sane laudandus est auctor tum quia clare perspexit quam arcte inter se sint connexae sententiae de conscientia Christi humana et sententiae de constitutione eiusdem ontologica,[17] tum quia accurate iudicavit unionem quae in linea naturae non esset eatenus esse realem quatenus in linea entis inveniretur, tum quia acute intellexit quantum in theologia hodierna desideraretur methodus explicita, tum quia tanta ei inerat animi fortitudo ut non solum methodologiam theologicam confecerit[18] sed etiam magno tractatu ipsam methodum applicaverit.[19]

For transcendentals are applicable to absolutely everything that exists: there exist the being, unity, truth, and goodness of the divine Word as divine; there exist the being, unity, truth, and goodness of the assumed human nature as a human nature; and there also exist the being, unity, truth, and goodness of the incarnate Word, which is itself one being.

Now if the Word supplies the transcendentals of the human nature, then it supplies the very reality of the human nature. But if the Word supplies the very reality of the human nature, then the human nature has no reality of its own. There follows, of course, that remarkable interpenetration which this author enthusiastically proposes; however, it is not the divine and human realities that interpenetrate, but the divine reality and the predicamental attributes of the human nature.

Fourth, the objection has already been raised against this author that he has slipped into monophysitism in the same way that he himself claims that Scotus had slipped into Nestorianism.[16] This, however, needs to be understood in the right way.

Just as Scotus's intention was in no way Nestorian, neither is Xiberta intentionally a Monophysite.

One can arrive at Nestorianism from Scotus's position by adding principles that are true in themselves but rejected by Scotus, and similarly by adding principles that are true in themselves but not admitted by Xiberta, one can arrive at monophysitism.

Nevertheless, while Scotus's position is worked out most skillfully to avoid the danger of erroneous conclusions, Xiberta's method and manner of expression seem quite different.

Fifth, Xiberta is certainly to be commended for several reasons: for his clear understanding of the close relationship between opinions on the human consciousness and opinions on the ontological constitution of Christ;[17] for his accurate judgment that a union that does not exist in the area of nature is real only insofar as it takes place in the area of being; for his acute realization of the need for an explicit method in theology today; and for having had the courage not only to devise a theological methodology,[18] but also to apply it in a treatise of considerable length.[19]

---

16 F. Lakner, 'Eine neuantiochenische Christologie?' *Zeitschrift für katholische Theologie* 77 (1955) 228.

17 Bartolomé M. Xiberta, *El Yo de Jesucristo* (Barcelona: Herder, 1954) 101–103.

18 Bartolomé M. Xiberta, *Introductio in sacram theologiam* (Madrid: Instituto Francisco Suárez, 1949).

19 Xiberta, *Tractatus de Verbo incarnato*; see vol. 1, pp. 5–7.

Quae tamen methodus, quasi crucis experimento examinata, in hoc videtur deficere quod ad specificam differentiam cognitionis scientificae (per causas) non satis attendit; unde necessitatem philosophiae tamquam ancillae insufficienter inculcat, et proprietatem secundum quam theologia ita est synthetica ut omnium scientiarum sit regina in clara luce non ponit.

68 Quibus omnibus perspectis, adhuc quaerenda manet ratio seu causa ipsius unionis hypostaticae. Non enim sufficit relatio inter duo entia completa sive sine fundamento ponitur sive in modo fundatur. Neque sufficit analogia quae ex compositione entis finiti repetitur cum eatenus perfectibile et perfectio in unum coalescant quatenus perfectibile se habet ad perfectionem sicut potentia ad actum. Neque illud totum quod R.P. Diepen proposuit magis causam habet quam totum Tiphani. Neque attributorum divisio in transcendentalia et praedicamentalia ad rationem causae realis pertingit.

Quae cum ita sint, analogiam petimus non ex iis quae de ente finito componendo naturaliter cognoscimus sed ex iis quae de ipso Deo naturaliter cognoscimus. Nam

(i) eiusmodi est ens infinitum ut per nihil aliud quam per eundem (entitative) actum sciendi non solum necessaria sed etiam contingentia cognoscat, et per nihil aliud quam per eundem (entitative) actum volendi non solum necessaria sed etiam contingentia velit;

(ii) et ideo pari ratione per eundem (entitative) actum essendi non solum est quod necessario est sed etiam est quod contingenter factum est.

Iam vero illud per quod aliquis vel scit vel vult vel est, causa seu in divinis ratio nominatur. Praeterea, cum eadem est duorum simul causa, eadem etiam est duorum unionis causa. Quare

(iii) sicut realiter uniuntur divina necessariorum scientia et divina contingentium scientia quia per eundem actum utraque habetur scientia, et realiter uniuntur divina necessariorum volitio et divina contingentium volitio quia per eundem actum utraque habetur volitio,

(iv) ita etiam in Verbo realiter uniuntur 'esse Deum' et 'esse hominem' quia per eundem essendi actum Verbum et Deus est et homo est.

Naturarum ergo divinae et humanae unionem realem fundat atque constituit ipsum Verbi esse divinum quia per hoc unum esse una eademque persona et necessario Deus est et contingenter homo factus est.

This method, however, when put to a crucial test, as it were, appears to be deficient in that it does not pay sufficient attention to the specific difference of scientific knowledge, that is, knowledge through causes. As a result, he does not sufficiently stress the importance of philosophy as handmaiden to theology, nor does he show clearly how the synthetic nature of theology makes it queen of all sciences.

68 With all the foregoing points firmly understood, the question of the reason for or cause of the hypostatic union itself is still before us. A relation between two complete beings is not enough, whether this relation is said to be without a foundation or to be founded upon a mode. Nor is an analogy drawn from the composition of a finite being sufficient, since perfectible and perfection form a unity only insofar as the perfectible is related to the perfection as potency to act. Nor does that whole proposed by Diepen have any more of a cause than that of Tiphanus. Finally, the division of attributes into transcendental and predicamental does not bring us any closer to the formality of a real cause.

This being the case, we go for our analogy not to what we naturally know about the composition of a finite being but to what we naturally know about God. Thus:

(1) infinite being is such that solely through what is entitatively the same act of knowing it knows not only necessary but also contingent beings, and that solely through what is entitatively the same act of willing it wills not only necessary but also contingent beings;

(2) and so by the same line of reasoning it is solely through entitatively the same act of being that it not only is what it necessarily is but also is what it has contingently become.

Now that through which someone knows or wills or exists is called a cause, or, in the Godhead, a reason. Moreover, when two things together have the same cause, the union of the two also has the same cause. Therefore:

(3) just as divine knowledge of necessary beings and divine knowledge of contingent beings are really one because both are had through the same act, and divine willing of necessary beings and divine willing of contingent beings are really one because both are had through the same act,

(4) so also in the Word 'to be God' and 'to be man' are really one because it is through the same act of being that the Word is both God and man.

Therefore, the real union of the divine and human natures in Christ is grounded upon and constituted by the divine act of existence of the Word, because through this one act of existence one and the same person is both necessarily God and has contingently become man.

69 Quod tamen rite intelligi oportet. Obici enim solet quod, si incarnatio per esse divinum constituitur, cum hoc esse non sit proprium Filio sed tribus personis commune, non solus Filius sed omnes tres personae incarnentur necesse est. Praeterea, si incarnatio per esse divinum constituitur, cum hoc esse sit idem prorsus ac divina essentia et divina natura, unio non fit in persona sed in natura et non fit secundum personam sed secundum naturam.

Quae sane argumenta valerent vel si esse divinum principium quoddam materiale esset quod caeca necessitate secundum leges sibi inditas sub iisdem adiunctis idem semper faciat, vel etiam si esse divinum esset sicut esse finitum quod aliud sit ac intelligere et velle, vel etiam si ipsa unio fundaretur in analogico quodam theoremate secundum quod esse divinum et essentia humana assumpta se habeant ut actus eminens et potentia.

Qua de causa, sedulo considerandum est Deum esse non solum 'agens per intellectum' sed etiam 'ens per intellectum.' Agens per intellectum Deus est quia eius agere seu producere nihil est aliud quam eius intelligere et velle ut aliquid producatur. Ens per intellectum Deus est quia sua essentia est suus intellectus et sua voluntas, et suum esse est suum intelligere et suum velle.

Si ergo Deus trinus intelligit et vult solum Filium ita incarnari ut unio sit et in persona et secundum personam, per hoc intelligere et velle et (1) producuntur ea finita quae ad incarnationem requirantur, cum Deus sit agens per intellectum, et (2) constituitur ipse Filius ut hypostatice unitus secundum esse suum infinitum, cum hoc esse nihil sit aliud ac illud intelligere et velle.

Eatenus ergo esse infinitum Filii est ratio et causa intrinseca atque constitutiva unionis hypostaticae, quatenus hoc esse tantummodo secundum modum significandi, nullatenus autem realiter, est aliud ac divinum intelligere et divinum velle.

Quae quidem positio necessaria videtur. Unio enim hypostatica est unio in persona et secundum personam. Sed persona divina non realiter distinguitur sive ab esse divino sive ab essentia divina sive a natura divina. Iam vero quae realiter inter se non distinguuntur, solummodo secundum intellectum sunt distincta. Et ideo unio hypostatica constitui non potest nisi per illud esse reale quod etiam per identitatem intelligere et velle est.

69 All this, however, must be correctly understood. The usual objection is that if the incarnation is constituted by the divine act of existence, then not only the Son but all three persons would necessarily be incarnate, since the divine act of existence is not proper to the Son but is common to all three. Again, if the incarnation is constituted by the divine act of existence, then since this act of existence is exactly the same as the divine essence and divine nature, the union is effected not in the person but in the nature and takes place on the basis not of the person but of the nature.

Now these arguments would, it is true, be valid if the divine act of existence were some kind of material principle that always acts the same way by blind necessity in accordance with innate laws under identical conditions, or again, if the divine act of existence were like a finite act of existence, which is not identical with its acts of understanding and willing, or if the union itself were grounded in some analogical theorem according to which the divine act of existence and the assumed human essence were related to each other as eminent act and potency.

For this reason it must be carefully borne in mind that God is not only 'an agent through intellect' but also 'a being through intellect.' God is an agent through intellect because divine acting or producing is nothing other than divine understanding and willing that something be produced. God is a being through intellect because the divine essence is the divine intellect and will, and the divine act of existence is the divine act of understanding and the divine act of willing.

Therefore, if the triune God understands and wills that only the Son should become incarnate and this in such a way that the union should take place in the person and on the basis of the person, then by this understanding and willing (1) everything finite required for the incarnation is produced, since God acts through intellect, and (2) the Son is constituted as hypostatically united through the infinite act of existence, since this act of existence is nothing else than that understanding and willing.

Accordingly, the infinite act of existence of the Son is the intrinsic constitutive reason and cause of the hypostatic union, inasmuch as this act of existence is different from the divine act of understanding and of willing only in concept and not at all in reality.

In fact, it could hardly be otherwise. The hypostatic union is a union in the person and on the basis of the person. But a divine person is not really distinct either from the divine act of existence or from the divine essence or from the divine nature. Now what are not really distinct from one another are distinguished only in the mind. The hypostatic union, therefore, can be constituted only by that real act of existence that is also identical with the act of understanding and of willing.

Quibus perspectis, iam elucet quid esse debeat actus eminens, nempe, id quod est et constituit id quod intelligit et vult se esse et se constituere. Quod si habetur, prorsus superfluit mendicatum adiutorium quod ex dubie analogica entis finiti compositione repetitur.

Sectio Quarta: Ex Principio Compositionis Compositi Deductio

70 Unionem hypostaticam primo proposuimus prout dogmate catholico docetur et deinde in potentiam et actum tum ex parte subiecti assumentis tum ex parte obiecti assumpti resolvimus. Quae multa quemadmodum in unum componenda sint iam consideravimus, ita ut nihil remaneat nisi illa deductio in via doctrinae quae ex multis resolutis secundum principium compositionis ad ipsum dogma redeat.

Primo, ergo, ratio seu causa constitutiva unionis hypostaticae non dicit cur Filius sit persona, vel cur sit Deus, vel cur sit homo, sed cur idem sit qui est Deus et qui est homo. Persona enim est Filius per relationem subsistentem; Deus est Filius per essentiam divinam; homo est Filius per essentiam humanam; sed idem est ille qui Deus est et qui homo est per rationem seu causam constitutivam unionis hypostaticae.

Deinde, quod Deus trinus secundum infinitam suam sapientiam et bonitatem de se ipso intelligere et velle potest, hoc (1) Deus esse potest et (2) per esse suum divinum esse potest.

Ad primum: Deus hoc esse potest quia intelligentia divina est infallibilis et volitio divina est efficax.

Ad alterum: hoc per esse suum divinum esse potest, nam non aliud est divinum esse et aliud divinum intelligere et aliud divinum velle sed unum idemque; et ideo eo ipso quod Deus per suum intelligere aliquid de se ipso intelligit, iam per suum esse est illud; iterum, eo ipso quod Deus per suum velle aliquid de se ipso vult, iam per suum esse est illud. Quod sane in nulla creatura esse potest cum in omni creatura aliud est esse et aliud intelligere et aliud velle;[20] et nihilominus in Deo omnino est necessarium cum in Deo simplici unus idemque sit actus essendi, intelligendi, et volendi.

Tertio, Deus trinus intelligit et vult non Patrem neque Spiritum sanctum sed solum Filium unionem hypostaticam inire. Sed quod Deus trinus intelligit et vult,

In view of this, it is now clear what that eminent act must be: it is that which is and constitutes that which it understands and wills itself to be and to constitute. If you have such an act, it is quite unnecessary to go a-begging for help from a dubious analogy with the composition of a finite being.

4 Deducing the Composite from the Principle of Composition

70 Our first step was to set forth the hypostatic union as taught in Catholic dogma, and then we resolved it into potency and act both on the side of the assuming subject and on that of the assumed object. We have now considered how all these combine in a unity, so that all that remains to be done is to make that deduction in the way of teaching that, according to the principle of composition, brings us back to the dogma itself from the various elements into which it was resolved.

In the *first* place, then, the constitutive reason or cause of the hypostatic union does not tell us why the Son is a person, or why he is God, or why he is man, but why it is the same one who is God and who is man. For the Son is a person through a subsistent relation; the Son is God through the divine essence; the Son is man through a human essence; but it is through the constitutive reason or cause of the hypostatic union that the same one who is God is also man.

In the *second* place, whatever the triune God in the divine infinite wisdom and goodness can understand and will about himself, God (1) can be, and (2) can be through the divine act of existence.

As to (1): God can be this because the divine understanding is infallible and the divine willing effective.

As to (2): God can be this through the divine act of existence because the divine act of existence and divine understanding and divine willing are all one and the same reality. And by the very fact that through the divine act of understanding God understands something about God, God already is that something through the divine act of existence. Again, by the very fact that through the divine act of willing God wills something about God, God already is that something through the divine act of existence. This, of course, is impossible in any created being, since in every creature act of existence, understanding, and willing are different.[20] But in God this must absolutely be so, since in God, an utterly simple reality, the acts of being, understanding, and willing are one and the same.

In the *third* place, the triune God understands and wills only the Son to enter into the hypostatic union, not the Father or the Holy Spirit. But what

20 Thomas Aquinas, *Summa theologiae* 1, q. 54, aa. 1–3.

etiam intelligere et velle potest; neque quicquam intelligere potest nisi secundum infinitam suam sapientiam neque quicquam velle potest nisi secundum infinitam suam bonitatem. Ergo secundum infinitam suam sapientiam et bonitatem Deus trinus hoc de se ipso intelligere et velle potest quod non Pater neque Spiritus sed solus Filius unionem hypostaticam ineat.

Quarto, ex altero et tertio simul sumptis concluditur, tum (1) fieri posse ut solus Filius unionem hypostaticam ineat, tum (2) hoc fieri posse per esse divinum quod idem est realiter ac divinum intelligere et divinum velle.

Ulterius, cum nihil aliud sit potentia quam id per quod aliquid fieri possit, potentia ad unionem hypostaticam est divinum esse prout realiter identificatur cum divino actu intelligendi et volendi.

Praeterea, cum divinum esse sit tribus personis commune, etiam potentia ad unionem hypostaticam ineundam est tribus personis communis.[21]

Notate denique totum argumentum inquantum unionem hypostaticam respicit in facto unionis fundari; ex hoc enim facto ad posse in tertio gressu conclusimus.

Quinto, intra ipsum ens infinitum, simplex, necessarium, immutabile, non realiter distinguuntur potentia ad aliquid et actus eiusdem. Sed potentia ad unionem hypostaticam constituitur per esse divinum quod est idem ac divinum intelligere et divinum velle. Ergo etiam ipse actus unionis hypostaticae constituitur per esse divinum quod est idem realiter ac divinum intelligere et divinum velle.

Sexto, sicut per entitative eundem infinitum sciendi actum Deus scit et necessaria et contingentia, sicut per entitative eundem infinitum volendi actum Deus vult et necessaria et contingentia, ita etiam per entitative eundem infinitum essendi actum tum esse potest Deus trinus tum est Deus Filius non solum id quod necessario est sed etiam id quod contingenter factus est.

Quae comparatio non tantum analogia quaedam est, cum in Deo non aliud sit intelligere et velle et aliud sit esse. Sed illa sola intercedit differentia quod, cum Deus de aliis intelligat et velit, per intelligere et velle suum alia producit, sed cum Deus de se ipso intelligat et velit, per intelligere et velle et esse suum est quod de se intelligat et velit.

the triune God does understand and will the triune God also can understand and will, and God cannot understand anything except in accordance with the infinite divine wisdom nor will anything except in accordance with the infinite divine goodness. Therefore in accordance with that infinite wisdom and goodness, the triune God can understand and will this about God, that the Son alone and not the Father or the Holy Spirit should enter into hypostatic union.

In the *fourth* place, from the foregoing second and third points taken together it follows (1) that it is possible for the Son alone to enter the hypostatic union, and (2) that this is possible because of the divine act of existence, which is really identical with divine understanding and divine willing.

Further, since potency is simply that through which something is possible, it follows that the potency to the hypostatic union is the divine act of existence as really identical with the divine act of understanding and willing.

Again, since the divine act of existence is common to the three persons, the potency to enter into the hypostatic union is also common to all three.[21]

Note, finally, that the entire argument regarding the hypostatic union is based on the fact of the union; for it was from this fact that in the third point we concluded to its possibility.

In the *fifth* place, within that infinite, simple, necessary, and immutable being there is no real distinction between a potency to something and its act. But the potency to the hypostatic union is constituted by the divine act of existence, which is identical with divine understanding and divine willing. Therefore the act of the hypostatic union is also constituted by the divine act of existence, which is really identical with divine understanding and divine willing.

In the *sixth* place, just as by what is entitatively the same infinite act of knowing God knows both what is necessary and what is contingent, and just as by what is entitatively the same act of willing God wills both what is necessary and what is contingent, so too by what is entitatively the same infinite act of being the triune God is able to be, and God the Son is, not only what he necessarily is but also what he has contingently become.

This comparison is not just some kind of analogy, since in God it is not one thing to understand and to will and another to be. The only difference is that in understanding and willing concerning other beings, by divine understanding and willing God produces them, whereas in understanding and willing concerning himself, by divine understanding and willing and act of existence God is what he understands and wills about himself.

21 Ibid. 3, q. 3, a. 5.

Septimo, nemo vere et realiter est aliquid nisi per proprium suum esse est illud. Sed Filius vere et realiter est homo. Ergo per proprium suum esse Filius est homo.

Octavo, quia per suum esse sibi identicum Filius et Deus est et homo est, vere et realiter perficitur unio duarum naturarum in una persona et secundum eandem personam.

Neque obstat quod esse est commune tribus vel quod esse identificatur cum natura divina. Illud enim esse est idem quod divinum intelligere et divinum velle. Quare si Deus trinus intelligit et vult solum Filium ita incarnari ut unio sit in persona et secundum personam, per idem intelligere atque velle, quia etiam esse est, et solus Filius incarnatur et unio non in natura sed in persona neque secundum naturam sed secundum personam est.

71   *Nono*, circa incarnationem triplex invenitur contingentia: nam (1) fieri potuit absolute ut nulla facta sit incarnatio; (2) fieri potuit absolute ut facta sit incarnatio in alia natura quam in illa quae ex Maria fuit; et (3) fieri potuit absolute ut Pater vel Filius vel Spiritus vel duae quaelibet vel omnes tres personae divinae incarnarentur.

Iam vero omne quod contingenter verum est de Deo vel de persona divina, adaequationem veritatis non habet nisi ponitur terminus quidam ad extra creatus, contingens, conveniens. Non enim habetur verum contingens nisi habetur ens contingens; et ipse Deus nullo modo est entitative contingens.

Exigit ergo ipsa veritas incarnationis non solum causam constitutivam, quae est esse Verbi infinitum, sed etiam talem terminum ad extra productum ut salvetur a parte rei triplex verum contingens qua contingens.

Decimo, terminus aut operationis est aut relationis. Terminus operationis est inquantum scire terminatur ad scitum, velle terminatur ad volitum, producere terminatur ad productum. Terminus relationis est inquantum omnis relatio terminatur ad relationem oppositam.

Iam vero in Verbo incarnato, inquantum entia creata importat, duplex invenitur aspectus. Aliud enim est incarnari quod in Verbo solo invenitur. Aliud autem est omnia creata producere quae ad incarnationem requiruntur, et hoc non solius Verbi est sed Dei trini (DB 704).

In the *seventh* place, no one is really and truly anything except by his or her own act of existence. But since the Son is really and truly human, he is so by his own proper act of existence.

In the *eighth* place, because the Son is both God and man through his own act of existence, which is identical with himself, the union of the two natures is really and truly brought about in the one person and on the basis of that same person.

Nor does the fact that act of existence is common to the three persons and is identified with the divine nature present any obstacle, for that act of existence is the same as divine understanding and divine willing. Hence if the triune God understands and wills that only the Son become incarnate in such a way that the union take place in and on the basis of the person, then by the same understanding and willing, since they are the same as the divine act of existence, only the Son becomes incarnate and the union takes place not in the nature but in the person and on the basis not of the nature but of the person.

71 In the *ninth* place, with respect to the incarnation there are three contingent truths: (1) absolutely speaking it was possible for there to be no incarnation; (2) absolutely speaking it was possible for there to be an incarnation in a nature other than that derived from Mary; and (3) absolutely speaking it was possible for the Father or the Son or the Spirit or any two or all three to become incarnate.

Now anything that is contingently true of God or of a divine person lacks the correspondence needed for truth unless there is posited some external, created, contingent, appropriate term; for a contingent truth is impossible without a contingent being, and God is in no way entitatively contingent.

The truth of the incarnation, therefore, demands not only a constitutive cause, which is the infinite act of existence of the Word, but also the production of an extrinsic term as the condition in the real order for these three contingent truths as contingent.

In the *tenth* place, a term belongs either to an operation or to a relation. You have the term of an operation when knowing terminates in what is known, when willing terminates in what is willed, when producing terminates in a product. You have the term of a relation in that every relation terminates in an opposite relation.

Now there are two aspects in the incarnate Word vis-à-vis created beings. One is the fact of becoming incarnate, which belongs to the Word alone; the other is the production of all the created things requisite for the incarnation, and this pertains to the triune God and not to the Word alone (DB 704; DS 1331).

Qua de causa, inquantum Deus trinus scit et vult et producit incarnationem, et Deus trinus ratione refertur ad naturam assumptam et natura assumpta realiter refertur ad Deum trinum ut ad causam extrinsecam.

Praeterea, inquantum solus Filius incarnatur, et ipse Filius naturam humanam assumens ad hanc naturam ratione refertur, et ipsa natura assumpta ad solum Filium assumentem refertur realiter tamquam ad causam Verbo incarnato intrinsecam.

Quae realis relatio naturae assumptae ad solum Filium est terminus ad extra creatus, contingens, conveniens secundum quem salvatur triplex verum contingens. Quia enim haec relatio est realis, salvatur veritas realis incarnationis. Quia haec realis relatio in illa natura invenitur quae ex Maria fuit, salvatur veritas circa naturam quae assumpta est. Quia haec realis relatio solum Filium respicit, salvatur veritas circa personam assumentem.

Undecimo, eatenus haberi potest realis relatio, quatenus habetur reale eiusdem fundamentum. Sicut enim creatio passiva non esset realis relatio nisi subiectum eius ex nihilo sui et subiecti produceretur, ita etiam relatio ex parte obiecti assumpti non esset realis nisi illud obiectum vere et realiter esset assumptum.

Qua de causa, terminus qui ad extra exigitur non solum est realis relatio assumptionis proprie dictae sed etiam importat atque praesupponit quod vere et realiter a solo Verbo assumpta est illa natura quae ex Maria fuit.

Duodecimo, hoc reale assumi non est idem quoad rem ac reale posse assumi. Etsi enim in ipso Deo infinito et immutabili idem sit quoad rem et posse assumere et actu assumere, aliter prorsus in ente mutabili atque finito res se habet. Secus enim vel omnis natura humana esset assumpta, vel nulla alia natura assumi potuisset nisi illa quae assumpta est; quod est contra fidem cum Christus homo sit nobis non assumptis similis quoad omnia absque peccato (DB 148).

Decimo tertio, actu assumi est actus quidam absolute supernaturalis. Nam absolute supernaturale est quod excedit naturalem proportionem cuiuslibet essentiae substantialis et finitae; et nihil magis excedit naturalem proportionem cuiuslibet essentiae substantialis et finitae quam ut fiat essentia substantialis Verbi Dei.

Qua de causa, potentia ad hunc actum supernaturalem est obedientialis. Quod enim fieri non potest in aliquo secundum naturalem eius proportionem, absolute tamen in eo fieri potest inquantum omnis creatura nihil antiquius habet quam ut Deo ad nutum obediat.

Decimo quarto, haec potentia obedientialis est essentia humana substantialis atque individualis. Id enim potest assumi quod actu assumitur. Sed actu assumpta

Thus, since the triune God knows, wills, and produces the incarnation, the triune God is conceptually related to the assumed nature, and the assumed nature is really related to the triune God as to its extrinsic cause.

Again, since the Son alone became incarnate, the Son in assuming a human nature is conceptually related to this nature, and the assumed nature is really related to the Son alone, who assumed it, as to a cause intrinsic to the incarnate Word.

This real relation of the assumed nature to the Son alone is the external, created, contingent, appropriate term that guarantees the three contingent truths. Because this relation is real, it guarantees the truth of the reality of the incarnation; because this real relation exists in the nature derived from Mary, it guarantees the truth about the nature that is assumed; and because this real relation regards only the Son, it guarantees the truth about the person assuming.

In the *eleventh* place, a real relation is possible only when a real foundation for that relation exists. For just as passive creation would not be a real relation unless its subject were produced from nothing, so too the relation on the side of the object assumed would not be real unless that object were really and truly assumed.

Hence the required external term not only is the real relation of the assumption properly so called, but also implies and presupposes that the nature derived from Mary was really and truly assumed by the Word alone.

In the *twelfth* place, this fact of being really assumed is not the same in reality as the real possibility of being assumed. For although in God, who is infinite and immutable, the ability to assume and the actual assuming are really the same, the situation is completely different for a finite being that is subject to change. Otherwise either every human nature would have been assumed, or no other nature could have been assumed than the one that was assumed; and this is contrary to faith, since the man Christ is like us, who have not been assumed, in all respects save sin (DB 148; DS 301–302).

In the *thirteenth* place, to be actually assumed is an absolutely supernatural act. For whatever exceeds the natural proportion of any substantial finite essence is absolutely supernatural; and nothing more greatly exceeds the natural proportion of any substantial finite essence than to become the substantial essence of the Word of God.

Hence the potency to this supernatural act is obediential; for what is impossible to any creature according to its natural proportion can happen to it absolutely speaking, inasmuch as the highest priority for every creature is obedience to God upon command.

In the *fourteenth* place, this obediential potency is the substantial individual human essence. For what is actually assumed can be assumed. But that sort of

est eiusmodi essentia humana. Ergo etiam potuit assumi eiusmodi essentia humana.

Unde concludes potentiam naturalem et potentiam obedientialem inter se distingui (1) circa actus ad quos ordinantur et (2) circa causas proportionatas ad illos actus producendos; sed non realiter distingui quoad entitatem iis intrinsecam, secus nulla natura ne obedientialiter quidem actum supernaturalem recipere posset.

Decimo quinto, substantialis est ille actus quo actu assumitur natura humana Christi. Nam proprius actus fit in propria potentia. Sed potentia ad hunc actum supernaturalem est essentia substantialis. Ergo ipse actus etiam substantialis est.

Praeterea, ille actus supernaturalis aut substantialis est aut accidentalis. Sed non est accidentalis. Ergo est substantialis.

Ad minorem: si accidentalis est, aut recipitur in potentia intelligendi aut in potentia volendi aut in ipsa essentia animae.

Sed si recipitur in potentia intelligendi vel in potentia volendi, sequitur naturam humanam esse a Verbo assumptam secundum unionem circa verum et bonum; quod quidem non potest excedere unionem moralem.

Si autem recipitur in ipsa essentia animae, sequitur naturam humanam esse a Verbo assumptam eo modo quo donum increatum Spiritus sancti per gratiam sanctificantem iustis conceditur; quod quidem non potest excedere unionem accidentalem quam Nestoriani coniunctionem vel *synapheian* nominaverunt.

Relinquitur ergo quod ille actus supernaturalis quo actu assumitur natura Christi humana non accidentalis est sed substantialis.

Decimo sexto, hic actus supernaturalis et substantialis ita recipitur in essentia humana substantiali et individuali ut ab illa essentia excludat actum substantialem seu esse ad quod recipiendum naturaliter proportionatur.

Si enim in illa essentia adesset esse naturaliter proportionatum, eo ipso adesset esse proprium; nam esse proprium alicuius essentiae nihil est aliud quam esse ad quod illa essentia naturaliter proportionatur.

Si in illa essentia adesset esse proprium, resultaret ens stricte dictum et unum stricte dictum quod est simpliciter indivisum in se et simpliciter divisum ab omni alio. Quare haberentur et subsistens et distinctum et, cum illa essentia sit humana, natura intellectualis, ita ut constitueretur persona finita.

human essence actually was assumed, so it was also possible for such a human essence to be assumed.

From this one may conclude that natural potency and obediential potency are distinguished (1) with regard to the acts to which they are ordered and (2) with regard to the causes proportionate to the production of those acts; but they are not really distinct as to their intrinsic entity, for otherwise no nature would ever be capable, even obedientially, of receiving a supernatural act.

In the *fifteenth* place, the act whereby the human nature of Christ is actually assumed is substantial. For an act and its potency are proportionate to each other. But the potency to this supernatural act is a substantial essence, and hence the act itself also is substantial.

Besides, that supernatural act is either substantial or accidental; but it is not accidental; hence it is substantial.

For if accidental, it is received either in the potency to understand or in the potency to will, or in the very essence of the soul.

Now if it is received in the potency to understand or in the potency to will, it follows that the human nature was assumed by the Word in a union concerned with truth and goodness, which could be no more than a moral union.

And if it is received in the very essence of the soul, it follows that the human nature is assumed by the Word in the same way as the uncreated gift of the Holy Spirit is conferred upon the just through sanctifying grace; but that could be no more than an accidental union which the Nestorians called *synapheia* or 'conjunction.'

We conclude, therefore, that the supernatural act whereby the human nature of Christ is actually assumed is not accidental but substantial.

In the *sixteenth* place, this supernatural substantial act is received in a substantial individual human essence in such a way as to make it impossible for that essence to receive the substantial act, the act of existence, to which that essence is naturally proportionate.

For if a naturally proportionate act of existence were present in that essence, by that very fact it would have its own proper act of existence, since the proper act of existence of any essence is simply the existence to which that essence is naturally proportionate.

And if that essence had its proper act of existence, there would result a being in the strict sense and a unity in the strict sense, that which is simply undivided in itself and simply divided from everything else. Accordingly you would have a distinct subsistent being and, since that essence is human, you would have an intellectual nature, and this would constitute a finite person.

Iam vero Verbum non assumpsit personam humanam, cum in unione Verbi incarnati non invenitur nisi una persona eaque divina. Et ideo ab essentia humana assumpta excludi oportet actum substantialem seu esse ad quod illa essentia naturaliter ordinatur et proportionatur.

Dixerit tamen quispiam quod pariter constituitur persona finita per actum substantialem et supernaturalem in essentia humana receptum. Quod minime sequitur. Eatenus enim unum subsistens constituitur per esse in essentiam receptum quatenus idem et per essentiam est in potentia et per esse est in actu. Iam vero essentia Christi humana considerari potest vel prout est potentia naturalis vel prout est potentia obedientialis. Sed secundum quod est potentia naturalis, non actuatur, et ideo quamvis subsistens finitum per essentiam sit in potentia, numquam tamen fuit actu. Et secundum quod est potentia obedientialis, actuatur quidem, sed sic in potentia erat non subsistens finitum sed natura a Verbo assumpta.

72 Iam sunt inter se comparanda quae separatim consideravimus, nempe, causam constitutivam unionis hypostaticae (§ 70) et terminum ad extra qui per verum contingens exigitur (§ 71).

Decimo septimo, ergo, correlativa simul concipiuntur. Sed assumere et assumi sunt correlativa. Et ideo in ordine conceptionum simultaneae sunt et relatio rationis quae in Verbo ponitur et relatio realis quae in natura assumpta ponitur.

Praeterea, verum logicum conceptibus coniunctis vel separatis constat. Et ideo sicut simul concipiuntur assumere et assumi, ita simul veritatem habent et quod Verbum naturam humanam assumit et quod natura humana a Verbo assumitur.

Praeterea, non prius habetur verum contingens quam habeatur ens contingens. Et ideo quia Verbum potuit non incarnari, non prius habetur veritas incarnationis quam habeatur terminus ad extra creatus, contingens, et conveniens.

Nihilominus in ipso ordine ontologico simpliciter prius est esse Verbi infinitum et simpliciter posterius seu omnino secundarium est illud esse seu actus substantialis et supernaturalis quo natura humana constituitur ut actu assumpta.

Sicut enim persona divina per nihil aliud quam per suum scire scit et per nihil aliud quam per suum velle vult, ita etiam per nihil aliud quam per suum esse est. Sicut autem scientia contingentis et volitio contingentis terminum contingentem non solum exigit sed etiam facit ita ut scientia et volitio sint simpliciter priores et terminus sit simpliciter

But the Word did not assume a human person, since in the union of the incarnate Word there is only one person, and that divine. Hence there must be ruled out from the assumed human essence that substantial act or act of existence to which that essence is naturally ordered and proportionate.

One might argue, however, that a finite person would likewise be constituted by a substantial supernatural act received in a human essence. But that does not follow at all. A subsistent unity is constituted by an act of existence received into an essence only when what is in potency by essence is the same as what is in act by existence. Now the human essence of Christ can be considered either as a natural or as an obediential potency. But as a natural potency it is not actuated, and so although by its essence there is potentially here a subsistent finite being, it never actually came to be. As obediential potency it is indeed actuated, but what was in potency in this case was not a finite subsistent but the nature assumed by the Word.

72 Let us now consider together in their mutual relationship what we have so far been considering separately, namely, the constitutive cause of the hypostatic union (§ 70) and the extrinsic term required by a contingent truth (§ 71).

In the *seventeenth* place, then, correlatives are conceived simultaneously. Now 'to assume' and 'to be assumed' are correlatives, and so in the conceptual order the relation of reason in the Word and the real relation in the assumed nature are simultaneous.

Furthermore, logical truth consists of concepts that are either joined or separated. Thus, just as 'to assume' and 'to be assumed' are conceived simultaneously, so too that the Word assumes a human nature and that a human nature is assumed by the Word are simultaneously true.

Again, there is no contingent truth prior to the existence of a contingent being. Hence, since it was possible that the Word not become incarnate, the truth of the incarnation is not to be had prior to the existence of an external, created, contingent, and appropriate term.

In the ontological order, however, the infinite act of existence of the Word is simply prior, while that act of existence or substantial supernatural act whereby the human nature is constituted as actually assumed is simply posterior or altogether secondary.

For just as a divine person knows by the divine act of knowing and by nothing else, and wills by the divine act of willing and by nothing else, so also a divine person *is* by the divine act of existence and by nothing else. But just as divine knowledge and willing of a contingent being not only requires a contingent term but also causes it to be, so that the knowing and willing are simply prior and the

posterior, ita etiam hoc, quod persona divina est id quod contingenter facta est, terminum contingentem non solum exigit sed etiam ipsa hac exigentia reddit terminum formaliter talem. Quatenus enim per prius infinita perfectio constituit hoc quod dicitur assumere, eatenus finita perfectio sufficit ad constituendum hoc quod dicitur actu assumi.

Quibus perspectis, non ex aequo concludes et esse Verbi infinitum et terminum ad extra positum ad unionem hypostaticam concurrere.

Esse enim infinitum est unica ratio et causa constitutiva ipsius unionis quia per esse suum infinitum Verbum non solum est id quod necessario est sed etiam est id quod contingenter factum est. Sic enim neque aliter salvatur et quod Verbum ipsum vere et realiter homo est et quod idem et Deus et homo est.

Terminus autem, qui est actu assumi, (1) non est causa unionis tum quia ipsum esse infinitum est unica causa tum quia superfluit alia causa ubi adest causa infinita, neque (2) est conditio ontologica sive praevia sive simultanea quia esse infinitum est absolute independens et ad omnia sufficiens, et ideo (3) est simpliciter posterior, consequens, resultans, tum quia neque causa est neque conditio ontologica sive praevia sive simultanea tum etiam quia eatenus 'assumi' realiter haberi potest quatenus per prius in ordine ontologico habetur realiter assumere.

Decimo octavo, actus substantialis et supernaturalis in essentia Christi humana receptus, cum ideo sit 'assumi' quia exigitur ab infinito actu Verbi assumentis, fundat realem relationem naturae assumptae ad solum Verbum.

Decimo nono, non ponitur hic actus substantialis seu esse secundarium ut essentia Christi humana sit realis; neque ponitur ut essentia illa existat.

Non ponitur ut illa essentia sit realis. Nam aliud est ens rationis quo essentia concipitur, et aliud est principium reale quod cum esse componitur. Sed essentia Christi humana non est merum ens rationis sed aliquod principium entis reale; et quod iam est aliquod principium reale non alio indiget ut reale fiat.

Neque ponitur ut illa essentia existat, nam nulla essentia finita existit. Quod enim est vel existit est ens stricte dictum. Ipsa autem principia entis (materia, forma; essentia, esse; etc.) non sunt vel existunt, sed iis aliquid (ens, nempe) est vel existit. Quare, sicut Petrus vel Paulus existit, non autem essentia Petri vel essentia Pauli, ita etiam Christus Deus existit et Christus homo existit, non autem essentia Christi humana quae finita est.

term simply posterior, so too the fact that a divine person is what that person has contingently become not only necessitates a contingent term but this very necessity makes that term formally such a term. For as infinite perfection constitutes in advance what is termed 'to assume,' so also a finite perfection suffices to constitute what is termed 'being actually assumed.'

In view of this, you cannot attribute an equal role in the hypostatic union to the infinite act of existence of the Word and to the external term.

The infinite act of existence is the sole reason and constitutive cause of this union because by the infinite act of existence the Word is not only what the Word necessarily is but also what the Word has contingently become. Only in this way can you maintain that the Word is really and truly man and that the same one is both God and man.

The term, however, which is the fact of being actually assumed, (1) is not the cause of the union, both because the infinite act of existence is the sole cause and because in the presence of an infinite cause any other cause is superfluous; (2) nor is it an ontological condition, whether prior or simultaneous, since an infinite act of existence is absolutely independent and all-sufficient; and therefore (3) it is simply posterior, consequent, a resultant, and this for two reasons: first, because it is neither a cause nor a prior or simultaneous ontological condition, and secondly, because 'being assumed' is really possible only if there is an ontologically prior real 'assuming.'

In the *eighteenth* place, since the 'being assumed' exists because it is required by the infinite act of the assuming Word, the substantial supernatural act received in Christ's human essence is the foundation of the real relation of the assumed nature to the Word alone.

In the *nineteenth* place, this substantial act or secondary act of existence is not required for the human essence of Christ to be real, nor is it required for the existence of that essence.

It is not required for the reality of that essence. For the 'being of reason' whereby an essence is conceived is quite different from the real principle that enters into composition with an act of existence. But the human essence of Christ is not a mere 'being of reason' but a real principle of being, and what is already a real principle does not need anything else to become real.

Nor is it required for the existence of the essence, because no finite essence exists. Whatever is or exists is a being in the strict sense of the word. But the components or principles of being (matter and form, essence and existence, and so forth) are not, do not exist; rather, they are that by which something, namely a being, is or exists. Peter and Paul exist; the essence of Peter and the essence of Paul do not. In just the same way, the finite human essence of Christ does not exist; Christ our God exists, and Christ the man exists.

Vigesimo, hic actus substantialis seu esse secundarium non est causa constitutiva ut Christus homo existat. Sicut enim per esse suum infinitum Christus est Deus, ita etiam per idem esse infinitum Christus est homo. Sed quia esse infinitum est necessarium, et contingenter Christus est homo, ad hoc quod Christus per esse infinitum est homo consequitur per modum termini simpliciter posterioris illud esse quod ideo prorsus secundarium est.

Vigesimo primo, non ponitur hic actus substantialis seu esse secundarium tamquam intermedium quod coniungat atque uniat divinitatem et humanitatem. Unio enim hypostatica est unio in persona et secundum personam ita ut intermedium inter duas naturas sit persona Verbi quae et Deus est et homo est. Praeterea, nisi coniungens atque uniens esset ipsa persona Verbi, non haberetur idem reale quod et Deus est et homo est. Patet autem esse illud secundarium non esse sive Deum sive hominem; et ideo nullo modo potest esse id quod coniungit atque unit duas naturas in una persona.

Ulterius, sicut persona Verbi est illud idem *quod* et Deus et homo est, ita esse Verbi infinitum est illud *quo* persona Verbi et Deus est et homo est. Et ideo esse Verbi infinitum ponitur tamquam unica causa unionis hypostaticae; e contra, esse secundarium sicut non est id *quod* coniungit et unit, ita etiam non est id *quo* coniungens et uniens coniungit et unit. Remanet ergo ut esse secundarium nullo modo sit intermedium coniungens et uniens. Sed inquantum coniungens persona per esse suum infinitum contingenter se constituit ut homo, consequitur illud esse secundarium per modum termini simpliciter posterioris, sicut etiam dicitur quod ultima dispositio ad formam receptionem formae consequitur.

Vigesimo secundo, quia hoc esse secundarium est absolute supernaturale, etiam est gratia quaedam. Sed non est gratia unionis hypostaticae quasi hanc unionem constitueret. Gratia enim unionis quae unionem constituit est illa unica causa constitutiva unionis quae est esse Verbi infinitum. Attamen dici potest hoc esse secundarium gratia unionis inquantum a causa unionis constitutiva exigitur et eam consequitur.

Vigesimo tertio, ideo inter se differunt esse proprium ad quod essentia humana naturaliter proportionatur et esse hoc secundarium ad quod essentia humana non est nisi potentia obedientialis, quia (1) esse proprium omnem suam determinationem ex illa essentia accipit in qua recipitur et per quam limitatur sed (2) hoc esse secundarium determinationes suas ex duplici fonte accipit. Nam inquantum

In the *twentieth* place, this substantial act or secondary act of existence is not the constitutive cause whereby Christ the man exists. For just as Christ is God through his infinite act of existence, so too he is man through that same infinite act. But because infinite existence is necessary and Christ is man contingently, consequent upon the fact of his being a man by his infinite act of existence there follows, as a simply posterior term, that act of existence that accordingly is altogether secondary.

In the *twenty-first* place, this substantial act, this secondary act of existence, is not some intermediary linking and uniting the divinity and humanity. The hypostatic union takes place in the person and on the basis of the person, so that the intermediary between the two natures is the person of the Word who is God and is man. Besides, if the person of the Word were not that which links and unites the two natures, there would not be one and the same reality that is God and is man. Clearly, the secondary act of existence is neither God nor man, and so it is quite impossible for it to be that which links and unites the two natures in one person.

Furthermore, as the person of the Word is that one same reality *which* is both God and man, so the Word's infinite act of existence is that *by which* the person of the Word is both God and man. The infinite act of existence of the Word, therefore, is the sole cause of the hypostatic union; on the other hand, the secondary act of existence, as it is not that *which* links and unites, neither is it that *by which* the link and unifier links and unites. We must conclude, then, that the secondary act of existence is in no way a linking and uniting intermediary. But inasmuch as the conjoining person constitutes himself contingently as a man through the infinite act of existence, that secondary act follows by way of a simply posterior term – just as the final disposition to a form is said to follow upon the actual reception of that form.

In the *twenty-second* place, because this secondary act of existence is absolutely supernatural, it is also a grace. However, it is not the grace of the hypostatic union as though constituting that union. The grace of union constituting the union is that sole constitutive cause of the union that is the infinite act of existence of the Word. Nevertheless, this secondary act of existence can be said to be the grace of union inasmuch as it is required by and consequent upon the constitutive cause of the union.

In the *twenty-third* place, the proper act of existence to which a human essence is naturally proportionate differs from this secondary act of existence to which a human essence is only obediential potency in that (1) the proper act of existence is entirely determined by the essence in which it is received and by which it is delimited, whereas (2) this secondary act of existence receives its determinations

resultat ex eo quod Verbum per esse suum infinitum est hic homo, determinatur per habitudinem suam ad solum Verbum incarnatum; inquantum autem resultat in hac essentia, etiam determinatur per essentiam quae illud recipit atque limitat.

73 Cum iam considerata sint quae respiciant tum causam quae unionem constituit (primo ad octavum), tum terminum qui ad extra exigitur (octavo ad decimum sextum), tum comparationem causae atque termini inter se (decimo septimo ad vigesimum tertium), remanet ut haec omnia simul considerentur secundum quod ad finem inquisitionis theologicae conducant.

Vigesimo quarto, ex potentia unionis hypostaticae incipientes ratiocinando processimus ad actum unionis et ad terminum creatum qui ex actu concluditur. Sed ideo quis ratiocinatur et discurrit ut ad intelligentiam perveniat; ad intelligentiam autem pervenit inquantum non solum singulas conclusiones ex praemissis consequi perspicit sed etiam omnes conclusiones per modum unius in ipsis principiis intelligibiliter contentas apprehendit. Quae quidem omnium per modum unius apprehensio vel formalis esse potest vel virtualis. Et virtualis quidem est inquantum quis habet habitum ut prompte, faciliter, et saltem sine tristitia ad quamlibet quaestionem usque ad ultimum 'cur' respondere possit. At formalis non est sine quodam artificio; hac enim in vita nihil intelligere possumus nisi per conversionem ad phantasma; at in quaestione longiori atque difficiliori phantasma conveniens haberi non potest nisi per diagramma quoddam adiuvatur ipsa imaginatio; et ideo qui omnia per modum unius apprehendere velit, diagramma quoddam faciat in quo et elementa quaestionis omnia omnesque inter elementa nexus symbolice repraesententur.

Vigesimo quinto, haec sive formalis sive virtualis omnium per modum unius apprehensio ad quod totum ratiocinium terminatur imperfecta est nostra mysterii intelligentia. Nam totum ratiocinium circulo quodam agitur, et circulus sicut a vero revelato incipit ita in vero revelato terminatur.

Ordientes enim posuimus ipsum dogma, nempe, eundem esse Deum et hominem, unam personam eamque divinam, unum ens, unam rem.

Deinde, in via inventionis in qua fides rationem illuminat deduximus et quaenam sit potentia et quinam sit actus ex parte subiecti assumentis et iterum quaenam sit potentia et quinam sit actus ex parte obiecti assumpti.

Tertio, inter viam inventionis in qua fides rationem illuminat et viam doctrinae in qua ratio per fidem illustrata imperfectam fidei intelligentiam assequitur,

from two sources. As resulting from the fact that the Word through his infinite act of existence is this man, it is determined by its relation to the incarnate Word alone; and as coming into existence in this essence, it is also determined by the essence that receives and delimits it.

73 Having considered all that concerns the constitutive cause of the union (arguments 1–8 above), the requisite external term (arguments 9–16), and the comparison of the cause and the term (arguments 17–23), what remains for us now is to consider all these points together as leading us towards the goal of theological inquiry.

In the *twenty-fourth* place, with the potency for the hypostatic union as our starting point, we have through a process of discursive reasoning arrived at the act of the union and the created term in which that act terminates. But the aim of discursive reasoning is to understand; and it arrives at understanding not only by grasping how each conclusion follows from premises, but also by comprehending in a unified whole all the conclusions intelligibly contained in those very principles. Now this comprehension of everything in a unified whole can be either formal or virtual. It is virtual when one is habitually able to answer readily and without difficulty, or at least 'without tears,' a whole series of questions right up to the last 'why?' Formal comprehension, however, cannot take place without a construct of some sort. In this life we are able to understand something only by turning to phantasm; but in larger and more complex questions it is impossible to have a suitable phantasm unless the imagination is aided by some sort of diagram. Thus, if we want to have a comprehensive grasp of everything in a unified whole, we shall have to construct a diagram in which are symbolically represented all the various elements of the question along with all the connections between them.

In the *twenty-fifth* place, this comprehensive grasp of everything in a unified whole, whether formal or virtual, in which the whole process of reasoning terminates, is our imperfect understanding of a mystery. For our reasoning followed a circular course, so to speak, beginning as it did from revealed truth only to terminate in revealed truth.

First, we started out by stating the dogma itself, namely, that one and the same is God and man, one person and that a divine person, one being, one reality.

Next, proceeding along the way of discovery in which faith illumines reason, we deduced what were the potency and the act on the side of the assuming subject and then again what were the potency and the act on the side of the object assumed.

Third, between the way of discovery in which faith illumines reason and the way of teaching in which reason so illumined attains an imperfect understanding

requiritur momentum syntheticum in quo quodammodo perspicitur quemadmodum ex multis ad unum redeundum sit. Quo in momento ad mysterium incarnationis ea extendimus quae communiter de ipso Deo per distinctionem inter
'entitative' et 'terminative' agnoscuntur, nempe, quod personae divinae per actum suum infinitum non solum necessario in divina natura sunt sed etiam in alia
quam volunt natura esse possunt.

Quarto, posita hac radice in quam terminatur illuminatio rationis per fidem
et ex qua incipit intelligentia fidei per rationem illuminatam, ordinate consideravimus tum ea quae Filium assumentem respiciunt tum ea quae circa naturam
assumptam consequuntur, tum ea quae in comparatione utriusque quaeri possunt, tum denique fructum intelligentiae ex toto motu percipiendum.

Quo in motu proceditur, non aliunde ad factum incarnationis demonstran-
dum, sed ex facto incarnationis per fidem suscepto ad imperfectam eiusdem facti
intelligentiam.

Vigesimo sexto, haec fidei intelligentia non in eo est quod perspicientes quid sit
Deus concludimus quid persona divina esse possit; nam hac in vita quid sit Deus
nescimus. Est ergo haec fidei intelligentia eiusmodi quae ex multorum conver-
gentia in centrum quoddam ignotum haberi possit; et ut magis specifice loquar,
est haec intelligentia tum ex analogia eorum quae naturaliter cognoscuntur tum
ex nexu mysteriorum inter se et cum fine hominis ultimo.

Et quantum ad analogiam eorum quae naturaliter cognoscimus, intelligentiam
quandam non petivimus ex ente finito et composito ut, sicut ens finitum essentia
atque esse componitur, ita Verbum incarnatum quasi essentia humana et esse divino simili quodam modo componatur; sed analogiam inde sumpsimus quod quae
contingenter de Deo vera sunt et in ipsum actum infinitum tamquam in causam et
in ens quoddam contingens tamquam in terminum consequentem resolvi oportet.
Quod enim in theologia naturali notissimum est tum circa actionem divinam tum
circa volitionem divinam tum circa scientiam divinam, post revelatam unionem
hypostaticam etiam ad esse divinum extendi posse atque debere opinati sumus.
Praestare autem hanc analogiam tum ex ipsa sua claritate elucet tum ex eo quod
ipsam unionem hypostaticam non in theoremate quodam de entibus finitis com-
ponendis sed in ipsa Dei perfectione fundat.

Quantum autem attinet ad nexum mysteriorum inter se et cum fine hominis
ultimo, cum hic finis sit visio beatifica in qua ipsa divina essentia intellectui creato
illabatur, cum in finem elevemur per iustificationem in qua donum increatum

of faith, a moment of synthesis is needed in which in some way one grasps how to return from multiplicity to unity. It was in this moment that we applied to the mystery of the incarnation what is commonly accepted concerning truths about God in distinguishing between 'entitatively' and 'terminatively'; that is, that the divine persons through their infinite act not only necessarily exist in their divine nature but are also capable of existing in any other nature they might wish to assume.

Fourth, having determined this foundational point at which the illumination of faith by reason ends and from which the understanding of faith by illumined reason begins, we considered in due order what pertains to the Son as the one who assumes, what the consequences are for the nature assumed, what questions can be asked in looking at the two together, and finally what fruitful understanding can be gathered from the process as a whole.

The aim of this process has been, not to prove the fact of the incarnation by something extraneous to it, but to go in faith from an acceptance of the fact of the incarnation to an understanding, albeit imperfect, of that fact.

In the *twenty-sixth* place, this understanding of the faith is not a matter of grasping the nature of God and drawing a conclusion about what a divine person can be, for in this life we do not know the nature of God. Hence this understanding of the faith is of the sort that can be had from the convergence of several elements upon some unknown central point. To put it more specifically, this understanding is derived both from an analogy with things known by the natural light of reason and from the interconnection among the mysteries themselves and with our ultimate end.

As to an analogy with what we know in a natural way, we have not sought understanding from a finite composite being to say that, just as a finite being is composed of essence and existence, so the incarnate Word is in some similar fashion composed of a human essence and the divine act of existence. Our analogy, rather, has been derived from the fact that what is contingently true of God must necessarily be resolved into that infinite act as its cause and some contingent being as a consequent term. Our thinking was that what is very well known in natural theology concerning divine action, divine volition, and divine knowledge, now with the revelation of the hypostatic union can and must be extended to the divine act of existence as well. This analogy is manifestly superior both because of its clarity and because it grounds the hypostatic union not on some theorem about composite finite beings but on the very perfection of God.

Now as to the connection of these mysteries among themselves and with our ultimate end: (1) since this end consists in the beatific vision in which the divine essence itself enters into a created intellect, and (2) since we are elevated to this

nobis detur, cum unio denique hypostatica causa atque origo sit tum nostrae iusti-
ficationis tum per iustitiam perseverantem finis adeptionis, mirabilis illa invenitur
similitudo quod in his tribus non solum infinita Dei perfectio creaturis coniungitur
sed etiam ipsa coniunctio terminum quendam creatum, contingentem, convenientem importat. Sicut enim in unione hypostatica praeter esse Verbi infinitum
habetur tamquam terminus esse substantiale et secundarium in essentia Christi
humana receptum, ita in iustificatione impii praeter donum increatum Spiritus
sancti habetur tamquam terminus gratia sanctificans quae est accidens in anima
receptum, et in visione beatifica praeter divinam essentiam quae vicibus speciei
intelligibilis quodammodo fungitur etiam habetur tamquam terminus lumen
gloriae.

Vigesimo septimo, sicut progressus in aliis scientiis per multorum collaborationem
et successionem saeculorum pedetentim efficitur, ita etiam profectus scientiae,
intelligentiae, sapientiae circa mysteria Dei. At quamvis progressus scientiarum
aliarum in novas semper sententias tendat, profectus intelligentiae theologicae in
eodem est sensu, eadem sententia, eodem dogmate (DB 1800).

Qua de causa, non aliud verum nobis erat intelligendum quam quod S. Ioannes
docuit Verbum carnem factum esse et Chalcedonense concilium iteravit unum
eundemque et Deum esse et hominem. Cuius unionis non aliam invenimus
causam unicam nisi unicum illud esse quod in Christo semper agnoverunt S.
Thomas eiusque discipuli. Neque alium posuimus terminum qui hac a causa constitutiva exigitur praeter esse illud secundarium non accidentale quod in *Quaestione
disputata de unione Verbi incarnati* agnovisse videtur Aquinas. Neque aliam assig-
navimus rationem cur natura assumpta non sit persona quam quod esse proprio
careat.

end through justification, in which an uncreated Gift is given to us, and finally (3) since the hypostatic union is the cause and source both of our justification and of our attainment of this end through perseverance in justice, one can discover this remarkable similarity in these three instances, namely, that in them not only is God's infinite perfection united to creatures, but also this very union involves the existence of an appropriate created contingent term. In the hypostatic union there is present besides the infinite act of existence of the Word a secondary substantial act of existence as a term received in Christ's human essence, just as in the justification of a sinner besides the uncreated gift of the Holy Spirit there is also present as a term sanctifying grace received in the soul as an accident, and in the beatific vision in addition to the divine essence, which in a way fulfills the function of an intelligible species, there is just such a term in the light of glory.

In the *twenty-seventh* place, as progress in other branches of knowledge takes place gradually over the centuries through the collaboration of many persons, so it is with the growth of our knowledge, understanding, and wisdom concerning the mysteries of God. But whereas in the case of other sciences progress leads to ever new findings, progress in theological understanding occurs within the same dogma, the same meaning, the same pronouncement (DB 1800; DS 3020).

That is why there was no truth for us to understand other than that enunciated by John, 'The Word was made flesh,' and repeated in the statement of Chalcedon that one and the same is both God and man. No sole cause of this union have we found other than that sole act of existence that St Thomas and his followers have always recognized in Christ. Nor have we affirmed the existence of any term required by this constitutive cause other than that secondary, non-accidental act of existence that Aquinas seems to have acknowledged in his *Quaestio disputata de unione Verbi incarnati*. And our only reason for denying that the assumed nature is a person is that it lacks its own proper act of existence.

De Conscientia Humana

74 Antequam de conscientia Christi humana quaeratur, omnino scire oportet et (1) quid sit conscientia, et (2) quid per hoc pronomen 'ego' significari soleat vel possit, et (3) in quasnam causas intrinsecas atque constitutivas hoc ens concretum, nempe, homo sui conscius, resolvatur.

Utrum tamen vera sint quae in hac parte quinta proponantur, et inter philosophos disputatur, et inter theologos qui de conscientia Christi conscripserint, vel existere quaestionem disputabilem haud attenditur.

Quibus perspectis, sic nobis procedendum esse videtur ut in hac parte quinta conscientiam esse experientiam stricte dictam exponatur, in parte vero sexta (sectione prima ad quartam) concludatur quid de conscientia Christi dicendum sit secundum quod conscientia ut experientia concipiatur, denique in sectione quinta (partis sextae) secundum consectaria theologica iudicetur utrum conscientia concipi debeat ut experientia an ut perceptio.

Quod argumentum in favorem conscientiae-experientiae quamvis extrinsecum atque theologicum sit, tamen peremptorium inventum iri credo.

Sectio Prima: Quid Sit Conscientia

75 Conscientia est sui suorumque actuum experientia stricte dicta atque interna.

Experientia dicitur et late et stricte: late, est fere idem ac cognitio vulgaris; stricte, est notitia quaedam praevia atque informis quae ab inquisitione intellectuali praesupponitur et per eam completur.

PART 5

Human Consciousness

---

74 Before we begin our inquiry into the human consciousness of Christ, the following three points should be thoroughly understood: (1) what consciousness is, (2) what is generally meant or can be meant by the pronoun 'I,' and (3) what the intrinsic constitutive causes are into which is resolved this concrete being, namely, a human being conscious of himself or herself.

The truth of what we are proposing in this fifth part is a matter of debate among philosophers, while those theologians who have written about the consciousness of Christ seem hardly aware that a debatable question here even exists.

In view of this it would seem that the best way to proceed is to show in part 5 that consciousness is experience in the strict sense of the word, then in part 6, sections 1 to 4, to draw conclusions concerning the consciousness of Christ in the light of consciousness conceived as experience, and finally in section 5 of part 6 to determine from theological corollaries whether consciousness is to be conceived as experience or as perception.

Our argument in favor of consciousness-as-experience, although drawn from another field, that of theology, nevertheless, we believe, will prove to be quite conclusive.

1 The Nature of Consciousness

75 Consciousness is interior experience of oneself and one's acts, where 'experience' is taken in the strict sense of the word.

'Experience' may be taken in a broad sense or in a strict sense. Broadly speaking it is roughly the same as ordinary knowledge; strictly speaking it is a preliminary unstructured sort of awareness that is presupposed by intellectual inquiry and completed by it.

Inquisitio intellectualis (1) explicite formulatur per quaestiones, Quid sit? Cur ita sit? An sit? Utrum ita sit? sed (2) consistit in illa admiratione intellectuali quam Aristoteles initium duxit omnis scientiae atque philosophiae.

Iam vero inquisitio reflexiva (An sit? Utrum ita sit?) primam intellectus operationem praesupponit in qua quaestionibus (Quid sit? Cur ita sit?) per actus intelligendi et concipiendi respondere conamur. Secus enim deesset obiectum clare et distincte conceptum de quo iudicaremus.

Praeterea, ipsa directa inquisitio (Quid sit? Cur ita sit?) notitiam quandam aliam praesupponit. Secus deesset quod admirati per quaestiones, Quid sit? Cur ita sit? investigaremus.

Existit ergo notitia quaedam et praevia et informis; praevia quidem quia ab inquisitione intellectuali praesupponitur; informis autem quia superflueret inquisitio intellectualis si iam intelligibiliter formata esset. Quam notitiam praeviam atque informem nominamus experientiam stricte dictam.

Quae experientia in externam et internam dividitur. Nam etsi ipsa experientia in se ipsa sit indivisa et quodammodo confusa, tamen inquirendo et intelligendo, reflectendo et diiudicando, ad hanc in ea divisionem agnoscendam pervenimus.

Quae enim externe experimur, tum actu quodam proprio tum per modum obiecti apprehendimus.[1] Tamquam obiecta enim et colores videmus et sonos audimus et sapores gustamus et odores olfacimus et dura et mollia, calida et frigida, gravia et levia, lenia et aspera tangendo sentimus. In quibus omnibus cum nondum inquiratur et intelligatur, concipiatur et iudicetur, non adest nisi notitia illa praevia atque informis quae stricte dicitur experientia.

Quae autem interne experimur, neque actu quodam proprio nobis innotescunt neque per modum obiecti. Eo enim ipso quod colorem video, non solum color ex parte obiecti sed etiam ex parte subiecti innotescunt et videns et videre. Eo ipso quod quidditatem intelligo, non solum quidditas ex parte obiecti sed etiam ex parte subiecti innotescunt et intelligens et intelligere. Eo ipso quod rem esse iudico, non solum esse rei ex parte obiecti sed etiam ex parte subiecti innotescunt

Intellectual inquiry (1) is explicitly formulated by the questions, What is it? Why is it so? Is it? and Is it so? But (2) it consists in that intellectual wonder that Aristotle considered to be the beginning of all knowledge and philosophy.

Reflective inquiry, expressed in the questions, Is it? and Is it so?, presupposes the first operation of the intellect in which we try to answer by acts of under-standing and conceiving the questions, What is it? and Why is it so? Without this prior step we should have no clearly and distinctly conceived object about which to make a judgment.

Again, direct inquiry (What is it? Why is it so?) presupposes in turn awareness of another sort, for without it we should have nothing to wonder about and so inquire into by asking the questions, What is it? and Why is it so?

There is such a thing, therefore, as this preliminary unstructured awareness. It is preliminary in that it is a prerequisite to intellectual inquiry; it is unstructured, because if it were already intelligibly formed, further inquiry would be super-fluous. This preliminary unstructured sort of awareness is what we call experience in the strict sense of the word.

Experience in this sense can be either exterior or interior. Although experience in itself forms a sort of continuous and rather confused whole, yet if we inquire and understand and reflect and judge, we shall readily conclude that this division of experience is valid.

For what we experience exteriorly we apprehend both by some special act and as an object.[1] It is as objects that we see colors, hear sounds, taste flavors, smell odors, and feel things as hard or soft, hot or cold, heavy or light, smooth or rough. In all of these cases, since we have not yet inquired and understood, or formed concepts and judgments, we have only that preliminary unstructured awareness that we have called experience in the strict sense of the term.

What we experience interiorly, however, is known to us neither by some special act nor as an object. In the very act of seeing a color I become aware not only of that color on the side of the object but also, on the side of the subject, of both the one seeing and the act of seeing. In the very act of understanding an intelligibility there becomes known not only that intelligibility on the side of the object but also, on the side of the subject, the one who understands and the act of understanding. In the very act of judging that a certain thing exists there becomes known not only the existence of that thing on the side of the object, but also, on

---

1 [Lonergan uses two distinct Latin expressions, 'per modum obiecti' and 'ex parte obiecti.' The former (used here and in one other place a few lines later) is translated 'as an object,' and the latter (used frequently) 'on the side of the object.' He also uses the expression 'ex parte subiecti,' which is translated 'on the side of the subject.']

et iudicans et iudicare.² Et cum haec notitia, videntis nempe et videndi, intelligentis et intelligendi, iudicantis et iudicandi, et praesupponitur et completur tum inquantum quaeruntur quid sit videns, intelligens, iudicans, et quid sit videre, intelligere, iudicare, tum inquantum de quidditatibus inventis iudicatur, etiam haec notitia est praevia illa atque informis quae stricte dicitur experientia.

Quibus perspectis, conscientiae definitio explicata est. Distincta enim sunt (1) experientia late et stricte dicta et (2) experientia stricte dicta tum externa tum interna. Et cum experientia interna sit sui suorumque actuum, omnes definitionis partes elucidantur. Qua de causa et ulterius concludi possunt sequentia.

76 *Primo*, conscientia non est quaelibet notitia sui suorumque actuum, sed ea tantum quae praevia atque informis est. V.g., per primam intellectus operationem oritur notitia sui inquantum intelligitur et definitur quid sit homo; et per eandem operationem oritur notitia suorum actuum inquantum intelligitur et definitur quid sit videre, intelligere, iudicare, velle, appetere, timere, delectare, dolere, etc. Similiter per alteram intellectus operationem oritur notitia sui suorumque actuum inquantum aliquis iudicat se esse hominem, se videre, se intelligere, etc. Quae tamen omnia cum per inquisitionem intellectualem innotescant, ad conscientiam minime pertinent. Nam conscientia est praevia ad inquisitionem intellectualem et, sicut experientia externa, per inquisitionem intellectualem complenda.

Deinde, quod per conscientiam innotescit, non sub ratione veri et entis, neque sub ratione intelligibilis et quidditatis, sed sub ratione experti attingitur.³

the side of the subject, the one who judges and the act of judging.² And when this awareness of the one seeing and of the act of seeing, of the one understanding and of the act of understanding, of the one judging and of the act of judging is presupposed and completed, first, by asking *what* is one who sees, understands, judges, and also *what* it is to see, to understand, to judge, and then by making a *judgment* about what one has understood through this inquiry, this awareness also is that preliminary unstructured awareness that we have defined as experience in the strict sense.

With all this thoroughly understood, the definition of consciousness becomes clear. We have made a distinction (1) between experience in the broad sense and experience in the strict sense, and (2) between exterior and interior experience taken in the strict sense. Since interior experience is experience of oneself and one's acts, all the elements of the definition have been explained. Consequently, we may proceed to draw the following conclusions.

76 *First,* consciousness is not just any awareness of oneself and one's acts, but only that awareness that is preliminary and unstructured. For example, by way of the first operation of the intellect you acquire an awareness of yourself when you grasp and define what a human being is; and through the same operation of the intellect you come to an awareness of your own acts when you grasp and define what is meant by seeing, understanding, judging, willing, desiring, fearing, enjoying, grieving, and so on. Similarly, through the second operation of the intellect you come to an awareness of yourself and your acts in making the judgment that you are a human being, that you see, that you understand, and so forth. All this knowledge comes through intellectual inquiry, and so is not at all what we have referred to as consciousness. For consciousness is prior to intellectual inquiry and, like exterior experience, needs to be completed by it.

Second, what is known by consciousness is attained not under the formality of the true and of being, nor under the formality of the intelligible and definable, but under the formality of the experienced.³

2 [The verb 'innotescunt' is used in the three sentences that are translated beginning 'In the very act.' In reference to the objects of understanding and judgment, it has a fuller sense of 'there becomes known' than in connection with the object of seeing and with the subject of all three acts. In these latter cases it means 'there is experienced' or 'I become aware of.' The experience is exterior in seeing color, but interior in attaining the subject, whether of seeing or of understanding or of judging. This interior experience or awareness is precisely what Lonergan means by 'consciousness.']

3 [Here too, as with 'ex parte obiecti' and 'ex parte subiecti,' regularly recurring phrases are translated uniformly throughout: 'sub ratione experti' as 'under the

Non sub ratione veri et entis: quod enim sic attingitur per secundam intellectus operationem innotescit inquantum quis quaerit an res sit vel utrum ita sit, et evidentiam ponderat, et ad iudicium verum pervenit, et per verum tamquam medium-in-quo ens attingit.

Non sub ratione intelligibilis et quidditatis: quod enim sic attingitur per primam intellectus operationem innotescit inquantum quis quaerit quid sit hoc vel cur ita sit, et intelligibile in sensibilibus perspicit, et perspectam intelligibilitatem definiendo concipit.

Sub ratione experti attingitur: ideo enim sive externa sive interna experimur ut inquirentes intelligamus et reflectentes iudicemus; quare expertum est id (1) quod praerequiritur ut inquisitio intellectualis oriri possit et (2) quod subsequentem inquisitionem intellectualem postulat atque exigit ut cognitio hominis fiat vere et proprie cognitio humana, nempe, intellectualis et rationalis.

Tertio, experientia stricte dicta attingit ens sed non sub ratione entis, et verum sed non sub ratione veri, et intelligibile sed non sub ratione intelligibilis, et quidditatem habens sed non sub ratione quidditatis; sub ratione experti enim attingit vere id quod est ens et intelligibile et quidditatem habens.

V.g., qui videt colorem, non videt non-ens sed ens videt; tamen ens quod videt, non sub ratione entis sed sub ratione coloris videt; non enim oculis cernendo sed rationaliter iudicando ad esse (unde ens nominatur) pertingitur. Pariter qui est conscius sui suorumque actuum, non est conscius non-entis sed est conscius entis (sui) et entium (actuum suorum); et tamen ens et entia quorum est conscius non sub ratione entis sed sub ratione experti attinguntur.

Iterum, visio coloris est vera, cum inter colorem et visionem intercedat adaequatio in qua ratio veritatis consistit; non tamen ipsa haec adaequatio oculis cernitur cum veritas formaliter in solo iudicio intellectus inveniatur; et ideo quamvis vere colorem videat, non tamen sub ratione veri sed tantummodo per actum exercitum vere videt. Pariter, interna experientia sui suorumque actuum et vera est et tamen neque ipsum subiectum neque actus subiecti sub ratione veri attingit.

Not under the formality of the true and of being: for what is attained in this way is known through the second operation of the intellect inasmuch as one asks whether something is or is so, then weighs the evidence and makes a true judgment, and so through the true, as a medium-in-which, arrives at being.

Not under the formality of the intelligible and the definable: for what is attained in this way is known through the first operation of the intellect inasmuch as one asks what this is or why it is so, grasps the intelligible in the sensible, and in defining conceives the intelligibility one has grasped.

But under the formality of the experienced: for we experience external or internal data in order that through inquiry we might understand and through reflection we might judge. The experienced, therefore, (1) is a prerequisite for the emergence of intellectual inquiry, and (2) demands and requires subsequent intellectual inquiry if our knowledge is to be truly and properly human, that is, intellectual and rational.

Third, experience in the strict sense attains being, but not under the formality of being; it attains the true, but not under the formality of the true; it attains the intelligible, but not under the formality of the intelligible; and it attains the definable, but not under the formality of the definable. Rather, under the formality of the experienced it truly attains being, the intelligible, and the definable.

Some examples will help here. If you see a color, you see not non-being but being; but the being that you see, you see not under the formality of being, but under the formality of color; for being, or existence (*esse*, from which we get the noun 'being,' *ens*), is not found by taking a look with one's eyes, but by making a rational judgment. By the same token, if you are conscious of yourself and your acts, you are conscious not of non-being but of a being (yourself) and of beings (your acts); but the being and beings of which you are conscious are attained not under the formality of being but precisely under the formality of the experienced.

Again, the seeing of a color is true, since between color and vision there is that correspondence in which truth essentially consists. But this correspondence is not discerned by one's eye, since truth is formally found only in the intellectual act of judging. Hence, although the eye truly sees color, it does not see it under the formality of the true, but it truly sees it only through the exercise of its act of seeing. Likewise, the interior experience one has of oneself and one's acts is a true experience, and yet it does not attain the subject of these acts or the acts of the subject under the formality of the true.

---

formality of the experienced,' 'sub ratione intelligibilis et quidditatis' as 'under the formality of the intelligible and definable,' and 'sub ratione veri et entis' as 'under the formality of the true and of being.']

Iterum, qui videt colorem, non videt inintelligibile sed intelligibile videt; aliud tamen est colorem videre et aliud est colorem intelligere; et ideo qui colorem videt, non sub ratione intelligibilis sed sub ratione coloris intelligibile attingit. Pariter, qui est sui conscius vel suorum actuum, non rei inintelligibilis conscius est sed rei intelligibilis; at aliud est esse conscium subiecti vel conscium actuum, et longe aliud est intelligere subiectum vel actus subiecti; et ideo quamvis per conscientiam intelligibile attingatur, tamen non sub ratione intelligibilis sed sub ratione experti attingitur.

Denique tandem sicut aliud est videre colorem et aliud colorem definire, ita aliud est esse conscium sui suorumque actuum et aliud est definire se suosque actus. Nihilomus color qui videtur definibilitatem seu quidditatem habet; et similiter subiectum actusque quorum quis est conscius definibilitatem et quodammodo quidditatem habent. Et ideo sicut per visionem ita etiam per conscientiam attingitur quod quidditatem habet, non sub ratione quidditatis sed sub ratione vel coloris vel experti.

Quarto, alia ergo est conscientia et alia est introspectio sive vulgaris sive technica et scientifica.

Conscientia enim est praevia atque informis quaedam notitia et sui et suorum actuum. Introspectio autem est consequens inquisitio intellectualis in qua sub ratione intelligibilis, quidditatis, veri, et entis attingitur id quod per conscientiam sub ratione experti attactum est. Nec quicquam refert utrum consequens haec inquisitio intellectualis modo technico et scientifico peragatur an ea sit quae in quolibet homine fieri possit et soleat. Pariter enim etsi diversimode ultra conscientiam in subsequentem inquisitionem intellectualem progrediuntur tum technica et scientifica introspectio tum communis et vulgaris reflexio.

Quinto, alia in nobis conscie, alia autem inconscie peraguntur. Conscie enim fieri solent apprehensiones et appetitiones tum in parte sensitiva tum in parte intellectuali. Inconscie autem fiunt cellularum metabolismus, sanguinis circulatio, capillorum crescentia, aliaque eiusmodi.

Sexto, pro qualitate operationis distinguuntur conscientia empirica, intellectualis, rationalis, moralis. Inquantum enim quis secundum partem sensitivam apprehendit et appetit, sui suorumque actuum est empirice conscius. Inquantum autem inquirit, intelligit, definit, cum iam qua intelligens operetur, sui suorumque actuum est intellectualiter conscius. Inquantum vero reflectitur, evidentiam scrutatur atque ponderat, et secundum evidentiam iudicat, cum iam secundum suam rationalitatem operetur, rationaliter dicitur conscius. Inquantum denique ultra

Further, if you see a color, you do not see something that is unintelligible, but something that is intelligible. But it is one thing to see a color and another thing to understand color. To see a color is to attain something intelligible, not under the formality of the intelligible but under the formality of color. Similarly, if you are conscious of yourself or your acts, you are conscious not of something unintelligible but of something intelligible. But to be conscious of the subject or of one's acts is not at all the same as understanding the subject or the acts of the subject. Hence, although consciousness attains what is intelligible, it does so not under the formality of the intelligible but under the formality of the experienced.

Finally, as it is one thing to see color and another to define it, so it is one thing to be conscious of yourself and your acts and another to define yourself and your acts. Yet the color that is seen is definable, that is, possesses 'quiddity'; similarly, the subject and the acts of which you are conscious also possess definability, or quiddity. And so, like vision, consciousness also attains that which is definable, not, however, under the formality of the definable, but under the formality of color or of the experienced.

Fourth, it follows that consciousness is not the same as introspection, either in the ordinary sense of that word or in the technical scientific sense.

Consciousness, as we have said, is a preliminary unstructured awareness of oneself and one's acts. Introspection, on the other hand, is a further intellectual inquiry in which what consciousness has attained under the formality of the experienced is attained under the formality of the intelligible, of the definable, of the true, and of being. It makes no difference whether this further intellectual inquiry is carried out in a technical and scientific manner or is something that can be, and commonly is, done by anyone. Both the technical and scientific introspection and the common everyday reflection go beyond consciousness to further intellectual inquiry, though in different ways.

Fifth, some processes go on within us consciously, others unconsciously. Apprehensions and appetitive movements at both the sensitive and the intellectual levels are generally conscious, while the metabolism of our cells, the circulation of blood, the growth of hair, and the like, occur unconsciously.

Sixth, consciousness is divided into empirical, intellectual, rational, and moral according to the quality of its operations. In sense perception and sensitive appetition, consciousness of oneself and one's acts is empirical. When you engage in intellectual inquiry and in acts of understanding and defining, operating as an intelligent person, you are intellectually conscious of yourself and your acts. When you reflect, examine and weigh the evidence, and judge in accord with the evidence, operating by way of your rationality, you are said to be rationally conscious. When, finally, you go beyond truth and being to consider a good that

verum et ens in considerationem boni intelligibilis et quodammodo obligantis procedit, cum iam secundum suam moralitatem agat, moraliter conscius dicitur.

Ubi tamen illud non est praetermittendum quod subiectum eiusque actus sicut per conscientiam empiricam ita etiam per conscientiam intellectualem et rationalem et moralem nisi sub ratione experti non attinguntur. Nisi enim quis per prius intellectualiter conscius redditur, nondum inquirere vel intelligere vel definire potest quid sit inquirens et inquirere, intelligens et intelligere, definiens et definire. Similiter, nisi quis per prius rationaliter conscius redditur, nondum reflecti et ponderare et iudicare potest utrum ipse sit rationalis.

Septimo, pro statu subiecti distinguuntur conscientia somniantis et vigilantis, sani et insanientis, etc.

Octavo, pro gradu attentionis distinguuntur gradus claritatis et distinctionis in ipsa conscientia. Ita qui videt, non inconscius sui per videre inconscium videt; tamen communiter homines vident quin ullatenus ad videre suum vel ad se videntes attendant. At si quis hoc nomen 'videre' pronuntiat, si quid 'videre' significet intelligit, si utrum ipse videat quaerit, iam per multos et diversos actus in unum directos convertitur attentio subiecti videntis in se ipsum atque suum videre.

Attamen aliud est conscium esse sui suorumque actuum, et aliud est attendere ad se suosque actus. Nisi enim per prius essemus conscii, frustra, per attentionem magis concentratam, clariorem atque distinctiorem conscientiam reddere conaremur. Et ideo graviter errare ii videntur qui conscientiam ponant non in praevia illa atque informi notitia sed in subsequente attentionis directione atque concentratione.

Nono, quamvis homo sit magis sui conscius quam suorum actuum, non tamen est conscius sui nisi secundum actus suos.

Homo est magis concius sui quam suorum actuum. Nam longe facilius illud unum attingimus quod videt et audit et tangit et sentit et admiratur et inquirit et intelligit et definit et reflectitur et evidentiam scrutatur et iudicat et appetit et vult, etc., etc., quam singulos hos actus inter se distinguimus et in se sub ratione experti attingimus.

Homo non est conscius sui nisi secundum suos actus. Non enim datur moralis sui conscientia nisi inquantum quis de bono intelligibili et quodammodo obligante considerat, deliberat, iudicat, eligit. Non datur rationalis sui conscientia nisi

is intelligible and in some way a matter of obligation, exercising the moral aspect of your being, you are said to be morally conscious.

Here, however, one must not overlook the fact that as through empirical consciousness, so also through intellectual, rational, and moral consciousness a subject and a subject's acts are attained only under the formality of the experienced. For unless you are first intellectually conscious, you cannot ask or understand or define what it is to be a questioner and to inquire, or to be intelligent and to understand, or to be one who defines and to define. So also, unless you are first rationally conscious, you cannot reflect and weigh the evidence and judge whether you are rational.

Seventh, consciousness can be distinguished as being that of someone dreaming or awake, sane or insane, and so on, according to the condition or state of mind of the subject.

Eighth, according to one's attention level, consciousness can have various degrees of clarity and distinctness. For example, when you are seeing something, you are doing so neither as unconscious of yourself nor by an act of seeing that is unconscious; nevertheless, people usually see without adverting at all to their act of seeing or to themselves as seeing. Yet if you utter the word 'see,' understand the meaning of this word, and ask whether you yourself see, then by focusing many different acts on this one point you, as a seeing subject, turn your attention to yourself and your act of seeing.

To be conscious of oneself and one's acts, however, is not the same as attending to oneself and one's acts. If we were not first conscious, it would be futile for us to try to render our consciousness more clear and distinct by concentrating our attention. That is why it is a serious error to think that consciousness consists not in that preliminary unstructured awareness that we have spoken of, but rather in the subsequent focusing and concentrating of attention.

Ninth, although we are more conscious of ourselves than of our acts, nevertheless we are conscious of ourselves by reason of our acts.

We are more conscious of ourselves than of our acts, since it is much easier for us to attain the one who sees and hears and touches and feels and wonders and inquires and understands and defines and reflects and examines evidence and judges and desires and wills, and so forth and so on, than to distinguish all these acts from one another and to attain them in themselves under the formality of the experienced.

However, we are not conscious of ourselves except by way of our acts. Moral consciousness of oneself is had only inasmuch as one considers some good that is intelligible and in some way obligatory, deliberates about it, judges, and makes a choice. Rational consciousness of oneself is had only inasmuch as one inquires

inquantum quis quaerit an res sit vel utrum ita sit et evidentiam ponderat et secundum evidentiam sententiam fert suam. Non datur intellectualis sui conscientia nisi inquantum quis admiratur et inquirit et intelligit et perspectam intelligibilitatem definiendo concipit. Non datur empirica sui conscientia nisi inquantum quis secundum partem suam sensitivam operatur. Unde hominem illum simpliciter inconscium dicimus qui per laesionem organorum vel per altissimum somnum ab omni operatione sensitiva et intellectuali cessat.

Sectio Secunda: Quid Sit 'Ego'

Considerari potest sensus huius nominis 'ego,' vel secundum actum significandi, vel secundum id quod significatur, vel secundum fontes significandi.

77 Secundum actum significandi distinguuntur (1) verbum exterius, (2) verbum interius incomplexum, et (3) verbum interius complexum.

(1) Secundum verbum exterius, 'ego' est ipsum vocabulum sive ore prolatum sive scriptis consignatum sive imaginatione repraesentatum.

(2) Secundum verbum interius incomplexum, 'ego' est id quod intenditur quando 'ego' concipitur, definitur, hypothetice explicatur.

Cum verbum ideo sit incomplexum quod a vero et falso, ab esse et non esse praescindat, tot sunt 'ego' secundum verbum interius incomplexum quot sunt sententiae vel philosophicae vel psychologicae vel vulgares secundum quas respondetur ad quaestionem, quid sit 'ego.'

(3) Secundum verbum interius complexum, 'ego' est id quod intenditur quando secundum aliquam conceptionem, definitionem, hypothesin, theoriam 'ego' esse affirmatur.

Inquantum verbum interius complexum a vero et falso, ab esse et non esse, non praescindit, hoc 'ego' unicum est neque dantur diversitates nisi secundum conceptiones plus minus evolutas atque adaequatas. Inquantum autem homines sunt fallibiles, hoc 'ego' multiplex videri potest cum alii aliter iudicent et unusquisque in sua sententia se certum credat.

78 Deinde considerandum est 'ego' secundum id quod significatur et, cum id quod significatur diversificetur secundum eum qui significat, distinguendum videtur 'ego' significatum secundum usum communem, secundum usum psychologorum, et secundum usum philosophorum.

(4) Secundum usum communem id quod significatur per 'ego' est 'hic homo qui sum.' Quod etiam magis explicite declarari potest; cum enim 'hic homo qui sum' sit ultimum

whether some thing exists or is so, weighs the evidence concerning it, and makes a judgment on the basis of the evidence. Intellectual consciousness of oneself is had only inasmuch as one is wondering about something, inquires into it, grasps its intelligibility, and by defining expresses this understanding conceptually. Empirical consciousness of oneself is had only inasmuch as one is operating by way of one's sensitive nature. And so we say that someone is simply unconscious when because of some physical trauma or because one is in a deep sleep all sensitive and intellectual activity is suspended.

2 The Word 'I'

The meaning of this pronoun 'I' can be approached in various ways: according to the act of meaning, or according to what is meant, or according to the sources of meaning.

77 In considering 'I' according to the act of meaning, we distinguish three things: the outer word, the simple inner word, and the compound inner word.

(1) As an outer word, the pronoun 'I' is the word itself as either uttered orally or written or represented in the imagination.

(2) As a simple inner word, 'I' is that which is intended when 'I' is conceived, defined, or hypothetically explained.

Since an inner word is simple because it prescinds from truth and falsity, from existence and non-existence, there are as many simple inner 'I's' as there are opinions among philosophers, psychologists, or ordinary people about the answer to the question, What do you mean by 'I'?

(3) As a compound inner word, 'I' is what is intended when 'I' is affirmed to be in accordance with some conception or definition or hypothesis or theory.

Since a compound inner word does not prescind from truth and falsity, from existence and non-existence, this 'I' is unique, and all variations from it result from more or less adequate and more or less developed conceptions. To err is human, and so this 'I' might seem to have multiple meanings inasmuch as people have different opinions and all are sure they are right.

78 Next, let us consider what is meant by 'I.' The meanings given to it are different depending on who gives them, and so we have to distinguish between the meaning of 'I' in common usage, in psychological parlance, and in philosophical discourse.

(4) In common usage, 'I' means 'this one who I am.' To put it more explicitly, since 'this one who I am' is the ultimate subject of attribution, that is, that to which

subiectum attributionis seu id cui attribuo omnia quae mihi attribuo, 'ego' quod significatur est idem quod ultimum subiectum attributionis et ideo est idem quod 'persona'
inquantum persona vulgo definiri solet ultimum subiectum attributionis.

(5) Secundum usum psychologorum id quod significatur per 'ego' variatur secundum
scholas, theorias, hypotheses.

In genere, dici potest quod 'ego' connotat quandam unitatem intelligibilem in eventibus
interne expertis perspectam, ubi tamen eventus generatim sunt sensitivi et unitas quae in
eventibus intellectu conspicitur saepe non est nisi unitas ordinis.[4]

(6) Secundum usum philosophorum id quod significatur per 'ego' maximas patitur differentias neque tantum secundum diversitatem scholarum sed etiam secundum gradum
ex-sistentiae ab hoc vel illo philosophante adeptum qui opiniones talis scholae se sequi
credit et profitetur quin tamen eas accurate intelligat.

Inter scholasticos, ut caetera omittamus, communiter id quod significatur per 'ego' est
id quod significatur secundum usum communem. Ita ergo 'ego' est 'hic homo qui sum,'
et ultimum subiectum attributionis, et hoc sensu persona.

Attamen sub hac uniformitate latent differentiae sat graves quae in quaestionibus Christologicis plus minus clare statim appareant.

Quamvis enim idem agnoscatur 'ego' quod 'hic homo existens,' nihilominus alia ab aliis
analysis metaphysica 'huius hominis existentis' defenditur.

Dicimus quidem nos quod 'hic homo existens' est 'ens,' 'id quod est,' 'subsistens,' 'persona,' 'principium quod operationum,' 'ego ontologicum.'

Ulterius, dicimus 'ens-quod' non esse idem adaequate quod essentia humana individua
et concreta, neque idem adaequate quod natura humana individua et concreta.

Agnoscimus tamen alios aliter sentire quia, uti credimus, reale qua reale eis videtur
non id quod mediante vero iudicio innotescit sed id quod ante iudicium per nescio quem
intuitum conspicitur. Ubi enim iis evidentia videtur ipsa realitas evidenter perspecta quam

I attribute whatever I attribute to myself, in this common usage 'I' is the same
as the ultimate subject of attribution and therefore is the same as 'person,' where
'person' is taken in a non-technical sense as the ultimate subject of attribution.

(5) The meaning of 'I' among psychologists varies according to various schools
and theories and hypotheses.

In general, the psychologists' 'I,' *ego*, can be said to connote a certain intelligible unity discerned among interiorly experienced events. Such events, however,
usually belong to the sensitive part of a person, and the unity seen by the intellect
in these events is very often no more than the unity of order.[4]

(6) Among philosophers there is the greatest divergence of opinion about 'I,' not
only because of the different schools of philosophy but also because of the level of
Existenz achieved by various devotees of philosophy who believe and declare that
they are following the opinions of a particular school without, however, having
an accurate understanding of them.

To take just the case among Scholastic philosophers, the pronoun 'I' is commonly understood in the sense it has in common usage. Accordingly, 'I' means
'this one who I am,' the ultimate subject of attribution, and in this sense, 'person.'

But underneath this uniformity of opinion lurk serious differences that immediately surface more or less clearly when dealing with certain questions in Christology.

Even though 'I' is acknowledged to be the same as 'this existing human being,' nevertheless different philosophers espouse divergent metaphysical analyses
of 'this existing human being.'

Our position is that 'this existing human being' is a 'being,' 'that which is,' a
'subsistent,' a 'person,' a 'principle that operates,' an 'ontological I.'

Furthermore, we maintain that a 'being which' (*ens quod*) is not totally identical
with an individual concrete human essence or with an individual concrete human
nature.

We recognize that others have different opinions. The reason for this difference, we believe, lies in the fact that for them the real as real is not that which
is known by the mediation of a true judgment, but rather that which prior to
judgment is discerned in some sort of intuition. Whereas for them evidence seems
to be the reality itself as manifestly perceived that a judgment merely enunciates,

---

4 See the distinctions between the psychological and the deep 'I' and 'me' that are
  mentioned by Paul Galtier, *L'Unité du Christ* (Paris: Beauchesne, 1939) 339-44.
  (Latin: Consuli possunt distinctions inter 'ego' et 'me' psychologica et profunda
  quas narrat P. Galtier, *L'Unité du Christ*, 1939, pp. 339 ss.) [See below, p. 261, where
  there are discussed Galtier's empirical 'I' and empirical 'me,' and then his deep 'I'
  and deep 'me.']

iudicium tantummodo enuntiat, nobis evidentia est unde vere affirmetur aliquid esse, neque reale qua reale (seu ens) innotescit nisi mediante hoc 'esse' vere affirmato.

79 Denique considerandum est 'ego' secundum fontes significandi internos, nam secundum hos fontes aliud et aliud connotant 'ego' et 'hic homo existens.' Qui enim dicit quis sit 'hic homo existens' parentes nominat et ortus locum et familiares et opera praeclare facta. Qui autem dicit quis sit hic 'ego' totam experientiam externam missam facit et unice ex interna experientia loquitur. Fontes ergo de quibus hauritur ut 'ego' significetur sunt, brevi quodam vocabulo, conscientia. Neque vel hic a diversitate philosophorum opinantium effugere possumus, cum ipsa conscientiae structura aliter ab aliis concipiatur. Alii enim conscientiam ducunt perceptionem quandam in qua 'ego' aliaque interna ex parte obiecti directe et immediate conspiciuntur. Alii autem conscientiam ducunt experientiam stricte sumptam uti superius determinatum est.

(7) Qui conscientiam perceptionem ducunt reapse talem perceptionem non habent sed suam experientiam internam et intelligunt et concipiunt et etiam iudicant ut id, quod ex parte subiecti datur, ex parte obiecti sistatur et tamquam 'perceptum' habeatur. Qua de causa, tot tantasque patiuntur difficultates quandocumque determinare volunt utrum hoc vel illud directe et immediate a conscientia percipiatur an forte intercesserit quoddam ratiocinium. Verbi gratia, utrum per conscientiam percipiatur tantummodo 'ego' phaenomenale an etiam 'ego' profundum; utrum 'ego' profundum sit idem quod natura, substantia, anima, persona, etc.

(8) Qui conscientiam experientiam ducunt omnem talem quaestionem superfluam et fere absurdam habent. Conscientia non percipit quidquam sive directe sive indirecte sive immediate sive mediate, nam quod per conscientiam innotescit non ex parte obiecti sistitur ut 'perceptum' dici possit sed ex parte subiecti se habet, neque tantum ex parte subiecti percipientis sed etiam ex parte subiecti vel somniantis vel vigilantis, vel apprehendentis vel appetentis, vel sensitive operantis vel intellective.

Praeterea, haec experientia non describitur sed indicatur. Omnis enim descriptio et inquisitionem intellectualem supponit et id quod intelligendo et concipiendo innotescit includit. Indicatur autem conscientia-experientia inquantum methodus describitur secundum quam reditur ex experientia, quae intelligendo et

for us evidence is that which grounds the affirmation that some thing exists, and we do not know the real as real (that is, we do not know being) save through the true affirmation of this 'act of existence.'

79   Finally, we must consider the meaning of 'I' according to interior sources of meaning, for on the basis of these sources 'I' and 'this existing human being' have different connotations. To say who 'this existing human being' is, we refer to someone's parents, birthplace, relationships, and achievements. But in telling you who this 'I' is, we omit all references to exterior experience and speak only from inner experience. Thus the source from which 'I' derives its meaning is, in one word, consciousness. And even here we cannot escape from the diversity of opinion among philosophers, since they conceive the structure of consciousness in different ways. Some take consciousness to be a type of perception in which the 'I' and other interior data are directly and immediately perceived on the side of the object, while others understand consciousness as experience in the strict sense, as we have defined it above.

(7) Those who understand consciousness as a type of perception do not in fact have such a perception. Rather, they understand, conceive, and even judge their interior experience in such a way as to take what is a datum on the side of the subject and transpose it to the side of the object, and so it becomes a 'percept.' As a result, they run into many enormous difficulties whenever they try to determine whether this or that is directly and immediately perceived by consciousness or whether some process of reasoning may have intervened. An example of this would be in determining whether consciousness perceives only the phenomenal 'I' or the deep 'I' as well, and whether this deep 'I' is the same as nature, substance, soul, person, and the like.

(8) Those who understand consciousness as experience consider such questions superfluous, and even rather absurd. Consciousness does not perceive anything, either directly or indirectly, mediately or immediately; for what is known through consciousness is not found on the side of the object, so as to be referred to as a 'percept,' but on the side of the subject, and not only on the side of a perceiving subject but also on the side of a dreaming or waking subject, or of a knowing or desiring subject, or of a subject operating sensitively or intellectually.

Moreover, this type of experience is not described but only indicated. Description supposes intellectual inquiry and includes what is known through insight and conception. But consciousness-as-experience is indicated inasmuch as a method is described by way of which one can go from an experience structured by understanding and conception back to that experience itself in the strict sense.

concipiendo formata est, ad ipsam experientiam stricte dictam; neque conscientia est methodus redeundi vel ipse reditus sed id ad quod reditur.

Est autem haec experientia (a) id quod habetur sine ulla inquisitione psychologica vel philosophica, (b) materia in qua perspiciuntur unitates intelligibiles atque relationes sive a psychologicis sive a philosophis, (c) evidentia materialis propter quam conceptiones sive vulgares sive psychologicae sive philosophicae dici possunt verae.

80 Quibus perspectis, brevia quaedam statuimus theoremata.

Theorema I

Ad sententias Christologicas determinandas maxime interest utrum quis supponat conscientiam esse perceptionem vel experientiam stricte dictam.

Qui enim conscientiam perceptionem supponit, quaerit utrum natura assumpta, humanitas assumpta, anima huius hominis, conscientia Christi humana perceperit divinam personam. Sistitur nempe ex parte subiecti aliquid creatum et quaeritur utrum ex parte obiecti persona divina innotescat.

Qui autem conscientiam experientiam supponit, quaerit utrum persona divina in humana natura subsistens conscie an inconscie videat, audiat, delectetur, patiatur, intelligat, iudicet, velit, eligat, appetat. Sistitur nempe ex parte subiecti persona divina; indifferens prorsus habetur quod ex parte obiecti ponatur; et unice quaeritur utrum subiectum experiatur in operationibus psychologicis eliciendis.

Quam oppositionem radicalem in sectione quinta partis sextae, 'Opinionum Dialectica,' plenius exponemus. In aliis vero sectionibus quae hanc praecedunt, ne quaestio nimis complexa evadat, auctorum opiniones omittemus et conscientiam esse experientiam supponemus.

Theorema II

Quemadmodum subiectum seu 'ego' multipliciter et tamen cohaerenter dicatur.
    Quinque qui sequuntur sensus distinguuntur:
    (a) hic homo existens,
    (b) hic homo existens et psychologice operans,
    (c) hic homo existens et psychologice operans, qua ex parte subiecti et sub ratione experti innotescens,

Consciousness, however, is not that method of returning nor the return itself, but that to which one returns.

This experience, then, is (a) what is had without any psychological or philosophical inquiry, (b) the material in which intelligible unities and relationships are grasped whether by psychologists or by philosophers, and (c) the material evidence by reason of which either ordinary or psychological or philosophical concepts can be said to be true.

80 We are now in a position to state some brief theorems.

Theorem I

It is of the utmost importance in Christology whether one considers consciousness to be perception or experience strictly so called.

On the supposition that consciousness is perception, the question arises whether the assumed nature, the assumed humanity, the soul of this man, the human consciousness of Christ, perceived the divine person. In other words, something created is placed on the side of the subject, and the question is asked whether a divine person comes to be known on the side of the object.

On the supposition, however, that consciousness is experience, the question is whether it is consciously or unconsciously that a divine person subsisting in a human nature sees, hears, enjoys, suffers, understands, judges, wills, chooses, desires. That is, a divine person is placed on the side of the subject, and it is quite irrelevant what is given on the side of the object. The question is simply and solely whether a subject in eliciting psychological operations is experiencing.

We shall explore more fully this radical opposition in section 5 of part 6, 'The Dialectic of Opinions.' In the sections preceding it, however, to avoid overly complicating the question, we shall omit the opinions of other authors and take consciousness to be experience.

Theorem II

How the subject, or 'I,' has many different yet coherent meanings.

We may distinguish the following five meanings:

(a) this existing human being;

(b) this human being existing and operating psychologically;

(c) this human being existing and operating psychologically, considered as known on the side of the subject and under the formality of the experienced;

(d) hic homo existens et psychologice operans, qua ex parte obiecti et sub ratione intelligibilis innotescens,

(e) hic homo existens et psychologice operans, qua ex parte obiecti et sub ratione veri et entis innotescens.

Theorema in eo est quod perspicitur quemadmodum hi quinque et inter se conveniant et inter se differant. Quod theorema cum multis constet partibus, per adnotationes infra numeratas declarabimus.

(i) Alterum (b) super primum (a) addit 'psychologice operans.'

Illud intendimus esse 'psychologice operans' quod vel sensitive vel etiam intellective sive apprehendit sive appetit.

Cum in omni tali operatione habeatur experientia stricte dicta atque interna, id quod ita additur est conscientia. Unde definiri possunt:

Subiectum ontologicum vel *'ego' ontologicum* est hic homo existens.

Subiectum psychologicum vel *'ego' psychologicum* est hic homo existens et psychologice operans.

(ii) Tertium (c), quartum (d), et quintum (e) super alterum (b) addunt reduplicationem, 'qua sub tali ratione innotescens.'

Unde brevitatis causa poni possunt definitiones:

Subiectum seu *'ego' qua conscium* est hic homo existens et psychologice operans qua ex parte subiecti et sub ratione experti innotescens.

Subiectum seu *'ego' qua conceptum* est hic homo existens et psychologice operans qua ex parte obiecti et sub ratione intelligibilis seu quidditatis innotescens.

Subiectum seu *'ego' qua affirmatum* est hic homo existens et psychologice operans qua ex parte obiecti et sub ratione veri et entis innotescens.

(iii) Differunt subiectum psychologicum et subiectum qua conscium sola reduplicatione.

Scilicet, nemo est conscius nisi psychologice operatur. Et nemo qui psychologice operatur est inconscius quamvis generatim ad se sui conscium non advertat.

(iv) Si de eodem materialiter subiecto agitur, differunt subiectum qua conscium, qua conceptum, et qua affirmatum sicut tres gressus in eadem cognitione eiusdem rei.

Nam quod intelligimus et concipimus est id ipsum quod experimur, cum in ipsis quae experimur intelligibiles unitates atque relationes inspiciamus.

(d) this human being existing and operating psychologically, considered as known on the side of the object and under the formality of the intelligible;

(e) this human being existing and operating psychologically, considered as known on the side of the object and under the formality of the true and of being.

The theorem consists in grasping how these five meanings are coherent with one another and how they differ from one another. The several parts of this theorem will be indicated by the nine numbered sections below.

(1) Meaning (b) adds to (a) the words 'operating psychologically.'

By 'operating psychologically' we refer to cognitive and appetitive operations both sensitive and intellectual.

Since in every operation of this sort there is had interior experience in the strict sense of the word, what is added is consciousness. Hence the following definitions:

The *ontological subject* or *ontological 'I'* is this existing human being.

The *psychological subject* or *psychological 'I'* is this existing human being operating psychologically.

(2) Meanings (c), (d), and (e) each reduplicate (b), by adding 'considered as known under such-and-such a formality.'

Thus, for the sake of brevity we may formulate the following definitions.

The *subject* or the *'I' as conscious* is this existing human being operating psychologically, considered as known on the side of the subject and under the formality of the experienced.

The *subject* or the *'I' as conceived* is this existing human being operating psychologically, considered as known on the side of the object and under the formality of the intelligible and the definable.

The *subject* or the *'I' as affirmed* is this existing human being operating psychologically, considered as known on the side of the object and under the formality of the true and of being.

(3) The only difference between a psychological subject and a subject as conscious is in the reduplication.

That is to say, no one is conscious unless operating psychologically; and no one operating psychologically is unconscious even though one generally does not advert to oneself as conscious of oneself.

(4) Although we are dealing here with a subject that is materially one and the same, still when we speak of the subject as conscious, as conceived, and as affirmed, we are referring to three different levels of the same knowledge of the same reality.

For what we understand and conceive is precisely what we experience, since we discern, so to speak, intelligible unities and relationships in the data of experience.

Praeterea, quod reflectentes et iudicantes affirmamus est id ipsum quod experti intel-ligimus et concipimus, cum ideo rationaliter affirmemus quia ipsa experta sunt in quibus verificatur quod intelligimus et concipimus.

Neque conceptio sine iudicio est cognitio humana proprie dicta, et multo minus est pura experientia sine intelligenti conceptione et sine iudicio. Sola conceptio non est cognitio quia, verbi gratia, centauros quidem concipimus quin vere et proprie eos cognoscamus. Pura experientia non est cognitio cum in pura experientia desint non solum omnes dis-tinctiones, quae per iudicia comparativa et negativa innotescunt, sed etiam omnis proxima distinguendi possibilitas, quae in eo consistit quod quaedam concipimus et inter se com-paramus.

Brevi, idem est quod per tres gressus unius cognitionis innotescit, primo, sub ratione experti, deinde, sub ratione intelligibilis, tertio, sub ratione veri et entis.

Quod sane perspici non potest ab iis qui experientiam ducant cognitionem quandam in se completam; unde nec perspicere possunt quemadmodum inter se habeant conscientia Christi humana et visio eiusdem beata.

(v) In subiecto qua conscio innotescit quidem hic homo existens et psychologice operans, non tamen formaliter neque ex parte obiecti sed sub ratione experti et ex parte subiecti.

Non formaliter: nisi enim per intelligentiam et conceptionem non formaliter innotescunt vel 'homo' vel 'hic' vel 'existens' vel 'et' vel 'psychologice' vel 'operans.'

Non ex parte obiecti: quod enim ex parte obiecti innotescit, aut per sensus externos aut per conceptionem aut per iudicium innotescit.

Ex parte subiecti: attendit enim subiectum conscium ad obiectum quodlibet quod sen-tit, imaginatur, appetit, investigat, intelligit, definit, iudicat, vult, eligit, efficit. At quamvis subiectum ad quodlibet obiectum cuiuslibet operationis psychologicae attendat, nihilomi-nus non in statu inconscio versatur sed eo ipso quod attendit ideo conscius sit necesse est.

Sub ratione experti: scilicet, habetur id in quo intelligi posset et id propter quod af-firmari posset 'hic homo existens et psychologice operans.' Nam in qualibet operatione psychologica id quod sentit, appetit, intelligit, eligit, etc., non est sensus neque appetitus neque intellectus neque voluntas neque natura humana neque essentia humana sed hic

Again, what we affirm upon reflection and judgment is precisely what we experience, understand, and conceive, since we make rational affirmations precisely because it is in what we experience that we verify what we have understood and conceived.

Nor can conception without judgment be properly called human knowledge, and much less can pure experience without intelligent conception and judgment be considered such. Conception alone is not knowledge: we can, for example, form a concept of centaurs, but we cannot truly and properly be said to know them. Pure experience is not knowledge either, because pure experience not only lacks all distinctions, which are arrived at through comparative and negative judgments, but even any proximate possibility of making distinctions, which consists in the fact that we conceive certain things and compare them with one another.

Briefly: it is one and the same thing that is known at three levels of a single cognitional operation; it is known first under the formality of the experienced, then under the formality of the intelligible, and thirdly under the formality of the true and of being.

All of this, of course, cannot possibly be understood by those who consider experience to be some knowledge that is complete in itself; hence neither can they grasp the relation between Christ's human consciousness and his beatific vision.

(5) In a subject as conscious this existing human being operating psychologically is indeed known, not, however, formally or on the side of the object but under the formality of the experienced and on the side of the subject.

Not formally: 'human being' and 'this' and 'existing' and 'and' and 'psychologically' and 'operating' are known formally only by understanding and conception.

Not on the side of the object: what is known on the side of the object is known only through the external senses or by conception or in a judgment.

But on the side of the subject: for conscious subjects attend to whatever object they are feeling, imagining, desiring, investigating, understanding, defining, judging, willing, choosing, or effecting. But even though subjects may attend to any object of any of their psychological operations, they do not do so in an unconscious state; rather the very fact that they are attentive necessarily means that they are conscious.

And under the formality of the experienced: that is, there is present that in which 'this existing human being operating psychologically' can be understood and that on the basis of which it can be affirmed. For in any psychological operation whatever, that which senses, desires, understands, chooses, and so forth, is not the sense or the appetite or the intellect or the will or a human nature or a

homo existens et psychologice operans; praeterea, non datur vel videns inconscium vel videre inconscium, et similiter de aliis operationibus.

(vi) Minime confundenda sunt subiectum qua conscium et subiectum qua feliciter introspiciens.

Subiectum qua feliciter introspiciens dicit non solum subiectum qua conscium sed etiam subiectum quod systema quoddam psychologicum intellexerit atque conceperit, et quod hoc systema in ipsa sua experientia et intelligere et verificare eventu felici secuturo quaerit.

(vii) Subiectum qua conscium distingui potest multiplex.

Nam multae sunt operationes psychologicae, multi sunt status subiecti psychologice operantis, multi sunt fines quos subiectum prosequi potest, et diversae sunt qualitates ipsius conscientiae quae esse potest vel empirica vel intellectualis vel rationalis vel moralis, etc.

(viii) Quamvis subiectum qua conscium semper sit hic homo existens et psychologice operans, tamen pro diversitate huius subiecti hoc vel magis vel minus conspicitur.

Magis conspicitur cum subiectum per diversas potentias simul operatur, v.g., quando de sensibilibus intellectu inquirit, in sensibilibus intelligibile percipit, secundum sensibilia de conceptibus iudicat, contra appetitum sensitivum et secundum iudicium morale voluntate determinat quid ipse per corpus facturus sit.

Minus conspicitur quando subiectum secundum habitus acquisitos in situationibus consuetis operatur, quando parte sensitiva praecipue operatur, quando somniat, quando graviores morbos psychicos patitur, etc.

(ix) Propter hanc multiplicitatem, diversitatem, et saepe etiam obscuritatem, dici solet hoc subiectum qua conscium quoddam 'ego' apparens, phaenomenale (*Erscheinungs-Ich*).

Quod quidem nisi male intelligitur, nullatenus est reprobandum.

Cave tamen ne hic loquendi modus in errorem ducat, nempe, aliud esse hoc 'ego' apparens et aliud esse 'ego' reale quod per modum cuiusdam X ignoti sub apparentiis lateat. Uti enim diximus, idem est quod sub ratione experti innotescit et quod sub ratione vel intelligibilis vel veri et entis innotescit.

Etiam notate hoc erroris periculum valde augeri si quis conscientiam non experientiam sed perceptionem quandam arbitratur; cum enim per conscientiam nihil ex parte obiecti innotescat, praelucente errore radicali in quamlibet fere conclusionem perveniri potest.

human essence, but this existing human being operating psychologically. Besides, there is no such thing as an unconscious seer or unconscious seeing, and the same holds for all other such operations.

(6) A subject as conscious is not to be confused with a subject engaged in successful introspection.

By a subject engaged in successful introspection we mean not only a subject as conscious but also a subject that has understood and conceived some psychological system and is seeking to understand and verify this system in his or her own experience by a successful outcome of this inquiry.

(7) There are many ways in which the subject as conscious can be distinguished.

For there are many psychological operations, many states of a subject operating psychologically, and many goals that a subject might pursue, and the quality of consciousness itself, which can be empirical or intellectual or rational or moral, and so on, can vary greatly.

(8) Although a subject as conscious is always this particular existing human being operating psychologically, this fact will be more or less noticeable depending upon the variations within this subject.

It is more noticeable when a subject is operating through several faculties at the same time; for example, when one is inquiring intellectually into sensible data, grasping the intelligible in those data, judging one's concepts according to those data, and deciding what external action to take in accordance with one's moral judgment and against one's sensitive appetite.

It is less noticeable when a subject is operating according to ingrained habits and in familiar situations, or when one is operating mainly at the sensitive level of one's being, or when one is dreaming, or when one is suffering from severe mental illness, and so forth.

(9) On account of this multiplicity, diversity, and also frequent obscurity, the subject as conscious is frequently referred to as an 'apparent I' or 'phenomenal I' (*Erscheinungs-Ich*).

Such an expression is quite acceptable when correctly understood.

But one must be careful not to be misled by this expression into thinking that this 'apparent I' is not the same as the real 'I' which like a certain unknown 'X' underlies these appearances. As we have said, what is known under the formality of the experienced is the same as what is known under the formality of the intelligible or under the formality of the true and of being.

Note also that this misunderstanding is all the more dangerous when one thinks of consciousness not as experience but as a kind of perception. For through consciousness nothing is known on the side of the object, and so if guided by this radical error, one can come to just about any conclusion.

Section Tertia: Conscientiae Finitae Constitutio Ontologica

Quaenam sint causae intrinsecae atque constitutivae ut sit persona finita, iam pridem consideravimus. Nunc ergo quaeritur quaenam causae constitutivae sint addendae ut persona finita fiat conscia.

81 Et primo negative procedimus statuentes (1) personam finitam non esse consciam per se ipsam, (2) personam finitam non esse consciam per potentias vel habitus accidentales, et (3) personam humanam non esse consciam per operationem quandam distinctam atque specialem qua ipsa se ex parte obiecti intueatur.

Primo, ergo, persona finita non est conscia per se ipsam, secus semper conscia esset, quod contra factum est.

Deinde, persona finita non est conscia per potentias vel habitus accidentales, nam existentia potentiarum et habituum tantummodo indirecte concluditur ex eo quod actus vel fieri possunt vel prompte, faciliter, delectabiliter fieri solent.

Tertio, persona humana non est conscia per operationem quandam distinctam atque specialem qua ipsa se ex parte obiecti intueatur. Nam talis operatio non existit; neque ullum argumentum in eius favorem invenitur nisi confunduntur praevia atque informis notitia sui suorumque actuum et consequens inquisitio intellectualis in quidditatem et existentiam tum sui tum suorum actuum.

Praeterea, etiamsi existeret distincta illa atque specialis operatio, nihil ad conscientiam humanam constituendam conferret. Conscientia enim humana non est notitia ex parte obiecti quod inspicitur sed ex parte subiecti quod inspicit; et talis notitia ex parte subiecti neque specialem actum exigit neque ipsum subiectum tamquam obiectum actus supponit.

Non exigit actum specialem, nam quicumque sit actus, idem semper est subiectum quod agit; et ideo sive video sive audio sive appeto sive timeo, etc., cum semper idem sim, semper idem conscius fio.

Neque supponit ipsum subiectum tamquam obiectum actus, nam ea notitia est conscientia quae fit non ex parte obiecti quod videtur vel auditur vel appetitur vel timetur, etc., sed ex parte subiecti quod videt vel audit vel appetit vel timet, etc.

82 Quibus perspectis, remanet ut persona finita fiat conscia per omnes et quaslibet operationes partis sive sensitivae sive intellectivae. Quod tamen ut clarius et distinctius proponatur, sequentibus assertis complectimur.

3 The Ontological Constitution of Finite Consciousness

We have already considered the intrinsic causes that constitute a finite person. Now we go on to ask what causes have to be added to constitute a finite person as conscious.

81 First, by way of negation, we state the following: (1) finite persons are not conscious in and of themselves; (2) a finite person is not conscious through accidental potencies or habits; (3) a human person is not conscious through some distinct and special operation by which one looks at oneself on the side of the object.

First, if finite persons were conscious in and of themselves, they would be conscious at all times, which is not the case.

Second, a finite person is not conscious through any accidental potencies or habits; for it is only indirectly that we conclude to the existence of potencies and habits, from the fact that certain acts either can occur or regularly do occur readily, easily, and pleasurably.

Third, a human person is not conscious through some distinct and special operation by which one intuits oneself on the side of the object. No such operation exists; nor is there any argument in its favor unless one confuses the preliminary unstructured awareness of oneself and of one's acts with subsequent intellectual inquiry into the nature and the existence of oneself and of one's acts.

Besides, even if such a distinct and special operation did exist it would contribute nothing to constituting human consciousness. Human consciousness is not awareness on the side of the object that is observed, but on the side of the subject that observes; and such awareness on the side of the subject does not require a special act nor does it presuppose the subject itself as the object of an act.

It does not require a special act, for whatever act is performed, it is always the same subject who is acting. Hence, whether I see or hear or desire or fear, or whatever, it is always the same I who become conscious, since I am always the same.

Nor does it presuppose the subject itself as the object of an act, for consciousness is the awareness that is had, not on the side of the object that is seen or heard or desired or feared, and so forth, but on the side of the subject that sees, hears, desires, fears, and so forth.

82 In view of this, we are left with the conclusion that a finite person becomes conscious through any and all operations of both the sensitive and the intellectual part of one's being. In order to expound this more clearly and distinctly, we make the following assertions.

Primo, accidentales sunt operationes entis finiti quae in parte sive sensitiva sive intellectiva peraguntur.[5]

Deinde, hae operationes, quamvis ex parte obiecti inter se differant, tamen ex parte subiecti-conscii-per-actum-conscium inter se conveniunt.

Differunt ex parte obiecti: aliud enim est color qui videtur, aliud prorsus est sonus qui auditur, aliud omnino est quidditas quae intelligitur, etc.

Conveniunt ex parte subiecti conscii per actum conscium: absonum enim et absurdum est cogitare vel subiectum inconscium per videre inconscium vere et realiter videre colores, vel subiectum inconscium per audire inconscium vere et realiter audire sonos, vel subiectum inconscium per intelligere inconscium vere et realiter perspicere intelligibile in sensibilibus, etc.

Unde concludes conscientiam sub aspectu empirico in eo consistere quod simile invenitur quando inter se comparantur operationes vel sensitivae vel intellectivae quae circa obiecta diversa fiant. Quamvis enim videre et audire tantum ex parte obiecti inter se differant quantum color et sonus, tamen simillima sunt quatenus uterque actus intra campum conscientiae iacet et subiectum conscium reddit.

Tertio, aliter subiectum dicitur conscium et aliter actus dicitur conscius.

Principia enim entis finiti ipsa non sunt sed iis aliquid est. Quare operationes sensitivae et intellectivae in ente finito, sicut ipsae non sunt, ita non sunt consciae; et sicut his operationibus aliquid est, ita iisdem operationibus aliquid est conscium.

Unde concludes subiectum esse conscium ut quod est conscium, operationes vero esse conscias ut quibus subiectum est conscium.

Et pari ratione concluditur ex eodem principio quod sensus non sentit sed homo per sensum, et intellectus non intelligit sed homo per intellectum; sensus enim et intellectus sicut ipsi non sunt sed iis aliquid est, ita ipsi non operantur sed iis aliquis operatur.

Quarto, vere et realiter subiectum redditur conscium per operationes accidentales. Sicut enim accidentis est subiecto inesse, ita etiam subiecti est per accidentalia perfici.

First, both the sensitive and intellectual operations of a finite being are accidents.[5]

Second, although these operations are different from one another on the side of the object, still on the side of the subject that is conscious through a conscious act they have much in common.

They are different on the side of the object: a color that is seen is quite different from a sound that is heard, an intelligibility that is understood, and so forth.

On the side of the subject that is conscious through a conscious act, however, they have much in common. For it is incongruous and absurd to think that an unconscious subject through an unconscious act of seeing really and truly sees colors, or that an unconscious subject through an unconscious act of hearing really and truly hears sound, or that an unconscious subject through an unconscious act of understanding really and truly grasps an intelligibility in sense data, and so forth.

Hence we conclude that consciousness viewed in its empirical aspect consists in the fact that there is something similar when sensitive or intellectual operations having different objects are compared to one another. For although on the side of the object seeing and hearing are as different from each other as color is different from sound, they are nevertheless very similar inasmuch as each act lies within the field of consciousness and renders the subject conscious.

Third, the subject and the act are said to be conscious, but in different ways.

The principles of a finite being do not exist themselves, but are that by which something exists. In a finite being, therefore, just as the operations of sense or intellect do not exist themselves, so they are not conscious themselves; and just as by these operations something exists, so by these same operations something is conscious.

We conclude, therefore, that a subject is conscious as that which is conscious, while operations are conscious as that by which the subject is conscious.

With equal reason we conclude from the same principle that it is not the senses that sense but the human being through the senses, nor is it the intellect that understands but the human being through the intellect; for just as sense and intellect do not exist themselves but are that by which something exists, so too they do not operate themselves but are that by which someone operates.

Fourth, a subject is really and truly rendered conscious through accidental operations. As it belongs to an accident to exist in a subject, so also it belongs to a subject to be perfected through its accidents.

5 Thomas Aquinas, *Summa theologiae,* 1, q. 54, aa. 1–3.

Sicut ergo non augetur quantitas Petri quin ipse Petrus vere et realiter augeatur et sicut non alteratur qualitas Petri quin ipse Petrus vere et realiter alteretur, ita non recipitur actus videndi in visu Petri quin Petrus et vere et realiter per suum videre videat et vere et realiter per suum videre conscium conscius videat, etc.

Quinto, operationes accidentales in parte sensitiva et intellectiva peractae rationem conscientiae includunt ex ipsa ontologica earum perfectione.

Sicut enim 'inconscium' non negat ens, ita etiam 'conscium' non addit super ens. 'Inconscium' enim nihil est aliud quam ens in inferiori gradu perfectionis, et ideo inconscia est capillorum crescentia, sanguinis circulatio, vel cellularum metabolismus. 'Conscium' pariter nihil est aliud quam ens in superiori gradu perfectionis ontologicae, et ideo ex ipsa sua perfectione intrinseca et videre est conscium ut quo, et subiectum facit conscium ut quod, et similiter de aliis his operationibus.

Unde concludes radicem conscientiae non esse petendam ex mira quadam qualitate causalitatis efficientis. Causa enim efficiens est principium motus vel mutationis in alio secundum quod aliud; notitia autem illa praevia atque informis, quae conscientia est, adeo non aliud respiciat ut potius quaedam sui-praesentia-sibi describitur.[6]

Sexto, subiectum per suas operationes redditur conscium secundum perfectionem ipsarum operationum.

Ita per operationes sensitivas redditur empirice conscium, per inquisitionem, intelligentiam, conceptionem redditur intellectualiter conscium, per reflectionem, evidentiae ponderationem, iudicium redditur rationaliter conscium, per consilia de bono intelligibili, deliberationem, electionem redditur moraliter conscium.

Praeterea, cum hi conscientiae gradus alius alium supponant, haberi possunt conscientia empirica sine intellectuali, et intellectualis sine rationali, et rationalis sine morali; sed haberi non possunt moralis sine rationali, rationalis sine intellectuali, intellectualis sine empirica. Quae tamen regula ordinem naturalem respicit qui quodammodo invertitur cum Deus per gratias infusas magis voluntatem quam intellectum et magis intellectum quam sensum movere possit et soleat.

Thus, as Peter's quantity does not increase without Peter himself really and truly increasing, and his quality does not change without a real and true change in Peter, in the same way, no act of seeing takes place in Peter's sense of sight without Peter really and truly seeing through his act of seeing, and really and truly consciously seeing through this conscious act of seeing, and so for the other operations.

Fifth, it is by reason of their ontological perfection that these accidental operations of sense and intellect have the character of consciousness.

For just as 'unconscious' does not negate being, so 'conscious' adds nothing to being. 'Unconscious' is simply being, at a lower level of perfection, and so such processes as the growth of hair, the circulation of the blood, and the metabolism of cells are unconscious. By the same token, 'conscious' is simply being, at a higher level of ontological perfection, and so by reason of its intrinsic perfection the act of seeing is conscious as that by which [one is conscious], and renders a subject conscious as that which [is conscious]; and the same holds for these other operations.

We conclude, therefore, that the root of consciousness is not to be sought in some marvelous quality of efficient causality. An efficient cause is the principle of motion or change in another as other; but that preliminary unstructured awareness that is consciousness, so far from regarding some other, is even described as a certain presence of oneself to oneself.[6]

Sixth, a subject is rendered conscious through its operations in accordance with the perfection of the operations themselves.

Thus, through sensitive operations one is rendered empirically conscious; through inquiry, understanding, and conception one becomes intellectually conscious; through reflection, weighing the evidence, and judgment one becomes rationally conscious; and through seeking intelligible good, deliberating about it, and choosing it one becomes morally conscious.

Moreover, since there is an order among these levels of consciousness, in which the higher presupposes the lower, it is possible to have empirical consciousness without intellectual, intellectual without rational, and rational without moral; but you cannot have moral consciousness without rational, rational without intellectual, or intellectual without empirical. This, however, describes the natural order – which, in a way, is reversible, since God by the infusion of supernatural graces can and usually does affect the will more than the intellect and the intellect more than the senses.

6 Ibid. 1, q. 87, a. 1

Septimo, subiectum fit conscium normaliter vel abnormaliter secundum perfectionem vel defectum ordinis qui viget tum in parte infra-sensitiva tum in habitibus acquisitis tum in finibus ad quos vel habitualiter orientatur vel actu tendit.

Quod assertum, cum ad psychologiam spectet, ideo tantum ponitur ne quis erronee credat abnormalitatem conscientiae ex defectu obscurae cuiusdam perfectionis ontologicae provenire.

Octavo, aliud est esse conscium empirice, intellectualiter, rationaliter, moraliter, et aliud longe est conscientiae analysin intelligere et concipere et appropriare et applicare.

Qua de causa, si quis hanc conscientiae analysin in se ipso verificare velit, non ei sufficit conscium esse, sed insuper requiritur ut non solum ipsam analysin intelligat atque systematice secundum suas implicationes concipiat sed etiam ut hunc complexum abstractum atque universalem modo concreto per exempla ex propria experientia hausta illustret atque artem seu technicam introspectionis psychologicae aliquatenus addiscat.

Nono, ut denique tandem hanc quaestionem concludamus, in easdem resolvitur causas persona finita et conscia in quas resolvitur persona finita sentiens, intelligens, iudicans, eligens. Nam 'conscium' non addit super ens sed nihil dicit nisi ens in tali gradu perfectionis ontologicae. Neque per operationem quandam distinctam et specialem ipsi nos intuemur, sed eo ipso quod sentimus, intelligimus, iudicamus, eligimus, iam nobis inest praevia quaedam atque informis notitia nostri nostrorumque actuum. Neque aliter ex experientia interna quam ex experientia externa procedimus inquirendo et intelligendo, reflectendo et iudicando, ut nos ipsos iam sub ratione experti notos etiam sub ratione intelligibilis et quidditatis, veri et entis apprehendamus.

Seventh, a subject becomes conscious normally or abnormally depending on the order or disorder that obtains at the infra-sensitive level of one's being or in one's acquired habits or in the goals to which one is habitually oriented or actually tending.

Although this assertion is a matter of psychology, we are adding it here simply to guard against the error of thinking that abnormalities in consciousness stem from the lack of some hidden ontological perfection.

Eighth, it is one thing to be empirically, intellectually, rationally, and morally conscious, and quite another to understand, conceive, appropriate, and apply an analysis of consciousness.

For this reason, if you want to verify this analysis of consciousness in yourself, it is not enough for you to be conscious; you also need not only to understand the analysis and conceive it systematically with its implications, but also to take this abstract universal scheme and illustrate it by concrete examples drawn from your own experience and learn to some extent the art or technique of psychological introspection.

Ninth, to conclude this question at last: a finite conscious person is made up of the same causal elements as a finite person sensing, understanding, judging, or choosing. 'Conscious' adds nothing to being; it simply denotes being of a certain degree of ontological perfection. Nor do we intuit ourselves through some distinct and special operation; by the very fact of our sensing, understanding, judging, or choosing we already have a certain preliminary unstructured awareness of ourselves and our acts. Further, we proceed from interior experience just as we do from exterior experience, by inquiring and understanding, by reflecting and judging, so as to apprehend ourselves, already known under the formality of the experienced, also now under the formality of the intelligible and the definable, of the true and of being.

De Conscientia Christi

83 Primo, secundum quod conscientia concipitur ut experientia, determinatur (1) de conscientia Christi divina, (2) de conscientia Christi humana, (3) de constitutione ontologica conscientiae Christi humanae, et (4) de unitate psychologica unius conscii per duas conscientias.

Deinde, cum conscientia etiam concipiatur quasi perceptio quaedam esset, (5) proponuntur duae simul sententiae, nempe, conscientiae-experientiae et conscientiae-perceptionis, et cum utriusque sententiae consectaria sint deducta satis perspicitur tum conscientiam-experientiam cum dogmate catholico et sensu fidelium congruere tum conscientiam-perceptionem in eas conducere difficultates quas theologi de hac re disputantes in alterius quisque sententia et iam pridem clare perspiciant et vehementer denuntient.

Sectio Prima: De Conscientia Christi Divina

84 In primis quaerendum est utrum vere etsi analogice Deus sit conscius.

Et Deum vere esse conscium nobis est affirmandum, cum rationem conscientiae in perfectione ontologica operationum sensitivarum atque intellectualium posuerimus. Deus enim est actus purus, ipsum intelligere, et ipsum amare. Sed actus purus non est caecus ac stolidus sicut vel lapis cadens vel planta crescens, neque ipsum intelligere est inconscium cum Archimedes propter finitum quoddam intelligere 'Eureka!' exclamaverit, neque ipsum amare est inconscium cum et spirituale et voluntarium secundum infinitam sapientiam infinite bonum sit.

PART 6

The Consciousness of Christ

83 In this part, taking consciousness as experience, we shall first of all deal with (1) the divine consciousness of Christ, (2) his human consciousness, (3) the ontological constitution of Christ's human consciousness, and (4) the psychological unity of one who is conscious through two consciousnesses.

Then, since consciousness is also conceived as if it were a certain kind of perception, we shall (5) set forth these two opinions together, namely, consciousness-as-experience and consciousness-as-perception; and when the consequences of each opinion have been deduced, it will become evident that consciousness-as-experience squares with both Catholic doctrine and the *sensus fidelium*, while on the other hand consciousness-as-perception gets one into those difficulties that the theologians who have argued this question have for some time now clearly perceived and vigorously denounced in each other's opinions.

1 The Divine Consciousness of Christ

84 The first question is whether God is truly, albeit analogically, conscious.

We must indeed assert that God is truly conscious, since we have maintained that consciousness as such belongs to the ontological perfection of sensitive and intellectual operations. God is pure act, the subsistent act of understanding, the subsistent act of loving. But pure act is not blind or inert like a falling rock or a growing plant. Nor is the subsistent act of understanding unconscious: even Archimedes, with his finite act of understanding, exclaimed, 'Eureka!'; and the subsistent act of loving is not unconscious either, since being both spiritual and willed in accordance with infinite wisdom it is infinitely good.

Analogice tamen conscientia de Deo dicatur necesse est. Non enim in Deo aliud realiter est subiectum conscium et aliud realiter est actus quo est conscium et aliud realiter obiectum primarium quod per actum attingitur; sed haec tria unum idemque sunt. Neque per multos actus est Deus conscius cum in eo non inveniatur nisi unus actus isque infinitus. Qua de causa, non alia in eo est praevia quaedam atque informis notitia sui et alia subsequens inquisitio intellectualis; neque ulla in eo invenitur conscientia mere empirica cum sensibus careat; neque per aliud est conscius intellectualiter et per aliud rationaliter et per aliud moraliter, cum in eo non alia sit prima intellectus operatio et alia secunda, neque alia operatio intellectus et alia operatio voluntatis, neque ullus processus ex potentia in actum; neque in eo augentur vel minuuntur claritas atque distinctio conscientiae prout subiectum per multos actus inter se ordinatos in se ipsum reflectitur vel in alia obiecta fertur.

Quae tamen differentiae minime excludunt radicalem illam similitudinem quae ad veram analogiam asserendam et requiritur et sufficit. Non enim fundatur ratio conscientiae in illa multiplicitate quam a Deo excludimus sed in illa perfectione superioris gradus ontologici quae in lapidibus et plantis deest, in animalibus secundum conscientiam empiricam invenitur, in hominibus secundum conscientiam empiricam, intellectualem, rationalem, et moralem habetur, in angelis secundum haec tria posteriora. Quod si in animalibus et hominibus et angelis multiplicitas conscientiam non impedit, quanto magis modo suo eminentiori Deus sit conscius necesse est.

Dixerit tamen quispiam ad mentem P. Galtier[1] cognitionem divinam esse essentialiter directam neque ullo modo illam reflexionem admittere quae conscientiae proprie dictae inhaereat.

Concedimus sane in Deo super cognitionem directam non supervenire aliam cognitionem reflexam.

Negamus tamen in nobis rationem conscientiae in eo inveniri quod cognitio reflexa super cognitionem directam superveniat.[2] Secundum hanc enim opinionem id quod innotescit ex parte obiecti in cognitione directa non innotescit per conscientiam; sed id quod innotescit ex parte obiecti in cognitione reflexa innotescit per conscientiam. Secundum autem opinionem eorum quos sequimur id quod innotescit ex parte obiecti sive in

Consciousness, however, must be predicated of God analogically. In God, the subject that is conscious, the act by which it is conscious, and the primary object of this act are not really distinct from one another: these three are one and the same. Nor is God conscious through a multiplicity of acts, for in God there is but one act, an act that is infinite. Hence in God there is no preliminary unstructured self-awareness followed by a really distinct intellectual inquiry. Having no senses, God has no merely empirical consciousness; nor is God intellectually conscious through one operation, rationally conscious through another, and morally conscious through a third, since in God there is no distinction between the first operation of the intellect and the second, or between the operations of the intellect and those of the will; nor is there any process from potency to act. Finally, in God the clarity and distinctness of consciousness neither increase nor decrease as the subject through a series of interrelated acts reflects on itself or turns its attention to other objects.

These differences, however, by no means exclude the radical similarity that is both required and sufficient for affirming a true analogy. True consciousness is not based on that multiplicity that we have excluded from God but on that higher level of ontological perfection that is absent in rocks and plants and that is found at the empirical level in animals, at the empirical, intellectual, rational, and moral levels in humans, and at the last three levels in angels. Now if such multiplicity in animals, in humans, and in angels does not prevent them from being conscious, how much more must God be conscious in God's own more eminent way.

Here someone might say along with Paul Galtier[1] that God's knowledge is essentially direct and in no way admits of that reflexive character inherent in consciousness properly so called.

We fully agree that in God there is no reflexive knowledge in addition to direct knowledge.

But we deny that what constitutes consciousness in us is some reflexive knowledge superadded to direct knowledge.[2] For according to that opinion, what is known on the side of the object in direct knowledge is not known through consciousness, whereas what is known on the side of the object in reflexive knowledge is known through consciousness. However, according to the opinion we are

1 Paul Galtier, *L'Unité du Christ* 238, note 1.
2 [Distinguish Lonergan's use of 'reflexa' (reflexive) from his use of 'reflective' in 'reflective understanding.' The latter falls under what he is here calling 'direct' knowledge: we reflect on the contents of intellectual activity in order to form a judgment. But the former refers to reflection on the activity itself and on its conscious subject.]

cognitione directa sive in cognitione reflexa non innotescit per conscientiam; et id quod innotescit ex parte subiecti tum in cognitione directa tum in cognitione reflexa innotescit per conscientiam. Secundum primam opinionem quam sequitur P. Galtier, sumus conscii quatenus in nos ipsos reflectimur et nos ipsos ex parte obiecti apprehendimus. Secundum alteram opinionem quam amplectimur, sumus conscii quia sumus actu sentientes, intelligentes, iudicantes, eligentes; neque quidquam refert quid sit obiectum quod sentitur, intelligitur, iudicatur, eligitur; neque quidquam refert utrum actus sit directus an reflexus; conscientia enim est sentientis, intelligentis, iudicantis, eligentis, et reflectentis, et semper est ex parte subiecti qui sentit, intelligit, iudicat, eligit, reflectitur.

Et ideo Deum dicimus vere etsi analogice conscium non quia Deus in se ipsum reflectatur sed quia Deus intelligit et iudicat et vult et eligit.

85 Deinde quaeritur utrum personae divinae sint consciae non solum secundum actus essentiales sed etiam secundum actus notionales.

Essentiales dicuntur actus qui tribus divinis personis sunt communes. Ita Pater, Filius, Spiritus sanctus et intelligunt et iudicant et volunt et eligunt.

Notionales dicuntur actus qui uni alterive personae divinae sunt proprii. Ita solus Pater dicit Verbum; Pater et Filius, non autem Spiritus sanctus, spirant[3] seu 'producunt' Amorem procedentem, qui est Spiritus sanctus. Solus Filius dicitur. Solus Spiritus sanctus spiratur.

Ex antecessis sequitur omnes tres personas divinas esse conscias secundum actus essentiales. Demonstratum enim est Deum esse conscium secundum suum intelligere et amare. Sed Pater est Deus, Filius est Deus, Spiritus est Deus. Ergo Pater, Filius, Spiritus sunt conscii secundum divinum intelligere et divinum amare essentiale.

At ulterius quaeritur utrum personae divinae sint consciae secundum actus notionales, scilicet, utrum Pater conscie an inconscie dicat Verbum, utrum Verbum conscie an inconscie dicatur, utrum Pater et Filius conscie an inconscie spirent Spiritum sanctum, utrum Spiritus sanctus conscie an inconscie spiretur.

Ubi notandum est: (1) quaestionem non esse utrum personae divinae ex parte obiecti sciant actus notionales, cum agatur non de scientia sed de conscientia quae

following, what is known on the side of the object, whether in direct knowledge or in reflexive knowledge, is not known through consciousness, whereas what is known on the side of the subject in both direct knowledge and reflexive knowledge is known through consciousness. In the former opinion, followed by Galtier, we are conscious inasmuch as we reflect upon ourselves and apprehend ourselves on the side of the object. In the latter opinion, to which we subscribe, we are conscious because we are actually sensing, understanding, judging, choosing; and it does not matter at all what the object is that is sensed, understood, judged, chosen; nor does it matter at all whether our act is direct or reflexive. For consciousness belongs to the one sensing, understanding, judging, choosing, and reflecting, and is always on the side of the subject who senses, understands, judges, chooses, reflects.

Accordingly, we conclude that God is truly, albeit analogically, conscious, not because God engages in self-reflection but because God understands, judges, wills, and chooses.

85 The next question is whether the divine persons are conscious not only through their essential acts but through their notional acts as well.

The essential acts are those that are common to all three persons. Thus the Father, the Son, and the Holy Spirit understand, judge, will, and choose.

The notional acts are those that are proper to one or other of the divine persons. Thus, only the Father utters the Word; both Father and Son, but not the Holy Spirit, spirate[3] or 'produce' Proceeding Love, which is the Holy Spirit. Only the Son is uttered, and only the Holy Spirit is spirated.

From the foregoing it follows that all three divine persons are conscious through the essential acts. For we have shown that God is conscious through divine understanding and loving. But the Father is God, the Son is God, and the Holy Spirit is God. Therefore the Father, the Son, and the Holy Spirit are conscious through essential divine understanding and divine loving.

But the further question here is whether the divine persons are conscious through the notional acts: that is, whether the Father consciously or unconsciously utters the Word, whether the Word consciously or unconsciously is uttered, whether the Father and the Son consciously or unconsciously spirate the Holy Spirit, and whether the Holy Spirit consciously or unconsciously is spirated.

At this point the following observations should be made. (1) At issue here is not whether the divine persons know the notional acts on the side of the object, since

3 [Consistently in the Collected Works translation of Lonergan's Latin theology 'spirare' will be translated 'to spirate.']

ex parte subiecti sit; (2) quaestionem non esse de conscientia concomitante, scilicet, utrum Pater dum Verbum inconscie dicat saltem conscie intelligat et conscie amet; sed (3) quaestionem esse de conscientia proprie dicta et secundum ipsum actum notionalem.

Quare qui negative respondet, concedit quidem Patrem conscie intelligere et conscie amare, scire se intelligere et scire se amare, dicere Verbum et scire primam personam SS. Trinitatis Verbum dicere, sed negat Patrem conscie dicere Verbum et negat Patrem scire se (secundum proprietatem reflexivi) Verbum dicere.

Qui autem affirmative respondet, tenet Patrem et conscie intelligere et conscie amare et conscie Verbum dicere et conscie Spiritum spirare et scire se (secundum proprietatem reflexivi) et intelligere et amare et dicere et spirare.

Qua de quaestione non magis abundant auctores quam de conscientia Christi Dei et hominis. At secundum ea quae exposuimus tum apud *Theological Studies*, 1946–49,[4] tum opere *De Deo trino*, Pars systematica, 1964, pp. 186 ss.,[5] omnino affirmative respondendum est.

Quibus perspectis, sequitur personas divinas esse conscias non solum secundum quod sunt Deus sed etiam secundum quod sunt personae distinctae. Si enim Pater conscie dicit Verbum, cum solus Pater dicat, solus Pater conscie dicit Verbum. Si Pater et Filius conscie spirant Amorem, cum soli Pater et Filius spirent, soli Pater et Filius conscie spirant. Pariter si Verbum conscie dicitur, cum solum dicatur, solum conscie dicitur; et si Spiritus conscie spiratur, cum solus spiretur, solus conscie spiratur.

Dixerit tamen quispiam: omnia in divinis unum sunt ubi non obviat relationis oppositio (DB 703). Sed conscie dicere, conscie dici, conscie spirare, conscie spirari non tantum sunt

we are discussing not knowledge but consciousness, which is on the side of the subject; nor (2) does the question here have to do with concomitant consciousness, that is, whether the Father while unconsciously uttering the Word is at least consciously understanding and consciously loving; but (3) the question deals with consciousness properly so called and on the basis of the notional act itself.

Those who answer this question in the negative concede that the Father consciously understands and consciously loves, that the Father knows indeed that the Father understands and loves, that the Father utters the Word and knows that the first person of the most holy Trinity utters the Word; but they deny that the Father consciously utters the Word, and they deny that the Father knows himself (in accord with the proper force of this reflexive pronoun) to be uttering the Word.

Those who give an affirmative answer to this question hold that the Father consciously understands and consciously loves and consciously utters the Word and consciously spirates the Spirit and knows himself (in accord with the proper force of this reflexive pronoun) to be understanding and loving and uttering and spirating.

Those who have written on this point are no more numerous than those who have written on the consciousness of Christ as God and man. However, in conformity with what we have written in *Theological Studies*[4] and in *De Deo trino, Pars systematica*, 1964, chapter 5, assertion 12,[5] this question must definitely be answered in the affirmative.

From this it follows that the divine persons are conscious not only inasmuch as they are God but also inasmuch as they are distinct persons. If the Father consciously utters the Word, since only the Father utters, only the Father consciously utters the Word. If the Father and the Son consciously spirate Love, then since only the Father and the Son spirate, only the Father and the Son consciously spirate. Similarly, if the Word is consciously uttered, then since it alone is uttered, it alone is consciously uttered; and if the Spirit is consciously spirated, then since it alone is spirated, it alone is consciously spirated.

To this, however, one may make the following objection: in God all things are one except where there is opposition of relation (DB 703; DS 1330); but to utter consciously, to be consciously uttered, to spirate consciously, and to be consciously

---

4 [Bernard Lonergan, *Verbum: Word and Idea in Aquinas*, volume 2 in Collected Works of Bernard Lonergan (Toronto: University of Toronto Press, 1997). Lonergan's reference was to the original *Theological Studies* articles. See above, p. 5, note 2.]

5 [Bernard Lonergan, *De Deo trino: Pars systematica* (Rome: Gregorian University Press, 1964) 186–93.]

relationes oppositae. Ergo non datur sive conscie dicere sive conscie dici sive conscie spirare sive conscie spirari.

Conceditur maior et negatur minor.

Dicere enim nihil est aliud nisi relatio quae advenit intelligenti inquantum ab intelligente procedit verbum; et spirare nihil est aliud nisi relatio quae advenit ei qui bonum intelligibile intelligit et concipit inquantum ab eo procedit amor. Similiter, dici nihil est aliud quam relatio quae conceptui inest inquantum ab intelligente procedit; et spirari nihil est aliud quam relatio quae amori inest inquantum ab eo procedit qui bonum intelligibile intelligit et concipit.

Ulterius, sicut conscie intelligere non addit super intelligere, ita conscie dicere non addit super dicere; et similiter in aliis, nam 'conscium' non addit super ens sed ipsam entis perfectionem modo magis explicito declarat.

Qua de causa, quod asseritur in minore est simpliciter falsum. Nam 'conscie dicere' distinguitur a paternitate non quoad rem sed quoad modum significandi tantum; quod enim paternitas significat per modum relationis, 'conscie dicere' significat per modum actus notionalis; et simile est in aliis.

Instatur: conscientia est quoddam scire; sed scire divinum est commune tribus; ergo conscientia divina est communis tribus.

Ad maiorem: conscientia est quoddam scire, *distinguitur*: ex parte obiecti, *negatur*; ex parte subiecti scientis, *subdistinguitur*: solus sciens est conscius, *negatur*; etiam sciens est conscius, *conceditur*.

Ad minorem: scire divinum est commune tribus, *distinguitur*: ex parte obiecti, *conceditur*; ex parte subiecti, *subdistinguitur*: ita ut sicut Pater scit et concipit, etiam Filius sciat et concipiat, *negatur*, ita ut sicut Pater scit, etiam Filius sciat, sed sicut Pater concipit, Filius non concipiat, *conceditur*.

Ad conclusionem: conscientia divina est communis tribus, *distinguitur*: omnes tres personae et conscie intelligunt et sciunt et volunt et eligunt, *conceditur*; singulae tres personae conscie et dicunt et dicuntur et spirant et spirantur, *negatur*.

Nam Pater et Filius et Spiritus per actum essentialem ex parte obiecti communiter sciunt solum Patrem non-inconscie dicere et solum Fillum non-inconscie dici et solum Spiritum non-inconscie spirari.

spirated are not just opposed relations; therefore, [in God] there is no conscious uttering or conscious being uttered or conscious spirating or conscious being spirated.

We grant the major premise of the objection but deny the minor.

For to utter is simply the relation that accrues to one who understands inasmuch as a word proceeds from the one who understands; and to spirate is simply the relation that accrues to one who understands and conceives an intelligible good inasmuch as love proceeds from that one. In the same way, to be uttered is simply the relation that belongs to a concept inasmuch as it proceeds from one who understands; and to be spirated is simply the relation that belongs to love inasmuch as it proceeds from one who understands and conceives an intelligible good.

Moreover, just as consciously understanding adds nothing to understanding, so consciously uttering adds nothing to uttering, and so for all the rest; for 'conscious' adds nothing to being but simply expresses more explicitly the perfection of a being.

Hence what is stated in the minor premise is simply false. 'Uttering consciously' is distinct from 'paternity' not in reality but only in the way we give them meaning; for what 'paternity' expresses as a relation, 'uttering consciously' expresses as a notional act; and so for all the rest.

One may further object: consciousness is a kind of knowledge; but divine knowledge is common to the three persons; therefore divine consciousness is common to the three.

To this we reply: the major premise, that consciousness is a kind of knowledge, we distinguish as follows: knowledge on the side of the object, we deny; knowledge on the side of the knowing subject, we further distinguish: that only the knower is conscious, we deny; that also the knower is conscious, we grant.

As to the minor premise, we reply: that divine knowledge is common to the three persons, we distinguish as follows: knowledge on the side of the object, we grant; knowledge on the side of the knowing subject, we further distinguish: knowledge wherein the Son knows and conceives just as the Father knows and conceives, we deny; knowledge wherein the Son knows in the same way as the Father knows, but does not conceive as the Father conceives, we grant.

As to the conclusion: that divine consciousness is common to the three persons, we distinguish as follows: that all three persons consciously understand and know and will and choose, we grant; that each of the three persons consciously utters and is uttered and spirates and is spirated, we deny.

For the Father and the Son and the Spirit through essential act know in common on the side of the object that only the Father not-unconsciously utters, that only the Son not-unconsciously is uttered, and that only the Spirit not-unconsciously is spirated.

Instatur: saltem nulla datur analogia ut affirmari possit Verbum conscie dici et Spiritum conscie spirari.

Respondetur: non datur analogia directa quia in homine uno una tantum est persona, *conceditur*; non datur analogia indirecta inquantum in uno homine una persona et conscie dicit et conscie spirat unde in divinis ubi tres sunt personae perfectione infinitae etiam tres secundum proprios actus notionales sunt consciae, *negatur*.

86 Denique tandem ad corollarium maximi momenti perventum est. Unus enim idemque Christus ita Deus et homo est ut natura divina et natura humana neque mutentur neque confundantur sed in persona et secundum personam uniantur. Qua de causa, cum de conscientia Christi agatur, maxime refert utrum ipsa Christi persona qua persona sit conscia. Si enim ipsa persona qua persona est inconscia, unio hypostatica est et in inconscio et secundum inconscium. Si autem ipsa persona qua persona est conscia, unio hypostatica est et in conscio et secundum conscium.

Iam vero personas divinas esse conscias vidimus non solum secundum actus essentiales, uti intelligere et velle, sed etiam secundum actus notionales, uti dicere et dici, generare et generari, spirare et spirari.

Porro, actus notionales non sunt tribus personis communes et ideo, quia personae sunt consciae secundum hos actus, aliter Pater est conscius et aliter Filius est conscius et aliter Spiritus est conscius.

Ulterius, cum personae inter se per solas relationes originis distinguantur, fieri non potest ut alia persona aliter sit conscia nisi inquantum ipsae relationes sint consciae.

At ipsae personae per relationes constituuntur. Et ideo cum relationes sint consciae, etiam ipsae personae qua personae sint consciae necesse est.

Neve credas illud mirum valde quod dixi, nempe, relationes esse conscias. Exemplum maxime elementare sumatur. Quilibet homo vel bona conscientia gaudet vel mala torquetur. Iam vero ipsa persona hominis gaudet et torquetur, neque sane de inconscio gaudet vel ab inconscio torquetur. Gaudet ergo vel torquetur circa actum bonum vel malum. Qui sane actus non absolute consideratur sed relative; non enim de quolibet actu sed de suo proprio gaudet vel torquetur. Neque conscius est actus sui inquantum actus est sed non

A still further objection: at least there is no analogy allowing us to say that the Word is consciously uttered and the Spirit consciously spirated.

To this objection we reply that it is true there is no direct analogy, since in an individual human being there is only one person; but we deny that there is no indirect analogy, since one person in one human being consciously utters and consciously spirates, and hence in God where there are three persons of infinite perfection these three also are conscious through the proper notional acts.

86 Finally, we have now come to a most important corollary. One and the same Christ is both God and man in such a way that the divine nature and the human nature are neither changed nor mixed but are united in the person and on the basis of the person. In treating the consciousness of Christ, therefore, the question whether the person of Christ as person is conscious is very pertinent. If the person as person is unconscious, then the hypostatic union exists in what is unconscious and on the basis of what is unconscious. If, however, the person as person is conscious, then the hypostatic union exists in what is conscious and on the basis of what is conscious.

But we have seen that the divine persons are conscious not only through essential acts, such as understanding and willing, but also through the notional acts, such as uttering and being uttered, begetting and being begotten, spirating and being spirated.

Furthermore, the notional acts are not common to all three persons, and therefore, since the persons are conscious through these acts, the Father and the Son and the Spirit are conscious each in a different way.

Again, since the persons are distinct from one another solely by relations of origin, it would be impossible for them to be conscious in different ways if the relations themselves were not conscious.

But the persons themselves are constituted by the relations; therefore, since the relations are conscious, the persons themselves as persons must necessarily be conscious.

This matter of the relations being conscious is not all that strange. Let us take a simple example. Peter, for example, either enjoys a good conscience or is tormented by a bad conscience. But it is his person that enjoys and is tormented, and he surely does not enjoy a good conscience because of something unconscious, nor is he tormented because of something unconscious: his enjoyment and his torment stem from his good or his evil action. And he certainly does not look at these actions absolutely, but relatively: that is, he does not experience joy or torment over just any such action, but over his own. Nor is he conscious of his action inasmuch as it is an action but not conscious of it inasmuch as it is his; indeed it

inquantum suus est; quinimmo, praecise inquantum conscius est sui actus tamquam sui gaudet vel torquetur. Ille enim actus ab ipso processit, neque solus actus ad ipsum refertur, sed etiam ipse ad suum actum. Conscie enim ab ipso conscio processit actus conscius; neque tantum empirice conscius erat inquantum actus ita ab ipso processit ut se sic agentem experiretur; neque tantum intellectualiter conscius erat inquantum actus ita ab ipso processit ut quid sit ita agere intelligeret; neque tantum rationaliter conscius erat inquantum actus ab ipso processit ut iudicaret talem actum esse in tali genere et specie; sed etiam moraliter conscius erat inquantum actus ita ab ipso processit ut iudicaret et se sic agentem et ipsum suum actum vel bonum esse vel malum. Conscie ergo refertur homo ad suum actum secundum conscientiam et empiricam et intellectualem et rationalem et moralem. Et propter hanc relationem consciam et conscie actus est suus et conscie de ipso actu suo homo ipse vel gaudere vel torqueri potest.

Quibus perspectis, si vere homo ad imaginem Dei factus est, ex iis relationibus humanis atque consciis analogice procedendum est ad relationes personarum divinarum constitutivas concipiendas. Et ideo Patrem, Filium, et Spiritum sanctum dicimus conscios non solum secundum quod sunt subiecta actus divini essentialis sed etiam secundum quod sunt subiecta actuum notionalium. Quod si conscii sunt secundum actus notionales, conscii sunt secundum relationes mutuo oppositas, scilicet, secundum paternitatem et filiationem, spirationem activam et passivam. Denique cum in divinis idem realiter sint abstractum et concretum, ut Deitas sit Deus, etiam hae consciae relationes sunt subsistentes ut paternitas sit Pater, et filiatio sit Filius, et spiratio passiva sit Spiritus sanctus. Qua de causa, personae divinae secundum totam suam realitatem sive absolutam sive relativam sunt consciae; et ideo quamvis unio hypostatica facta sit non in natura neque secundum naturam sed in persona et secundum personam, nihilominus in quodam conscio et secundum quoddam conscium facta est, cum nihil in persona divina sit quod inconscium sit.

Sectio Secunda: De Conscientia Christi Humana

Asserta

1 Christus ut homo sub ratione experti se ipsum attingit per operationes suas humanas et secundum perfectionem ipsarum operationum.

is precisely because he is conscious of it as his own action that he experiences joy or torment. For that action proceeded from him, and so not only is that action related to him, but he himself is also related to the action. This conscious action consciously proceeded from one who was conscious. He was not just empirically conscious, so that the act proceeded from him in such a way that he experienced himself acting in such a way; nor was he merely intellectually conscious, so that the act proceeded from him in such a way that he understood what it was to act in this way; nor was he just rationally conscious, so that the act proceeded from him in such a way that he judged that such an act is of such and such a genus and species; but he was also morally conscious, so that the act proceeded from him in such a way that he judged that he was acting in this way and that this deed of his was good or evil. Peter, therefore, is consciously related to his action by way of empirical, intellectual, rational, and moral consciousness; and because of this conscious relationship, it is true both that the act is consciously his and that he himself can consciously either rejoice in or be tormented by his act, as the case may be.

In view of this, if in fact human beings are made in God's image, we may proceed by way of analogy from these conscious human relations to conceiving the relations that constitute the divine persons. That is why we say that the Father, the Son, and the Holy Spirit are conscious as subjects not only of essential divine acts but also as subjects of notional acts. Now if they are conscious through their notional acts, they are conscious through mutually opposed relations, that is, through paternity and filiation, active and passive spiration. Finally, since in God the abstract and the concrete are really the same, so that divinity is God, these conscious relations too are subsistent, so that paternity is Father, filiation is Son, and passive spiration is the Holy Spirit. Hence the divine persons are conscious in the totality of their being, both absolute and relative; and therefore the hypostatic union, although effected not in a nature or on the basis of a nature but in a person and on the basis of a person, nevertheless was effected in something conscious and through something conscious, for in a divine person there is nothing that is not conscious.

2 The Human Consciousness of Christ

Assertions

1 Christ as man, through his human operations and in proportion to the perfection of those operations, attains himself under the formality of the experienced.

2 Christus ut homo per conscientiam suam humanam atque scientiam suam beatam clare intelligit et certo iudicat se esse Filium Dei naturalem et verum Deum.

87 *Divisionis ratio*

Praesupponitur conscientia Christi secundum naturam divinam et secundum personam divinam, et quaeritur de conscientia Christi humana. Proinde cum homo se cognoscat, primo inquantum experientiam sui stricte dictam habeat, et deinde inquantum ipse se intelligat et affirmet, primum assertum supra positum internam Christi hominis experientiam respicit et veritatem humanitatis assumptae tuetur, assertum vero alterum subsequentem intelligentiam atque affirmationem respicit et unitatem personae in duabus naturis tuetur.

Ad terminos (1)

Christus: is qui et Deus et homo est.

ut homo: secundum suam humanitatem.

Christus ut homo: includuntur divina persona et humana natura sed praescinditur a natura divina.

sub ratione experti: secundum praeviam illam atque informem notitiam quae est experientia stricte dicta atque interna. Quatenus est experientia stricte dicta, opponitur ei quod innotescit ex ratione obiecti[6] per actus intelligendi, concipiendi, reflectendi, iudicandi. Quatenus est experientia interna, opponitur ei quod innotescit ex parte obiecti per sensus exteriores, imaginationem, memoriam, etc.

se ipsum attingit: ipse sibi innotescit ex parte subiecti.

operatio: aequivoce dicit vel (1) perfectionem, actum, actum secundum, *energeian*, vel (2) exercitium causalitatis efficientis, factionem, *poiêsin*. In thesi intelligitur operatio primo sensu, sed alter sensus non excluditur cum homo conscius sit non solum secundum actus sed etiam secundum emanationes intelligibiles actus ex actu.

operationes humanae: sive primo sensu, uti sentire, appetere, inquirere, intelligere, concipere, reflecti, evidentiam perspicere, iudicare, velle, eligere; sive altero sensu, inquantum

2 Christ as man, through his human consciousness and his beatific knowledge, clearly understands, and with certainty judges, himself to be the natural Son of God and true God.

87 *Reason for This Division*

Taking for granted that Christ is conscious on the basis of the divine nature and on the basis of the divine person, we go on to inquire about his human consciousness. Now, one knows oneself, first inasmuch as one has experience strictly so called of oneself, and then inasmuch as one understands and affirms oneself. Therefore the first assertion above regards the interior experience of Christ the human being and safeguards the truth of the assumed humanity; the second assertion regards his subsequent understanding and judgment, and safeguards the unity of the person in two natures.

Definition of Terms, Assertion 1

Christ: he who is both God and man.

as man: through his humanity.

Christ as man: includes both the divine person and the human nature, while prescinding from the divine nature.

under the formality of the experienced: through that preliminary unstructured awareness that is internal experience in the strict sense of the word. As experience strictly so called, it is opposed to what is known on the side of the object[6] through acts of understanding, conceiving, reflecting, and judging. As internal experience, it is opposed to what is known on the side of the object through the external senses, imagination, memory, and so on.

attains himself: he becomes aware of himself on the side of the subject.

operation: can mean either (1) perfection, act, second act, *energeia*, or (2) the exercise of efficient causality, making, *poiêsis*. In this thesis 'operation' is taken in the first sense, while the second sense is not excluded, since one is conscious not only through one's acts but also through the intelligible emanations of one act from another.

human operations: both in the first sense, such as sensing, desiring, inquiring, understanding, conceiving, reflecting, grasping the evidence, judging, willing, and choosing; and in the second sense, in that one who inquires produces his or her

---

6 [Lonergan's Latin is 'ex ratione obiecti'; this is the only occurrence in the work of that phrase; the translation is the same as for the usual 'ex parte obiecti.']

inquirens suum intelligere producit, intelligens definitionem producit, reflectens evidentiae perspicientiam producit, evidentiam perspiciens iudicium producit, deliberans electionem producit.

per operationes: scilicet, sicut sensus non sentit, sed homo per sensum, ita sensus non est conscius, sed homo per suum sentire. Et similiter Christus homo per operationes humanas
conscius sui redditur.

secundum perfectionem ipsarum operationum: scilicet, habet conscientiam sui ut sentientis per
suum sentire, ut intelligentis per suum intelligere, ut iudicantis per suum iudicare, ut
eligentis per suum eligere, denique tandem ut hominis per suam humanitatem diversimode operantem.

[Ad terminos (2)]

conscientia sua humana: cf. assertum primum.

scientia beata: scire Deum trinum per suam essentiam, et pro perfectione huius scientiae
caetera etiam in Deo per modum obiecti secundarii cognoscere.[7]

intelligere: prima operatio intellectus unde quis conceptionem dicere et ad quaestionem,
Quid sit, respondere potest.

iudicare: dicere verbum interius quod ex secunda intellectus operatione procedit et ad quaestionem, An sit, respondet.

se: ipsum subiectum quod conscie intelligit et conscie iudicat.

per conscientiam et scientiam beatam: omnis beatus videt Deum trinum et Verbum incarnatum;
sed Christus ut homo non solum ex parte obiecti videt Deum trinum et Verbum incarnatum sed etiam ex parte subiecti est sui conscius; unde ex coniunctione et scientiae et
conscientiae se esse Verbum incarnatum et intelligit et affirmat.

Sensus primi asserti

Primo asseritur (1) quis sit conscius, (2) cuius sit conscius, (3) cur sit conscius, (4)
quatenus sit conscius, et (5) qua ratione conscius conscium attingat.

Nam (1) is qui conscius est, Christus ut homo est.

act of understanding, one who understands produces a definition, one who reflects produces the grasp of the evidence, one who grasps the evidence produces
a judgment, and one who deliberates produces a choice.

through operations: that is, just as it is not the sense that senses but a human being
through the sense, so it is not the sense that is conscious but a human being
through sensing. Similarly, Christ as human is rendered conscious through his
human operations.

in proportion to the perfection of these operations: he is conscious of himself as sensing
through his sensitive operations, as understanding through his act of understanding, as judging through his act of judging, as choosing through his making
a choice, and ultimately as human through the various operations of his humanity.

Definition of Terms, Assertion 2

his human consciousness: see above, first assertion.

beatific knowledge: to know the triune God through the divine essence and, in proportion to the perfection of this knowledge, to know all other things in God as
secondary objects.[7]

understands: the first operation of the intellect by which one can form a concept
and answer the question, What is it?

judges: to utter an inner word that proceeds from the second operation of the
intellect and answers the question, Is it?

himself : the very subject that consciously understands and consciously judges.

through his consciousness and beatific knowledge: all the blessed see the triune God and
the incarnate Word; but Christ as human not only sees the triune God and the
incarnate Word on the side of the object but is also conscious of himself on the
side of the subject; hence by a combination of knowledge and consciousness he
understands and judges himself to be the incarnate Word.

The Meaning of Assertion 1

The first assertion states the following: (1) who is conscious, (2) what he is conscious
of, (3) why he is conscious, (4) to what extent he is conscious, and (5) under what
formality the one who is conscious attains the one who is conscious. For:

(1) The one who is conscious is Christ as man.

---

7 DB 530; DS 1000; Thomas Aquinas, *Summa theologiae*, 1, q. 12; 3, q. 10.

Iterum (2) is cuius conscius est, Christus ut homo est; per conscientiam enim conscius se ipsum attingit.

Ideo (3) conscius est quia sensitive et intellective operatur; nam per operationes eiusmodi homines sunt conscii, et Christus ut homo est per omnia nobis similis absque peccato.

Eatenus (4) conscius est quatenus facit ipsa harum operationum perfectio; quatenus ergo Christus ut homo sentit, empirice est conscius; quatenus intelligit, intellectualiter est conscius; quatenus iudicat, rationaliter est conscius; quatenus eligit, moraliter est conscius.

Denique (5) cum conscientia sit praevia quaedam atque informis notitia sui suorumque actuum, sub ratione experti Christus ut homo Christum ut hominem attingit. Quamvis enim Christus ut homo et se intelligat et se affirmet, tamen per suam intelligentiam se intelligit et per suum iudicium se affirmat.

Sensus asserti alterius

Deinde asseritur, cum Christo homini innotescat (1) ex parte subiecti per conscientiam humanam ipse sibi et (2) ex parte obiecti per visionem beatam Filius Dei naturalis, inquantum haec duo in consideratione ipsius Christi hominis simul sumuntur, Christum ut hominem ex parte obiecti et clare intelligere et certo affirmare se (secundum proprietatem huius reflexivi) esse Filium Dei naturalem et verum Deum.

Quid significet 'Christus ut homo'

Cum in tota hac quaestione difficultas principalis sit quisnam cuiusnam sit conscius, et clarius et distinctius declarandum esse videtur quid praecise significet 'Christus ut homo.' Dicimus enim Christum ut hominem Christi ut hominis esse conscium.

Omnibus ergo consentientibus, 'Christus ut homo' est persona divina in natura humana subsistens; et ideo distinguitur tum contra personam divinam nude sumptam tum contra personam divinam in divina natura subsistentem; quae sane distinctiones, cum Christus Deus et homo sit unum ens et una res, non sunt maiores reales quibus alia res a re alia separatur, sed inquantum divina persona et divina natura distinguuntur, rationis cum fundamento in re, inquantum autem divina et humana in ipso Christo distinguuntur, ad modum realis minoris.

(2) The one of whom he is conscious is Christ as man; it is through consciousness that one who is conscious attains oneself.

(3) Therefore he is conscious because he is operating sensitively and intellectually; for it is through these kinds of operations that human beings are conscious, and Christ as man is like us in every way, sin excepted.

(4) The level of one's consciousness depends upon the perfection of these operations. Insofar, therefore, as Christ as man senses, he is empirically conscious; insofar as he understands, he is intellectually conscious; insofar as he judges, he is rationally conscious; insofar as he chooses, he is morally conscious.

(5) Finally, since consciousness is a preliminary unstructured awareness of oneself and one's acts, Christ as man attains Christ as man under the formality of the experienced. Christ as man, of course, both understands and affirms himself, but it is through his intelligence that he understands himself and through his judgment that he affirms himself.

The Meaning of Assertion 2

The second assertion states that, since Christ the man (1) is aware of himself on the side of the subject through human consciousness and (2) knows the natural Son of God on the side of the object through beatific vision, inasmuch as these two are taken together in considering Christ the man, it follows that Christ the man clearly understands and with certainty, on the side of the object, affirms himself (in the proper meaning of this reflexive pronoun) to be the natural Son of God and true God.

The Meaning of 'Christ as Man'

Since the main difficulty in this whole question is to know who is conscious of whom, it seems that we ought to state more clearly and distinctly just exactly what is meant by 'Christ as man.' For our position is that Christ as man is conscious of Christ as man.

There is universal agreement that 'Christ as man' means a divine person subsisting in a human nature; 'Christ as man,' therefore, is in contradistinction both to the divine person taken by itself and to the divine person subsisting in the divine nature. But since Christ, God and man, is one being and one reality, these distinctions are not major real distinctions, by which one thing is separated from another. The distinction between the divine person and the divine nature is a rational distinction with a foundation in reality, while the distinction between divine and human in Christ is a minor real distinction.

Quia ergo Christus ut homo personam divinam in se includit, idem est ponere Christum ut hominem sui conscium ac ponere personam divinam sui consciam. Qua de causa, asserto nostro adversantur omnes qui subiectum conscientiae humanae Christi ponant sive (1) hominem quendam assumptum, sive (2) subiectum quoddam psychologicum seu 'ego' psychologicum quod cum persona divina non identificetur, sive (3) animam Christi humanam, sive (4) naturam Christi humanam, sive (5) conscientiam Christi humanam. Attamen in ipsis auctoribus legendis sedulo distinguendum est inter modum loquendi et veram eorum intentionem, praesertim cum haec quaestio omnino sit recentior et perpauci perspectum habeant quid sit conscientia.

Proinde quamvis omnino necessarium sit in Christo homine personam divinam personae divinae esse consciam, tamen hoc solum affirmare non sufficit. Sicut enim vera et propria est humanitas Christi, ita etiam vere et proprie humana est conscientia Christi ut hominis. Qua de causa, *per conscientiam vere et proprie humanam persona divina est personae divinae conscia*. En difficultas! En problematis nodus!

Cuius difficultatis solutio in ipso incarnationis mysterio fundatur. Nisi enim persona divina vere et realiter esset homo, nullo modo fieri potuit ut per conscientiam vere et proprie humanam persona divina esset personae divinae conscia. Per conscientiam enim humanam homo est hominis conscius. At persona divina vere et realiter homo est. Et ideo per conscientiam vere et proprie humanam persona divina est sui conscia inquantum ipsa persona divina homo est.

Argumentum ad primum assertum

(1) Omnis homo sub ratione experti se ipsum attingit per operationes suas humanas et secundum perfectionem ipsarum operationum.

Atqui Christus ut homo (persona divina in humana natura subsistens) vere et proprie est homo.

Ergo Christus ut homo sub ratione experti se ipsum attingit per operationes suas humanas et secundum perfectionem ipsarum operationum.

Maior: constat ex analysi conscientiae humanae.

Minor: constat ex conc. Chalcedonensi, '... consubstantialem nobis eundem secundum humanitatem, per omnia nobis similem absque peccato' (DB 148).

Since, therefore, Christ as man includes in himself a divine person, there is no difference between stating that Christ as man is conscious of himself and that a divine person is conscious of himself. It follows, then, that all those will be opposed to our assertion who take the subject of Christ's human consciousness to be either (1) an assumed human being, or (2) some psychological subject or psychological 'I' that is not identified with the divine person, or (3) the human soul of Christ, or (4) the human nature of Christ, or (5) the human consciousness of Christ. However, in reading these authors one must carefully distinguish between their way of speaking and what they really intend, especially since this question is relatively recent and the nature of consciousness is not widely understood.

Again, although it is absolutely necessary to maintain that in Christ the man a divine person is conscious of a divine person, this affirmation by itself is not sufficient. For just as Christ's humanity is a true and proper humanity, so also is the consciousness of Christ as human a true and proper human consciousness. Therefore, *through a consciousness that is truly and properly human, a divine person is conscious of a divine person.* Here is the difficulty! This is the crux of the problem!

The solution to this difficulty is rooted in the mystery of the incarnation. If a divine person were not really and truly human, it would be quite impossible for a divine person to be conscious of a divine person through a true and proper human consciousness. For it is through human consciousness that a human being is conscious of a human being. Now, a divine person is really and truly human; therefore through a true and proper human consciousness a divine person is conscious of himself inasmuch as that divine person is human.

Argument for Assertion 1

(1) Every human being attains himself or herself under the formality of the experienced through his or her human operations and in proportion to the perfection of those operations.

But Christ as man – a divine person subsisting in a human nature – is truly and properly a human being.

Therefore Christ as man attains himself under the formality of the experienced through his human operations and in proportion to the perfection of those operations.

The major premise is clear from an analysis of human consciousness.

The minor premise is clear from the Council of Chalcedon: '... the same one consubstantial with us in his humanity, and like us in all things save sin' (DB 148; DS 301–302).

(2) In humana natura sensus non sentit sed homo per sensum, appetitus non appetit sed homo per appetitum, intellectus non intelligit sed homo per intellectum, voluntas non vult sed homo per voluntatem.

Ulterius, in homine sentiente, appetente, intelligente, volente, ipse homo est conscius ut quod est conscium et operationes sunt consciae ut quibus ille est conscius.

Ulterius, non datur conscientia intellectualis per sensationes, neque rationalis per actus intelligendi, neque moralis per iudicia speculativa; sed secundum sensationes habetur conscientia empirica, secundum actus intelligendi habetur conscientia intellectualis, secundum iudicia speculativa habetur conscientia rationalis, et secundum deliberationes et electiones habetur conscientia moralis.

Quae omnia nihil aliud dicunt quam hominem se ipsum sub ratione experti attingere per operationes humanas et secundum perfectionem operationum humanarum.

Atqui in Christo homine persona Verbi divina est qui sentit et appetit et intelligit et vult secundum operationes finitas et humanas.

Ergo persona Verbi divina in humana natura subsistens est conscia sui qua modo humano sentientis, appetentis, intelligentis, volentis.

(3) Qui vere patitur, per sensationes dolorosas ipse sui conscius est.
Atqui Christus ut homo vera carnis passione passus est (DB 462).
Ergo Christus ut homo per sensationes dolorosas ipse sui conscius erat.

N.B. Quid significet argumentum primum (1) per argumentum alterum (2) magis explicite declaratur et illustratione particulari in tertio (3) argumento proponitur.

Obicitur

(1) Fieri non potest ut persona divina ipsa se attingat per operationes mere sensitivas ut videre, esurire, flagellari, cruce torqueri.

Respondetur: si persona divina non vere et proprie homo est, *conceditur*; si vere et proprie homo est, *distinguitur*, non se ita attingit sub ratione quidditatis et intelligibilis vel sub ratione veri et entis, *conceditur*, non se ita attingit sub ratione experti, *negatur*. Iam vero persona divina facta est nobis similis quoad omnia absque peccato; et ideo sicut ipsi nos attingimus inquantum conscie sentimus, ita etiam persona divina inquantum facta est per omnia nobis similis.

(2) In a human nature it is not the sense that senses, but a human being through the senses, not the appetite that desires but a human being through the appetite, not the intellect that understands but a human being through the intellect, and not the will that wills but a human being through the will.

Furthermore, in the case of a human being who senses, desires, understands, and wills, that same human being is conscious as that which is conscious, and the operations are conscious as that through which the human being is conscious.

Again, intellectual consciousness does not come about through sensations, nor rational consciousness through insights, nor moral consciousness through speculative judgments; rather, sensations give rise to empirical consciousness, insights to intellectual consciousness, speculative judgments to rational consciousness, and deliberations and choices to moral consciousness.

All of this is just another way of saying that a human being attains himself or herself under the formality of the experienced through his or her human operations and in proportion to the perfection of these operations.

But in Christ the man the divine person of the Word senses, desires, understands, and wills by way of finite human operations.

Therefore the divine person of the Word subsisting in a human nature is conscious of himself as sensing, desiring, understanding, and willing in a human manner.

(3) One who is truly suffering is conscious of self through painful sensations.

But Christ as man truly suffered bodily pain (DB 462; DS 852).

Therefore Christ as man was conscious of himself through painful sensations.

Note that the meaning of the first argument is stated more explicitly in the second and given a particular illustration in the third.

Objections

(1) A divine person cannot possibly attain himself through merely sensitive operations such as seeing, being hungry, being scourged, being crucified.

Reply: If that divine person is not truly and properly human, we concede; if that person is truly and properly human, we distinguish: that he does not attain himself under the formality of the definable and intelligible or under the formality of the true and of being, we concede; that he does not attain himself under the formality of the experienced, we deny. A divine person has become one like us in all things but sin; so just as we attain ourselves inasmuch as we have conscious sensations, a divine person does likewise, since that person is like us in every way.

(2) Homo non est sui conscius per solas operationes sensitivas vel intellectuales sed reflectione quadam ulteriori indiget ut sui conscius fiat.

Respondetur: eo ipso quod homo sentit, non se attingit hoc sensu quod se sentire neque intelligit neque concipit neque iudicat, *conceditur*, eo ipso quod homo sentit, non se attingit sub ratione experti, *negatur*.

Exemplo sit qui flagellatur: nisi enim intellectu operatur, se flagellari neque intelligit neque concipit neque iudicat; nihilominus, etiamsi tanta esset agonia ut nullatenus intellectu operaretur, ipse conscius se ipsum dolentem experiretur.

(3) Haec expositio est praeter quaestionem: illud enim quod quaeritur est quemadmodum Christus per conscientiam humanam suae divinitatis conscius fuerit.

Respondetur: est praeter quaestionem prout erronee, uti nobis videtur, concipi posset, *transeat*; est praeter ipsam quaestionem statuere personam divinam esse personae divinae consciam per conscientiam vere et proprie humanam, *negatur*.

(4) *Instatur*: secundum expositionem non attingitur persona divina qua divina; ergo manet difficultas.

Respondetur: persona divina qua divina est persona divina qua in divina natura subsistens; quae qua talis non attingitur nisi per conscientiam divinam. Secundum expositionem vero per conscientiam humanam attingitur persona divina in natura humana subsistens neque plus desiderari potest nisi a monophysitis.

Argumentum ad assertum alterum

Ut Christus homo et clare intelligat et certo iudicet se esse Filium Dei naturalem et verum Deum, requiruntur et sufficiunt

(1) conscientia sui,

(2) in qua subiectum (quod per conscientiam sibi innotescit) est Filius Dei naturalis et verus Deus;

(3) clara intelligentia quidditatis Filii Dei naturalis et Dei veri, et

(4) perspicientia identitatis et subiecti conscii et obiecti quidditative intellecti.

Atqui hae conditiones necessariae atque sufficientes per conscientiam Christi humanam et scientiam eiusdem beatam implentur.

(2) A human being is not conscious of self simply through sensitive or intellectual operations but needs further reflection to become conscious of self.

Reply: It is true that by the mere fact that one senses, one does not attain oneself, if by that you mean that one neither understands nor conceives nor judges that one is sensing; but we deny that by the mere fact that one senses one does not attain oneself under the formality of the experienced.

Take for example one who is being scourged: if his intellect is not functioning he neither understands nor conceives nor judges that he is being scourged; but even if his torment is so great as to render his intellect inoperative, he is still conscious of himself experiencing pain.

(3) Your explanation misses the point of the question. What we are asking is how Christ was conscious of his divinity through his human consciousness.

Reply: It could, perhaps, miss the point if the question is, as it seems to me, misunderstood; but that it misses the point to state that a divine person is conscious of a divine person through a consciousness that is truly and properly human, we deny.

(4) But again, according to the explanation given, a divine person is not attained as divine; the difficulty therefore remains.

Reply: A divine person as divine is a divine person as subsisting in the divine nature, and as such is not attained except through divine consciousness. But according to our explanation, what is attained through human consciousness is a divine person subsisting in a human nature, and only the monophysites could ask for anything more.

Argument for Assertion 2

For Christ as man to understand clearly and to judge with certainty himself to be the natural Son of God and himself true God, the following conditions are required and sufficient:

(1) consciousness of himself;

(2) in which the subject (that which is aware of itself through consciousness) is the natural Son of God and himself true God;

(3) a clear understanding of the quiddity of the natural Son of God and of the true God; and

(4) a grasp of the identity between the conscious subject and the object thus quidditatively understood.

But these necessary and sufficient conditions are fulfilled by Christ's human consciousness and his beatific knowledge.

Ergo per conscientiam Christi humanam et scientiam suam beatam Christus ut homo et clare intelligit et certo iudicat se esse Filium Dei naturalem et Deum verum.

Ad maiorem

Requiritur (1) conscientia sui propter proprietatem reflexivi 'se';

requiritur alterum (2), secus erronea esset intelligentia et erroneum iudicium quod asseritur;

requiritur tertium (3), nam qui non clare intelligit quid sit Filius Dei naturalis, non potest clare intelligere se esse Filium Dei naturalem;

requiritur quartum (4), nam qui hanc identitatem non perspicit, eam non clare intelligit.

Sufficiunt vero haec quattuor. Nam quod intelligitur et iudicatur, ex parte obiecti ponitur; quare cum Christus homo intelligat et iudicet se esse Filium Dei naturalem, ex parte obiecti ponitur (a) identitas inter (b) Filium Dei naturalem et (c) subiectum ex parte subiecti sibi innotescens; et ideo sufficit ut (1) subiectum ex parte subiecti sibi innotescat, (2) Filius Dei naturalis ex parte obiecti clare intellecti innotescat, (3) subiectum sit Filius Dei naturalis, et (4) haec identitas a subiecto perspiciatur.

Ad minorem

Conditio prima (1) per conscientiam Christi humanam impletur, uti ex primo asserto constat. Neque aliter impleri potest.

Conditio altera (2) est dogma Incarnationis.

Conditio tertia (3) et per scientiam beatam impletur et sine scientia beata impleri non potest. Qui enim quidditatem rei intelligit, rem per essentiam cognoscit; et Deum per essentiam cognoscere intellectui creato non contingit nisi per visionem beatam.[8]

Conditio quarta (4) statim impletur cum aliae conditiones implentur. Nam per scientiam suam beatam Christus ut homo non solum ipsum Deum trinum

Therefore through his human consciousness and beatific knowledge Christ as man clearly understands and with certainty judges himself to be the natural Son of God and true God.

The major premise

(1) Consciousness of himself is required on account of the proper force of the reflexive '*himself*';

(2) the second condition is required, since otherwise the understanding and the judgment stated above would both be erroneous;

(3) the third condition is required, since one who does not understand what the natural Son of God is cannot clearly understand himself to be the natural Son of God;

(4) the fourth condition is required, since without a grasp of this identity one cannot be said to understand it clearly.

These four requirements are sufficient. For that which is understood and affirmed is on the side of the object. When, therefore, Christ the man understands and judges himself to be the natural Son of God, there are on the side of the object (a) the identity between (b) the natural Son of God and (c) the subject aware of himself on the side of the subject. Therefore it suffices (1) that the subject be aware of himself on the side of the subject, (2) that the natural Son of God be known on the side of the clearly understood object, (3) that the subject be the natural Son of God, and (4) that this identity be grasped by the subject.

The minor premise

Condition (1) is fulfilled by Christ's human consciousness, as is clear from the first assertion; it cannot be fulfilled in any other way.

Condition (2) is the dogma of the incarnation.

Condition (3) is fulfilled by beatific knowledge and cannot be fulfilled without this knowledge. For to understand the quiddity of something is to know that thing in its essence; and no created intellect can know God in his essence save through the beatific vision.[8]

Condition (4) is fulfilled immediately upon the fulfilment of the other conditions. For through his beatific knowledge Christ as man knew not only the triune

---

8 Thomas Aquinas, *Summa theologiae*, 1, q. 12. [Note that (2) and (3) here correspond to (2) and (3) in the argument itself, but that they are reversed in the paragraph above beginning 'These four requirements.']

tamquam obiectum primarium sed etiam Verbum incarnatum qua incarnatum tamquam obiectum secundarium cognovit. Qua de causa, in obiecto secundario visionis beatae Christus ut homo omnia vidit quae per conscientiam suam humanam ipsi innotescebant.

Obicitur: Si necessaria est visio beata ut Christus homo sciat se esse Filium Dei, sequitur conscientiam Christi humanam esse erroneam.

Atqui nullus error admitti potest in conscientia Christi humana.

Ergo non requiritur visio beata ut Christus homo sciat se esse Filium Dei.

Respondetur: Ad maiorem: aequivocatio adest in voce 'scire.'

Si enim 'scire' dicitur proprie, significat cognitionem ex parte obiecti et sub ratione quidditatis, veri, et entis. Iam vero ad scientiam proprie dictam sive divinae essentiae sive filiationis aeternae, requiritur in intellectu creato visio beata. Sed ex hac necessitate visionis minime sequitur error in conscientia quia conscientia non est ex parte obiecti sed ex parte subiecti, neque per conscientiam humanam attingitur quidquam sub ratione quidditatis, veri, et entis.

Si autem 'scire' dicitur improprie pro qualibet notitia, tunc etiam includit notitiam ex parte subiecti et sub ratione experti. Sed ad talem notitiam sui Christus ut homo non indiget visione beata, cum per solam conscientiam humanam persona divina Verbi iam sit sui conscia, seu ipsa se attingat ex parte subiecti et sub ratione experti. Quare etiam si 'scire' improprie sumatur, nullus invenitur error in conscientia Christi humana.

Minor conceditur et conclusio pariter distinguitur.

88   *Circa subiectum ontologicum et psychologicum*

Quaeri solet utrum Christus sit unum ontologice et duo psychologice.

Quam quaestionem omisit Pius xii, *Sempiternus Rex*,[9] uti videtur, deliberate.[10]

God as primary object but also the incarnate Word as incarnate as a secondary object. In this secondary object of his beatific vision, therefore, Christ as man saw everything that became manifest to him through his human consciousness.

Objection: If beatific vision is needed for Christ the man to know himself to be the Son of God, it follows that his human consciousness is erroneous.

But we cannot admit error in Christ's human consciousness.

Therefore beatific vision is not required for Christ the man to know himself to be the Son of God.

Reply: In the major premise the word 'to know' [*scire*] is equivocal.

Taken in its proper sense, 'to know' signifies knowledge [*cognitio*] on the side of the object and under the formality of the definable, of the true, and of being. Now, for knowledge [*scientia*] in a proper sense, whether of the divine essence or of eternal filiation, a created intellect has to have the beatific vision. But the necessity for this vision by no means implies an error in consciousness, since consciousness is not on the side of the object but on the side of the subject, and human consciousness does not attain anything under the formality of the definable, of the true, and of being.

But in an improper sense, 'to know' refers to any kind of knowing [*notitia*] and thus includes awareness on the side of the subject and under the formality of the experienced. For this sort of awareness of himself Christ as man needs no beatific vision, since the divine person of the Word is already conscious of himself through his human consciousness alone, that is, attains himself on the side of the subject and under the formality of the experienced. Hence even if 'to know' is taken in this improper sense, there is no error to be found in the human consciousness of Christ.

We concede the minor premise, and distinguish the conclusion according to the distinction introduced into the major premise.

88 *The Ontological and Psychological Subject*

The question is often raised whether Christ is ontologically one and psychologically two.

Pope Pius XII in *Sempiternus Rex*[9] omitted this question, deliberately, it seems.[10]

---

9 8 September 1951; *Acta Apostolicae Sedis* 43 (1951) 638.

10 Paul Galtier, 'La conscience humaine du Christ,' *Gregorianum* 32 (1951) 562, note 68; Karl Rahner, 'Chalkedon – Ende oder Anfang?' in Aloys Grillmeier and Heinrich Bacht, *Das Konzil von Chalkedon* (Würzburg: Echter-Verlag, 1954), vol. 3, p. 12; Pietro Parente, *L'Io di Cristo*, 2nd ed. (Brescia: Morcelliana, 1955) 356, note 537.

Respondetur quod in Christo Deo et homine habetur unum ratione personae et duo ratione naturarum. Qua de causa, cum una sit persona, nulla est distinctio facienda ratione ipsius subiecti quasi aliud esset subiectum divinae naturae vel conscientiae et aliud esset subiectum humanae naturae vel conscientiae. Attamen, cum duae sint naturae, cumque ipsum subiectum ad naturam (cuius subiectum est) habitudinem importet, omnino distinguere oportet inter subiectum prout in natura divina subsistit et idem subiectum prout in natura humana subsistit. Quod quidem nihil est aliud quam distinguere inter Christum ut Deum et Christum ut hominem.

Ulterius, subiectum prout in natura divina subsistit per conscientiam divinam ipsum sibi innotescit, et idem subiectum prout in natura humana subsistit per conscientiam humanam ipsum sibi innotescit. Et sicut idem non est in natura divina subsistere quod in natura humana subsistere, ita etiam idem non est sibi innotescere qua Deum ac sibi innotescere qua hominem.

Quibus perspectis, non est dicendum Christum esse unum ontologice et duo psychologice, sed est dicendum quod uno modo Christus est unum et ontologice et psychologice et alio modo Christus est duo et ontologice et psychologice. Unum enim est Christus (1) ontologice quia una eademque est persona et (2) psychologice quia una eademque persona sibi innotescit tum per conscientiam divinam tum per conscientiam humanam. Duo autem est Christus (1) ontologice quia tum in natura divina tum in natura humana subsistit et (2) psychologice quia per divinam conscientiam sibi innotescit qua subsistens in divina natura et per conscientiam humanam sibi innotescit qua subsistens in humana natura.

89   *Ontologicum et psychologicum in Christo ut homine*

Praeterea, circa ipsum Christum qua hominem duplex aspectus ontologicus et psychologicus subtilius distingui potest.

Nam in ordine essendi prius est esse quam operari, et ideo per prius Christus est homo quam ut homo operetur. At homo est conscius per suas operationes. Et ideo in ordine essendi per prius Christus constituitur ontologice ut homo quam psychologice ut homo conscius.

In ordine autem cognoscendi per prius homo sibi innotescit per conscientiam sub ratione experti quam per inquisitionem intellectualem sibi innotescat sub ratione intelligibilis et quidditatis, veri et entis. Quod autem sibi sub ratione experti innotescit, subiectum

In answer to this question we say that in Christ, God and man, there is one by reason of the person, and there are two by reason of the natures. It follows, then, that since the person is one, no distinction by reason of the subject is to be made, as if there were one subject of the divine nature or consciousness and another subject of the human nature or consciousness. However, since there are two natures, and since a subject bears a relationship to the nature whose subject it is, one must by all means distinguish between the subject as subsisting in the divine nature and that same subject as subsisting in a human nature. This, of course, is simply the distinction between Christ as God and Christ as man.

Furthermore, the subject subsisting in the divine nature is aware of himself through divine consciousness, and this same subject as subsisting in a human nature is aware of himself through human consciousness. And since to subsist in the divine nature is not the same as to subsist in a human nature, so also to be aware of oneself as God is not the same as to be aware of oneself as a human being.

In view of this, we should not speak of Christ as ontologically one and psychologically two, but rather as in one way both ontologically and psychologically one and in another way as both ontologically and psychologically two. He is ontologically one because his person is one and the same, and he is psychologically one because this one and the same person is aware of himself through both divine consciousness and human consciousness. But Christ is ontologically two in that he subsists in both a divine nature and a human nature, and psychologically two in that through divine consciousness he is aware of himself as subsisting in a divine nature and through human consciousness he is aware of himself as subsisting in a human nature.

89 *The Ontological and the Psychological in Christ as Man*

Here we may go further and draw a more subtle distinction between the ontological and psychological aspects in Christ as man.

In the order of being, existence is prior to operation, and so Christ exists as a human being before he operates as a human being. But a human being is conscious through his or her operations. Therefore in the order of being Christ is constituted first ontologically as a human being and then psychologically as a conscious human being.

In the cognitional order, however, a human being becomes aware of himself or herself first through consciousness under the formality of the experienced and only subsequently becomes known to himself or herself through intellectual inquiry under the formality of the intelligible and definable, of the true and of being.

psychologicum dicitur. Quod vero sibi sub ratione entis innotescit, subiectum ontologicum dicitur. Et ideo in ordine quo homo sibi innotescit, prius est subiectum psychologicum et posterius est idem subiectum sub ratione entis seu ontologicum. Qua de causa, primum posuimus assertum de Christo inquantum ipse se attingit sub ratione experti, et alterum posuimus assertum de Christo prout ipse se attingit sub ratione entis.

90   Utrum in Christo inveniatur exinanitio quaedam psychologica

Quod in Christo sit quaedam exinanitio, omnino patet secundum illud 'exinanivit semetipsum' (Phil. 2.7).

Quae quidem exinanitio non est depositio sive personae divinae sive naturae divinae sive conscientiae quae ad personam naturamque divinam pertineat.

Sed exinanitio haec in accessione quadam consistit inquantum qui Deus est etiam vere et proprie homo factus est.

Prima ergo in Christo invenitur exinanitio ontologica inquantum vere et proprie homo est. Ad quam sequitur etiam exinanitio psychologica. Qui enim vere et proprie homo est, non est sui conscius quasi homo non esset, sed per conscientiam suam humanam est sui conscius secundum quod homo est.

Praeterea, cum in Christo Deo et homine naturae divina et humana neque mutentur neque commisceantur, pariter ex unione hypostatica neque mutantur neque commiscentur conscientiae divina et humana. Et ideo sicut Dei Filius per conscientiam suam divinam secundum infinitam suam perfectionem sibi innotescit, ita etiam idem Dei Filius per conscientiam suam humanam secundum inopiam humanae naturae sibi innotescit. Qua de causa, quae prima et ontologica est exinanitio per assumptionem naturae humanae effecta, per consequentem exinanitionem psychologicam in plena luce sistitur inquantum Christus non solum est homo sed etiam ipse se ut hominem experitur.

91   Utrum in Christo sit 'ego' quoddam humanum

Quod 'ego' quoddam in Christo inveniatur, ex ipsa sua loquela patet; dixit enim 'antequam Abraham fieret, ego sum,' etc.

Quod quidem 'ego' est (1) vox quaedam exterior ab ore Christi prolata, (2) verbum interius in mente Christi humana conceptum tum complexe ('ego sum') tum per prius incomplexe, (3) id quod sub ratione veri et entis per vocem significatur et per verbum

Now that which is aware of itself under the formality of the experienced is called the psychological subject. But that which is known to itself under the formality of being is called the ontological subject. Therefore in the order in which a human being comes to know himself or herself, there is first the psychological subject and then the same subject under the formality of being, the ontological subject. It was for this reason that our first assertion concerned Christ as attaining himself under the formality of the experienced while our second assertion concerned Christ as attaining himself under the formality of being.

90   *Is There in Christ a Psychological Kenosis?*

That there is some sort of self-emptying in Christ is quite clear from Philippians 2.7: he 'emptied himself ...' (*heauton ekenôsen*).

This kenosis is certainly not a laying aside of the divine person or of the divine nature or of the consciousness that belongs to a divine person and nature.

Rather, this kenosis consists in a certain acquisition, in that he who is God has also become human in the true and proper sense.

The first kenosis to be found in Christ, therefore, is ontological in that he is truly and properly human. Consequent upon it is a psychological kenosis. For one who is truly and properly human is not conscious of himself as if he were not human, but through his human consciousness he is conscious of himself in his human condition.

Besides, since in Christ, God and man, the divine and human natures are neither changed nor mixed, the divine and the human consciousnesses are likewise neither changed nor mixed as a result of the hypostatic union. Hence as the Son of God is aware of himself in his infinite perfection through his divine consciousness, so also the same Son of God is aware of himself through his human consciousness in the poverty of human nature. As a result, that first, ontological kenosis, brought about by the assumption of a human nature, becomes very evident through the consequent psychological kenosis inasmuch as Christ not only is human but also experiences himself as human.

91   *Is There a Human 'I' in Christ?*

Christ's own words clearly indicate the presence of some 'I' in him: for example, 'Before Abraham was, I am,' and similar sayings.

This 'I' is (1) an outer word uttered by Christ; (2) the inner word conceived in the human mind of Christ, both in its compound form ('I am') and in its prior simple form ['I']; (3) that which under the formality of the true and of being is

interius intenditur, quod quidem, cum 'ego' dicatur, idem est ac ipse qui significat et intendit, (4) ille ipse significat et intendit secundum potentiam harum operationum, et (5) ille ipse qui significat et intendit secundum actum harum operationum.

Iam vero primum et alterum sunt simpliciter humana.

Tertium autem est persona divina Verbi; haec enim est persona quae significat et intendit; quod ex ipso textu confirmatur cum humanitas Christi non ante sed post Abraham fuerit.

Quartum autem et quintum sunt persona Verbi divina prout in natura humana subsistit. Nam secundum suam naturam humanam persona Verbi et dicere potest et actu dicit. At secundum suam naturam divinam persona Verbi neque dicere potest neque dicit sed dicitur tantum, cum in divinis 'dicere' sit actus notionalis (importat relationem personalem) qui Deo Patri proprius est.

At ulterius 'ego' sumitur ad significandum subiectum psychologicum. Eo ergo modo quo in Christo agnovimus unum tantum et ontologice et psychologice, etiam unum 'ego' idque divinum in Christo est ponendum. Eo autem modo quo in Christo duo agnovimus et ontologice et psychologice, etiam duo 'ego' secundum quid, nempe, ego ut divinum et ego ut humanum, in Christo ponenda sunt et agnoscenda.

Quare inquantum idem subiectum sibi innotescit tum per conscientiam divinam tum per conscientiam humanam, unum 'ego' simpliciter in Christo est sicut et una persona.

Inquantum autem 'ego,' seu subiectum psychologicum, non solum ipsum subiectum dicit sed etiam habitudinem importat ad naturam atque conscientiam cuius subiectum est, cum in Christo duae sint naturae atque conscientiae, ideo in Christo distinguendum est inter 'ego ut divinum' quod sibi secundum infinitam suam perfectionem innotescit, et 'ego ut humanum' quod se experitur secundum limitationes naturae assumptae. Quae sane distinctio nihil est aliud quam ad campum psychologicum eam transferre distinctionem quae inter Christum ut Deum et Christum ut hominem notissima est.

Praeterea, hoc 'ego' qua humanum in Christo diversificatur secundum diversos conscientiae status atque actus ita ut (1) idem semper sit subiectum etiam psychologicum et (2) alius et alius sint conscientiae status et (3) ipsum idem subiectum per diversos status diversimode se habeat et diversimode sibi innotescat. Eundem ergo dicimus etiam psychologice cuius olim anima usque ad mortem erat tristis et nunc per visionem plene redundantem perfunditur gloria; quae differentiae non ita ad accessorium quendam conscientiae statum

meant by the outer word and intended by the inner word, and that which in fact, when the word 'I' is spoken, is identical with the one who signifies and intends; (4) the very one who means and intends in the way proper to the potency of these operations; and (5) the very one who means and intends in the way proper to the act of these operations.

The first and second 'I' above are simply human.

The third is the divine person of the Word, for this is the person who means and intends; this is confirmed by the text quoted, since the humanity of Christ did not exist before Abraham but after.

The fourth and fifth are the divine person of the Word as subsisting in a human nature. The person of the Word can speak and actually does speak in accordance with his human nature. But in his divine nature the person of the Word neither can nor does speak but is only spoken, since in the Godhead 'to speak' is a notional act – one that implies a personal relation – that is proper to God the Father.

But 'I' can be further taken to signify the psychological subject. In the sense, therefore, in which we have recognized that in Christ there is only one, both ontologically and psychologically, we should also speak of only one 'I' in Christ, and that is the divine 'I.' On the other hand, in the sense in which we recognized that there are two in Christ, both ontologically and psychologically, so also there is a qualified sense in which two 'I's' are to be recognized in him, 'I' as divine and 'I' as human.

Thus, inasmuch as the same subject is aware of himself through both the divine consciousness and the human consciousness, there is, absolutely speaking, only one 'I' in Christ just as there is only one person.

But inasmuch as 'I', the psychological subject, not only denotes that subject but also implies a relationship to the nature and the consciousness whose subject he is, and since in Christ there are two natures and two consciousnesses, we must distinguish between the 'I as divine,' which is aware of itself in its infinite perfection, and the 'I as human,' which experiences itself with the limitations of the assumed nature. This is simply transferring to the psychological realm the familiar distinction between Christ as God and Christ as man.

Moreover, Christ's 'I' as human undergoes variation according to his various states and acts of consciousness in such a way that (1) even the psychological subject always remains the same while (2) the states of consciousness change, and (3) through these changing states this same subject exists in different ways and experiences himself in different ways. We say therefore that even psychologically he is the same one whose soul was once sorrowful even unto death and who now experiences the radiance of glory through his altogether overflowing vision. These variations are not so restricted to some superficial state of consciousness that they do

restringuntur ut ipsum subiectum qua humanum non afficiant atque penetrent; neque adeo ipsum subiectum immutant ut alius psychologice olim fuerit tristis et alius psychologice nunc sit beatus.

At quamvis in Christo homine agnoscamus 'ego' qua humanum etiam secundum diversos conscientiae status modificatum, nullatenus in Christo admittendum credimus 'ego' mere humanum quod a divina persona distinguatur saltem psychologice. Haec enim opinio (quamvis ex errore circa communicationem idiomatum oriri possit) in errore saltem psychologico fundatur. Nam si conscientia non ut experientia subiecti sed ut obiecti perceptio concipitur, non solum praetermittitur persona divina sibi innotescens quatenus ipsa vitam humanam experitur, sed etiam in perceptis humanae vitae eventibus frustra quaeritur infinitum et ideo ad subiectum mere humanum concluditur. E contra, si conscientia non ut obiecti perceptio sed ut experientia subiecti concipitur, statim habetur quod persona divina vitam humanam experiens sibi ex parte subiecti et sub ratione experti innotescit. Nam sensus non sentit, sed homo per sensum; neque inconscie sentit homo sed conscie; neque alius hodie sentit et alius heri, sed idem; neque haec psychologica atque conscia identitas per diversitatem statuum tollitur, cum certo sciamus non alium vel aliud sed nos ipsos somniare et, qui quandoque amentes fuerint, quid in statu amentiae *sibi* visum sit describere possint. Neque plus quam fallaciam proferunt qui inter experientiam stricte dictam et subsequentem inquisitionem intellectualem non distinguant et ideo psychologicam subiecti identitatem negent quia in morbis psychicis (quae caeterum in Christo defuerunt) deesse possint et plena sui intelligentia et adaequata sui affirmatio.

92 *Quid in Christo homine significetur ut principium quod operetur*

In Christo Deo et homine sunt inconfuse et immutabiliter tum duae naturae (DB 148) tum duae operationes (DB 292), et secundum hoc significantur (1) divina natura ut principium quo operationis divinae et (2) humana natura ut principium quo operationis humanae.

At in eodem Christo Deo et homine invenitur una tantum persona quae operatur tum divina tum humana, et ideo secundum hanc personae unitatem agnoscendum est unum tantum principium quod operatur, nempe, ipsa divina persona.

not affect and indeed deeply penetrate the subject himself as human; on the other hand, they do not so alter the subject that the one who psychologically once was sorrowful is not the same as the one who psychologically now is in a state of bliss.

But, although we recognize in Christ the man an 'I' as human, even one that is modified according to varying states of consciousness, we believe that there is not to be admitted in Christ a merely human 'I' that is at least psychologically distinguished from the divine person. Such an opinion, although it might arise from an error regarding the interchange of properties, is founded on an error that is at least psychological. For if you conceive consciousness not as the experience of a subject but as the perception of an object, then not only do you overlook the divine person who becomes aware of himself inasmuch as he experiences human life, but also you seek in vain for something infinite in the perceived events of human life, and so you conclude that there is a merely human subject here. If, on the other hand, you conceive consciousness not as the perception of an object but as the experience of a subject, you immediately see that the divine person experiencing human life is aware of himself on the side of the subject and under the formality of the experienced. For it is not the sense that senses but a human being through the sense; and one does so not unconsciously but consciously. Nor is it one human being who sensed yesterday and another who senses today, but the same one; and this conscious psychological identity is not lost through variations in the states of consciousness, since we know for certain that it is we ourselves who are dreaming and not someone or something else, and people who were previously insane are able to describe what being insane was like *for them*. Those are guilty of a fallacy who fail to distinguish between experience strictly so called and subsequent intellectual inquiry, and so they are led to deny the psychological identity of the subject on the grounds that in mental illnesses (which Christ did not have in any event) full understanding and adequate affirmation of oneself can be lacking.

92 *What Is the Principle That Operates in Christ the Man?*

In Christ, God and man, the two natures (DB 148, DS 301–302) and the two sets of operations (DB 292, DS 557) are both present unchanged and unmixed. This means (1) that the divine nature is the 'principle by which' (*principium quo*) of divine operation, and (2) that the human nature is the 'principle by which' of human operation.

But in this same Christ, God and man, there is but one person that performs both divine and human operations; in view of this oneness of person, therefore, only one principle that operates (*principium quod operatur*) is to be admitted, namely, the divine person itself.

Quibus perspectis atque firmiter retentis, quaeritur utrum illud principium-quod concipiendum sit tamquam ipsa divina persona nude spectata cum praecisione ab utraque natura an concipiendum sit tamquam ipsa divina persona prout in aliqua subsistit natura.

Quod idem aliis verbis iterum quaeritur, nempe, utrum principium quod operatur sit persona sine respectu ad naturam qua operatur an sit persona cum respectu ad naturam.

Quod iterum secundum consequentia aperitur. Si enim persona nude spectata sit principium quod, sufficit dicere principium quod esse Christum vel personam Verbi. Sin autem persona cum respectu ad naturam sit principium quod, semper dicendum est principium quod esse vel Christum ut Deum vel Christum ut hominem secundum quod operatio sit divina vel humana.

Respondetur principium quod operatur semper esse personam cum respectu ad naturam; unde operans semper est aut Christus ut Deus aut Christus ut homo; vel iterum operans semper est persona divina aut qua subsistens in divina natura aut qua subsistens in humana natura.

Cuius responsionis prima ratio est quod quae secundum abstractam mentis considerationem ponuntur, sicut non sunt, ita non operantur. Sed persona divina non est sive sine divina natura sive (post incarnationem) sine humana natura. Ergo persona divina non est quod operatur sine respectu sive ad divinam sive ad humanam naturam.

Altera deinde est ratio quod 'esse et operari est personae a natura.'[11]

Tertia est ratio quae ex ipsa notione principii petitur. Principium enim est primum in aliquo ordine. Unde in ordine essendi distinguuntur et principium quod est et principia quibus est; et principium quod est est primum in ordine resolutionis cum ab ente concreto incipiatur et ad causas quibus componitur procedatur; in ordine autem compositionis prima sunt principia quibus componitur et ad ipsum compositum terminatur. Similiter in ordine operandi distinguuntur principium quod operatur et principia quibus operatur; et in ordine resolutionis primum est ipsum operans a quo incipit resolutio; in ordine autem compositionis prima sunt principia quibus operatur (natura, potentia, habitus).

Iam vero haberi non potest primum in aliquo ordine sine ullo ordine; et haberi non potest ordo sine respectu; et ideo cum principium sit primum in aliquo ordine, haberi non potest principium quod operatur sine respectu ad principia quibus operatur.

With this clearly and firmly in mind, we may ask whether this principle that operates is to be conceived as the divine person taken by itself while we prescind from both natures, or as the divine person considered as subsisting in some nature.

In other words, is the principle that operates the person without reference to the nature by which it operates or the person with reference to a nature?

Again, the implications of this question help to clarify it. For if the person taken by itself is the principle that operates, then one may simply say that the principle that operates is Christ, or the person of the Word. But if the principle that operates is the person with reference to a nature, one must always say that the principle that operates is Christ as God or Christ as man according to whether the operation is divine or human.

Our answer to this question is that the principle that operates is always the person with reference to a nature. The operator, therefore, is always either Christ as God or Christ as man; or again, the operator is always the divine person either as subsisting in the divine nature or as subsisting in the human nature.

The first reason for this answer is that whatever is stated as an abstract consideration of the mind neither exists in reality nor operates. But the divine person of the Word does not exist apart from the divine nature nor, after the incarnation, apart from the human nature. Therefore the divine person is not something that operates without reference to either the divine nature or the human nature.

The second reason is that 'being and operating belong to a person by reason of a nature.'[11]

The third reason is drawn from the very notion of a principle. A principle is that which is first in some order. Hence in the order of being there is a distinction between the principle that is and the principles by which it is; and the principle that is is first in the order of resolution, since this order begins from concrete being and proceeds to the causes by which it is constituted; while the order of composition starts from the principles by which a being is constituted and ends at the composite being itself. Similarly, in the order of operation there is a distinction between the principle that operates and the principles by which it operates; and in the order of resolution that which is first is the operator itself from which the resolution begins, while in the order of composition the principles by which it operates – nature, potency, habit – are first.

Now there cannot be a first in some order unless there is an order, and there cannot be an order without some reference. Therefore since a principle is a first in some order, there cannot be a principle that operates without reference to the principles by which it operates.

11 Thomas Aquinas, *Summa theologiae*, 3, q. 19, a. 1, ad 4m.

93 *Utrum persona Verbi exerceat causalitatem efficientem in operationes suas humanas*

Quae quaestio tripliciter intelligi potest. Primo modo, ut persona Verbi nude spectata sine respectu ad naturam sive divinam sive humanam exerceat causalitatem efficientem in operationes suas humanas.

Alio modo, ut persona Verbi prout in divina natura subsistat exerceat hanc causalitatem efficientem.

Tertio modo, ut persona Verbi prout in humana natura subsistat exerceat causalitatem efficientem in proprias operationes humanas.

Si primo modo intelligitur, negative respondetur. Nam id quod exercet causalitatem efficientem est id quod operatur secundum quod operatio intelligitur de operatione effectus. Iam vero, secundum ea quae superius sunt dicta, persona Verbi nude spectata non est principium quod operatur.

Si secundo modo intelligitur, respondetur affirmative sed cum distinctione. Quod enim a divina persona per causalitatem efficientem producitur, per divinam potentiam producitur; quae divina potentia est eadem realiter ac divina essentia; quae divina essentia est communis tribus personis. Qua de causa inter catholicos agnoscitur opera omnia divina ad extra a tribus personis divinis communiter procedere.[12] Et ideo quidquid efficienter operatur Filius qua in divina natura subsistens, pariter omnino operantur et Pater et Spiritus sanctus.

Si denique tertio modo intelligitur quaestio, respondendum est affirmative. Nam multae operationes nostrae a nobis efficienter producuntur, e.g., per intellectum agentem producimus et speciem intelligibilem et operationem quae speciem consequitur; et similiter, volendo finem producimus volitionem mediorum; et aperiendo oculos producimus actum videndi secundum exercitium actus; etc. Sed Filius Dei factus est 'similis nobis per omnia absque peccato.' Et ideo persona Verbi qua subsistens in natura humana, seu Christus ut homo, exercet causalitatem efficientem in operationes suas humanas.

Sectio Tertia: De Constitutione Ontologica Conscientiae Christi Humanae

94 Cum 'psychologicum' et 'conscium' non addant super ens sed tantummodo ens dicant in tali gradu perfectionis ontologicae, iisdem prorsus rationibus seu

93 *Does the Person of the Word Exercise Efficient Causality upon His Human Operations?*

This question can be understood in three ways. The first is, Does the person of the Word taken by itself without reference to either the divine nature or the human nature exercise efficient causality upon his human operations?

The second is, Does the person of the Word as subsisting in the divine nature exercise this efficient causality?

The third is, Does the person of the Word as subsisting in a human nature exercise efficient causality upon his own human operations?

If the question is understood in the first sense, the answer is no. For that which exercises efficient causality is that which operates in the sense of operating an effect. Now according to what we said above, the person of the Word taken by itself is not a principle that operates.

If the question is understood in the second sense, the answer is yes, but with a distinction. Whatever is produced by a divine person by way of efficient causality is produced by divine power; this divine power is really identical with the divine essence, and the divine essence is common to all three persons. For this reason Catholic theology recognizes that all divine works produced outside the Godhead proceed in common from the three divine persons.[12] Whatever, therefore, the Son as subsisting in the divine nature does by way of efficient causality is likewise and entirely the work of the Father and the Holy Spirit too.

Finally, if the question is understood in the third sense, the answer is yes. For many of our operations are produced by us through efficient causality: for example, by our agent intellect we produce both the intelligible species and the operation that results from that species; similarly, by willing the end we produce our willing of the means; and by opening our eyes we produce the act of seeing with respect to the exercise of that act; and so on. But the Son of God has become 'like us in all things but sin.' Hence it follows that the person of the Word as subsisting in a human nature, that is, Christ as man, exercises efficient causality upon his human operations.

3 The Ontological Constitution of Christ's Human Consciousness

94 Since 'psychological' and 'conscious' add nothing to being but merely indicate being of a certain degree of ontological perfection, a divine person is constituted

---

12 DB 77, DS 171; DB 254, DS 501; DB 281, DS 531; DB 285, DS 535; DB 421, DS 790; DB 428, DS 800; DB 703, DS 1330; DB 2290, DS 3814.

causis intrinsecis constituitur persona divina ut homo conscius ac constituitur persona divina ut homo sentiens, intelligens, iudicans, volens, etc.

Iam vero constituitur persona divina ut homo (1) per esse suum infinitum tamquam unicam causam constitutivam et (2) per actum substantialem et supernaturalem in natura assumpta receptum tamquam per terminum consequentem. Quod iam pridem determinatum est.

Deinde, constituitur persona divina ut homo sentiens inquantum in sensibus illius hominis, qui persona Verbi est, eliciuntur operationes sentiendi. Et similiter est de caeteris operationibus. Sicut enim persona Verbi est id quod est hic homo, etiam persona Verbi est id quod per has operationes huius hominis sentit, intelligit, iudicat, vult, eligit, etc.

Tertio, cum is qui sentiat conscie sentiat, et is qui intelligat conscie intelligat, et is qui eligat conscie eligat, eo ipso quod persona Verbi est id quod sentit etiam est id quod conscie sentit, et eo ipso quod persona Verbi est id quod intelligit etiam est id quod conscie intelligit, et similiter de aliis. Nam 'conscium' non addit super ens sed dicit ens in tali gradu perfectionis ontologicae.

95 Quae tamen ut plenius et accuratius intelligantur, considerantur obiectiones quae sequuntur.

(1) Id quod sibi innotescit per operationes finitas et secundum perfectionem finitam harum operationum, non potest esse nisi finitum. Sed secundum assertum primum in sectione praecedenti, persona infinita sibi innotescit per operationes finitas et secundum perfectionem harum operationum. Ergo assertum illud statuit impossibile.

Respondetur: Ad maiorem: quod sic sibi innotescit, non potest esse nisi finitum, *distinguitur*: si persona divina non potest esse homo, *conceditur*; si persona divina potest esse homo, *negatur*; nam si persona divina potest esse homo, etiam potest esse homo conscius; sicut enim 'homo conscius' finitum dicit, etiam 'homo' finitum dicit.

Conceditur minor et pariter distinguitur conclusio. Nam assertum primum statuit non impossibile sed ipsum mysterium incarnationis quo Verbum Dei factum est et homo et quidem homo sui conscius.

as a conscious human being by the very same intrinsic causes or reasons that constitute a divine person as a human being who senses, understands, judges, wills, and so forth.

Now a divine person is constituted as a human being (1) through his infinite act of existence as the sole constitutive cause, and (2) through a substantial supernatural act received in the assumed nature as through a consequent term. This point has already been settled.

Second, a divine person is constituted as a sensitive human being inasmuch as sensitive operations are elicited in the senses of that human being that the person of the Word is; and the same holds for all the other operations. For just as the person of the Word is what this human being is, so also the person of the Word is that which through these operations of this human being senses, understands, judges, wills, chooses, and so forth.

Third, since one who senses senses consciously and one who understands understands consciously and one who chooses chooses consciously, then by the very fact that the person of the Word is that which senses, the person of the Word is also that which consciously senses, and by the very fact that the person of the Word is that which understands, the person of the Word is also that which consciously understands, and similarly for the rest. For 'conscious' does not add anything to being but denotes being at a certain level of ontological perfection.

95 To understand this more fully and accurately it will help to consider the following objections.

(1) That which is aware of itself through operations that are finite and in proportion to the finite perfection of such operations cannot be anything but a finite being. But according to the first assertion in the previous section, it is an infinite person who is aware of himself through finite operations and in proportion to the perfection of these operations. Therefore, that assertion states the impossible.

Reply: Regarding the major, that what is aware of itself in this way cannot be anything but finite, a distinction must be made. If it is impossible for a divine person to be a human being, then the statement is true. But if it is possible for a divine person to be a human being, then the statement is false. For if a divine person can be a human being, that divine person can also be a conscious human being, for just as 'conscious human being' denotes something finite, so also does 'human being.'

The statement in the minor is true. The conclusion calls for a similar distinction. For the first assertion does not state the impossible; it states the very mystery of the incarnation by which the Word of God became a human being and indeed a human being conscious of himself.

(2) Quod nihil personae intrinsecum addit, non potest personam constituere ut consciam sui. Atqui operationes humanae in potentiis accidentalibus humanis elicitae nihil ponunt personae divinae intrinsecum. Ergo non possunt constituere personam divinam ut sui consciam.

Respondetur: Ad maiorem: Quod nihil addit intrinsecum sive ipsi personae sive naturae secundum quam persona est, non potest personam constituere ut consciam sui, *conceditur*; quod ita nihil addit intrinsecum personae ut tamen addat naturae secundum quam persona est, non potest constituere personam ut consciam sui, *negatur*.

Minor contradistinguitur et negantur consequentia et consequens.

(3) *Instatur*: atqui persona infinita entitative eadem est sive aliam naturam assumit sive nullam aliam naturam assumit; ergo fieri non potest ut per operationes in natura assumpta elicitas persona infinita vere et realiter sit sui conscia.

Respondetur: Ideo persona infinita entitative eadem est sive incarnatur sive non, quia per actum infinitum tamquam per unicam causam constitutivam constituitur ut incarnata, *conceditur*; ideo eadem entitative est, quia non vere et realiter incarnatur, *negatur*.

Ergo persona infinita non potest esse vere et realiter sui conscia per operationes finitas, pariter *distinguitur*; si vere et realiter non facta est homo, *conceditur*; si vere et realiter per ipsum suum esse facta est homo, *negatur*.

(4) *Iterum instatur*: per solutionem eiusmodi constituitur persona infinita tamquam subiectum attributionis logicae vel ontologicae sed non constituitur persona infinita tamquam subiectum psychologicum.

Respondetur: Per solutionem eiusmodi non constituitur subiectum nisi logicum vel ontologicum, ad mentem empiristarum, *conceditur*, ad mentem realistarum, *negatur*.

Nam secundum realistas id est reale quod innotescit per verum tamquam medium in quo innotescit. Neque realitas psychologica ullam facit exceptionem. Qua de causa, si vere persona Verbi est homo, etiam ontologice et realiter est homo; et si vere persona Verbi est hic homo sui conscius, etiam realiter realitate psychologica persona Verbi est hic homo sui conscius.

(5) Quamvis persona divina sit subiectum conscientiae Christi humanae, tamen per talem conscientiam non sibi innotescit nisi ut merus homo.

(2) That which adds nothing intrinsic to a person cannot constitute that person as conscious of self. But human operations elicited in accidental human potencies add nothing intrinsic to a divine person. Therefore, they cannot constitute a divine person as conscious of self.

Reply: Regarding the major, it is true that that which adds nothing intrinsic either to a person or to the nature according to which the person exists cannot constitute the person as conscious of self; but it is false that that which adds nothing intrinsic to a person but does add to the nature according to which the person exists cannot constitute a person as conscious of self.

So we distinguish the minor accordingly, and we deny the validity of the argument and the conclusion.

(3) An infinite person is entitatively the same whether he assumes another nature or assumes no other nature; therefore it is impossible for an infinite person to be really and truly conscious of self through operations elicited in an assumed nature.

Reply: We agree that an infinite person, whether incarnate or not, is entitatively the same, since he is constituted as incarnate through infinite act as the sole constitutive cause; but we deny that the reason that he is entitatively the same is that he is not really and truly incarnate.

Therefore regarding the statement that an infinite person cannot be really and truly conscious of himself through finite operations, we have to make a distinction. The statement would be true if that person did not really and truly become human; but the statement would be false if that person really and truly has become human through his own act of existence.

(4) But in this sort of solution an infinite person is constituted as a subject of logical or ontological attribution but not as a psychological subject.

Reply: On the empiricist position, there is constituted in this sort of solution only a logical or ontological subject, but not on the realist position.

According to realists, the real is what is known through the true as the medium in which it is known. Psychological reality is no exception. If, therefore, the person of the Word is truly a human being, he is also ontologically and really a human being; and if the person of the Word is truly this human being conscious of himself, then the person of the Word is in psychological reality really this human being conscious of himself.

(5) Although the divine person is the subject of Christ's human consciousness, nevertheless through such consciousness he is not aware of himself except as just a human being.

Nam ex operationibus accidentalibus humanis non innotescit nisi natura humana.

Et ex nota natura humana non legitime concluditur nisi ad personam humanam.

Respondetur: *Ad assertum*: 'per conscientiam humanam persona divina non sibi innotescit nisi ut merus homo,' videtur negandum simpliciter. Per conscientiam enim subiectum sibi innotescit sub ratione experti; et quod innotescit sub ratione experti (1) non innotescit secundum rationem quandam formalem (ut merus homo), nam talis notitia per primam intellectus operationem et ex parte obiecti attingitur, et (2) non innotescit secundum rationem quandam exclusivam (nisi ut merus homo), nam talis negatio per alteram intellectus operationem et ex parte obiecti attingitur.

Ad primam rationem additam: ex operationibus accidentalibus humanis non innotescit nisi natura humana, *distinguitur*: ex operationibus eiusmodi etiam innotescit natura humana quando ad primam intellectus operationem proceditur, *conceditur*; ex operationibus eiusmodi non innotescit ipsum subiectum seu persona operans, *negatur prorsus*. Longe enim clarius per operationes nostri sumus conscii quam operationum conscii.

Ad alteram rationem additam: ex nota natura humana non legitime concluditur nisi ad personam humanam. Quasi concludere esset conscientiae, *negatur*, nam per conscientiam non concludimus sed experimur. Quasi natura sit eadem ac persona, *iterum negatur*, nam natura est quo et persona est quod est. Quasi per conscientiam innotesceret natura et non persona, *iterum negatur*; nam natura non innotescit per conscientiam sed ex conscientia per inquisitionem intelligitur; ipsa autem persona per conscientiam se sub ratione experti attingit.

(6) *Instatur*: per conscientiam Christi humanam non sibi innotescit nisi subiectum quoddam conscie sentiens, appetens, patiens, intelligens, volens, etc. Atqui eiusmodi est notitia sui quae in qualibet persona humana invenitur. Qua de causa dicere personam divinam per conscientiam humanam esse sui consciam nihil est aliud ac dicere personam divinam esse non divinam sed humanam.

For we are aware of nothing in accidental human operations except a human nature.

And from an awareness of human nature one cannot legitimately conclude to anything except a human person.

Reply: The assertion that 'through human consciousness a divine person is not aware of himself except as just a human being' must, it seems, be simply denied. For through consciousness a subject is aware of himself under the formality of the experienced; and what is known under the formality of the experienced (1) is not known by way of some formal characteristic, for example, 'as just a human being,' since such knowledge is attained through the first operation of the intellect and on the side of the object; and (2) is not known by way of some exclusive characteristic, for example, 'not aware of himself *except* as just a human being,' for such a negation is attained through the second operation of the intellect and on the side of the object.

As to the first reason adduced in support of the objection, that 'nothing is known from accidental human operations except a human nature,' a distinction is in order. We grant that when one proceeds to the first operation of the intellect, a human nature is also known from such operations. But we flatly deny that the subject, the person operating, is not manifest in such operations. For we are far more clearly conscious of ourselves through our operations than we are conscious of the operations themselves.

The second reason adduced is that 'from knowledge of a human nature one cannot legitimately conclude to anything except a human person.' If this is taken to mean that concluding belongs to consciousness, then we deny it, for through consciousness we do not draw conclusions: we experience. If it is taken to mean that nature and person are the same, again we deny it, for nature is that by which one is, and person is that which is. If it is taken to mean that through consciousness nature is known and not person, again we deny it; for nature is not known through consciousness but rather is understood through inquiry into the data of consciousness, while a person attains himself or herself through consciousness under the formality of the experienced.

(6) But through the human consciousness of Christ the one who becomes aware of himself is just a certain subject consciously sensing, desiring, suffering, understanding, willing, and so on. But this is the sort of self-awareness found in any human person. To say, therefore, that a divine person is conscious of self through human consciousness is the same as to say that the divine person is not divine but human.

Respondetur: Conscientia Christi humana est *similis* conscientiae nostrae, *conceditur*, nam persona Verbi facta est 'similis nobis per omnia absque peccato' (DB 148). Conscientia Christi humana est *eadem* ac alia quaelibet conscientia humana, *negatur*, nam nulla conscientia humana est eadem ac ulla alia sed unusquisque homo habet suam.

Proinde ad conclusionem: dicere personam divinam per conscientiam humanam esse sui consciam est (1) agnoscere personam divinam vere et realiter factam esse hominem, *conceditur*, et (2) addere aliam conscientiam praeter conscientiam divinam, *iterum conceditur*, et (3) tollere identitatem personae quae sui conscia sit per duas naturas et duas conscientias, *negatur*.

Iam vero id quod obicientem fugit est hoc: per conscientiam non solum innotescunt operationes sed etiam ipsa subiecti identitas seu ipsum subiectum sibi identicum; et quamvis in aliis hominibus subiectum sibi identicum (quod ex parte subiecti et sub ratione experti sibi innotescit) non sit nisi homo, nihilominus in Christo homine subiectum sibi identicum (quod ex parte subiecti et sub ratione experti sibi innotescit) est persona divina.

(7) *Instatur*: Attamen non sibi innotescit persona divina sed tantummodo subiectum sibi identicum quod qua conscium non est nisi humanum. Ergo manet difficultas.

Respondetur: Non sibi innotescit persona divina eo modo quo sibi innotescit inquantum subsistit in divina natura, *conceditur*; non sibi innotescit persona divina secundum quod ipsa vere et realiter facta est homo, *negatur*.

(8) *Instatur*: Ita habetur identitas ontologica quae divisim est conscia tum modo divino tum modo humano, sed non habetur idem subiectum psychologicum sui conscium tum modo divino tum modo humano.

Respondetur: Ita habetur identitas ontologica, *conceditur*; ita non habetur identitas psychologica, *distinguitur*: per solam conscientiam humanam, *conceditur*; per utramque conscientiam divinam et humanam, *subdistinguitur*: si unio (facta in persona et secundum personam) est unio facta in inconscio et secundum inconscium, *conceditur*; si unio facta est in conscio et secundum conscium, *negatur*. Vide quae superius dicta sunt de conscientia Christi divina.

Reply: We agree that Christ's human consciousness is *like* our consciousness, for the person of the Word is 'like us in all things but sin' (DB 148, DS 301–302). But we deny that Christ's human consciousness is exactly the *same* as any other human consciousness, since no human consciousness is the same as any other, but each of us has his or her own.

As to the conclusion, we agree that to say that a divine person is conscious of self through a human consciousness is (1) to acknowledge that a divine person has really and truly become a human being, and (2) to add in him another consciousness besides divine consciousness. But we do not agree (3) that this does away with the identity of the person who is conscious of himself through two natures and two consciousnesses.

What the objector overlooks is this, that through consciousness one becomes aware not only of operations but also of the identity of the subject, that is, the subject as self-identical; and although in other human beings this self-identical subject, aware of self on the side of the subject and under the formality of the experienced, is merely human, in the case of Christ the man the self-identical subject, manifest to himself on the side of the subject and under the formality of the experienced, is a divine person.

(7) It is not a divine person who is thus aware of himself but only a self-identical subject which, as conscious, is only human. The difficulty therefore remains.

Reply: We grant that the divine person is not aware of himself in the same manner in which he is aware of himself as subsisting in the divine nature; but we deny that the divine person is not aware of himself in a manner consistent with having really and truly become a human being.

(8) According to this, you have an ontological identity that is separately conscious in two ways, divine and human, but not the same psychological subject conscious of himself in both a divine way and a human way.

Reply: We agree that there is thus an ontological identity, but as to the statement that there is no psychological identity, we make the following distinction. We agree that there is no psychological identity through human consciousness alone; but what about a psychological identity through both human and divine consciousness? Another distinction is needed. We agree that there would also be no psychological identity if the hypostatic union, which was effected in and on the basis of the person, had been effected in and on the basis of something that is not conscious. But we deny that there is no psychological identity if the union is effected in and on the basis of something conscious. See what was said previously concerning the divine consciousness of Christ.

(9) Si in Iesu Nazareno ponitur subiectum sibi identicum et sui conscium, ponitur 'assumptus homo,' quod in Litt. Encycl. *Sempiternus Rex* reprobatur.

Respondetur: Si ponitur in Iesu Nazareno aliud subiectum sive ontologicum sive psychologicum praeter personam divinam, ponitur 'assumptus homo,' *conceditur*; si ponitur persona divina tamquam subiectum et ontologicum et psychologicum, ponitur 'assumptus homo,' *negatur*.

(10) Attamen persona divina non potest esse subiectum psychologicum conscientiae humanae.

Nam tale subiectum est principium-quod operationum; principium-quod operationum est causa efficiens operationum; et omne exercitium causalitatis efficientis est non unius sed trium personarum divinarum. Si ergo Verbum est subiectum psychologicum operationum humanarum, etiam Pater et Spiritus sanctus pariter sunt subiecta psychologica; quod est contra fidem cum unus tantum de Trinitate passus sit (DB 222).

Respondetur: Conceditur tum subiectum esse principium-quod operationum tum omne exercitium causalitatis efficientis ad extra esse per potentiam divinam quae est eadem ac essentia et ideo communis tribus personis.

Negatur autem (1) principium-quod qua tale dicere exercitium causalitatis efficientis et (2) principium-quod operationum humanarum Christi hominis esse personam Verbi vel nude spectatam vel qua in divina natura subsistentem.

Circa primum, distinguendum est inter operationem ut actum, perfectionem, *energeian*, et operationem ut factionem, *poiêsin*, exercitium causalitatis efficientis. Iam vero si operatio sumitur hoc secundo modo, principium-quod est causa efficiens operationis, et sic qui per intellectum agentem producit speciem intelligibilem et consequentem intelligendi actum, operari dicitur. Si autem operatio sumitur primo modo, principium-quod operationis qua tale non dicit causam efficientem operationis sed potius patientem et recipientem, et sic qui intelligit vel sentit est quidem principium-quod operatur sed, qua tale, non efficit sed patitur, cum sentire et intelligere secundum Aristotelem et S. Thomam sint quoddam pati.

Circa alterum autem satis iam dictum est ubi supra de principio quod operatur et quod exercet causalitatem efficientem. Praeterea, secundum definitiones ibi datas, ponere personam Verbi qua in divina natura subsistentem esse principium quod in Christo homine

(9) To assert that in Jesus of Nazareth there is a subject that is identical to himself and conscious of himself is to affirm the presence of an 'assumed human being,' an opinion condemned in the encyclical letter *Sempiternus Rex* (DB 2334; DS 3905).

Reply: We agree that, if there is affirmed in Jesus of Nazareth another onto-logical or psychological subject besides the divine person, then there is affirmed an 'assumed human being.' But if the divine person is affirmed to be both the ontological and psychological subject, then no 'assumed human being' is affirmed.

(10) And yet a divine person cannot be the psychological subject of human con-sciousness.

The reason is that such a subject is the principle that operates; the principle that operates is the efficient cause of the operations; and all exercise of efficient causality is to be attributed not to one divine person alone but to all three. If, therefore, the Word is the psychological subject of human operations, so also must the Father and the Holy Spirit be psychological subjects [of those operations] – which is contrary to the faith, since only one member of the Trinity has suffered (DB 222; DS 432).

Reply: We grant that the subject is the principle that operates and that all effi-cient causality exercised externally to God is the work of the divine power, which is identical with the divine essence and therefore common to all three persons.

But we deny (1) that a principle that operates means as such an exercise of efficient causality, and (2) that the principle that operates the human operations of Christ as human is the person of the Word either taken by himself or as subsisting in the divine nature.

As to (1), we must distinguish between operation as act, perfection, *energeia*, on the one hand, and operation as making, *poiêsis*, exercise of efficient causality, on the other hand. Now if operation is taken in this second sense, the principle that operates is the efficient cause of the operation, and thus one who by his agent in-tellect produces an intelligible species and a consequent act of understanding is said to be operating. If, however, operation is taken in the first sense, the prin-ciple that operates, as such, denotes not the efficient cause of the operation but rather something affected, something receptive, and thus one who understands or senses is indeed the principle that operates, but, as such, does not effect but rather is affected, since sensing and understanding are, according to Aristotle and St Thomas, a certain 'being affected' (*quoddam pati*).

As to (2), this has already been sufficiently dealt with above in speaking about the principle that operates and that exercises efficient causality. Besides, according to the definitions given there, the position that the person of the Word as sub-sisting in the divine nature is the principle that in Christ the man understands,

intelligit, eligit, sentit, patitur, a monophysismo, monenergismo, monothelismo distingui non potest.

(11) *Instatur*: persona divina Verbi non realiter distinguitur a natura divina Verbi. Qua de causa, si persona divina in humana natura subsistit, id quod in humana natura subsistit realiter est persona divina in divina natura subsistens.

Respondetur: Unio hypostatica facta est non in natura neque secundum naturam sed in persona et secundum personam.

Et ideo persona divina qua in humana natura subsistens (1) dicit personam divinam *quae* etiam est in divina natura subsistens, sed (2) non dicit personam divinam *qua* in divina natura subsistens.

Circa possibilitatem vero eius quod divina persona incarnatur quin divina natura incarnetur, satis supra est dictum ubi ponitur tamquam causa constitutiva unica esse Verbi infinitum qua cum divino intelligere et velle identicum.

Sectio Quarta: De Unitate Psychologica Christi Dei et Hominis

96 Iam constat unam Verbi personam esse subiectum et ontologicum et psychologicum tum conscientiae suae divinae tum conscientiae suae humanae.

Constat praeterea has duas conscientias inter se communicare ex parte obiecti ut Christus ut Deus sciat se esse hunc hominem et Christus ut homo sciat se esse Filium Dei naturalem.

Nunc ulterius quaeritur utrum hae duae unius conscientiae etiam ex parte subiecti communicent ut sit nexus non tantum ontologicus sed etiam psychologicus inter subiectum psychologicum conscientiae divinae et subiectum psychologicum conscientiae humanae.

Qui nexum ontologicum sed non psychologicum poneret, diceret eandem ontologice personam esse divisim subiectum conscientiae divinae et divisim subiectum conscientiae humanae.

Qui nexum et ontologicum et psychologicum poneret, diceret eandem ontologice personam non inconscie sed conscie duas habere conscientias.

97 Primo, ergo, videtur quod nexus sit ontologicus sed non psychologicus.

chooses, senses, and suffers is quite indistinguishable from monophysitism, mon-
energism, and monotheletism.

(11) The divine person of the Word is not really distinct from the divine nature of
the Word. Therefore, if the divine person subsists in a human nature, that which
subsists in a human nature is in reality the divine person subsisting in the divine
nature.

   Reply: The hypostatic union has been effected not in a nature nor on the basis
of a nature but in the person and on the basis of the person.

   Hence it follows that a divine person as subsisting in a human nature (1) denotes
a divine person *who* is also subsisting in the divine nature, but (2) does not denote
a divine person *as* subsisting in the divine nature.

   As to the possibility of a divine person being incarnate without the divine nature being incarnate, it suffices to refer to what we have said above where we
stated that the sole constitutive cause [of the hypostatic union] was the divine
Word's infinite act of existence as identical with the divine acts of understanding
and of willing.

4 The Psychological Unity of Christ, God and Man

96 It is now clear that the one person of the Word is the ontological and psychological subject of both his divine consciousness and his human consciousness.

   It is clear, moreover, that these two consciousnesses mutually communicate on
the side of the object, so that Christ as God knows himself to be this human being
and Christ as man knows himself to be the natural Son of God.

   Now the further question arises as to whether these two consciousnesses of one
reality also communicate on the side of the subject, so that there is not only an
ontological but also a psychological connection between the psychological subject
of divine consciousness and the psychological subject of human consciousness.

   To affirm an ontological connection while denying a psychological one is to
hold that the ontologically identical person is separately the subject of divine
consciousness and separately the subject of human consciousness.

   To affirm a connection that is both ontological and psychological is to hold
that the ontologically identical person consciously and not unconsciously has two
consciousnesses.

97 First, therefore, here are some arguments maintaining that there is an ontological but no psychological connection.

(1) Nam conscientia est personae a natura. Sed in Christo Deo et homine non habetur tertia quaedam natura composita secundum quam Christus sit duarum suarum conscientiarum conscius. Ergo divisim est conscius ut Deus et divisim est conscius ut homo.

(2) Praeterea, conscientia est per operationes et secundum perfectionem operationum. Sed in Christo Deo et homine, sicut sunt duae naturae (DB 148), etiam sunt inconfuse et inconvertibiliter duae operationes (DB 292). Ergo divisim Christus est conscius ut Deus et divisim Christus est conscius ut homo.

(3) Praeterea, conscientia non est conscientiae. Ergo quamvis Christus duas habeat conscientias, tamen non est conscius duarum conscientiarum.

98 Sed contra est quod 'agit utraque forma cum alterius communione quod proprium est' (DB 144). Sed inconvenienter ista communio ponitur inconscia. Ergo nexus est non tantum ontologicus sed etiam psychologicus.

Respondendum videtur quod post considerationem praecisivam in qua successive agitur de Christo inquantum est Deus et de Christo inquantum est homo, institui oportet considerationem concretam in qua de Christo agitur prout re vera est, nempe, simul et Deus et homo. Proinde quamvis in Christo et inconfuse et inconvertibiliter sint et duae naturae et duae operationes, etiam in Christo, iisdem testantibus conciliis, una est persona et indivisa et inseparata. Sed conscientia maxime personam respicit, cum et persona sit *quae* est conscia et principaliter persona sit *cuius* persona conscia est. Et ideo, sicut duas distinguimus conscientias propter duas naturas et duas operationes, ita etiam unum subiectum et ontologicum et psychologicum agnoscimus propter indivisionem personae.

Praeterea, ut superius dictum est, persona Verbi qua Deus sui conscia est tum secundum suam personam distinctam tum secundum suam naturam ita ut tota conscia sit secundum totam suam realitatem. Cui personae totaliter sui consciae, cum adveniat alia conscientia sui humana, sane non inconscie advenit. Non enim in inconscio additur conscientia ei qui totaliter conscius est. Quod si conscie conscientia humana personae divinae et consciae additur, sequitur ipsam personam divinam esse consciam duarum suarum conscientiarum.

Praeterea, unio hypostatica facta est et in persona et secundum personam. Sed persona Verbi secundum se est conscia. Et ideo unio hypostatica facta est et in conscio et secundum conscium. Iam vero si ponitur nexus tantum ontologicus

(1) Consciousness belongs to a person from the person's nature. But in Christ, God and man, there is no such thing as some third composite nature according to which Christ would be conscious of his two consciousnesses. Therefore, he is separately conscious as God and separately conscious as man.

(2) Again, consciousness is had through operations and in proportion to the perfection of those operations. But in Christ, God and man, as there are two natures (DB 148, DS 301–302), so also there are two sets of operations (DB 292, DS 557), unmixed and unchanged. Therefore Christ is separately conscious as God and separately conscious as man.

(3) Again, there is no such thing as consciousness of consciousness. Therefore, although Christ has two consciousnesses, he is not conscious of the two consciousnesses.

98 Against this opinion is the statement, 'Each nature performs the functions proper to itself, yet in concert with the other nature' (DB 144, DS 294). It would be incongruous, however, to hold such a concert to be unconscious. Therefore, the connection is not ontological only, but psychological as well.

Our response to the question is that, after the consideration in which we treated Christ as God and then Christ as man, one after the other and each by itself, we should go on to a concrete consideration of Christ as he is in reality, that is, as both God and man at the same time. So although in Christ two natures and two sets of operations coexist unmixed and unchanged, there is also in Christ, according to these same councils, but one person, undivided and unseparated. Now consciousness has to do especially with the person, since it is the person *who* is conscious, and it is the person, principally, *of whom* a person is conscious. Therefore, as we distinguish two consciousnesses on account of the two natures and the two sets of operations, so also we recognize one subject both ontological and psychological on account of the undividedness of the person.

Besides, as we said above, the person of the Word as God is conscious of himself both as to his distinct person and as to his nature, so that he is totally conscious as to his total reality. When to this person totally conscious of himself there is added a human consciousness of self, surely this does not come to him unconsciously. For to one who is totally conscious, consciousness is not added in something that is unconscious. But if a human consciousness is consciously added to a conscious divine person, it follows that that divine person is conscious of both his consciousnesses.

Again, the hypostatic union was effected in the person and on the basis of the person. But in himself the person of the Word is conscious; the hypostatic union, therefore, was effected in what is conscious and on the basis of what is conscious.

inter subiectum psychologicum divinae conscientiae et subiectum psychologicum humanae conscientiae, unio hypostatica facta esset et in inconscio et secundum inconscium; et cum persona Verbi nullatenus sit inconscia, unio non esset facta in persona.

Praeterea, persona stat in quodam indivisibili, et ideo in definitione personae ponitur subsistens quod est simpliciter indivisum in se et simpliciter divisum a quolibet alio. Sed in indivisibili non inveniuntur aliud et aliud. Et ideo in una Verbi persona non inveniuntur aliud secundum quod sit subiectum psychologicum conscientiae divinae et aliud secundum quod sit subiectum psychologicum conscientiae humanae. Qua de causa, sicut unum admittitur subiectum ontologicum etiam unum subiectum psychologicum admitti oportet.

Praeterea, et ipsa contraria opinio sensu caret. Nam inter subiectum psychologicum conscientiae divinae et subiectum psychologicum conscientiae humanae ponit quidem nexum ontologicum sed negat nexum psychologicum. Iam vero 'psychologicum' non dividitur contra ontologicum, secus 'psychologicum' esset nihil. Qua de causa necesse est affirmare 'psychologicum' esse ipsum ontologicum in tali gradu perfectionis ontologicae. Neque dubitari potest Christum Deum et hominem in debito gradu perfectionis ontologicae inveniri cum iam sit subiectum psychologicum non solum conscientiae divinae sed etiam conscientiae humanae. Neque de ipso nexu dubitari potest cum adsit identitas eiusdem personae quae est utriusque conscientiae subiectum psychologicum.

99 Praeterea, quae in favorem contrariae sententiae afferuntur, rem minime probant.

Verum sane est quod in Christo Deo et homine non est tertia quaedam natura composita. Et ex hoc sequitur quod conscientia Christi divina et conscientia Christi humana unum naturale non efformant, sicut conscientia intellectiva et conscientia sensitiva unum naturale in uno homine constituunt. Sed praeter unum naturale seu unum per se, etiam datur unum transcendentale quod definitur indivisum in se et divisum a quolibet alio. Et ideo quamvis duae Christi conscientiae inter se in unum naturale non coalescant, tamen in uno subiecto indivisibili coincidunt.

Praeterea, rite illud intelligi oportet quod conscientia est personae a natura. Non enim ipsa natura est conscia; neque natura est cuius quis est conscius; sed persona est conscia tum personae tum suorum actuum. Cum tamen 'conscium'

Now if there is only an ontological connection between the psychological subject of divine consciousness and the psychological subject of human consciousness, the hypostatic union would have been effected in what is unconscious and on the basis of what is unconscious; and since the person of the Word is in no way unconscious, that union would not have been effected in the person.

Furthermore, a person is one indivisible reality; hence the definition of person includes the notion of a subsistent that is absolutely undivided in itself and absolutely divided from everything else. But in a reality that is indivisible there is not present one thing that is not another, and thus in the one person of the Word there is not one reality by reason of which he is the psychological subject of divine consciousness and another reality by reason of which he is the psychological subject of human consciousness. For this reason, then, just as we admit only one ontological subject we must also admit only one psychological subject.

Besides, the contrary opinion makes no sense. Between the psychological subject of divine consciousness and the psychological subject of human consciousness it places an ontological connection but denies a psychological connection. But 'psychological' is not the opposite of 'ontological,' for otherwise it would be nothing. Hence we must maintain that 'psychological' is the ontological itself at a certain level of ontological perfection. Now there is no doubt that Christ, God and man, is found at the level of ontological perfection proper to him, since he is a psychological subject now not only of divine consciousness but also of human consciousness. Nor can there be any doubt about the connection, since there is here the identity of one and the same person who is the psychological subject of each consciousness.

99 The arguments advanced in support of the contrary opinion do not prove their point at all.

It is certainly true that in Christ, God and man, there is no third, composite nature. From this it follows that the divine consciousness of Christ and the human consciousness of Christ do not form a natural 'one,' the way intellectual consciousness and sensitive consciousness constitute a natural 'one' in one human being. But besides a natural 'one' or a 'one per se' there is also such a thing as a transcendental 'one,' defined as undivided in itself and divided from everything else. And so although the two consciousnesses of Christ do not coalesce into a natural 'one,' nevertheless they do come together in one indivisible subject.

Besides, the statement that consciousness belongs to a person from nature must be correctly understood. A nature itself is not conscious, nor is a nature that of which someone is conscious; it is the person who is conscious both of the person and of the person's acts. Nevertheless, since 'conscious' adds nothing to being but

non addat super ens sed ipsum ens dicat in tali gradu perfectionis ontologicae, inquantum natura est mensura perfectionis ontologicae, in tantum conscientia dicitur esse personae a natura. Et ideo cum Christus sit unum quoddam ens in duplici gradu perfectionis ontologicae, etiam dicendum est Christum esse unum quoddam conscium secundum duplicem conscientiam.

Ulterius, verum quidem est personam esse consciam per operationes et secundum perfectionem operationum. Et etiam verum est quod ipsae operationes sunt quodammodo consciae. Attamen, operationes sunt consciae ut quibus, et persona est conscia ut quod. Et ideo cum in Christo ita distinguantur operationes ut non dividatur persona, distinguendae sunt conscientiae quibus Christus est conscius, sed dividendum non est subiectum quod est conscium.

Denique tandem verum sit quod conscientia non est conscientiae. Remanet tamen quod conscientia est conscii. Et ideo in Christo Deo et homine unius subiecti conscii sunt duae conscientiae.

Sectio Quinta: Opinionum Dialectica

100 Opinionum dialectica considerari potest vel materialiter vel formaliter.

Materialiter est ipsa historica successio in qua unaquaeque opinio vel insufficiens vel falsa aliam contrariam semper evocat donec ad plenam quaestionis solutionem perveniatur.

Formaliter vero opinionum dialectica est huius motus historici intelligentia. Ad quam intelligentiam assequendam duobus maxime proceditur gressibus. Primo enim ea requiruntur principia ut quis discernere possit in quibusnam deficiant singulae opiniones. Deinde autem quo accuratius hi defectus perspiciuntur, eo clarius elucent tum rationes cur opiniones contrariae sint ortae tum etiam ipsarum harum opinionum contrariarum defectus proprii, unde etiam aliae et ulteriores opiniones his contrariae proponantur.

Valor denique dialecticae formalis duplex esse videtur. Nam et ipsius motus historici seu controversiae intelligentiam sat profundam generat, et singulari quodam modo veritatem demonstrat principiorum quibus exacte discernantur uniuscuiusque opinionis defectus.

Quibus perspectis, nobis visum est notae controversiae de conscientia Christi dialecticam investigare. Quamvis enim fieri non possit ut omnes opiniones secundum omnes suos aspectus brevioribus his in notulis considerentur, nihilominus vel abbreviatam inquisitionem credimus duplicem ferre fructum, alium nempe generalem quatenus natura atque vis huius methodi in exemplo concreto

simply denotes being of a certain degree of ontological perfection, consciousness is said to belong to the person from nature inasmuch as nature is the measure of ontological perfection. Since Christ, therefore, is one being of two different degrees of ontological perfection, he must be said to be one being conscious through two consciousnesses.

Furthermore, it is indeed true that a person is conscious through operations and in proportion to the perfection of operations; and it is also true that the operations themselves are in a way conscious. But operations are conscious as that by which one is conscious while a person is conscious as that which is conscious. Since in Christ, therefore, operations are distinguished without dividing the person, so must the consciousnesses by which he is conscious be distinguished without dividing the subject that is conscious.

Finally, it is true that there is no such thing as consciousness of consciousness. Yet it remains true that consciousness belongs to one who is conscious. Therefore in Christ, God and human, there are two consciousnesses belonging to one conscious subject.

5 The Dialectic of Opinions

100 A dialectic of opinions can be considered materially or formally.

Materially, it is the historical succession of opinions in which each opinion that is false or inadequate always evokes a contrary view until a full solution of the question is arrived at.

In a formal sense, however, a dialectic of opinions is an understanding of this historical process. This understanding is attained mainly in two steps. First, those principles are required that will enable one to determine where each single opinion is deficient. But then, the more accurately such deficiencies are discerned, the more clearly will appear both the reasons why contrary opinions have arisen and the deficiencies inherent in these contrary opinions themselves that in turn call forth still further opinions contrary to them.

This formal dialectic would seem to be doubly valuable. It yields a quite profound understanding of the historical movement or controversy in question, and it is singularly effective in demonstrating the truth of those principles that enable us to pinpoint the weaknesses of any opinion.

In view of this, we have felt it worth while to examine the dialectic of the well-known controversy regarding the consciousness of Christ. Although in this brief sketch we cannot examine all the opinions in all of their aspects, we feel nevertheless that even a rather brief investigation will be of advantage in two ways: in a general way, in that the nature and effectiveness of this method can be

manifestantur, alium autem particularem quatenus lector perspicere potest non meram opinionum multitudinem de conscientia Christi sed dialecticum quendam progressum ex falsis, deficientibus, insufficientibus in sententiam magis completam, perfectam, veram.

101 Primus et brevior motus.

Primum et breviorem motum ducimus qui cum R.P. Seiller incipit et decreto Sacri Officii finitur.[13]

Ad hunc motum intelligendum notandum est quid significet et quid non significet communicatio idiomatum.

Nam communicatio idiomatum in eo est quod propter unitatem personae, divina de humanis et humana de divinis, praedicantur.[14] Ita Beata Virgo est Mater Dei, non quod divinam naturam pepererit, sed quia eum peperit qui vere Deus est.

At communicatio idiomatum non est quod vel divina vel humana de divina Verbi persona praedicantur. Haec enim persona est ille unus idemque qui vere et proprie Deus est et vere et proprie homo est.

Iam vero errasse videtur R.P. Seiller circa communicationem idiomatum et quidem plus minus systematice. Scripsit enim:

> Dieu le Verbe est, en effet, sujet adoré et non point sujet adorant, si ce n'est par communication des idiomes, par langage in obliquo; il est de même sujet prié et non point sujet priant.[15]

Iam vero in illo asserto non adest communicatio idiomatum. Praedicatur enim subiectum (sujet adorant, sujet adoré) de persona (Dieu le Verbe). Neque hic est merus quidam lapsus linguae sed regulariter ita distinguitur inter Verbum assumens et hominem assumptum. Sic, 'En effet, sous le vocable Jésus-Christ, nous pouvons avoir en vue, non plus directement l'Homme subjoint au Verbe (Homo assumptus), mais le Verbe surjoint à l'Homme (Verbum assumens).'[16] .

demonstrated in a concrete example, and more particularly in that the reader can be shown, not a mere catalogue of opinions about Christ's consciousness, but a dialectical progression from false, deficient, and inadequate opinions to one that is more complete, perfect, and true.

101 First, we examine a brief movement.

Let us look first at a shorter movement that begins with the Reverend Léon Seiller and ends with a decree of the Holy Office.[13]

To understand this process one must be very clear about what the interchange of properties means and what it does not mean.

The interchange of properties means that because of the unity of the person, divine attributes are predicated of what is human, and human attributes of what is divine.[14] So, for example, the Blessed Virgin is the Mother of God, not because she gave birth to the divine nature but because she gave birth to him who is truly God.

The interchange of properties does not mean that either divine or human properties are predicated of the divine person of the Word. For this person is the selfsame one who is truly and in the proper sense God and truly and in the proper sense man.

Now Fr Seiller seems to have been mistaken about the interchange of properties, and indeed more or less systematically. For he writes:

> God the Word is in fact the subject adored and not at all the subject adoring, except by reason of the interchange of properties, by an indirect manner of speaking; he is in the same way the subject prayed to and not at all the subject praying.[15]

Now, there is no interchange of properties here. For the subject ('subject adored,' 'subject adoring,') is predicated of the person ('God the Word'). Nor is this just a slip of the pen on his part; he regularly distinguishes between the Word who assumes and the man assumed: 'In fact, under the expression "Jesus Christ" we can discern, no longer directly the Man joined to the Word (*Homo assumptus*), but the Word joining itself to the Man (*Verbum assumens*).'[16]

13 [*Acta Apostolicae Sedis* 43 (1951) 561.]
14 See Charles Boyer, *De Verbo incarnato* (Rome: Pontificia Universitas Gregoriana, 1952) 233–38.
15 Léon Seiller, *La psychologie humaine du Christ et l'unicité de personne* (Rennes & Paris, 1949) 17. The same statement also appears in *Franziskanische Studien* 31 (1949) 49–76, 246–74.
16 Seiller, *La psychologie* ... 23.

Proinde de Verbo assumente et de homine assumpto diversa praedicantur quasi de duobus. Ita homo assumptus neque directe neque intuitive conscius est suae unionis ad Verbum; sed conscius est suae visionis beatae in qua scit se per relationem ordinis esse Deum et Filium Dei naturalem.[17] E contra, 'Jésus-Christ, Verbe surjoint à l'Homme … se voit Dieu (per scientiam divinam), a conscience d'être identiquement Dieu et connaît le mode mystérieux selon lequel l'Homme né de Marie lui est uni.'[18]

In his ergo et similibus assertis sat clare videtur mala intelligentia communicationis idiomatum in separationem seu divisionem ipsius unius personae conduxisse.

Unde mirum non est hoc opus in indicem librorum prohibitorum esse relatum (12 VII 1951). Sequebatur articulus R.P. Browne, tunc Sacri Palatii Magistri.[19] Denique in Litteris Encycl. *Sempiternus Rex*, contra opiniones eiusmodi dicitur:

> At Chalcedonense Concilium, Ephesino prorsus congruens, lucide asserit utramque nostri Redemptoris naturam 'in unam personam atque subsistentiam' convenire vetatque duo in Christo poni individua, ita ut aliquis 'homo assumptus' integrae autonomiae compos, penes Verbum collocetur.[20]

102 Alter atque longior motus dialecticus.

In altero et longiori motu distinguuntur (a) fundamentum theoreticum, (b) fundamenti applicatio, et (c) reactiones subsequentes.

(*a*) Fundamentum theoreticum
(*aa*) *Oppositio radicalis*

Oppositio radicalis est inter duas theorias gnoseologicas, quarum una cognitionem in identitate fundat, alia autem cognitionem in dualitate quadam radicatam contendit.

According to this, then, different things are predicated of the assuming Word and the assumed human being as if they were two. Thus the assumed human being is neither directly nor intuitively conscious of his being united to the Word; but he is conscious of his beatific vision in which he knows that through a relation of order he is God and the natural Son of God.[17] On the contrary, 'Jesus Christ, the Word joined to the Man ... sees himself as God (through divine knowledge), is conscious of being identical with God, and knows the mysterious way in which the Man born of Mary is united to him.'[18]

In these, therefore, and similar statements we may clearly see how a misunderstanding of the interchange of properties has led to separating or dividing the one person.

It was hardly surprising, therefore, that this book was placed on the Index of Forbidden Books (12 July 1951), followed by an article by the Reverend Michael Browne, at that time Master of the Sacred Palace.[19] Finally, the encyclical *Sempiternus Rex* contained the following condemnation of opinions of this kind:

> But the Council of Chalcedon, in full accord with that of Ephesus, states most clearly that the two natures of our Redeemer meet 'in one person and subsistence,' and forbids putting two individuals in Christ, in such a way that an 'assumed man,' enjoying complete autonomy, is placed with the Word.[20]

102 Next, we consider another and longer dialectical process.

In this more lengthy process we distinguish three elements: (a) the theoretical foundation, (b) the application of this foundation to the consciousness of Christ, and (c) subsequent reactions.

(*a*) Theoretical foundation
(*aa*) *Radical opposition*

There is a radical opposition between two gnoseological theories: one that bases knowledge upon an identity, and another that maintains that knowledge is rooted in some kind of duality.

17 Ibid. 20–21.
18 Ibid. 23.
19 *Osservatore Romano*, 19 August 1951.
20 *Acta Apostolicae Sedis* 43 (1951) 638.

Apud Aristotelicos cognitio in identitate fundatur. Ita sensus in actu dicitur esse sensibile in actu, intellectus in actu dicitur esse intellectum in actu, et in his quae sunt sine materia idem reputatur intelligens et quod intelligitur.[21]

Apud Platonicos cognitio in dualitate radicatur; ita post Ideas Platonici posuerunt deos qui Ideas contemplarentur; post Unum Plotinus posuit Mentem. Similiter Günther et Rosmini, quia realem distinctionem inter cognitum et cognoscentem duxerunt necessariam, processiones trinitarias a se demonstratas crediderunt. Similiter J.-P. Sartre ita *en-soi* et *pour-soi* separat ut Deum realem et simplicem se cognoscentem reputat contradictorium. Similiter generatim empiristae, sensistae, phenomenologici, et realistae nativi.

(ab) Conscientiae notiones oppositae

Si cognitio in identitate radicatur, etiam conscientia in identitate radicatur. Unde sine nimia difficultate conscientia concipitur ut experientia stricte dicta, quae subiecto operanti ex parte subiecti inest et per quam subiectum operans sub ratione experti sibi praesens efficitur.

Si cognitio in dualitate fundatur, sicut et omnis cognitio ita etiam conscientia est quaedam intuitio seu perceptio seu confrontatio per quam innotescit quoddam obiectum; ab aliis autem perceptionibus, intuitionibus, confrontationibus distinguitur conscientia inquantum obiectum quod ita attingitur sit id ipsum quod percipit, intuetur, conscium efficitur.

(ac) Prima differentia consequens

Conscientia-experientia latius patet quam conscientia-perceptio. Conscientia enim, si experientia ex parte subiecti concipitur, omnem operationem sive sensitivam sive intellectivam sive apprehensivam sive appetitivam concomitatur; nec quidquam refert quid sit operationis obiectum cum semper idem sit subiectum operans. Sin autem conscientia concipitur tamquam perceptio sui ex parte obiecti, non habetur conscientia nisi in illis operationibus in quibus obiectum est ipsum subiectum operans.

Aristotelians base knowledge upon an identity. Thus for them the sense in act is the sensible in act, the intellect in act is the understood in act, and in the case of immaterial beings that which understands is identical with that which is understood.[21]

For Platonists, on the other hand, knowledge is rooted in a duality. Thus, subsequent to the Ideas, Platonists posited gods to contemplate the Ideas; and subsequent to the One, Plotinus posited Mind. In a similar way, Günther and Rosmini, maintaining that there had to be a real distinction between the knower and the known, believed that they had proven the trinitarian processions. Likewise also Jean-Paul Sartre moves from his separation of the *en-soi* from the *pour-soi* to argue that for a real and simple God to know himself would be a contradiction. So also, generally speaking, empiricists, sensists, phenomenologists, and naive realists.

(ab) Divergent opinions on consciousness

If knowledge is rooted in identity, so also is consciousness. Hence it is not too difficult to conceive consciousness as experience strictly so called, which is in the operating subject on the side of the subject, and through which the operating subject is rendered present to itself under the formality of the experienced.

If knowledge is grounded upon duality, then consciousness, like all knowledge, is a kind of intuition or perception or confrontation through which an object is known; and consciousness is distinguished from all other perceptions, intuitions, or confrontations in that the object that is known is precisely that which is perceiving, intuiting, being made conscious.

(ac) First difference consequent upon the above

Consciousness-as-experience is a broader notion than consciousness-as-perception. For consciousness, conceived as experience on the side of the subject, accompanies every operation, whether sensitive or intellectual, cognitive or appetitive; nor does it matter what the object of the operation might be, since it is always the same subject that is operating. But if consciousness is conceived as a perception of oneself on the side of the object, then there is no consciousness except in those operations in which the object is the very subject operating.

21 Thomas Aquinas, *Summa theologiae*, 1, q.14, a. 2.

(ad) Altera differentia consequens

Aliter concipitur subiectum psychologicum si conscientia est experientia, et aliter concipitur idem subiectum psychologicum si conscientia est perceptio.

Si enim conscientia est experientia, subiectum psychologicum nihil est aliud nisi operationis psychologicae subiectum ontologicum. Nam eo ipso quod subiectum circa quodlibet obiectum operatur, semper sibi praesens efficitur ex parte subiecti et sub ratione experti.

Si autem conscientia est perceptio, nisi abusive non dicitur subiectum psychologicum. Nam in conscientia-perceptione habentur quidem et percipiens et perceptum, sed habetur conscientia non ratione percipientis sed ratione percepti, cum conscientia-perceptio non ex parte subiecti sit sed ex parte obiecti. Qua de causa, in ipsa conscientia-perceptione percipiens non est subiectum psychologicum sed ontologicum tantum, et perceptum, quamvis psychologicum sit, tamen non subiectum psychologicum est sed obiectum. Quod tamen obiectum psychologicum, propter identitatem materialem cum subiecto ontologico, abusive dicitur subiectum psychologicum.

(ae) Tertia differentia consequens

Si conscientia est experientia, non per se sola cognitionem quandam completam constituit sed cognitionis partem vel gressum vel elementum. Unum enim idemque est ens finitum ex diversis principiis compositum. Una pariter eademque cognitio est quae idem ens sub diversis aspectibus per successivos gressus cognoscit. Unum ergo idemque est quod sub ratione experti per experientiam et sub ratione quidditatis per intelligentiam et sub ratione veri et entis per iudicium cognoscimus. Neque aliud est quod experimur et aliud quod intelligimus, cum nihil intelligamus nisi in iis ipsis quae experiamur. Neque aliud est quod experimur et aliud quod affirmamus, cum evidentia careat iudicium nisi in iis ipsis fundetur quae experiamur.

Si vero conscientia est perceptio, ipsa per se sola cognitionem quandam directam atque immediatam constituit. Qua de causa, summopere enitendum est tum ut accurate dicatur quid per hanc conscientiam-perceptionem innotescat tum ut sedulo distinguatur hoc obiectum non solum ab obiectis aliarum perceptionum

(ad) Second consequent difference

The same psychological subject is conceived in different ways depending upon whether consciousness is taken to be experience or perception.

If consciousness is experience, the psychological subject is none other than the ontological subject of a psychological operation. For by the very fact that a subject is operating with regard to any object at all, it is always rendered present to itself on the side of the subject and under the formality of the experienced.

If, however, consciousness is perception, it is improper to speak of a psychological subject. For in consciousness-as-perception, although there is a perceiver and a perceived, there is consciousness not by reason of the perceiver but by reason of the perceived, since consciousness-as-perception is not to be found on the side of the subject but rather on the side of the object. Hence it follows that in consciousness-as-perception itself the perceiver is not a psychological subject but only an ontological subject, and that which is perceived, albeit psychological, is not a psychological subject but a psychological object. But it is improper to call a psychological object the psychological subject simply because it is materially the same as the ontological subject.

(ae) Third consequent difference

If consciousness is experience, then by itself alone it does not constitute a knowledge that is complete in itself; rather, it is only a part or an element of knowledge, a step in the cognitional process. Just as one and the same finite being is made up of different principles of being, so also that knowledge which knows one being under different aspects by way of successive steps is one and the same knowledge. What we know, therefore, through experience under the formality of the experienced is the very same thing that we know through understanding under the formality of the definable and through judgment under the formality of the true and of being. What we experience and what we understand are not two different realities, since we understand nothing except in the data of experience. Again, what we experience and what we affirm are not two different things, since a judgment lacks evidence if it is not grounded on what we experience.

If, however, consciousness is perception, then by itself alone it does constitute a knowledge that is direct and immediate. For this reason one has to bend every effort to state what precisely is known through this consciousness-as-perception, and to distinguish this object most carefully not only from the objects of other

sed etiam ab iis quae indirecte vel mediante ratiocinio ex ipsa conscientia-perceptione hauriantur. Quo tamen in labore non una omnium sententia est expectanda cum facile non credamus exacte determinare obiectum perceptionis quae non existat.

(af) Quarta differentia consequens

Si conscientia experientia est, alia et alia est secundum diversitatem opera-tionum. Aliter enim (empirice) sumus conscii inquantum sentimus, esurimus, cibis delectamur, etc.; aliter autem (intellectualiter) inquantum circa externe vel in-terne experta inquirimus, in iis quidditates intus legimus, et quod intelleximus definimus vel per modum hypotheseos proponimus; aliter proinde (rationaliter) sumus conscii, cum reflectimur utrum definita existant vel hypotheses verificentur, cum evidentiam ponderamus, cum evidentia compulsi iudicamus; aliter denique (moraliter) sumus conscii cum de bono intelligibili deliberamus, quid agendum sit a nobis determinamus, et ut faciamus per actum voluntatis eligimus.

In quibus omnibus unus idemque conscius sit necesse est. Frustra enim inquir-imus sine ulla praevia experientia; et nihil intelligimus nisi in iis ipsis quae experti sumus et imaginatione repraesentamus; neque reflectimur super definitiones vel hypotheses quin prius eas conceperimus; neque deliberamus vel eligimus nisi ea quae intellectu apprehendimus.

Qui unus idemque in omnibus non est merum quoddam postulatum ('ego' transcendentale) ut ipsa cogitatio (*Ich denke*) intelligibilis reddatur; sed sicut reales sint operationes sentiendi et intelligendi et volendi, ita etiam reale est ipsum op-erans.

Neque hoc operans est potentia quaedam accidentalis, cum simul per multas et diversas potentias operetur et intelligendo sensibilia et volendo intellecta et per corpus exsequendo quae per voluntatem elegit. Qua de causa dicitur quod sensus non sentit sed homo per sensum, et intellectus non intelligit sed homo per intellectum.

Qui homo operans ab aliis hominibus quidem non cognoscitur ut unum idemque nisi inquantum in sensibilibus externis intelligitur unitas quaedam nat-uralis quae iudicio affirmata sub ratione veri et entis apprehenditur.

perceptions but also from those that indirectly or through a process of reasoning are derived from such consciousness-as-perception. We cannot expect those who engage in this laborious task to be all of the same opinion, for it is rather difficult, we suspect, to identify with accuracy the object of a nonexistent perception.

(af) Fourth consequent difference

If consciousness is experience, it will vary according to the diversity of operations. We are conscious in one way (empirically) when we sense, are hungry, enjoy food, and so on; we are conscious in another way (intellectually) when we inquire into our external or interior experiences, grasp intelligibilities in them, and express what we have grasped either in a definition or as a hypothesis; we are conscious in another way (rationally) when we reflect upon whether what we have defined is so in reality or whether our hypotheses are verified, when we weigh the evidence, and are compelled by the evidence to make a judgment; and we are conscious in yet another way (morally) when we deliberate about an intelligible good, decide what we must do, and by an act of the will choose to do it.

In all of these operations it is necessarily one and the same person who is conscious. Inquiry is useless without some prior experience; we understand nothing except in those very data that we have experienced and that we represent in imagination; we cannot reflect upon definitions or hypotheses until we have conceived them; and we can deliberate about and choose only what we have intellectually apprehended.

That which is one and the same in all these operations is no mere postulate (a transcendental 'ego') to render thought (*Ich denke*) intelligible; rather, just as the operations of sensing, understanding, and willing are real, so also is the one who operates real.

Nor again is this operator some accidental potency, since one operates simultaneously through several different potencies, understanding sense data, willing what one has understood, and physically carrying out what one has chosen by an act of the will. For this reason we say that it is not the sense that senses but a human being through the sense, nor is it the intellect that understands, but a human being through the intellect.

This operating human being, it is true, is not known by other human beings as one and the same except insofar as a certain natural unity is grasped in external sense data and, having been affirmed in a judgment, is apprehended under the formality of the true and of being.

At idem homo operans a se ipso non solum intelligendo et iudicando innotescit sed etiam per ipsam internam experientiam ex parte subiecti operantis tamquam unum-idemque-sub-ratione-experti cognoscitur.

(*af '*) Si vero conscientia est quaedam perceptio eius quod ex parte obiecti sistitur, ad analysin supra positam haud perveniri potest. Incipitur ab obiectis ut ad actus perveniatur qui, cum multi et diversi sint, de eorum unitate quaeritur. Cum in multis et diversis actibus unitas quaedam ordinis inveniatur, ipsa haec unitas 'ego' vel 'me' empiricum nominatur.

> L'une, le Moi, répond aux phénomènes de la vie psychique, aux impressions, aux états d'âme perçus comme se succédant en nous. L'autre, le Je, à ce qui en est perçu comme le principe actif et unificateur. Aussi ont-ils beau être perçus simultanément par la conscience, tandis que le Moi se présente à elle comme un objet de connaissance, le Je lui apparaît comme le sujet qui possède et qui connaît.[22]

Quod si quis paulo profundius perceperit, ad 'ego' vel 'me' profundum perveniet. Hoc subiacet, antecedit, fundat 'ego' et 'me' empirica seu psychologica. Utrum sit substantia, inter philosophos generatim disputatur. Re vera, secundum P. Galtier, non est substantia qua talis sed substantia qua natura, qua principium operationum consciarum; neque nude secundum quod natura est per conscientiam percipitur sed tantummodo mediantibus 'ego' et 'me' psychologicis vel empiricis.[23]

Quamvis ergo sint qui ipsam animam per suam conscientiam sese percipere dicant, saltem per talem perceptionem solam determinari non potest utrum ipsa anima in se subsistat an in alio.[24] Qua de causa concludit quaestionem de persona extra ambitum conscientiae-perceptionis iacere.[25]

(*ag*) Binas distinximus notiones (*aa*) cognitionis, (*ab*) conscientiae, (*ac*) actuum in quibus conscientia occurrit, (*ad*) subiecti psychologici, (*ae*) habitudinis inter

But this same operating human being not only is known by himself or herself through understanding and judging, but also through interior experience itself is known to himself or herself on the side of the operating subject as 'one-and-the-same-under-the-formality-of-the-experienced.'

(*af '*) If, on the other hand, consciousness is a perception of what stands on the side of the object, it is impossible to arrive at the above analysis. One proceeds from objects to their acts, but since there are many different acts the question arises concerning their unity. And since in these many different acts a certain unity of order is to be found, this unity is labeled either an empirical 'I' or an empirical 'me.'

> One unity, the 'me,' corresponds to the phenomena of psychic life, to the impressions, to the interior states perceived as succeeding one another within us. The other unity, the 'I,' corresponds to what is perceived as their active principle and unifier. To be sure, both are perceived simultaneously by consciousness, but while the 'me' presents itself to consciousness as an object of knowledge, the 'I' appears before it as the subject which possesses and knows.[22]

Now if your perceiving goes a little deeper you will arrive at the deep 'I' or 'me.' This underlies, precedes, and grounds the empirical or psychological 'I' and 'me.' There is widespread disagreement among philosophers whether or not it is a substance. In fact, according to Galtier, it is not a substance as such but a substance as nature, as the principle of conscious operations; and as nature it is not perceived through consciousness directly as it is in itself, but only as mediated by the psychological or empirical 'I' and 'me.'[23]

Therefore, although there are some who claim that the soul perceives itself through its consciousness, at least this perception alone is not enough to determine whether the soul subsists in itself or in something else.[24] Hence he concludes that the question of person lies beyond the ken of consciousness conceived as perception.[25]

(*ag*) We have distinguished between two notions of (*aa*) knowledge, (*ab*) consciousness, (*ac*) acts in which consciousness occurs, (*ad*) the psychological subject,

22 Paul Galtier, *L'Unité du Christ* 339–40.
23 Ibid. 341–42.
24 Ibid. 342–43.
25 Ibid. 343.

contentum conscientiae et contentum intelligentiae et iudicii, et (*af*) descriptionum ipsius conscientiae humanae.

(*b*) Applicatio ad conscientiam Christi
(*ba*) *Applicatio conscientiae-experientiae*
(*baa*) *Applicatio ad conscientiam Christi divinam*

Cum subiectum psychologicum sit cuiuscumque operationis psychologicae subiectum ontologicum, cumque tres divinae personae sint subiecta ontologica (supposita) infiniti actus intelligendi et amandi, sequitur tres divinas personas esse subiecta psychologica unius actus tribus communis.

Ulterius secundum quod processiones divinae sunt intelligendae ad modum emanationum intelligibilium verbi a dicente et amoris ab utroque, etiam tres personae sunt subiecta psychologica secundum actus notionales singulis proprios.

Et ideo Christus ut Deus est sui conscius tum qua Deus tum qua persona distincta.

(*bab*) *Applicatio ad existentiam conscientiae Christi humanae*

Cum hic homo, Iesus Nazarenus, sit similis nobis per omnia absque peccato (DB 148), etiam ille sicut et nos erat videns per videre, audiens per audire, intelligens per intelligere, eligens per eligere, patiens per pati; neque alius erat videns et alius audiens et alius intelligens sed in diversis operationibus unus idemque; neque alius vespere et alius mane et alius heri sed semper ille idem; neque innotescebat ille idem per solam intelligentiam et conceptionem, reflectionem rationalem et iudicium, sed etiam per praeviam quandam atque in se informem experientiam internam; quae quidem experientia, sicut et nostra, et per operationes sensitive et intellectualiter apprehendendi et appetendi erat et secundum perfectionem harum operationum.

(*bac*) *Applicatio ad subiectum ontologicum et psychologicum*

Quaeritur utrum ille unus idemque, qui in Christo homine conscie sentiebat, intelligebat, eligebat, patiebatur, fuerit ipsa persona divina an forte 'ego' quoddam humanum.

(*ae*) the relation between the content of consciousness and the content of understanding and judgment, and (*af*) the descriptions of human consciousness.

(*b*) Application to the consciousness of Christ
(*ba*) *Application of consciousness-as-experience*
(*baa*) *Application to Christ's divine consciousness*

Since a psychological subject is the ontological subject of any psychological operation, and since the three divine persons are the ontological subjects (supposits) of an infinite act of understanding and loving, it follows that the three divine persons are the psychological subjects of one act common to all three.

Furthermore, inasmuch as the divine processions are to be understood after the manner of intelligible emanations of the word from the one who utters it and of love from both of these, the three persons are psychological subjects also with respect to the notional acts proper to each.

Christ as God, therefore, is conscious of himself both as God and as a distinct person.

(*bab*) *Application to the existence of Christ's human consciousness*

Since this man Jesus of Nazareth is like us in all things but sin (DB 148, DS 301–302), he also, like us, was one who saw by his act of seeing, heard by his act of hearing, understood by his act of understanding, chose by his act of choosing, and suffered through his suffering. There was not someone who saw and someone else who heard and yet another who understood, but one and the same in all these various operations; nor was there someone in the morning and someone else in the evening, someone yesterday and someone different today, but it was always one and the same. Again, that same one did not know himself only through understanding and conception and through rational reflection and judgment, but also through a preliminary interior experience unstructured in itself; and this experience, just like ours, occurred through his cognitive and appetitive operations of both sense and intellect, and in proportion to the perfection of these operations.

(*bac*) *Application to the ontological and psychological subject*

We come now to the question whether this same one who in Christ the man consciously sensed, understood, chose, and suffered was the divine person itself or was perchance some human 'I.'

Respondetur quod ipsa divina persona qua in divina natura subsistens erat subiectum ontologicum operationis divinae et qua in humana natura subsistens erat subiectum ontologicum operationis humanae.

Iam vero id ipsum quod est subiectum ontologicum operationis vel sensitivae vel intellectivae etiam est subiectum psychologicum et conscium eiusdem operationis.

Et ideo dicendum est quod ipsa divina persona in humana natura subsistens (Christus ut homo) conscie sentiebat, intelligebat, eligebat, patiebatur.

Quae conclusio confirmatur ex eo quod conscia passio seu conscius dolor connotatur in crucifixione et in vera carnis passione. Qua de causa, cum confiteri oporteat 'qui crucifixus est carne, Deum esse verum, et Dominum gloriae, et unum de Sancta Trinitate' (DB 222), et iterum 'Filium Dei ... impassibilem et immortalem divinitate, sed in humanitate pro nobis et pro nostra salute passum vera carnis passione' (DB 344), nullo modo ita distinguendum est ut Filius Dei ontologice et 'ego' quoddam humanum conscie sit passus, sed aperte est dicendum ipsum Dei Filium hominem factum et ontologice et psychologice esse passionis et crucifixionis subiectum.

(bad) *Applicatio ad habitudinem inter conscientiam Christi humanam et eiusdem scientiam beatam*

Cum per conscientiam humanam subiectum psychologicum se attingat, non ex parte obiecti sub ratione quidditatis vel veri vel entis, sed tantummodo ex parte subiecti et sub ratione experti, ideo ipsa conscientia humana non est cognitio quaedam in se completa sed ex ipsa sua ratione atque natura est notitia quaedam praevia et informis et per inquisitionem intellectualem informanda et complenda.

Praeterea, cum eiusmodi sit in Christo homine ipsum subiectum ontologicum et psychologicum ut quid sit innotescere non possit nisi per visionem beatam (i.e., per cognitionem Dei per essentiam), solummodo per hanc visionem potuit Christus homo ex parte obiecti et sub ratione quidditatis, veri, et entis, clare scire et certo iudicare quid sit illud subiectum quod erat et quod sub ratione experti iam cognoscebat.

Denique, cum experientia et intelligentia et iudicium non sint tres cognitiones de tribus obiectis sed una cognitio eiusdem rei sub diversis rationibus, omnino necessarium est ut idem Verbum incarnatum et per conscientiam sub ratione experti et per visionem beatam

Our answer is that this same divine person as subsisting in the divine nature was the ontological subject of divine operation, and as subsisting in a human nature was the ontological subject of human operation.

But the very one who is the ontological subject of sensitive or intellectual operations is also the psychological and conscious subject of these same operations.

We must conclude, therefore, that this divine person subsisting in a human nature – Christ as man – consciously sensed, understood, chose, and suffered.

This conclusion is confirmed by the fact that conscious suffering or conscious pain is connoted by crucifixion and real bodily suffering. Hence, since we are to believe that 'he who was crucified in the flesh is true God, the Lord of glory, one of the Holy Trinity' (DB 222, DS 432), and also to believe in 'the Son of God ... impassible and immortal by reason of divinity, but who in his humanity underwent real bodily suffering for us and for our salvation' (DB 344, DS 681), we must in no way draw any distinction between the Son of God having ontologically suffered and some human 'I' having consciously suffered; rather, we must state plainly that the very Son of God made human was both ontologically and psychologically the subject of the passion and crucifixion.

(bad) Application to the relationship between Christ's human consciousness and his beatific knowledge

Since through human consciousness a psychological subject attains himself or herself not on the side of the object under the formality of the definable or of the true and of being but only on the side of the subject and under the formality of the experienced, it follows that human consciousness is not a knowledge that is complete in itself but from its very formality and nature is a preliminary unstructured awareness that must be structured and completed by intellectual inquiry.

Furthermore, since in Christ the man the ontological and psychological subject is such that what it is cannot be known except through the beatific vision (that is, through knowing God by his essence), then only through this vision could Christ the man clearly know and with certainty judge, on the side of the object and under the formality of the definable, of the true, and of being, what that subject is that he was and that he knew under the formality of the experienced.

Finally, since experience, understanding, and judgment are not three knowledges about three objects, but one knowledge of the same reality under different formalities, it is absolutely necessary that the same incarnate Word be known to himself both through consciousness under the formality of the experienced and

sub ratione quidditatis et veri et entis innotesceret. Secus vel falso vel non secundum proprietatem reflexivi Christus homo affirmaret *se* esse Filium Dei.

(*bae*) *In quonam conscientia Christi humana a nostra differret ut nos esse meros homines vere dicamus sed ille se esse Filium Dei diceret*

In inquisitione intellectuali, quae conscientiam miratur et investigat, duo quaeri possunt. Nam universaliter quaeri potest, quid sim, et tunc de natura humana quaeritur; et particulariter quaeri potest, quis sim, et tunc de individuo quaeritur.[26]

Iam vero inquantum Christus homo ex sua experientia interna inquirebat quid esset, perfectam quandam humanitatem intelligebat atque affirmabat, secundum illud 'et eundem perfectum in humanitate' (DB 148).

Inquantum autem Christus homo ex sua experientia interna inquirebat quis esset, respondebat sicut et alius homo, 'Ipse ego unus idemque talia conscie sentiens, intelligens, volens, faciens, patiens.' Nam etiam ille erat 'per omnia nobis similis absque peccato' (DB 148).

Attamen ubi responsum 'ipse ego' ab alio homine prolatum nisi merum hominem non significat, idem responsum 'ipse ego' a Filio Dei prolatum Filium Dei significat. Praeterea, quamvis per solam visionem beatam Filius Dei sub ratione quidditatis, veri, et entis attingatur, nihilominus necesse est dicere eundem Filium Dei iam ex parte subiecti et sub ratione experti per conscientiam humanam esse cognitum. Quod quemadmodum fieri possit, totum fere problema est. Et quamvis multae et diversae solutiones sint propositae, de praesenti sufficit eam repetere quam credimus veram.

Primo ergo recolendum est conscientiam non esse ex parte obiecti sed ex parte subiecti, non esse ex parte percepti sed ex parte percipientis, et ideo ipsum Filium Dei seu Verbi personam esse sui consciam per conscientiam humanam non quia Filius Dei percipiatur sed quia Filius Dei percipit, neque quia Filius Dei se tamquam obiectum percipiat sed quia Filius Dei quodlibet obiectum vel sentit vel intelligit vel eligit vel prosequitur.

through beatific vision under the formality of the definable, of the true, and of being. Otherwise, in affirming *himself* to be Son of God, Christ the man would have been affirming falsely, or else affirming in a way that is not in keeping with the proper function of the reflexive pronoun.

(*bae*) *How Christ's human consciousness differs from ours, so that we truly say of ourselves that we are merely human beings, while Christ said of himself that he is the Son of God*

Intellectual inquiry, as it wonders about and ponders consciousness, can ask two questions. It may ask a universal question, What am I? and that is a question about human nature; it may also ask a particular question, Who am I? and that is a question about an individual.[26]

Now when, as a result of his interior experience, Christ as human asked, 'What am I?' he would understand and affirm a perfect humanity, in the sense of the statement 'and the same perfect in humanity' (DB 148, DS 301–302).

But when from his interior experience he asked, 'Who am I?' he would answer like any other human being, 'I myself am the very one consciously sensing, understanding, willing, doing, suffering these things'; for he was 'like us in all things but sin' (DB 148, DS 301–302).

However, any other human being who answers, 'I myself,' indicates nothing more than a mere human being; but when God's Son answers, 'I myself,' he indicates the Son of God. Furthermore, although it is only through the beatific vision that the Son of God is attained under the formality of the definable and the true and of being, nonetheless it must be said that the same Son of God is now known through his human consciousness on the side of the subject and under the formality of the experienced. Just how this can be – that is the whole problem. Many different solutions to it have been proposed, but let it suffice for us now to present the solution that we believe to be correct.

First of all, let us recall that consciousness is not on the side of the object but on the side of the subject, not on the side of the perceived but on the side of the perceiver. Hence it follows that the Son of God or the person of the Word is conscious of himself through human consciousness not because the Son of God is perceived but because the Son of God perceives, nor because the Son of God perceives himself as an object but because the Son of God either senses or understands or chooses or attends to any object whatsoever.

26 Thomas Aquinas, *Summa theologiae*, 1, q. 87, a. 1.

Deinde recolendum est ipsum incarnationis mysterium, nempe, 'Filium Dei, natum ex Patre unigenitum ... Deum ex Deo, lumen ex lumine, Deum verum de Deo vero ... per quem omnia facta sunt quae in caelo et in terra ... et homo factus est' (DB 54). Quod quidem mysterium exinanitionem quandam ontologicam affirmat, non quasi divinitas deponeretur, sed quia humanitas et vere et realiter assumitur.

Tertio, addendum est eundem Filium Dei hanc suam exinanitionem ontologicam experiri. Qui enim conscie per actum infinitum ab aeterno operatur, ex tempore per actus finitos conscie operari incipit ad modum hominis et sentiendo et intelligendo et volendo et faciendo et patiendo.

Quarto, quamvis haec ipsarum conscientiarum dissimilitudo Filio Dei innotescat inquantum est subiectum utriusque simul conscientiae, nihilominus remanet, etiamsi a conscientia Christi divina praescindatur, ipsum Filium Dei vere et proprie esse conscium per conscientiam humanam et ideo ex parte subiecti et sub ratione experti ipsum Filium Dei sibi innotescere.

Secundum hanc ergo solutionem persona divina per conscientiam Christi humanam innotescit, non quia differt conscientia Christi humana a conscientia humana alia, sed quia alius est conscius per conscientiam Christi humanam, nempe Christus homo, et alius est conscius per conscientiam humanam alterius, nempe merus homo. Quod iterum et aliter dici potest. Nam differt conscientia Christi humana non quia aliter ad quaestionem, quid sit, respondeatur, sed quia aliter ad quaestionem, quis sit, respondetur; et aliter respondetur non quia aliud per conscientiam Christi humanam percipiatur sed quia alius percipit.

(bb) Applicatio conscientiae-perceptionis
(bba) Applicatio ad conscientiam Christi divinam

Conscientia-perceptio in actu directo fieri non potest. Non sumus conscii nisi aliquid aliud iam facimus. Ergo concludendum est quod, antequam conscientia percipere possit, praerequiritur actuatio quaedam subiecti per aliam quamlibet operationem psychologicam.

Iam vero in Deo non sunt duo actus, alius directus et alius superveniens actus reflexus; et ideo in Deo non est ponenda conscientia stricte dicta quae utique est conscientia-perceptio.[27]

Second, recall to mind the mystery of the incarnation: 'Son of God, the only-begotten born of the Father ... God from God, light from light, true God from true God ..., through whom all things in heaven and on earth were made ... and was made man' (DB 54, DS 125). Indeed, this mystery affirms a certain ontological kenosis, not as if divinity were laid aside, but in that humanity is really and truly assumed.

Third, we must add the fact that this same Son of God had experience of this ontological kenosis of his. For he who operates consciously and from all eternity through infinite act now begins in time to operate consciously in human fashion through finite acts of sensing, understanding, willing, doing, and suffering.

Fourth, although this dissimilarity between the two consciousnesses is manifest to the Son of God inasmuch as he is the subject of both consciousnesses at once, nevertheless it remains true, even if we prescind from the divine consciousness of Christ, that the Son of God is truly and in the proper sense conscious through human consciousness and therefore that the Son of God is aware of himself on the side of the subject and under the formality of the experienced.

According to this solution, therefore, the divine person is manifest through Christ's human consciousness, not because his human consciousness is different from any other human consciousness, but because someone, namely, Christ the man, is conscious through the human consciousness of Christ, whereas someone else, one who is a mere human being, is conscious through the human consciousness that belongs to him. Or, to put it another way, Christ's human consciousness is different, not in that he gets a different answer to the question, What am I? but in that he gets a different answer to the question, Who am I? And this answer is different not because something else is perceived through Christ's human consciousness, but because someone else is doing the perceiving.

(*bb*) *Application of consciousness-as-perception*
(*bba*) *Application to Christ's divine consciousness*

Consciousness-as-perception cannot occur in a direct act. We are not conscious unless and until we do something else. We must conclude, therefore, that before consciousness can perceive there must be some prior actuation of the subject through some other psychological operation.

Now in God there are not two acts, one direct act and another, reflex act following upon it; hence no consciousness strictly speaking can be attributed to God, where consciousness, of course, is understood as perception.[27]

27 Paul Galtier, *L'Unité du Christ* 238, note 1.

(bbb) Applicatio ad existentiam conscientiae Christi humanae

Cum conscientia intelligatur 'facultas aut potius actus quo agens se ipsum in suis actibus percipit ut eorum principium et subiectum,'[28] primo determinandum est utrum in Christo homine habeatur praeter multos actus etiam quoddam unum quod in actibus percipiatur. Et omnino affirmative respondendum est; nam necessarium est ut

> ... apud Christum, sicut apud omnem personam, detur etiam unitas psychologica quae per conscientiam habetur; secus enim illius unitatis ontologicae quam de se profitetur maneret inconscius; sola porro conscientia ex qua oriri possit illa unitas psychologica est humana ...[29]

> Le Christ, en un mot, ne serait pas vraiment homme, s'il ne s'était pas produit en lui comme en nous des états de conscience propres à se grouper sous la forme de notre 'moi' empirique.[30]

Neque in Christo homine datur tantummodo unitas ordinis in ipsis operationibus sed etiam huius unitatis sat superficialis fundamentum antecedens, subiacens, profundum.

> La présence dans le Christ d'un 'moi' ainsi défini (empiricum, psychologicum) n'est donc qu'une conséquence naturelle de sa vie humaine. Mais il est de même pour le 'moi' substantiel correspondant. L'un a sa racine dans l'autre ... A proprement parler, il n'est que la nature humaine, cette nature humaine qui, dans le Christ comme ailleurs, est forcément consciente d'elle-même.[31]

(bbc) Applicatio ad subiectum ontologicum et psychologicum

Subiectum ontologicum est id quod est et operatur; subiectum psychologicum est id quod speciali quadam perceptione percipitur. Si enim conscientia est perceptio, non sufficit ut subiectum percipiat, sed requiritur ut sit obiectum quod percipiatur. Quod sequenti loco accurate illustratur.

(bbb) Application to the existence of Christ's human consciousness

Since consciousness is understood as 'the faculty, or rather the act, by which the agent perceives himself or herself in his or her acts as their principle and subject,'[28] the first thing to be determined is whether in Christ as human there is, in addition to a multiplicity of acts, also some unity that may be perceived in those acts. The answer, of course, must be in the affirmative; for it is necessary that

> in Christ, as in every person, there is also a psychological unity that is had through consciousness; for otherwise he would remain unconscious of that ontological unity that he claims for himself. Moreover, the only consciousness that can give rise to that psychological unity is human consciousness ... [29]

> In a word, Christ would not be truly human if there were not produced in him, as in us, states of consciousness apt to group themselves under the form of our empirical 'me.'[30]

Nor is there in Christ as human only a unity of order among the operations themselves, but this rather superficial unity itself has an antecedent and underlying deep foundation.

> The presence in Christ of a 'me' so defined (*empiricum, psychologicum*) is then but a natural consequence of his human life. But the same holds true for the corresponding substantial 'me.' The one has its roots in the other ... Properly speaking, it is simply human nature, this human nature, which in Christ as in all other cases is necessarily conscious of itself.[31]

(bbc) Application to the ontological and psychological subject

The ontological subject is that which is and operates; the psychological subject is that which is perceived through some special kind of perception. For if consciousness is perception, it is not enough that the subject perceive; it must also be the object perceived. This is clearly illustrated in the following passage.

28 Paul Galtier, *De incarnatione ac redemptione* (2nd ed., Paris: Beauchesne, 1947) 266, § 339.
29 Ibid. 267, § 340.
30 Paul Galtier, *L'Unité du Christ* 344.
31 Ibid. 345.

Humana enim in Christo, etsi vere et proprie sunt Verbi (*i*), tamen Verbum in se ipso non afficiunt: hoc sensu tantum Verbum dicitur nasci, pati, obedire, crescere aut mori quia eius est natura in qua et ex qua formaliter haec sunt (*ii*). Pariter igitur de cogitationibus et verbis humanis, quibus illa phaenomena seu operationes seu passiones cognoscuntur et exprimuntur. Cognoscuntur et dicuntur ab ipso Verbo personaliter (*iii*); sed nec necessitas est ulla ut haec eius sensa vel dicta illum in se attingant (*iv*). Sicut solius (*v*) corporis est nutriri et augescere, solius (*v*) voluntatis humanae mandatum accipere aut adimplere, ita solius (*v*) naturae humanae est percipere dolorem et dicere conscie: 'ego sitio,' 'ego rogo,' etc. Haec sane sunt personae (*vi*) quae eam (naturam) assumpsit, sed quia ea (natura) est illorum proprium et unicum principium formale, ei soli etiam inhaerent.[32]

Quamvis sint hoc in loco quae admirationem movere possint, praesertim quae numero (*v*) sed etiam quae numero (*ii*) adnotavimus, intentio auctoris esse videtur distinctionem inter subiectum ontologicum et psychologicum applicare. Quamvis dixerit 'solius corporis ... solius voluntatis ... solius naturae humanae,' statim addit 'haec sane sunt personae' (*vi*) sicut et immediate antea dixerat 'cognoscuntur et dicuntur ab ipso Verbo personaliter' (*iii*). Argumentum ergo esse videtur quod, quamvis Verbum divinum sit subiectum ontologicum operationum humanarum, tamen principium proximum elicitivum est corpus, voluntas, natura assumpta; et ideo quia conscientia est perceptio principii proximi elicitivi, conscientia Christi humana non est Verbi divini. Cui argumento duplici de causa non consentimus, nam primo conscientia non est perceptio obiecti sed experientia subiecti, et secundo subiectum experiens in hac natura est ipsum Verbum divinum qua homo factum.

Alia illustratio eius quod, si conscientia est perceptio, nisi abusive non dicitur subiectum psychologicum, habetur ex eo quod, supposita visione beata 'Christus intellectu suo humano percipit *se* esse personam compositam cuius vere sunt attributa et operationes utriusque naturae.'[33] Ubi clare pronomen reflexivum 'se' refertur non ad naturam humanam sui consciam sed ad Christum qui est

All that is human in Christ, even though truly and properly belonging to
the Word (*i*), nevertheless does not affect the Word in itself: the Word is
said to be born, suffer, obey, grow, or die only in the sense that to the
Word belongs the nature in which and by reason of which these things
formally exist (*ii*). It is the same, therefore, with the human thoughts and
words by which those phenomena or operations or sufferings are known
and expressed. They are known and are uttered by the Word himself
personally (*iii*); but there is no need whatsoever for these feelings and
words to attain the Word in itself (*iv*). Just as it belongs to the body alone
(*v*) to feed and grow, and to the human will alone (*v*) to accept or carry
out a command, so it belongs to human nature alone (*v*) to perceive pain
and consciously utter the words, 'I thirst,' 'I ask,' and so forth. These, of
course, belong to the person (*vi*) who assumed that (nature), but because
that (nature) is the sole proper formal principle of them, they inhere in it
alone.[32]

Although there are several points in this passage that are mystifying, especially
those we have indicated by number (*v*) and number (*ii*), the author's intention
seems to be to apply the distinction between the ontological and psychological
subject. Although he used the words 'belongs to the body alone ... the will alone
... human nature alone,' he immediately adds, 'These, of course, belong to the
person' (*vi*), just as immediately prior to this he had said, 'are known and are
uttered by the Word himself personally' (*iii*). So the argument seems to be that,
although the divine Word is the ontological subject of human operations, still the
proximate principle eliciting them is the body, the will, the assumed nature; and
therefore, since consciousness is a perception of the proximate eliciting principle,
Christ's human consciousness does not belong to the divine Word. There are two
reasons why we do not accept this argument: first, because consciousness is not
the perception of an object but the experience of a subject, and second, because
the subject who is undergoing experiences in this nature is the very Word of God
as having become man.

A further illustration that consciousness-as-perception involves an improper
use of the term 'psychological subject' is the following. The beatific vision being
presupposed, 'Christ by his human intellect perceives *himself* to be a composite
person to whom truly belong the attributes and operations of both natures.'[33]
But here the reflexive pronoun 'himself' clearly refers not to a human nature
conscious of itself but to Christ who is the ontological subject of both natures and

32 Paul Galtier, *De incarnatione ac redemptione* 268, § 342.
33 Ibid. 270, § 343.

subiectum ontologicum utriusque naturae et, quia percipitur per visionem, abusive subiectum psychologicum dici potest.

(bbd) Cur conscientia Christi humana non censeatur ipsius personae

Si conscientia est perceptio, persona non est conscia eo quod percipit sed eatenus tantum quatenus percipitur. Iam vero in Christo homine persona divina est conscia, non quia percipiatur, sed quia percipit. Et ideo hac in theoria (conscientiae-perceptionis) ad personam divinam sui consciam non pervenitur.

Quod tamen argumentum afferri non potest ab iis qui conscientiam esse perceptionem ducant. Et ideo aliter arguunt.

> Persona enim non directe in se, sed tantummodo indirecte, in suis actibus attingitur. Immo, ideo tantum ita attingitur quia, apud nos, identificatur realiter cum principio a quo formaliter et immediate illi actus procedunt. In Christo autem, subiectum personale operationum humanarum realiter et totaliter distinguitur ab earum principio formali. Ergo nulla ratio est cur in illis (operationibus) a conscientia percipiatur.[34]

Quod argumentum potius metaphysicum gnoseologice sic exponitur. Etsi concedatur 'ego' profundum per ipsam conscientiam percipi, etsi concedatur hoc 'ego' profundum esse ipsam animam existentem atque operantem, attamen hoc non sufficit ut determinetur utrum illa anima existens et operans in se subsistat an ab alio assumpta sit. Qua quaestione indeterminata, etiam quaestio de persona manet intacta.[35]

(c) Reactiones indirectae

Contra sententiam quae conscientiam esse perceptionem supponit, vel directe vel indirecte reagi potest. Directe quidem reagitur inquantum quis conscientiam non perceptionem sed experientiam esse affirmat et conclusiones inde profluentes deducit. Indirecte autem reagitur inquantum quis conscientiam esse perceptionem vel explicite vel tacite agnoscit sed, quia consequentias Christologicas accipere non vult, effugium quoddam quaerit.

who, because he is perceived by vision, can by a misuse of language be called the psychological subject.

(bbd) *Why Christ's human consciousness is not regarded as belonging to his person*

If consciousness is perception, a person is not conscious because he perceives, but only insofar as he is perceived. But in Christ the man, a divine person is conscious not because he is perceived but because he perceives. This theory of consciousness as perception, therefore, cannot account for the divine person conscious of himself.

Now this line of argument cannot be proposed by those who consider consciousness to be perception. So they argue in another way.

> The person is attained, not directly in itself, but only indirectly, in his or her acts. Moreover, it is only so attained because, with us, the person is really identical with the principle from which formally and immediately those acts proceed. In the case of Christ, however, the personal subject of his human operations is really and totally distinct from their formal principle. There is therefore no reason for it to be perceived by consciousness in those operations.[34]

This rather metaphysical argument is expressed as follows in a gnoseological way. Even though it be granted that the deep 'I' is perceived through consciousness, and also that this deep 'I' is the soul itself as existing and operating, this is nevertheless not sufficient to determine whether that existing and operating soul subsists in itself or has instead been assumed by something else. And so long as that question remains unresolved, the question about the person also remains untouched.[35]

(c) *Indirect refutations*

The opinion that consciousness is perception can be refuted either directly or indirectly. Direct refutation asserts that consciousness is not perception but experience and deduces the conclusions that follow from that position. Indirect refutation, on the other hand, occurs when one either explicitly affirms or takes it for granted that consciousness is perception and then, realizing that this leads to unacceptable conclusions about Christology, looks for a way out of this predicament.

34 Ibid. 267–68, § 341.
35 Galtier, *L'Unité du Christ* 342–43.

Quare in reactionibus indirectis, quia conscientia esse perceptio supponitur, non attenditur ad personam divinam percipientem sed viis diversis proceditur ut persona divina per conscientiam humanam et perceptibilis efficiatur et ideo percepta dicatur.

(ca) *Excell. Dom. P. Parente*[36]

(caa) Conscientiam Christi divinam non solum admittit sed etiam modo nimis emphatico asserit. Quamvis enim consentiamus Verbum divinum esse conscium tum secundum actum divinum essentialem tum secundum actum notionalem proprium, cum tamen in divinis solus Pater dicat, Verbum autem dicatur sed non dicat, ad litteram sumi non debet 'ciascuna delle tre Persone divine ... si afferma come Io.'[37]

(cab) Ita concipit conscientiam humanam ut perfecta sui conscientia in Christo homine inveniri non possit.

> Certamente per avere una perfetta autocoscienza è necessario che il soggetto e l'oggetto siano una stessa cosa, come l'anima nostra quando si ripiega su se stessa. Questa esigenza di identità tra soggetto e oggetto non si attua in Christo a causa della distinzione reale tra natura umana e Persona divina: l'autocoscienza umana in Lui ha come ogetto proprio l'umanità nel suo essere e nel suo operare.[38]

Quo in loco concipitur conscientia tamquam perceptio eius quod cum percipiente identicum est; et quia persona divina non identificatur cum natura humana eo modo quo anima humana identificatur cum se ipsa, excluditur in Christo homine perfecta sui conscientia. En problema eodem modo conceptum ac apud P. Galtier.[39]

(cac) Quam ob rem, causas et rationes quaerit ut natura Christi humana in se inveniat unde ipsa se esse naturam assumptam percipiat et saltem obscure assumentem attingat.

> La coscienza dunque ripiegandosi sulla natura non può non avvertire che questa natura esiste e opera in virtù di un Altro, cioè in dipendenza del Verbo, che la

In indirect refutation, therefore, because consciousness is taken to be perception, one's attention is not directed to the divine person as perceiving, but one proceeds in various ways to make that person out to be somehow perceptible through human consciousness and so to declare it to be perceived.

(ca) Pietro Parente[36]

(caa) Parente admits the divine consciousness of Christ but overstates his case. For though we agree that the divine Word is conscious both in the essential divine act and in the proper notional act, yet in the Godhead only the Father speaks while the Word is spoken and does not speak, and so we must not take literally Parente's statement that 'each of the three divine Persons ... affirms himself as I.'[37]

(cab) As to the human consciousness of Christ, he conceives it in such a way that Christ the man cannot have a perfect consciousness of himself.

> It is certain that to have a perfect consciousness of self the subject and object must be one and the same, as is the case with our soul when it reflects upon itself. This requirement of identity between subject and object is not realized in Christ because of the real distinction between his human nature and the divine Person: in him human consciousness of self has as its proper object his humanity in its existence and operation.[38]

In this passage, consciousness is conceived as the perception of that which is identical with the perceiver; and since the divine person is not identical with the human nature in the way the human soul is identical with itself, perfect consciousness of self in the Christ as human is ruled out. This is also the way Galtier conceived the problem.[39]

(cac) Consequently, Parente looks for causes and reasons by which Christ's human nature might be enabled to perceive itself as an assumed nature and apprehend, at least dimly, the one assuming.

> Consciousness then, turning back to itself to reflect upon nature, cannot but notice that this nature exists and functions in virtue of an Other, that is,

36 *L'Io di Cristo* (Brescia: Morcelliana, 1951, 1955). The second edition changes the order and adds more than one hundred pages. References here are to this second edition.

37 Ibid. 374.

38 Ibid. 375.

39 Galtier, *De incarnatione ac redemptione* 267, § 341.

investe col suo essere, la fa sussistere e la regge in tutta la sua attività. E siccome
è proprio della coscienza psicologica polarizzare l'essere e l'attività di una natura
intorno all'*Io* (persona), la coscienza umana di Cristo deve registrare un *Io*, che è
la sua personalità. Ora in Cristo non c'è altra personalità che quella del Verbo e
però in definitiva il termine di quella coscienza dev'essere il Verbo, attinto, sia pure
oscuramente, come *Io* proprio.[40]

Clarissime apparet differentia inter conscientiam-perceptionem et conscientiam-experientiam. Quamvis enim auctor, sicut et nos, esse et operari Verbi in-
vocet, tamen

(i) ubi ille ponit Verbum tamquam obscurum terminum perceptionis cuiusdam
indirectae et mediatae, nos ponimus Verbum clarum subiectum conscium cuiuscumque operationis psychologicae;

(ii) ubi ille ponit conscientiam Christi humanam tamquam subiectum perceptionis, nos ponimus conscientiam esse internam experientiam humanam Verbi;

(iii) ubi ille ponit naturam Christi humanam tamquam obiectum directum
conscientiae-perceptionis et modificationes conscientiae Christi humanae tamquam media unde Verbum indirecte et obscure percipiatur, nos indifferentia re-
putamus obiecta quae Verbum experitur (quidquid enim experitur, semper ipse
conscius experitur) et ideo, salva gratiarum et donorum abundantia, affirmare
possumus Christum hominem sicut in aliis naturalibus ita etiam in conscientia
esse per omnia nobis similem.

(*cad*) Concludit principium unitatis Verbi incarnati, sicut ontologice, ita etiam
psychologice esse ipsam Verbi personam;[41] et cum hac conclusione prorsus consentimus quamvis non esse concedendum credimus (i) conscientiam esse perceptionem, (ii) non solum Patrem sed etiam Verbum et Spiritum dicere, vel (iii) personam Verbi a conscientia humana percipi propter modificationes conscientiae
Christi humanae.

(*cb*)   H. Diepen[42]

Conscientiam supponit esse perceptionem. Filium Dei asserit suos actus humanos
percipere tamquam actus alicuius; quis sit ille 'aliquis' per visionem beatam

in dependence upon the Word who invests it with his own existence, makes it subsist, and regulates it in all its activity. And just as it is characteristic of psychological consciousness to polarize the existence and activity of a nature around the 'I' (the person), so the human consciousness of Christ must register an 'I' which is its personhood. Now in Christ there is no other personhood than that of the Word, and so, in the last analysis, the term of that consciousness must be the Word, attained, however dimly, as its proper 'I'.[40]

The difference between consciousness as experience and consciousness as perception appears here very clearly. Although the author appeals, as we do, to the existence and operation of the Word, yet

(i) where he has the Word as an obscure term of some indirect and mediated perception, for us the Word is the clear conscious subject of any psychological operation;

(ii) for him Christ's human consciousness is the subject of perception, but for us this consciousness is the Word's interior human experience;

(iii) for him Christ's human nature is the direct object of consciousness-as-perception and the changes in his human consciousness are the means whereby the Word is indirectly and dimly perceived; for us, on the other hand, it makes no difference what objects the Word experiences (for whatever he experiences he always does so consciously), and therefore we can affirm that Christ as human, granted his abundant graces and gifts, is like us in all that belongs to human nature, consciousness included.

(cad) Parente's conclusion is that the principle of unity of the incarnate Word is both ontologically and psychologically the person of the Word.[41] With this conclusion we completely agree, but feel we cannot admit the following: (i) that consciousness is perception; (ii) that not only the Father but also the Word and the Spirit speak (dicere); (iii) that the person of the Word is perceived by Christ's human consciousness because of modifications in that consciousness.

(cb) Herman Diepen[42]

This author also supposes consciousness to be perception. He maintains that the Son of God perceives his human acts as being the acts of someone and knows

---

40 Parente, *L'Io di Cristo* 375.
41 Ibid. 377.
42 Herman Diepen, 'La psychologie humaine du Christ selon saint Thomas d'Aquin,' *Revue thomiste* 50 (1950) 515–62.

innotescit; negat actus Christi humanos ita modificari ut in iis per conscientiam percipiatur persona divina; affirmat tamen actus humanos Christi percipi non qua autonomos sed qua dependentes.[43]

Manca sane est conscientia quae non subiecti est sed actuum dependentium ab aliquo per conscientiam ignoto.

Circa ipsam vero actuum dependentiam, clare est distinguendum. Dependent enim actus Christi humani ab aliquo dupliciter. Primo modo, dependent a persona Verbi in humana natura subsistente quae empirice, intellectualiter, rationaliter, et moraliter conscia ipsos actus suos conscios ponit, sicut et quilibet homo. Alio modo, dependent tum natura Christi humana tum actus in illa natura eliciti a Deo trino qui omnia ad extra creat, conservat, ad actionem applicat, et tamquam instrumentis utitur secundum infinitam suam sapientiam et bonitatem. Qui duo modi non sunt inter se confundendi quasi confusio elucidaret conscientiam Christi humanam.

(cc) B. Xiberta[44]

Conscientiam concedit esse perceptionem. Negat tamen hanc perceptionem in Christo homine fieri per solam naturam humanam sine interventione Verbi divini. Asserit praesentiam Verbi hypostaticam sentiri non minus universaliter in ordine dynamico quam in ordine statico. Duas ob causas asserit Verbum dominari operationes Christi humanas: primo, quia ponit de integro esse humanum[45] et, deinde, quia propter Verbum operationes Christi humanae elevantur ad illum apicem perfectionis quem potentia obedientialis possibilem facit. Concludit animam Christi humanam ita possessam atque elevatam exercere suam conscientiam-perceptionem.[46]

Post distinguit duas cognitiones: aliud enim fuit quod anima Christi per meram quandam cognitionem obiectivam se hypostatice esse Verbo unitam cognoscit; aliud autem fuit quod eadem anima subiective vidit et contemplabatur

who this 'someone' is through his beatific vision. Diepen denies that Christ's human acts are modified in such a way that the divine person is perceived in them through consciousness; yet he states that those human acts are perceived not as autonomous but as dependent.[43]

But a consciousness that is not of a subject but of acts dependent upon someone who is unknown through that consciousness is surely defective.

As to the dependency of these acts, a distinction must be clearly made. There are two ways in which Christ's human acts depend upon someone. First, they depend upon the person of the Word subsisting in a human nature who, like any human being, is empirically, intellectually, rationally, and morally conscious in performing those conscious acts. Second, both Christ's human nature and the acts elicited in that nature are dependent upon the triune God who creates all things external to God, conserves them, applies them to their action, and uses them as instruments in accordance with his infinite wisdom and goodness. These two kinds of dependence must not be confused – as if confusion would throw any light on the problem of Christ's human consciousness.

(cc) Bartolomé Xiberta[44]

This author takes for granted that consciousness is perception. Nevertheless, he denies that this perception in Christ the man is had solely through his human nature without any intervention on the part of the divine Word. He maintains that the hypostatic presence of the Word is felt no less completely in the dynamic than in the static order. He gives two reasons for the control of the Word over Christ's human operations: first, because Christ's human existence is whole and entire,[45] and second, because on account of the Word those human operations are raised to that peak of perfection made possible by obediential potency. He concludes that Christ's human soul thus possessed and elevated exercises its consciousness-as-perception.[46]

He goes on to distinguish two kinds of knowledge: it was one thing for Christ's soul through some purely objective knowledge to know that it was hypostatically united to the Word; but it was something else for this same soul subjectively to

---

43 Ibid. 532.

44 Bartolomé M. Xiberta, *El Yo de Jesucristo* (Barcelona: Herder, 1954).

45 [Xiberta's Spanish is 'porque posee integramente el ser humano.' A literal translation would be 'because he possesses human existence integrally.' Of course, Xiberta is not referring to an act of existence (nor does Lonergan mean an act of existence when he writes 'esse humanum.')]

46 Ibid. 143.

et tamquam obiectum perceptum possedit ipsam realitatem et Verbi sustentantis et Humanitatis per sustentationem Verbi sublimatae.[47]

In eadem ergo problematica involvitur hic auctor ac Excell. Dom. Parente et R.P. Diepen. Quantum autem ad subtitulum sui operis, 'Un conflicto entre dos cristologias,' satis forte lectori iam apparet conflictum esse inter duas gnoseologias. In sua sententia concedere non possumus vel conscientiam esse perceptionem, vel miram illam penetrationem dynamicam quam ponit ut in natura assumpta ipsa assumptio sit conscientiae-perceptioni perceptibilis, vel conclusionem non ipsum Verbum hominem sed animam humanam percipere et cognoscere, vel modum explicandi unionem hypostaticam.[48]

(cd) J. Ternus[49]

Dividit sententias secundum quod per conscientiam quandam divinitatis praeviam ad visionem (Parente, Diepen) vel per ipsam visionem beatam (Galtier, etc.) Christus dicitur conscious[50] et altiorem synthesin ad mentem P. de la Taille quaerit inquantum esse divinum Verbi non solum ontologice sed etiam psychologice naturam Christi humanam actuat ita ut persona divina sit sui conscia non solum secundum naturam suam divinam sed etiam secundum humanam suam naturam atque conscientiam.

> Dieses hypostatische Ich ist seiner selbst nicht nur nach seiner Gottnatur bewusst, sondern auch nach seinem menschlichen Sein in seine menschlichen Bewusstsein und durch das in ihm verwirklichte Selbstbewusstsein.[51]

Quibus tamen statim addit:

> Nicht als ob der Logos den Akt des menschlichen Selbstbewusstseins Jesu formell setzte oder virtuell bewirkte. Es ist sein Akt, sofern die Natur und Seele, die ihn

see and to contemplate and to possess as a perceived object the very reality of both the sustaining Word and the humanity elevated by the Word's sustaining power.[47]

Xiberta, therefore, is caught in the same problematic as Parente and Diepen. As for the subtitle of his work, 'Un conflicto entre dos cristologias,' the reader will perhaps have discerned rather a conflict between two gnoseologies. In connection with his opinion we cannot grant that consciousness is perception, nor that there exists that remarkable dynamic penetration that he postulates so that in the assumed nature the assumption itself may be perceptible to consciousness-as-perception, nor the conclusion that it is not the Word as human but his human soul that perceives and knows, nor his way of explaining the hypostatic union itself.[48]

(cd) Joseph Ternus[49]

This author divides opinions according to whether they affirm that Christ is conscious through a consciousness of divinity that is antecedent to the beatific vision (Parente, Diepen) or is had through that vision itself (Galtier and others).[50] He looks for a higher synthesis, following the thought of Maurice de la Taille, according to which the divine act of existence of the Word actuates Christ's human nature not only ontologically but also psychologically, so that the divine person is conscious of himself not only according to his divine nature but also according to his human nature and consciousness. Thus:

> This hypostatic 'I' is conscious of itself not only according to its divine nature but also according to its human existence in its human consciousness and through the self-consciousness realized in him.[51]

Yet he immediately adds:

> It is not as if the Word formally constitutes or virtually actuates the act of Jesus' human self-awareness. It is his act inasmuch as the nature and soul

47 Ibid. 154.
48 For longer reviews of Xiberta's book see F. Lakner, *Zeitschrift für katholische Theologie* 77 (1955) 212–28; M. Cuervo, *La Ciencia Tomista* 82 (1955) 105–25; P. Parente has a brief comment on it in *L'Io di Cristo* 379.
49 Joseph Ternus, 'Das Seelen- und Bewusstseinsleben Jesu,' in Grillmeier-Bacht, *Das Konzil von Chalkedon*, III, 81–237.
50 Ibid. 223–29.
51 Ibid. 231–32.

setzt, die ihm hypostatisch zu eigen gehörige Natur und Seele ist. Aber im
Akt des menschlichen Selbstbewusstseins Jesu wirkt sich die quasi-formale
Aktuation des Logos ontisch so aus, dass das psychologische Ich der menschlichen
Bewusstseinserfahrung Jesu das vom Logos aktuierte Erscheinungs-Ich ist.[52]

Quantum ad hanc positionem psychologice spectatam attinet, dicendum videtur auctorem limites conscientiae-perceptionis ita praetergredi ut conscientiae
Christi humanae non obiectum divinum perceptum sed subiectum divinum psychologicum astruat. Quod sane laudamus. Attamen ita loquitur idem auctor ut
haud dici possit eum nobiscum simpliciter consentire. Ita enim concipitur hoc
subiectum divinum psychologicum ut in conscientia humana per actuationem
eminentem 'ego' quoddam apparens sistatur dum, e contra, ipsi dicimus personam Verbi ideo per conscientiam humanam esse sui consciam quia ipsa divina
persona exinanitionem suam ontologicam experiatur.

Quantum autem ad constitutionem ontologicam eiusdem conscientiae, sicut
actuationem eminentem ad ipsam unionem hypostaticam exponendam iam pridem reicimus, ita etiam ad unionis conscientiam eam superfluere ducimus. Sicut
enim in quaestione ontologica problema aestimamus non quemadmodum hic
homo Deus sit sed quemadmodum Deus sit hic homo, ita in quaestione psychologica problema aestimamus non quemadmodum conscientia humana divinum habeat subiectum sed quemadmodum divinum subiectum per conscientiam
humanam experiatur. Sicut ad problema ontologicum respondemus secundum
principia quae in contingentibus de Deo praedicatis vigent, ita ad problema psychologicum respondemus secundum principia quae constitutionem ontologicam
conscientiae humanae regunt. Denique cum actuationem eminentem parum lucis et multum confusionis in quaestione ontologica adhibere iudicaverimus, etiam
sine illa actuatione divinam personam per hanc conscientiam humanam experiri
brevissimo hoc syllogismo concludimus quod hic homo conscie experitur atque
divina persona est hic homo.[53]

that constitute him are the very nature and soul that belong to him hypostatically. But in the act of Jesus' human self-consciousness, the quasi formal actuation of the Word is ontically operative so that the psychological 'I' of Jesus' human experience of self-consciousness is the phenomenal 'I' actuated by the Word.[52]

From a psychological point of view, we may say that the author gets beyond the confines of consciousness-as-perception in that he attributes to Christ's human consciousness not a divine object that is perceived but a divine psychological subject. All well and good. But he speaks in such a way that one could hardly say that he simply agrees with our opinion. His concept of this divine psychological subject is of some phenomenal 'I' present in human consciousness through an eminent actuation; for us, on the contrary, the person of the Word is conscious of himself through human consciousness precisely because this divine person experiences his ontological kenosis.

As to the ontological structure of this same consciousness, we feel that just as we have rejected eminent actuation as an explanation of the hypostatic union itself, so too must we consider it superfluous for understanding the consciousness of this union. As we consider the ontological question to be not how this human being is God but how God is this human being, so for us the psychological question is not how a human consciousness has a divine subject but how a divine subject experiences through a human consciousness. And as we answer the ontological question according to those principles that obtain regarding contingent predications about God, so we deal with the psychological question by way of principles that govern the ontological constitution of human consciousness. Finally, since we have judged that eminent actuation added little light and considerable confusion to the ontological question, our conclusion that even without that actuation a divine person experiences through this human consciousness is summed up in this brief syllogism: this human being consciously experiences, and a divine person is this human being.[53]

---

52 Ibid. 232.
53 The reader who is interested in examining and evaluating other opinions will find references to a number of different authors in B. Xiberta, *El Yo de Jesucristo*. [Latin: Diligentissimus lector qui etiam alias opiniones investigare atque iudicare voluerit, ad multos et diversos auctores referentias inveniet apud B. Xiberta, *El Yo de Jesucristo*.]

Concluditur

103 Tum in publica ecclesiae praedicatione tum in privatis fidelium contemplationibus illud communiter agnoscitur quod Filius Dei ita est homo factus et ita in humanitate perfectus ut ipse experiatur quid sit hominem esse. Nec catholicus quisquam scandalosam non iudicaret sententiam secundum quam diceretur Filius Dei ontologice quidem sed non conscie neque experiendo vitam humanam egisse.

Quod verum catholicum statim sequitur, si conscientia ponitur esse experientia.

At idem verum praetermittitur ab iis qui vel ponunt vel supponunt conscientiam esse perceptionem.

Cui omissioni accedit problematica erronea. Cum enim personam ex parte subiecti et sub ratione experti sibi praesentem omiserint, illud quaerunt utrum persona divina per conscientiam humanam ipsa se ex parte obiecti perceperit.

Cui quaestioni secundum veritatem negative respondendum est, cum per solam visionem beatam Deus ex parte obiecti intelligi possit.

At haec vera et negativa responsio intra erroneam problematicam ad hoc conducit dilemma, ut aut conscientia humana in Christo homine omnino negetur aut subiectum humanum quod non sit persona divina inveniatur.

Qua de causa, ut subiectum mere humanum evitetur, alii conscientiam-perceptionem ad perceptionem indirectam extendunt ut mediantibus donis supernaturalibus conscientia Christi humana suum subiectum divinum obscura quadam ratione ex parte obiecti percipiat; alii autem conscientiam in Christo homine mancam ponunt ut subiectum quidem non percipiatur sed actus sui humani, a

Conclusion

103 It is commonly accepted, both in the public preaching of the church and in private contemplation on the part of the faithful, that the Son of God became human in such a way and was perfect in humanity in such a way that he really experienced what it was to be a human being. Any Catholic would consider it scandalous to maintain that the Son of God ontologically lived a human life but did not do so consciously or experientially.

This truth of the Catholic faith follows immediately when consciousness is taken to be experience.

But this same truth is overlooked by those who either affirm or take for granted that consciousness is perception.

Their oversight is compounded by a false problematic. Having overlooked the concept of a person present to himself on the side of the subject under the formality of the experienced, they ask whether a divine person through human consciousness perceived himself on the side of the object.

In all truth, this question must be answered in the negative. Only in the beatific vision can God be understood on the side of the object.

Now, in the context of the false problematic, this true negative answer leads to the dilemma of either completely denying human consciousness in Christ the man or having a human subject that is not a divine person.

Hence, in order to avoid having a merely human subject, some extend consciousness-as-perception to an indirect perception so that by means of supernatural gifts Christ's human consciousness in some obscure way perceives its divine subject on the side of the object. Others attribute to Christ the man a truncated consciousness so that while no subject is perceived, his human acts, being totally

quodam ignoto prorsus dependentes, indicia subiecti praebeant; alii autem conscientiam-perceptionem supernaturaliter elevant ut mirum quendam intermedium
locum teneat inter visionem beatam et cognitionem mediatam; alii autem viam
metaphysicam incedentes, per actuationem eminentem non solum ontologicam
sed etiam psychologicam, introducunt subiectum divinum ratione substantiae
conscium; alii denique ita affirmant Filium Dei hominem factum se per visionem
beatam cognoscere ut neque subiectum conscium neque conscientiam humanam
clare et explicite agnoscant.

Cum vero alius alterius sententiam sine difficultate refutet, cum omnes in hoc
peccare videantur quod omittunt personam divinam humanam vitam experientia
sua cognovisse, conscientia-perceptio derelinquenda est et conscientia-experientia
affirmanda.

Quod si conscientia-perceptio derelinquitur, haud sustineri potest illud principium quod cognitio in dualitate radicatur. Et si hoc principium derelinquitur,
eo pervenietur ut principia, doctrina, methodus S. Thomae Aquinatis et melius
intelligantur et securius affirmentur et fidelius applicentur.

dependent upon some unknown, give indications of a subject. Still others super-naturally elevate consciousness-as-perception to a wondrous position intermediate between the beatific vision and mediated knowledge. Then there are those who take a metaphysical approach and by invoking an eminent actuation that is not only ontological but psychological as well, come up with a divine subject who is conscious by reason of substance. And finally there are those who maintain that the incarnate Son of God knows himself through the beatific vision, but they speak about this in such a way that they do not clearly and explicitly acknowledge either a conscious subject or a human consciousness.

Since the proponents of these various opinions refute one another without any difficulty, and since all appear to err in overlooking the fact that the divine person had experiential knowledge of his human life, consciousness-as-perception must be abandoned and consciousness-as-experience affirmed.

Now if consciousness-as-perception is abandoned, the principle that knowledge is rooted in duality can hardly be maintained. And if that principle is abandoned, we shall come to a deeper understanding, a firmer assertion, and a more faithful application of the principles, the thought, and the method of St Thomas Aquinas.

Index